D1453398

The Culture of Civil War in Kyoto

A

[signature: Philip E. Lilienthal]

Book

The Philip E. Lilienthal imprint
honors special books
in commemoration of a man whose work
at the University of California Press from 1954 to 1979
was marked by dedication to young authors
and to high standards in the field of Asian Studies.
Friends, family, authors, and foundations have together
endowed the Lilienthal Fund, which enables the Press
to publish under this imprint selected books
in a way that reflects the taste and judgment
of a great and beloved editor.

The Culture of Civil War in Kyoto

Mary Elizabeth Berry

UNIVERSITY OF CALIFORNIA PRESS

Berkeley / Los Angeles / London

105618 02

The Publisher gratefully acknowledges the financial support of the Center for Japanese Studies, University of California, Berkeley.

University of California Press
Berkeley and Los Angeles, California

University of California Press, Ltd.
London, England

©1994 by
The Regents of the University of California

Library of Congress Cataloging-in-Publication Data

Berry, Mary Elizabeth, 1947–
    The culture of civil war in Kyoto / by Mary Elizabeth Berry.
        p.   cm.
    Includes bibliographical references and index.
    ISBN 0-520-08170-6
    1. Kyoto (Japan)—History.   2. Japan—History—Period of civil
wars, 1480–1603.
    DS897.K857B47   1993
    952'.186—dc20   93-7452
                                                                   CIP

Printed in the United States of America
9 8 7 6 5 4 3 2 1

The paper used in this publication meets the minimum requirements of American National Standard for Information Sciences—Permanence of Paper for Printed Library Materials, ANSI Z39.48-1984.☉

For
Anne Shively Berry and
Catherine Shively Berry

Contents

LIST OF FIGURES, MAPS,
AND ILLUSTRATIONS   ix

ACKNOWLEDGMENTS   xi

INTRODUCTION   xv

PRELUDE: THEY COLLECTED
ONE HUNDRED FOURTEEN HEADS   1

1
The Culture of Lawlessness, the Politics of Demonstration   11

2
Dancing Is Forbidden: The Structures of Urban Conflict   55

3
Word Wars: The Refuge of the Past   106

4
Popular Insurrection   134

5
Work: The Structures of Daily Life   171

134403
0501802

6
Neighborhood: The Reconfiguration of Attachment   210

7
Play: The Freedom of Invention   242

AFTERWORD: SCENES IN AND
AROUND THE CAPITAL   285

NOTES   303

BIBLIOGRAPHY   347

INDEX   365

Figures, Maps, and Illustrations

FIGURES

1. The Ashikaga Shogunal Line, 1429–1573   44
2. The *Kanrei* Line of the Hosokawa House, 1445–1563   45
3. The Principal Transitions in Kyoto's Government, 1467–1568   46
4. Biographical Sketches of the Wartime Shogun   120
5. Chronology of Events, 1526–1532   136

MAPS

1. The Provinces of Japan   xiii
2. Kyoto Before the Ōnin War   65
3. Areas of Kyoto Burned During the Ōnin War   66
4. Kyoto During the Age of Warring States   67
5. The Configuration of the Block   211

ILLUSTRATIONS

Portrait of Hosokawa Sumimoto   124
"People of Skill"   174
Fūryū Dancing   246

Water Container   264
Tea Caddy   265
Scenes In and Around the Capital   289

Acknowledgments

I have received the best of help throughout my work on Kyoto from good colleagues and friends. Thomas C. Smith of the University of California and Fujiki Hisashi of Rikkyō University have influenced this book profoundly. Although they may not always recognize their marks here, their suggestions and their own work have everywhere shaped my historical imagination. Yokota Fuyuhiko read documents with me during a year at Kyoto University and really made this book possible—as much through his responses to the texts as through his elucidation of them. Marcia Yonemoto, who is now writing a dissertation on the Edo period, has been a wise assistant with the keenest historical sense. My colleague Mack Horton offered many thoughtful observations on, and corrections to, the first four chapters. His own research on this period often guided my judgment. Kimiko Nishimura assisted me with the research for Chapter 7 with immense resourcefulness and good counsel. Christy Bartlett's astute reactions to my interpretation of the tea culture, as well as her own analysis of the tea texts, also enriched Chapter 7. For splendid and often salty guidance, I thank Asao Naohiro, Thomas Brady, Robert Brentano, Paula Fass, Harry Harootunian, Mark Metzler, Irwin Scheiner, Randolph Starn, and Kozo Yamamura. I am forever indebted to Gerard Caspary, Carla Hesse, and Thomas Laqueur—who simply liked the book tremendously from the beginning (making any amount of salt easy to take). Jane Taylorson made the book happen in typescript, working through endless versions with unaccountable good cheer but fully predictable accuracy. Betsey Scheiner edited the manuscript with uncanny skill and even greater grace. As ever, Donald Shively has been my muse. For the financial support that created time for research and writing, I am grateful to the Fulbright Commission, the Social Science Research Council, and the University of California, Berkeley.

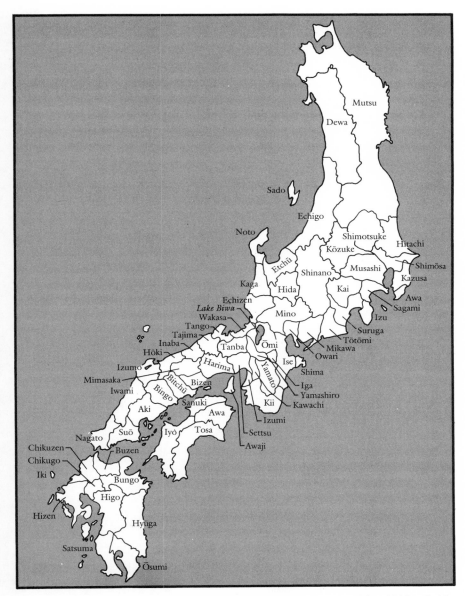

Map 1. The provinces of Japan. Based on Mary Elizabeth Berry, *Hideyoshi* (Cambridge: Harvard University Press, 1982). Courtesy of the publisher.

Introduction

Before the modern era, war was unusual in Japan. The fact is surprising, perhaps, since warriors figure so prominently in the national portrait. Japan nonetheless held at least a surface peace during much of the classical period (ca. 700–1180), and again during the early modern period (ca. 1615–1850). Even in the middle ages (ca. 1180–1467), which we associate tenaciously but often mistakenly with samurai disquiet, hostilities of significant duration and scope were departures from a more durable order. Conflict certainly did shoot throughout Japanese history. And conflict often resulted in local rebellions and uprisings, as well as armed quarrels across the spectrum of grievance. Words like *peace* and *order*, then, are imperfect measures. I use them to suggest not the unlikely ascendancy of social concord, but the uncommon absence of social convulsion.

This is a book about a convulsion that broke the surface of peace— about an unusual war that was fought for a century and more after 1467. Its length alone set the "Era of Warring States" apart from previous upheavals; the open warfare of classical and medieval times had rarely lasted more than five years. Yet in every way, the events of the warring states period moved outside past experience. Battle spread across place and station to test all attachments and configurations of power. The majority of the adult male population took up arms; major warlords could assemble tens of thousands, eventually hundreds of thousands, of troops.

Convulsion is one of the hardest historical experiences to understand, insofar as its purposes and structures emerge dynamically, often obscurely, through the process of confrontation itself. Search as we will for organizing stories about war, convulsion lacks any single plot that links obvious causes to consistent developments. Thus, those of us who write about the warring states tend to retreat, as we search for master themes, into characterizations of the period as "transitional." The label is fine in its way. Civil war clearly did separate the medieval and early modern polities. Japan looked very different in, say, 1450 and 1650, and we have traced the passage between those times through the war years— years of profound change, surely, even if we require the longest view to sort change out convincingly. Hence, by making transition our plot, we finesse the deep confusion of war to focus on the death of medievalism and the birth of early modernism. The last story has been most compelling among historians, since the relative clarity of the early modern settlement seems to illumine the terrain preceding it—showing us what to notice, to ignore, to judge as "aberrational."

Most scholarship has centered on the warring states themselves.[1] These were scores of local domains (finally numbering over two hundred) that warlords wrested from medieval landholdings, and medieval proprietors, as semi-autonomous fiefdoms. The hardiest of them would become the units of the national federation created by the "unifiers" of the early modern state. In this story of domainal formation, the end of the medieval polity recedes into a subsidiary motif, as does the wartime experiment with alternative political visions that survived unification (if at all) in mutant shapes.

The historical treatments of the warring states are abundantly vital and subtle. Yet we have found it difficult, perhaps undesirable in many cases, to escape a teleological narrative. In this work, too, themes of death and genesis arise that anticipate the seventeenth century. Certainly, I began the project looking for a coherent plot about wartime change and the passage into a new peacetime order. But I found something else: a record of pervasive yet indeterminate violence. Fracture seemed to defy coherence, the monotony of injury to defy change, the deflection of movement to defy linear passage. The documents of war led into a deracinated world where I began to look away from the long arcs of historical connection to the words and daily conduct of particular men and women. My subject became not transition but convulsion itself. And this book became an exploration of the distinctive experience, and the distinctive imagination, of a time apart from other time.

My territory is the city of Kyoto, Japan's capital since 794 and, throughout wartime, still the headquarters of a putatively national government that was nominally legitimated by the imperial house and administered by the Ashikaga shogun and their deputies. Like most history of the period, this one is local, although its attention to the urban scene, rather than the great provincial domains, is not common.[2] Nor were cities common. In a sparsely urbanized society where few towns numbered much more than 5,000 people, Kyoto stood apart in its immensity—for it embraced at least 100,000 residents—as well as its complexity. Gathered in the capital were the civil nobility, the military officials of the shogunate, a vast religious establishment attached to Buddhist temples and Shintō shrines, the elite among the country's artisans and traders, and an enormous population of workers in all categories. Kyoto's experience of war was not, then, emblematic of the national experience (although I believe it is suggestive). It was the experience of the nation's center in an increasingly centerless society. War began in Kyoto. Later, it began to end there as well.

Ending does not appear here. Just as my choice of locale is somewhat uncommon, my temporal framework may be disconcerting. The body of the book opens with the Ōnin war (1467–77), a rough yet serviceable marker for the commencement of widespread fighting.* Chronology variously intrudes and recedes thereafter, but rarely do I mention events after the 1550s. I appear to stop in midcourse, refusing to cross the divide of 1568. The year 1568 is another rough yet serviceable marker, indicating the commencement of the "unification" phase of civil war. It opened with the invasion of Kyoto by Oda Nobunaga; it closed around 1615 with the ascendancy of the Tokugawa house, and the gradual stabilization of early modern governance. The last period of war was also convulsive and unpredictable, as resistant to plot as the preceding century of upheaval. Yet still, the conflict after 1568 was sufficiently new in kind to signal a break from the past. We might measure the difference in scale: highly localized struggles were converging into national contests for hegemony. Behind this shift was a more profound change: the division of interest and force that had riven local politics (and kept politics local) was yielding to stunning concentrations of power. Several regional lords were building war machines of a size and cohesion adequate to suppress divergent contests in their home domains and then to

*Ōnin is an imperial era name (designating the years 1467–69) and thus an indication of the chronological framework of the war. Because this particular upheaval lasted until 1477, it is frequently called the Ōnin-Bunmei war to indicate its continuation into the following imperial era. (Bunmei designates the years 1469–87.)

move far beyond their borders. Just how this preponderance of force was achieved is a question we have yet to answer satisfactorily.

So I stop with the 1550s because the break occurring around 1568 separated two rather different worlds—not, in the end, two "phases" of a continuous movement. We can find numerous connections between the two periods. But my interest is in the particularity of the earlier years that connection distorts. The first century of war brought a diffusion of power and purpose that made a variety of political experiments possible. At least in Kyoto, this was a century of trial rather than of emergent resolutions. The 1550s represent a "midcourse" of warfare only if we insist on the union of beginning and ending.

The essential feature of the first century of warfare was rupture itself—rupture so extensive that it opened cleavages in every unit of the polity and society. Originally provoked by competition for high political office, war exposed divisions within the shogunal hierarchy of the Ashikaga and between the shogunate and its provincial officers; within and between martial houses across the country; within and between the networks of local magnates and common soldiers; within the manorial jurisdictions of civil proprietors and between those proprietors and military challengers. The dynamic of force also generated agrarian and sectarian and urban uprising. It came to license brute redress in every manner of quarrel. Bare numbers may suggest the dimensions of the upheaval. Kyoto went through seven bloody transitions in government between 1467 and 1568, as well as numerous failed coups and invasions. Marches on the city by debtors occurred almost annually for thirty years; a radical movement of townspeople under the banner of the Lotus sect reverberated for a decade. The landscape of war was stark: residents of a repeatedly burned and assailed city retreated into two separate enclaves that they protected with moats, walls, and watchtowers.

This experience of rupture was an experience of violence. The fact is central to the age but can be occluded in modern writing that makes war a backdrop for other, often abstract, developments. In our day, it is the filmmaker Kurosawa Akira who has laid firmest claim to the land of battle. I am not sure why injury has tended to fade from view, although I have wondered whether the scale of twentieth-century atrocity has reduced the gravity of our response to the past. Perhaps our attention to the institutional brutalities of modern states has also led us to slight premodern brutality. My own previous work has a bloodless quality, yet I have tried to convey here, through the words of contemporaries, some sense of war's violence. What diarists called "a world without the Way,"

I call the culture of lawlessness. The phrase has several meanings that I shall gloss later. Most immediately, it describes the unleashing of force in the service of particular interest, and the virtual equation of power and injury.

Yet for all its intensity, the wartime experience of rupture was not conclusive. It resulted neither in the full collapse of medieval institutions nor in the dominance of new ones. Particularly in Kyoto, where members of the old elite and their privileged subordinates remained concentrated, continuity with the past was affirmed by the survival (however halting) of shogunal and proprietary organs of rule as well as the persistence of medieval commercial organizations. And leaps into an uncharted future were deflected by the cycles of reprisal and cooptation that succeeded rebellion. Hence, the diarists whose voices we shall hear fastidiously chronicled the facts of convulsion, only to wonder about their always-elusive meanings and then to imagine some return to normalcy—or, as they put it, to "things as they should be." This very indeterminacy of events has blurred our own sense of period. Scholars who resist linking the early decades of war to the plot of unification and early modern transition link them, instead, to the middle ages. Warfare then becomes not an experience with a unique theme but a tumultuous coda to a continuous medieval history.[3]

This linkage to the past remains important to me, for I often follow the diarists in their concern for the fugitive nature of change, the tenacity of the old order. Finally, however, the indeterminacy of events defines rather than blurs my sense of period. Characterized first by rupture, the era of warring states was more deeply characterized by an exploration of possible political settlements.

One of these possibilities in Kyoto was the revival of some version of the medieval polity—and not simply because the obscure visions and divided interests of many contenders encouraged compromise on familiar terms. Despite resurgent coups and uprisings, the old order retained a practical appeal for warlords, aristocrats, and townspeople alike. I return throughout this book to the hold of the past on the men and women who struggled against it. Urgently intertwined with matters of identity and mentality, no less than with advantage, medieval institutions projected more than a vestigial presence in the wartime capital. Even so, we find those institutions transformed by violence, by the machinations of overlords as well as resisters, and by imagination. This last element is the most interesting. Through an artful politics of litigation conducted within traditional channels, residents of Kyoto invented a past that they used to remonstrate against misrule. Increasingly a mental construction rather than a continuous reality, the medieval order became a malleable instrument designed for protection or consolation, aggression or opposition, restoration or rebellion. It was no stable model of authority but a host of choices.

Yet even as they reinterpreted the legacy of the past, the residents of Kyoto also explored the possibilities of political and social reconfiguration. On occasion, such possibilities came sharply into view. Particularly in the Lotus uprising, townspeople shaped a radical vision of urban government that rejected the medieval settlement. Other, disparate visions of change led to direct assaults on the shogunal institution, the horizontal alignment of local soldiers against their overlords, and the organization of townspeople in neighborhood associations. More conspicuous than alternative visions, however, was an alternative politics, which I call the politics of demonstration. Although it was this politics that gradually formed movements like the Lotus, its emphasis fell on the process of search rather than on fixed objectives. Demonstration was an act of mass witness accompanied by exemplary displays of violence. It emerged as a form of public negotiation between nascent associates testing their own resolve and presumptive enemies compelled to assess their own loyalties. Usually staged in the streets with theatrical calculation, demonstration combined an immediate purpose (the cancellation of debts, for instance, or the intimidation of rival sectarians) with a broader probing of new social alliances (the alliances of class, locale, wealth, religion, and trade). We encounter it in many divergent situations: in the protocols accompanying battle, the rites of coup and purge, the conduct of major uprisings as well as more mundane protests, the execution of private justice. We encounter it most spectacularly in the forms of wartime play.

In its range and prominence, the politics of demonstration was new. Occupying a middle ground between the rule of faltering institutions and the rule of brute force, demonstration responded to convulsion by taking as given the intractably divided interests and unclear directions that made for convulsion in the first place. Then, through experimental confrontations that permitted retreat or regrouping, it provided a medium for actors who were neither ready nor even disposed to settle on any single formula of power and identification. This was a dangerous politics, certainly. In the act of opposition, no less than in the tentative alliances and movements it generated, demonstration inspired reprisal. And reprisal, in turn, inspired new trials. This process appears most vividly, in Kyoto, in the build up, repression, and deflection of the Lotus rebellion. Such jagged stories—none of them closed—are the content of Kyoto's wartime experience.

These stories belong to what I refer to as the culture of lawlessness. As I have suggested, the phrase partly describes the ascendancy of violence during the warring states period—the unleashing of force in the service of particular interest. But it describes something more elaborate as well: the state of being without, or lacking, the host of social assumptions intimated by the word *law*. Rather than mere transgression against presumptively normative rules of conduct, lawlessness indicates suspension in a world where rules have lost their cogency. It indicates the need to improvise new modes of association in a territory where precedents offered little guidance.

The medieval order (which I sketch more fully in the next section) had been sustained by a dense cordon of statute, institutional practice, custom, and attachment. Although approximate and frequently breached, the constraints of the polity included consent to shogunal decisions concerning appointment, landholding, and judicial actions; deference to the local authority of centrally confirmed governors; and subordination of the self to the corporate hierarchies of proprietorship, vassalage, patronage, and family. To varying degrees, these constraints continued to operate in the wartime capital, where the old order always retained a half-life. Yet they were under daily siege as rupture spread from assassination to riot, from attacks on abbots to attacks on children. Even though rupture was not complete, it nonetheless destroyed the expectations that had once organized everyday life and thoughts of the future. Thus, in many ways the most arresting feature of wartime documents is not their description of particular crises but their quality of apprehension. Writers presume that nothing can be presumed. Social relations and all the connections that had formed identities were a matter of constant reformulation.

Lawlessness was this process of invention, as men and women of all stations rejected stable definitions of selves, attachments, and values to test possibilities. Its hallmark was demonstration, which substituted for medieval constraints an alternative form of public conduct premised upon fluidity rather than stasis. In the culture of play, even more dramatically than in the culture of uprising, the transforming power of demonstration comes into view. Although the experience of the warring states defied closure, it did not preclude lasting, radical change. Urban residents began using political action as a mode of immediate, physical power in the streets. They began slipping out of the ties of proprietorship and patronage and into horizontal movements of class and wealth.

Throughout these introductory remarks, the medieval polity has been a quiet, seemingly fixed point of departure. It was nothing of the sort. But for readers new to Japanese history, and for fellow students interested in my own presumptions about the prewar years, a bald synopsis may be in order. The task is an awful one. Japan's medieval period was long, its histories were many, and a consensus about their meanings and convergences appears only to recede in recent scholarship. Thus my synopsis, although everywhere indebted to the great historians of this period, is not just bald but idiosyncratic.[4] Impatient readers should hasten on to the Prelude, where this book was always meant to begin.

The political order that prevailed in Japan when civil war broke out in 1467 was a product of accretion. Many disparate layers of historical experience overlapped and blended together in a system created less by design than by crisis and opportunity. Broadly speaking, the medieval settlement had two dimensions—one statist and one lordly—and both derived from the politics of the classical period.

As it emerged around A.D. 700, the classical state assigned sovereignty to a hereditary emperor. He, or for a time she, presided over a national system of government defined by statutory law and staffed by a civil aristocracy. Appointed within intricate hierarchies of power, these civil officials administered sixty-six provinces and their subdivisions, as well as the central ministries that oversaw local rule from the capital (first in Nara, later in Kyoto). They exercised the authority to allocate and tax land, to maintain order and execute justice, and to issue and codify continuing legislation. In addition, civil officials undertook an array of tasks indicative of the reach of state ambition. They conducted diplomatic and trade exchanges with China and Korea; they supervised public works, the minting of coins, and the standardization of weights and measures. They also established a university and a network of officially sponsored Buddhist temples. The cultural and ritual mission of the state was particularly conspicuous. From heroic architectural projects to the elaboration of imperial ceremony, from the compilation of national histories and poetic anthologies to the compilation of local gazetteers, the officials of the classical era cut a wide territory for public custody.

That territory was gradually overlaid, however, with private lordships. Through a range of legal and extralegal accommodations, noble families and religious institutions emerged as absentee proprietors of substantial provincial estates. These were variously, often tortuously, formed from reclaimed lands as well as publicly allocated fields that reverted to private control by commendation and other means. In the twelfth century, half of Japan's arable may have constituted estates of divergent size and organization. Yet in general terms, each estate was both a group of properties (ideally defined and removed from state control through official charters), and a hierarchical corporation that united cultivators, local managers, and intermediate sponsors under the jurisdiction of a major proprietor. All members shared income rights in the estate, and members above the cultivating stratum tended to belong to multiple corporations. The most expansive proprietors held scores of estates in different parts of the country and developed correspondingly large bureaucracies to oversee them.[5]

As estates grew in number and autonomy, the apparatus of the state calcified without collapsing. It awarded the titles that conveyed prestige as well as access to estate rights. Ministers and governors also continued to adjudicate land claims and to administer the still-extensive properties outside the manorial system. These properties too, however, came to be governed in a private fashion, insofar as officials regarded provincial resources as a personal benefice. Military power had a private dimension as well, and much of it eluded immediate state surveillance. Following the abandonment of national conscription in the late eighth century, martial responsibility devolved upon various constituencies: the small militias that policed estates under the authority of managers and proprietors; the corps of soldiers attached to provincial offices, who policed nominally public lands either in service to a governor or at their own initiative; and the bands of retainers (who might also belong to the first two groups) that formed around significant provincial families. Such families might hold estate positions at the managerial level, or public offices below the governor, or some combination of both. The greatest of them were descendants of the imperial house assigned commoner status with the surnames Taira and Minamoto. Linked to patrons in the capital, these families and their retainers served as a kind of national guard—recruited to suppress piracy or local rebellion. Yet they acted as frequently in their own interests and were the source of turmoil as well as its remedy, particularly in eastern and northern Japan.[6]

We associate the break between the classical and medieval eras with a civil war, fought between 1180 and 1185, that brought military power to the center of government. But like most transitions, this one too was fuzzy. At one level, the war focused on competition between the Taira and the Minamoto. The former house had been rewarded with land rights and high titles for several interventions in courtly crises; its head came to serve as Great Minister of State. Dishonored by its own reversals in these crises, the latter house used the occasion of a quarrel between the Taira and the imperial family to declare a war of vengeance. Yet this surface text conceals a far broader conflict between central organs of rule on the one hand (including both the ministries of the classical state and the offices of absentee proprietors) and their local agents on the other. The head of the Minamoto, a man named Yoritomo, attracted wide support with the vision of a new power, separate from the capital, that could vest land rights directly in response to local interests. By 1185, his partisans had defeated the Taira in campaigns across the country.[7]

The ensuing polity was a hybrid that established the character of medieval development. The imperial court survived in Kyoto as the source of political legitimacy and the center of a declining government with authority over "public" lands free of estate formation. Its ceremonial and cultural life retained considerable, if diminished, vitality. The noble and religious proprietors survived as well, although wartime confiscations and rewards had cut into their holdings. But imposed on the classical structures of state and lordship were analogous, eventually dominant, structures of shogunal rule.

"Shogun" is the abbreviation of an infrequently used classical title that was bestowed upon generals charged with internal pacification. One of several honors extended by a wary but compliant emperor to Minamoto no Yoritomo, it became the centerpiece of what would gradually evolve into a distinctive administration.[8] That administration began to take shape as Minamoto no Yoritomo established his headquarters in the city of Kamakura and assumed jurisdiction over the eastern provinces of the Kantō (a boon of victory that may not have produced dramatic changes in local governance). Nationally, the shogun played a peacekeeping role. Perceived by the court as a martial arm of the imperial state, Yoritomo was delegated to station officers in troubled areas as guarantors of order. Over time, officers in two categories spread across the nation: *jitō* (or military stewards) exercised police functions in individual estates and smaller units of public territory, such as districts or villages; *shugo* (or military governors) exercised jurisdiction over capital crimes at the provincial level. And again over time, responsibility for this network of subordinates prompted bureaucratic and institutional development. Particularly from the 1220s, the judicial organs of the shogunate grew in scope, and in sophistication, to handle not just the cases of military officers (their original province) but the cases of nobles, religious communities, and commoners as well.

The Kamakura shogunate lasted from 1185 until 1333, first under the authority of Minamoto no Yoritomo and his descendants and then under noble figureheads controlled by regents in the Hōjō house. In many ways it was an extension of the classical state, which undertook the public functions of peacekeeping and adjudication through offices sanctioned by the court. The public presence of the shogunate was enhanced, moreover, by additional functions that mimicked classical initiatives: the patronage of Zen Buddhist temples, the construction of monuments, the compilation of a history, the codification of laws, the maintenance of an elaborate ceremonial. Most important, the shogunate, rather than the court, received (and once executed) Mongol ambassadors demanding the submission of Japan and then supervised the national defense against the invasions of 1274 and 1281. The growing prominence of the shogunate inspired resistance virtually from its inception. An armed attempt at imperial restoration, supported by warriors disenchanted with Kamakura, failed in 1221. This crisis and continuing disquiet tilted the balance of power away from Kyoto. Following the restoration attempt, the shogunate disciplined members of the imperial family, confiscated estates, and stationed a garrison in the old capital.

The statist dimension of Kamakura rule was only one part of a complex settlement, however. The ambitions of armed men and local functionaries that brought the shogunate to power always underlay the exercise of public authority. Thus, at one level the officers of a national administration, military stewards and governors were also competitors for private advantage, which they sought through their official commissions. The search was variously eased and complicated by the conditions of their tenure: appointments tended to be hereditary, the surveillance of Kamakura remote, their incomes dependent on enterprise rather than fixed stipends, and their functions a matter of negotiation. The experience of military officers was predictably diverse.[9] Some failed to establish a presence; others—constrained alike by civil authorities and by litigation—assumed modest, often vulnerable roles. But still others became substantial powers who carved out landholdings and income rights from both estates and the nominally public domain—through reward and patronage, judicial actions, the reluctant concessions of proprietors, and outright aggression.

Let me trace the history of the succeeding shogunate before reflecting on the integral structures of the medieval polity. Kamakura fell in the 1330s as a result of two rather different movements, each indicative of competing directions in Japanese governance since the classical period. The emperor Go-Daigo mounted another attempt at imperial restoration, this one briefly successful between 1333 and 1336, which sought the recovery of national power by a throne committed to systematic public rule. Here was the statist model of universal, bureaucratic administration guided by statutory law. But Go-Daigo was dependent on supporters with divergent purposes. By 1336 one party had diverted the advantage to the martial house of Ashikaga in expectation of the increased rewards to warriors that the compromises of Kamakura and the imperial absolutism of Go-Daigo had foiled. Here was the lordly model of particular, personal administration guided by interest and accommodation.

The ensuing government was the familiar mixture, with both statist and lordly elements amplified. Eight shogun of the Ashikaga line held office between 1338 and the opening of civil war in 1467. (Seven more assumed the title during wartime.) They made their headquarters not in Kamakura but in Kyoto, where the imperial court, the civil nobility, and the community of aristocratic and religious proprietors also resided. Yet the authority that had once been contentiously shared by civilian and martial institutions was now exercised more securely by a dominant shogunate. Partisans of Go-Daigo mounted sporadic rebellions for two generations. Even so, courtly power waned as the Ashikaga resolutely occupied Kyoto and used Go-Daigo's legacy for their own purposes.

The emperor's vision of a cohesive rather than a bifurcated rule resulted in the creation under the Ashikaga of stronger *shugo*—military governors of the sixty-six provinces who came to preside, without the intervention of civil officials, as the chief administrators of the countryside. Delegated by the shogun to assume emergency powers that gradually became normalized, these *shugo* collected martial taxes, confiscated rebel holdings, conducted inquiries, and executed judgments on behalf of the judicial offices of the Ashikaga. They took direct control over what remained of public territories; they established a degree of power over local strongmen, such as the stewards (*jitō*) of the Kamakura era. They also cut into estates—through the imposition of martial taxes, through police actions that resulted from their jurisdiction over a grow-ing body of crimes. Perhaps the clearest symbols of a new *shugo* presence were the provincial capitals they established.[10]

Nor was the enhancement of the *shugo* the only indication of a pow-erful Ashikaga state. Heir to Kamakura's traditions, Ashikaga deputies also made and codified laws, maintained a judiciary and other central institutions, and conducted restored diplomatic relations with China. Their cultural enterprises outstripped the court's. Further, the shogun-ate assumed control of the money-lending establishment and issued an expanding corpus of commercial legislation. These and similar initiatives give the impression of a resurgent imperial state, this time under a mar-tial house (which had imperial ambitions of its own, in the judgment of some distinguished historians).[11] The impression is accurate in a sense, for the Ashikaga shogunate at its zenith (around the early fifteenth cen-tury) was a coherent national regime that influenced most aspects of public life. But the impression needs to be modified by two significant considerations. First, the shogunate retained limited authority over the court and surviving civil proprietors, and a quite erratic authority over parts of Kyushu and the northeast where entrenched local families held the preponderance of power.[12] Second, the shogunate functioned as an interdependent part—rather than as the sovereign body—in a system of lordly corporations.

As a practical matter, power was exercised at the local level within a variety of particularistic units forged in disparate ways. The old estates, uniting cultivators and managers and proprietors, numbered among these units; and some of them, especially those controlled by great temples, remained large and strong. The general decline in civil author-ity was replete with exceptions. Most other units were military proprie-torships—the holdings established by stewards of the Kamakura era, for example. The majority of military proprietorships arose in the Ashikaga era through the agency or compliance of the *shugo*.

In theory powerful officers of state, these *shugo* were also men of mixed backgrounds and personal resources whose authority derived from a shogunate with an insecure mandate of rule. The victory over Go-Daigo in the midst of considerable ferment had not provided a structure of military alliances. By vesting considerable provincial juris-diction in the *shugo*, a group that included Ashikaga collaterals as well as Kamakura houses and great rivals, the shogunate created a body of virtual peers to extend and consolidate its power. (A sort of peer rule was confirmed by the creation of a *shugo* council and the appointment of a chief administrative officer, the *kanrei,* from the *shugo* ranks.) But the problem of integration confronting the Ashikaga equally confronted these provincial governors. And the problem was exacerbated by the conditions of tenure: *shugo* frequently administered several, noncontiguous provinces; their assignments were rotated on occasion; and they were expected to reside for extended periods in the capital of Kyoto, where some of them jointly exercised central and provincial responsibilities. This diffusion of interest, combined with often-limited backing, made the *shugo* reliant on deputies. And thus, we find the spread of military proprietorships.

The *shugo* used the prerogatives of office to build alliances with a range of old and new men: with former *jitō,* with retainers who served or fought for their houses, with local magnates who had used estate or public commissions to establish land bases, with leagues of fighting men ready to exchange allegiance for reward. Sometimes called *shugo-dai* (deputy *shugo*), a term that properly refers to formal representatives of the governors, this complex stratum of agents is better called *kokujin*— or men of the land (alternately, men of the province). Alliance between them and a *shugo* involved the exchange of deference (and often of military support) for land or income privileges. And such privileges took multiple forms: custodianship of public lands, or properties confiscated from rebels and criminals, or estates conceded to the "protection" of *shugo,* or territories set aside from other holdings expressly to generate revenue for military actions. Allies of the *shugo* might also receive favorable judicial rulings that confirmed their holdings against rival claimants. They might exercise certain prerogatives—to collect field taxes, say, or to enforce punishments or police markets—that constituted private sinecures.

Some of these privileges were more secure than others. Some formed the basis of domainal rights (*chigyō-ken,* often translated as fiefs) while others did not. Most were hereditary and partible but others needed renewal. I nonetheless call them all proprietorships and associate them with lordly patterns of rule, to indicate several general points. The privileges derived from personal awards with an implicitly contractual function. They generated private resources rather than a public purse. They typically entailed a jurisdiction over several village communities that was randomly mediated by other authorities. But, of course, villages too were important mediators of authority.

No less complex than superior levels of power, villages included many layers of wealth, status, and land rights. Some, especially in the home provinces, had developed their own councils. Some were openly defiant of all overlords. Most were influenced by a stratum of armed peasants— the *jizamurai,* or soldiers of the village—who alternately provided support for and resistance to ambitious deputies of the *shugo.* Peasant uprising occurred with increasing frequency in the Ashikaga period, and few proprietors could prevail without the use of intimidating force or concessions to some element of the cultivating population. The spread of the Ikkō sect among peasants and the consequent growth of religious uprising provided one of the gravest challenges to civil and military proprietors alike.[13]

Thus, we find within the Ashikaga settlement four broad, internally varied tiers of power: the shogun and their immediate functionaries in the capital; the *shugo,* or military governors, who were charged with provincial rule; the *kokujin,* or men of the land, who actually exercised proprietorship over a range of discrete jurisdictions; and the cultivators who generated the resources of land and labor. We also find an imperial court that continued to legitimate martial authority and civil proprietors with their own ties to *kokujin* and cultivators.

Within some of these tiers of power, group identities and even a sense of solidarity found occasional expression (among courtiers, for example, or sectarian cells of farmers). But profoundly divided by wealth, influence, and interest, members of a tier were more often competitors whose primary concerns were organized by vertical alliances across tiers—what I call corporations—which first appeared in the estates of the classical era. Medieval corporations normally included cultivators, the *kokujin* proprietor of their villages, and the *shugo* protector of that *kokujin.* But there were many permutations. *Kokujin* leagues might form direct connections with a shogun; armed farmers might seek the patronage of a *shugo;* a *shugo* might be eclipsed by a formidable deputy; a great temple might unite with diverse *kokujin.* And so forth. Except for the lower strata of peasants, individuals also tended to belong to multiple corporations. Nor were these units confined to the tenurial relations of land. The China trade bound shogun, *shugo,* temples, and merchants in private exchanges for profit. Artisans and traders formed guilds linking themselves to peasant producers and proprietary authorities. City people were tenants of noble or military houses.

Corporation is another vexing term that I have bent somewhat out of shape here. I use it nonetheless to indicate several more general points. The operative units of power and social identification in medieval Japan were rarely class, station, wealth, occupation, and relationship to a universal entity like the state. Rather, they were particular units of attachment, formed through discrete negotiations, that bound persons of different status for the exchange of goods (including honor and service) in pursuit of private advantage. Although most had a territorial dimension, they united resident and absentee members through flexible contracts renegotiated by exigency and conflict. They emerged from above—as a lordly protector who represented the shogun or emperor vested authority in a subordinate proprietor; they also emerged from below—as strong cultivators or *kokujin* exacted concessions from superiors. Yet all corporations were premised on vertical alliances to distribute and regulate power rather than on impersonal public structures.

What, then, was the relationship between statist and lordly forms of rule in medieval Japan? Much of the scholarship on the period has centered on this question, with the implication that these apparently incompatible versions of governance were competitive or fitfully ascendant. A related question for historians across the spectrum concerns where, among the different tiers, power really lay. Was power hierarchical—flowing from the shogun to successively more dependent *shugo*, *kokujin*, and peasant cultivators? Or was one presumptively lower tier—the tier of *shugo*, for example, or of *kokujin*—the actual locus of power?[14]

Such questions have yielded a great deal of astute reflection, yet I increasingly find them unsatisfactory. Questions predicated on the anomalies and discordances in a system that lasted more than three centuries (without frequent convulsion) slight the possibility of integration. And efforts to find any single, stable configuration of power slight the dynamism of all political relations. Even though it carries its own clear problems, my formulation of the medieval polity tries to allow for integration and dynamism. I call this polity a complex corporatist state.[15]

State refers to the superstructure of the shogunate (and to the imperial court behind it) that could legitimately award or confirm claims to resources through appointment, judicial action, and edict. Frequently an interested party to these transactions that established its own network of influence, the shogunate was an executive and a mediator that set the frames within which local contests occurred. It was certainly heir to an imperial state that conceived the nation as a whole, with both a ceremonial and a legal center where precedents were defined and officers delegated. Yet it was not the custodian of any absolute value—the privilege of the sovereign, the public good, the universal rule of law. The shogunate remained a versatile, chameleon institution. Constrained by

its need for alliances and its distinctly mixed legacy of authority, the shogunate responded to opportunities with a blend of opportunism and
discretion that secured its mandate and became a model for local governance.

Corporatist refers to the vertical ties of attachment that were mediated by the state but forged between particular persons and groups. Patrons and clients created units of proprietary power, within which they
exchanged resources enjoyed privately. The prerogatives of office, including the office of the shogun, were the essential currency of these
exchanges. The units embraced persons of divergent status in variously
stable and volatile agreements. Agreements could be confirmed by the
state through decree, although they were often a matter of precedent;
injury could be pleaded before the state for melioration.

Complex refers to the diversity found within the corporatist state. It
refers, for example, to the primacy of negotiations over formulas in the
construction of its units, to the many forms and actors represented by
those units. It also refers to the differing advantages accorded to members in different units and hence discourages the assumption that vertical alliances entailed a strictly hierarchical distribution of power. An aggressive *shugo* might well dominate one corporation, while a *kokujin* or
a band of village soldiers might dominate another. Debates over which
tier captured the preponderance of influence in medieval Japan obscure
the variety of alliances that could alternately favor a superior or inferior
party, depending upon local conditions. Neither shogun nor *shugo*, neither *kokujin* nor villagers, were uniformly and continuously strong or
weak. Similarly, influence within the shogunal institution itself resided
at different times with its Ashikaga heads, the *kanrei* administrative officers, the *shugo* council, and bureaucratic magistrates. Debates over the
ascendancy of statist (sometimes called monarchical) and lordly (sometimes called feudal) models of rule obscure not only the functional coherence of the medieval polity but also the exigencies of personality and
crisis. Political roles invite interpretation. And an ambitious shogun with
an unusual opportunity—to resume diplomatic intercourse with China,
for example—might well project an image different from that of a reluctant heir confronted by rebellious *shugo*.

This complex corporatist state organized political and social relations
when war broke out in 1467. The broadest movements of wartime toppled the state—as power moved decisively from center to locale, from
the legitimating principle of office to the imperative of force. They also
toppled the corporations—as vertical alliances gave way to new config-

urations of class. But these movements took a devious course, and their consequences were explored for 150 years.

A last word about martial power. The designation of the medieval shogunates as military governments usefully indicates their responsibility for defense and their access to force through alliances with *shugo* and *kokujin* (and, in the case of the Ashikaga, a personal militia). The designation is nonetheless imperfect: civil activities dominated many regimes, and aristocratic concerns—from courtly marriages to the award of noble titles, from princely habits of cultivation to social exchanges with the throne—dominated the lives of many shogunal officials. A more stubborn problem involves the organization and training of armed men, which was not a systematic function of the shogunates. Nor did armed men constitute any single constituency. They ranged from erratically trained and equipped villagers to professional deputies of the *shugo*, schooled in advanced traditions of the martial arts. Their experience ranged from extensive campaigns in rebel provinces to sporadic interventions in local quarrels. And their command structures ranged from fairly tight systems of recruitment to ad hoc arrangements. Shogunal officials did not create formal structures of conscription or military service that contracted retainers for specific durations with well-defined responsibilities.

Military power was a matter of ambition and ingenuity, the nurturing of alliances over time, the conversion of lordship into command. Some men, including some shogun, became successful generals and built martial networks that survived in their houses for generations—particularly when occasions for battle (in the aftermath of the failed restoration, in breakaway provinces, in territorial disputes) kept their networks employed and rewarded. Yet there were profound divergences in force and the ability to rally it. To mount campaigns, the shogun remained as dependent as all other powers on resourceful connections. The dimensions of military force as well as the initial rallying powers of many *shugo* become clear in the exceptional crisis of the Ōnin war. But the continuing story of wartime is first one of strength fragmenting and then of consolidated armies forming, very slowly, under a new breed of warlords.

Prelude: They Collected
One Hundred Fourteen Heads

Sometime during an autumn evening in 1504, a Japanese aristocrat knelt down to record his thoughts about a troubling day. He turned to a diary that he kept in Chinese, the language of civility and learning. The entry is dense, economical, characteristically precise in the naming of names, as if precision itself could bring order to unseemly affairs.

Yakushiji Yōichi Motoichi, the deputy governor of the province of Settsu, who is a retainer of Hosokawa Ukyō Daibu Minamoto Masamoto Ason, has rebelled against Masamoto and turned enemy. He is marching toward Yodo in our province. All of Kyoto is in an uproar over these events; the exodus of residents carrying their valuables is shocking, people say.[1]

Over the following seventeen days, the diarist added to this record of rebellion, punctuating his account with rumor or hearsay. The entries evoke the brisk movement of news among neighbors as they exchanged details recovered from scouts or sightseers or their own memories of what now appeared foreboding events.

[The warrior Akazawa] Sōeki, another Hosokawa retainer, is of the same mind as the enemy and, they say, has fled Kyoto. . . . I hear that his difference of spirit with Masamoto arose last spring when Sōeki was at Mount Kōya and now, summoned by [Yakushiji] Yōichi, he has accordingly abandoned the capital. The world is ever more in upheaval. Battle has already occurred at Nishioka and we gaze at the smoke of scattered conflagrations. Because the roads to the south have become impassable, the number of men and women fleeing desperately to

1

the east is beyond knowing. They are virtually waging war for access to the roads, an unprecedented scene. . . . A provincial uprising is also exploding.

The litany of individual treachery and panic among the townspeople closes, two weeks after our diarist opened his account, with a terse entry.

Battle has now begun at Yodo where, we hear, the Kyoto party has the advantage.

Word of victory arrived within hours.

The castle at Yodo fell at daybreak. The principal in this affair, Yakushiji Yōichi, whose formal name is Motoichi, has been captured; the leader of the Shinomiya house and his son have cut their bellies. They say one hundred fourteen heads collected during this incident have been brought back to Kyoto. The unexpectedly swift victory is miraculous.

Our diarist offers his final words on the rebellion one day later.

I hear that the prisoner [Yakushiji] Motoichi, age twenty-nine, cut his belly at dawn. People are saying that this pacification of the world is like making night into day. It is remarkable. . . . A member of the Kyoto party, Kōzai Mataroku, had recruited men of the land from this vicinity by canceling half their taxes; he also deployed the people of southern Kyoto by excusing them from their land rents. These are the men, people say, who delivered the victory.

The quality of surprise, of awful transformations, in these passages provides much of their power. As the protagonist Yakushiji "turns enemy" and thus ruptures the presumptive order binding man and vassal, so confusion of a "shocking" and "unprecedented" character cuts Kyoto off from a presumptive normalcy. Things are not, to use the recurrent invective of our diarist's day, "as they *should* be," and, perhaps implicitly, as men and women quite *expected* them to be. Yet with alarming rapidity, rebellion and panic themselves become a new normalcy. Early victory (or any victory?) is miraculous, the recovery of peace as unlikely as the illumination of night.

But although surprise runs deeply through these passages, we also discover in the words of the writer and the actions of his characters some aspect of recognition. These people are not strangers to what surprises them. Residents of Kyoto know enough about armies approaching their province to hazard flight along crowded roads. A local league of armed farmers knows enough about the disarray attending rebellion to mount a timely uprising. The writer knows enough about the consequences of treachery immediately to imagine a world in upheaval. The sense of miraculous delivery is born, we suspect, not of the unfamiliarity of the peril but of the experience of grimmer encounters.

The tension between recognition and surprise in these passages has much to do with another tension—between simultaneous perceptions of catastrophe as discrete and pervasive. The immediate attention of our diarist remains on the singularity of the events he describes. A particular and nameable "principal" (known as Yōichi, this irreproachable diarist notes, but more formally designated Motoichi) has turned traitor against a particular and formidably named lord. But while the diarist initially acknowledges that lord with titles redolent of ancient pedigree and high office, he uses the simple personal name Masamoto to identify the object of Yakushiji Motoichi's defiance and, later, Sōeki's "difference of spirit." The last phrase, like the expression "sameness of mind" or even "rebellion" (literally, "turning the back" in Chinese), heightens the flavor of personal action.

And what began as an individual challenge ends with the suicide of an individual prisoner, named yet again as the man Motoichi and, this time, somehow amplified in character by the mention of his age. Notes about age are conventional in Japanese diaries, especially in moments of crisis, although not, I believe, as perfunctory embellishments. They hold, rather, a great mystery. What is it to die at twenty-nine?

The finality of individual death extends, in the last passage, to the events the rebel provoked. Dark has been made light. Victory has been delivered. This affair is closed.

If Motoichi's challenge was part of a more elaborate campaign, if its target was an institution or a body of ideas merely signified by the person Masamoto, if its conduct fitted a pattern of violent contests suggestive of social genesis, if in short it was "about" something other than personal differences of spirit—our diarist remains recalcitrant. When he or one of his newsbearers searches the past for meaning, it is the spring travels of the man Sōeki that alone invite remark. He does insistently associate Hosokawa Masamoto with "the Kyoto party" and his own sympathies, hence converting the rebel Motoichi into an enemy of the capital itself. But the loyalty of place, the union of insiders against outsiders, seems paramount here. If this loyalty has deeper roots (and, in passages ceaselessly alive with place where even the capital is named six times, our diarist compels us to wonder what could be deeper), he is again silent.

For all the particularity of the diarist's account, nonetheless, a context of war is unmistakable. Motoichi's "march" contains the image of an army soon joined in "battle" and finally routed at a "castle." The Kyoto party has ready a recruitment plan that quickly brings farmers and townspeople into the field. However surprising, discrete, and personal the contest between Motoichi and Masamoto, it is not played out in private duels or guerrilla raids. The adversaries prepare over two weeks or more for a full-dress encounter that eventuates in formal rites of victory: prisoners are taken, heads collected, trophies conveyed to the capital, the details of the critical suicide arranged. No strangers to surprise, neither are these men unaccustomed to singular quarrels.

The rebellion of Yakushiji Motoichi against Hosokawa Masamoto in 1504 has not loomed large in modern accounts of Japan's past. It occurred toward the middle of what we have come to call the Era of Warring States (1467–1568), and most of us who write of this time have fitted the event into its apparently appropriate place in the pattern of seemingly intelligible change that is conveyed by big words like *age* and *war.*

This is a book about Japan's age of war and, somewhat more specifically, about the capital of Kyoto during this century of upheaval. It is a book concerned, sometimes tentatively, sometimes insistently, with the sensibilities and the experiences that, given a long and distant perspective, help to locate the years between 1467 and 1568 as an "epoch." Yet I have begun with Yakushiji Motoichi, with a commonplace traitor who breaks my chronological path, because the diary that tells of this man and his death suggests the inadequacy of our terms of definition. Both "age" and "war," in their spurious clarity, muddle the significance of the events they describe.

Nakamikado Nobutane, the author of the diary I have cited, was sixty-two when Yakushiji Motoichi turned traitor. He was, then, a young man when battle broke out in the streets of Kyoto to "begin" our age of war in 1467, and he had known almost forty years of commotion since that date. But although we discover sharp traces of this background in the diary—in the sense of recognition that accompanies expressions of shock, in the presumption of a martial context for the individual act of treason—rawness remains a basic feature of the episode, which is never tamed by comparison or located on a continuum.

The long view is not the business of Nakamikado Nobutane, of course. It may be that the diarist's very disposition—to attend so closely to the moments of experience—precludes, if not the long view, then the flattening of detail that synoptic judgment can bring. But we may still be struck, in Nakamikado Nobutane's response to fresh trouble, by the absence of passing exclamations that hint at some habituation to violence. The lamentation of his narrative is the lamentation of novelty ("unprecedented," "remarkable"), not of familiarity ("yet again" or "as we expected"). His account remains innocent of a sense of grotesque tedium or even of the black humor that might come from savoring repeated suffering.

If some notion of an "age" is embedded in Nakamikado's words, it is (at least in part) one of a continuing past in which titles still bore meaning, in which relations of lords and vassals remained coherent, in which the nomenclature of time and place evoked a fixed order—an order now ruptured by treason. But precisely because Nakamikado sees the treachery as a rupture, not a routine misery so corrosive that it vanquishes the past and makes senseless its terms of reference, he feels it more keenly. Shock leads the diarist to expect a slide into madness, which is astonishingly halted, or delayed, by victory. Mixed with his belief in a continuing past, then, is a sense of utter vulnerability. Here we sense an echo of preceding threats. Yet the assumptions normally implicit in our use of the word *age*—that rebellion gave way to a collapse of the old order and a new universe of expectations—are not quite shared by Nakamikado Nobutane. He spins no web of meaning that binds any one time separable from other time. His age, insofar as the term is relevant, is one of imperiled continuity.

Alternatively, it is an age of episodes, each experienced intensely but independently of each other. Had Nakamikado Nobutane turned to historical narrative, I imagine him writing in the style of his distant contemporary, the Italian Guicciardini, who found in the repeated turmoil of sixteenth-century Florence neither pattern nor chaos. Guicciardini recovered, rather, the peculiarly new profile of each event, the power of singular personalities, the odd workings of caprice, the worried belief in a prevailing order, the resulting disbelief when order regularly gave way. His structure is the structure of the episode, his point of view immediate rather than retrospective. His meaning arises from the accretion of detail.[2] The historical narratives written in Japan during wartime are remarkably close in spirit to Guicciardini's work. The most ambitious of them are biographies, composed at what we now call the close of the period, about men we now find the authors of definitive change.[3] Yet they too, like the accounts of Nakamikado or Guicciardini, begin abruptly with the beginnings of their subjects, declining opportunities to sort out antecedents and put together frameworks; they proceed jaggedly with well-wrought scenes of action, declining opportunities to trace connections; and they end suddenly with personal turning points, declining opportunities to pass integrating judgments. In their attention (or, perhaps better, their inattention) to the fragmentary nature of experience, they remind us how fugitive a sense of "age" really is—how dependent the notion remains on beliefs in change and intelligible causal relations that tend to be discovered late and contentiously by those of us disposed to look for them.

An agreement that war was the seminal feature of a century of Japanese history gives greatest cogency to our notion of age. The word is charged with many meanings and, in the gravity of its associations, begins to evoke the scenes of flight, fire, havoc, and severed heads that Nakamikado Nobutane has drawn for us. But like all magisterial terms that grapple with immense realities, the word *war* has the ironic power of homogenizing and thus reducing experience. The word also tends to give shape—to impute beginning and end, discernible purpose, a sense of sides—to the least shapely of human ordeals.

Nakamikado Nobutane was quick enough to assign beginning and end and purpose and sides to the particular challenge of Yakushiji Motoichi. But his words are the words of battle in a vocabulary that lacked an unambiguous word for war—as if reflecting a resistance to imagining one more or less bearable calamity as an unbearable state of being, or insisting on the primacy of the intelligible part over an elusive whole. Battle (*kassen*) was a word that served equally well to describe street altercations between townspeople and tax collectors, religious feuds eventuating in attacks upon abbots, and mob actions against pawnbrokers; its emphasis was on the unexpected explosion of violence. And almost invariably, battle was linked in contemporary accounts to another ubiquitous but no less powerful word, quarrel (*kenka*), which rooted hostilities in an underlying anger—what Nakamikado Nobutane describes as "differences of spirit."

The perception of battle as discrete and born of personal injury helps temper the impulse, which I think is contained in the English word war, to understand serious conflicts in primarily abstract and structural terms. I find compelling the holistic analyses of Japan's age of war that center on fundamental changes in society and politics. We might describe the upheaval, for example, as a rejection by local agents of centralized authority and absentee proprietorship over land; as the denial of privileges legitimated by ancestry or office and the halting exploration of notions of a public interest and a common access to power; as a showdown between the forces of private justice and the defenders of institutions of law; and as a transforming reformulation of political life that occasioned varying degrees of self-rule and, more important, new modes of popular action. The very simplicity of such analyses gives them both their marvelous power to illuminate and their intractable (though not unwelcome) difficulty—for all, after all, are partial rather than holistic, most are disputable, and some are contradictory.

But they miss entirely the messiness and the fierce rage of conflict—particularly, perhaps, of the type of conflict Japan experienced after 1467. A civil war fought among a homogeneous island people, the struggle never focused, if struggles ever do find a clear focus, on comparatively well defined issues of race or religion or foreign challenge. It lacked, too, an obvious revolutionary cast: the high drama of war arrayed against each other the members of a political elite, armed holders of property who fought over the distribution of power within institutions they largely took for granted. The major contestants did not challenge the existence of the venerable centers of authority in the nation, the shogunate and the imperial court; nor did they take aim at any specific body of governing policies. Least of all did they generate an articulate ideology of protest. Perhaps the most important feature of their struggle (and the one that most clearly accounts for its shapelessness) was its phenomenal duration. The conflict extended over a century and more. With time, it moved throughout the country and across all social boundaries. Yet while long, it was also intermittent; while pervasive, it was also localized.

What, exactly, the conflict was "about" is hard to say, for it came to be about many different things in many different places as the initial convulsion within the elite opened fissures everywhere. Armed contests over political jurisdiction within the community of would-be governors gave way to brutal family quarrels, agrarian rebellion, clashes between religious sectarians, ferocious dissension over commercial privileges and indebtedness to moneylenders. With the licensing of violence and private justice at the highest levels of power, the rule of force became endemic to all quarrels: differences among villagers over water rights or among townspeople over wells resulted time and again in bloody resolutions that were hardly resolutions at all. The moorings of the world had slipped. In the process, something resembling a revolution—a stubbornly protracted, cumulative revolution—did occur. The institutions that adversaries took for granted were gradually but surely transformed; relations of power and class were substantially altered. As we struggle to put a name to this revolution, our holistic analyses are as much a refuge as a solution.

Yet the slipperiness of change must matter to us. The direction of conflict remained diffuse—creating different purposes in different groups, propelling forward ideas once barely formed. Certain contests receded while others gained prominence for a time. But a central and ascendant struggle that defined an "age" of "war" was spectral until the closing movement of the upheaval. And even after that, the variety of open struggles and the range of resolutions deferred for years a common awareness that one state of being was over and something else had begun.[4]

Hence, the attention of Nakamikado Nobutane to the discrete episode seems right. In capturing the shapeliness of the singular event, he moves us to consider the shapelessness of the whole, in which notions of purpose were yet inchoate, notions of cohesive sides hardly relevant, and notions of beginning and end presumptive of changes very slowly apparent. He captures, too, the force of personality that is missing in holistic analyses. Nakamikado Nobutane does not, perhaps cannot, tell us about the differences of spirit that moved Yakushiji Motoichi to turn his back on his lord. Ideas, causes, visions, dreams may well have been at stake. But abstractions take the form of a man acting against another man, who embodies the grievance. A sense of injury runs through the records of this time. Felt viscerally, injury is associated inexorably with human failing. Failing is linked inevitably with reprisal, and reprisal is extended invariably into mounting violence.

One hundred fourteen heads, Nakamikado Nobutane tells us, were transported back to the capital by Hosokawa Masamoto's victorious party. They may have been displayed in Kyoto on stakes but, displayed or not, people knew and talked of them. Nakamikado Nobutane was not the only diarist to make note of them.[5] Many residents, in fact, must have observed their arrival, for heads are large and heavy enough, particularly in such quantity, to require a substantial convoy. Probably displayed before the shogun or his representatives at the official mansion, they would have been borne, by horse or by hand, across the length of the city—from the southeastern corner of town where the road from Yodo castle joined the urban grid, to the north-central site where the shogun resided on Muromachi avenue.

The collection and presentation of such trophies was conventional in Japanese history, for heads served as a proof of victory and, more to the point, as evidence of the taking of enemy leaders—who were identified either by familiar features or by the distinctive hairstyles, blackened teeth, and cosmetics significant of high rank. They also suggested the extinction of the enemy's potency. Sundering head from body, the swordsman vanquished the spirit.

But there may be more here than a predictable rite of victory. Decapitation is hard and ugly work, so dishonoring that it was left to semi-outcastes on the fringes of military society. Yet the deepest dishonor befell the enemy dead—the mutilated and paraded bodies of fallen soldiers. Only criminals met this fate off the battlefield, and we miss a common element if we separate the ferocious humiliation dealt the felon from the confirmation of an enemy's defeat.[6] The equation of enemy and criminal made decapitation less a rite of victory than an act of vengeance. For the troops of Hosokawa Masamoto, the severing of heads appears a form of punishment directed not simply against the "leadership" of a "cause" but against many, many individual men who, sharing Yakushiji Motoichi's spirit, became personally complicit in an injury to Hosokawa Masamoto and the individual men he led. We find nothing here of a disposition to abstract the purposes of conflict from persons who are party to them or to treat as honorable opponents adversaries who act violently on grievance.

This exchange of injury for injury and the consequent kindling of new grievance surely belies whatever finality Nakamikado's diary imputes to Hosokawa Masamoto's victory, for a grudge is a Gorgon with heads in reserve. And, indeed, Nakamikado himself closes his tale of victory with an image of only fleeting closure: if "this pacification of the world is like making night into day," that world can (will) revolve again away from the light. The anticipation of returning darkness appears more vivid in his opening scenes of "uproar," "exodus," and the desperate flight of city people "waging war for access to the roads." Although spared on this occasion from the unnamed trials that would have accompanied a defeat of the "Kyoto party," these residents acted out of a fear that no parade of heads, no brief return of daylight, could easily dispel.

It is this sense of fear and uncertainty that, in the end, pervades the diary entries. The diary exhibits a mighty effort at control, to be sure—in its precision, its submission of rupture to narrative, its invocation of a continuing past. But these refuges dissolve in the almost-lunatic oscillations of perception that overpower the report. In part, the oscillations are traced in the contrasts of the diary: between surprise over violence and habituation to it; between the singularity and the pattern of conflict; between the personal and the societal roots of disorder; between the institutional identities of the protagonists and their individual "differences of spirit"; between the ragingly vengeful and the methodically orchestrated conduct of battle; between the resolution and the irresolution of victory; between the alternating ascendancies of the sun and the moon. In deeper part, the oscillations are traced in the diary's central question: what is normal? Or what can we expect? The frustration of expectation suspends Nakamikado in a mental universe where an "unprecedented" shattering of normalcy is routine enough to inspire a cool, seemingly normal recruitment of city soldiers. Thus if Nakamikado's diary plays against fixed notions of "age" or "war," it offers us no sanguine images as substitutes. Nakamikado's experience lacks a frame; it is less simple, more devious, than frames allow.

1

The Culture of Lawlessness, the Politics of Demonstration

The Age of Warring States began spectacularly with the "Upheaval of Ōnin," which brought up to 300,000 troops to battle in the streets of Kyoto between 1467 and 1477. The conflict centered on quarrels over succession in several of Japan's great military households, including the shogunal household itself, although many men with many purposes spread the crisis throughout the provinces before the fires of Ōnin had died. One formative account of the initial conflict emerges in the *Chronicle of Ōnin,* a roughly contemporary work by an anonymous historian. It opens with dazzling clarity.

In the first year of Ōnin [1467], the country was greatly disturbed and for a long time thereafter the five home provinces and the seven circuits were all in turmoil. The fault lay with the shogun, Yoshimasa. . . . Instead of entrusting the affairs of the nation to his worthy ministers, Yoshimasa governed solely by the wishes of politically inexperienced wives and nuns. . . . These women did not know the difference between right and wrong and were ignorant of public affairs and the way of government. Orders were given freely from the muddle of drinking parties and lustful pleasure seeking. Bribery was freely dispensed. After men like Ise Sadachika or Shinzui had been approached, lands which should have gone to one party went to another. . . .

There were other signs that forewarned of a great conflict. Both court nobles and warriors were steeped in luxury. . . . The opulence of the great houses and the suffering of the masses were beyond description. . . . If there were loyal subjects at this time, why did they not come forth with remonstrances? On the contrary, their attitude was "let the country break asunder, if it is going to break."[1]

These passages resound with a conviction old as the historical writing of China and Japan, that evil proceeds from evil men, particularly from self-indulgent and careless rulers who attend only to the counsel of bad ministers (and ignorant women). Their failings are moral failings—venality, caprice, sexual vice, profligate spending. And these provoke ever-graver discord among officials, foster injury and the pursuit of redress, inflict poverty on those taxed to support lordly opulence. The license of the ruler and his men sanctions the license of all.

Removing Ōnin to a generic realm of tragedy already charted by a long tradition of similar "war tales," the chronicler proceeds from personal invective to a sober treatment of the ensuing battles. Like earlier storytellers, he shows no disposition to ennoble conflict by locating it in lofty causes or compelling injustice or the visions of charismatic leaders. Nor does he tally the gains of war; they exist—if at all—beyond the universe of the tale. He marks instead the costs of violence—the death, the devastation of the landscape, the perversion of the spirit. The richness of the account comes from the actions of men and women enmeshed in trouble. Their conduct, always a mix of valor and weakness more human than heroic, does not redeem war; it makes somehow comprehensible and unbearably sad the consequences of irresponsible rule.

But while this tone of pathos is sustained throughout the *Chronicle of Ōnin,* its opening clarity is not. As the storyteller moves from the overture to the particular events of this specific war, he labors over too many quarrels among too many characters. He struggles for coherence—heaping episodes upon us as if to insist that plot and meaning must somehow emerge from one more account of one more battle or alliance or conspiracy or ancestral grudge. Yet the task appears finally to have overcome him, for the *Chronicle* dissolves without an ending in the middle of the Ōnin war.

My account of Ōnin and the conflicts that immediately succeeded it mimics the *Chronicle,* at least on one level. Dodging generic themes, I nonetheless grapple with a plot that suggests intelligible causes for the war, the motives of a substantial cast of characters, and the sequence of events that made local crises into a national ordeal. More deliberately than the *Chronicle,* this retelling combines the story of particular grievances with an exploration of the political tensions that helped provoke the war and the assumptions that helped license it. More expansively than the *Chronicle,* this retelling extends into later events—the provincial uprising in Yamashiro and a sequence of coups in the shogunate—

to expose the dynamic of violence set in motion by Ōnin. But like the *Chronicle,* this retelling uses details to evoke what the storyteller called the breaking of the country and what I shall call the culture of lawlessness.

The phrase describes, in part, the specific injuries of wartime: coup, assassination, personal assault and physical destruction, looting and arson. We need not share the loyalties or the perspective of the chronicler (who identified with the imperiled nobility) to recognize havoc. "The culture of lawlessness" further defines an essential feature of the world after Ōnin: the ascendancy of individual interest, which was loosed from traditional controls into frequently violent expression. Medieval law displayed a certain toleration for "private battle" in the service of uniquely compelling concerns. Yet with Ōnin the "force of the self" exploded across all boundaries of place and purpose to become a conventional recourse for persons with wrongs to avenge or causes to advance. In the process, it challenged all the constraints that had once (though contentiously and unevenly) ordered the medieval polity—the constraints not only of legal statute, precedent, and institution, but of attachment to lord and family as well.

But even though my account mimics the *Chronicle* on one level, it moves apart from that model on another to suggest the essential inadequacy of both plot and pathetic mode. Like the chronicler, I lose my struggle to make sense of the too many quarrels of too many characters. Unlike the chronicler, I find the meaning of Ōnin in this absence of coherence. The experience of wartime was the experience of plotlessness.

The most arresting aspect of Ōnin's events is their indeterminacy. This is partially a matter of discrete surprises: bizarre shifts in alliance, retreats from victory, betrayals of cause. It is more broadly a matter of unresolved endings: Ōnin fizzled without a victor; apparently successful uprising moved into failure; the plotters of repeated coups brutalized then rehabilitated the shogunal institution. Just what, we must often ask, did the contenders want? I don't think they knew. Certainly, they understood the particular enmities and prizes that moved them. Surely, too, they perceived links between their immediate purposes and the deeper strains in every relationship of power and personal attachment. All else remained obscure. The source and definition of the trouble, the extent of common cause in pursuing a remedy, the possibility or even desirability of systemic transformation, the ways that advantage could be imagined or measured—all such issues were matters of confusion.

Thus, Ōnin signaled a change in Japan's historical experience, but not one that could be apprehended in terms of clear meanings and obvious directions. Rather, Ōnin wrenched apart one political and social universe without quite destroying it or substituting something new. The first battles began a long process in which people of all stations explored desire and negotiated the terms of an emerging polity. This process is what I mean by "lawlessness." Men and women after Ōnin lacked a compass; their actions were lawless—bereft of guidance—as they explored a new terrain without directional markers and boundaries. The most conspicuous of these actions were violent unleashings of self-interest, but the most significant were mass spectacles of demonstration and witness. In demonstration, the new political culture of wartime first found form and, eventually, meaning.

The Ōnin War

Cast of Characters

Western Camp	*Eastern Camp*
Hatakeyama Yoshinari	Hatakeyama Masanaga
Shiba Yoshikado	Shiba Yoshitoshi
Ashikaga Yoshihisa	Ashikaga Yoshimi
Yamana Sōzen	Hosokawa Katsumoto

The succession quarrels that precipitated the Ōnin war originated in three military families. The first and most consequential of the quarrels came out of the Hatakeyama house, an old and singularly powerful family related to the shogunal line, whose heads served as governors (*shugo*) of three provinces (out of a total of sixty-six) and received high ministerial appointments in the shogunal administration. When it began, the contest involved two children: Hatakeyama Masanaga, the nephew, adopted son, and original heir of the long childless incumbent; and Hatakeyama Yoshinari, the natural son of the incumbent, who was born late in his father's lifetime to a minor concubine. The incumbent preferred Yoshinari and, with the consent of the shogun, transferred the family headship to him in 1454. The more powerful vassals of the Hatakeyama house, as well as influential officials outside the family, continued to prefer the nephew.[2]

The second quarrel came out of the Shiba house, another old family related to the shogun, whose heads also served as governors of three provinces. Although once prominent in the shogun's administration, the Shiba had been weakened by a series of succession conflicts. Their final trials took shape after 1452 when the incumbent head died young without a son or designated heir. The ensuing contest involved two distant relatives of the deceased: Shiba Yoshitoshi, a member of a minor branch house who was initially appointed by the shogun as family head; and Shiba Yoshikado, a descendant of an important collateral line who assumed the headship in 1461 following hostilities between Yoshitoshi and the Shiba vassals.

The third quarrel came out of the shogunal house itself—the house of Ashikaga—whose heads had controlled the military administration of Japan since 1338. This contest involved two heirs of Ashikaga Yoshimasa, the incumbent shogun: Ashikaga Yoshimi, a brother of the incumbent, who was persuaded to leave monastic orders in 1464 to succeed a still young but disaffected and childless shogun bent upon retirement; and Ashikaga Yoshihisa, the son of the incumbent, who was born in 1465 to Yoshimasa's principal consort. The brother had agreed to stand as heir only with assurances that no son eventually born to Yoshimasa would threaten his succession. But that succession was repeatedly postponed after Yoshihisa's birth.

Succession mattered enormously in medieval Japan because men who headed major houses and occupied high offices wielded great personal power. Provincial governors like the Hatakeyama appointed their own deputies and apportioned a wide range of land and tax rights. They also executed legal decisions and enjoyed final jurisdiction over their vassals. Higher administrative promotions within the shogunate brought them leverage over income and military resources in the capital area and over the appointment of governors across the country. Not least important to the calculus of power was the social suasion of resourceful heads—who arranged marriages, oversaw adoptions, selectively entertained ambitious men and women, gave and received significant gifts, and prayed at the right memorial services.[3]

There were institutional constraints on the exercise of power in late medieval Japan, notably a legal tradition that protected well-established rights in land. More critical was an underlying (if faltering) consent to shogunal authority that tempered conduct, as such consent always must, in elusive ways—sometimes by inspiring obedience to a shogun's orders, more often by inspiring imitation of a shogun's example or concern for a shogun's approbation. The consent of the great houses to shogunal authority appeared most clearly in formal appointments, which united the rightfulness of office with the pursuit of local rule. Deriving their own legitimacy from that of the shogunate, the Hatakeyama and the Shiba and their peers governed their domains as the shogun's men.

Nonetheless, both law and shogunal authority functioned best in support of prior negotiations about power, for medieval government retained the character of private accommodation. The shogun and his counselors, the great provincial families, and the local vassals of those families acted within a universe of mutual dependency whose members were variously ascendant and only fitfully aligned. A shogun's pronouncement about a family headship, let us say, might mean very little without the assent of both a man's peers and his formidable armed vassals. And in exercising the considerable prerogatives of his office, that head ruled successfully only when he balanced adroitly the expectations of lord, peer, and vassal.

These contentious interests weighed upon potentially powerful men from birth, when relations were forged that could determine personal fortunes. Each of the principals in our three succession quarrels began life as a leader of a faction. Maternal and paternal relatives, adoptive parents and sponsors, wet nurses and their families, the households of prospective brides, paternally appointed and self-announced vassals, patrons near and far—all formed ever-widening circles of attachment around boys who could be swayed into and throughout adulthood. The immediate attention of these factions focused on succession.

Medieval society preserved a dynamic approach to succession that had characterized elite Japanese households (in various forms) since antiquity. Despite a preference for selecting heirs to great families from among the sons of the incumbent head, the first son of the principal consort retained only an uncertain advantage over his full and half-brothers; and these siblings, particularly if born late to an aging father, retained only an uncertain advantage over their cousins and other paternal relatives (including uncles) and their adoptive brothers from either collateral or unrelated houses. Once selected, an heir might still be replaced by a preferred rival or forcibly eclipsed by a pretender. Several designated heirs might exist at once, typically in a specified order of ascent.[4]

Because of the variety of candidates for succession, the choice of an heir had to be made actively; because of the possibility of reversing a first decision, the choice of an heir had to be compelling. Although a strong head of a cohesive house might enjoy considerable freedom in naming his successor—particularly if he had a mature son—the openness of choice invited, and virtually required, negotiation over a broadly acceptable selection. Hence, we encounter the politics of faction—which was, I think, less a result of the succession system than the motive for its creation and survival. The system was bent to the collective interest in succession that centered on a single lineage but embraced many collateral, allied, and dependent groups. It implicated these groups in the choice, tending to deny sole dominion to an incumbent head, his main consort, and his favorite son. Although medieval society accorded great power to the head of a great house, it modulated that power from birth. The principals to the three quarrels, then, mattered as individuals—for, with the exception of the shogun's infant son, their characters and actions gave shape to the conflict. But they mattered, too, as representatives of many other men, and some women, whose characters and actions shaped the conflict just as surely.

There was a certain genius to the medieval approach to succession. It frustrated autocratic rule and, when it worked well, distributed power and enhanced the strength of warrior houses compelled to function cohesively. The approach also encouraged families to absorb dangerous outsiders—principally through adoption and marriage. The failure of factions disappointed by a particular choice of heir might be variously mitigated: by access to negotiations that a closed system would have precluded; by concessions that reflected both their influence and the need to retain their loyalties; and by the anticipation of happier outcomes to later decisions. But the system was perilous: it required exquisite compromise and a conviction that compromise would succeed. In the decades before Ōnin, uncommon pressures sent cracks through the foundation of compromise.

One problem was the overextension of families such as the Hatakeyama and the Shiba, who governed multiple, noncontiguous provinces and consequently depended on local deputies for local rule. Overextension tended to increase the number of retainers with substantial interests in a family heir and, more critically, contributed to the growth of major vassals who emerged as surrogate governors. By manipulating a variety of advantages—from a sustained local presence to repeated appointments, from propitious marriages to tenacity of character, from distinguished service in battle to large land holdings, from lucrative money-lending activities to connections with other military and courtly families—these vassals constructed, over time, complex households of their own.[5] Able to recruit hundreds of men for battle, they provided both the essential support for, and the inevitable threat to, absentee governors who lacked independent armies under their direct control.

The always-delicate relationship between governor and deputy, between lord and vassal, was tested uniquely by succession, when the obvious issues of power were joined to the equally explosive issues of prestige and affection. When the incumbent head of the Hatakeyama house pressed the claims of his young son, despite the allegiance to his nephew of two important vassal families (the Yusa and the Jinbo), he scorned his deputies and they declined his leadership. The greatest vassals of the Shiba house—the families of Kai and Asakura—had originally favored the appointment as head of Shiba Yoshitoshi, who was basically an outsider to local politics and, at seventeen, presumed to be both grateful for support and submissive to guidance. But an ungrateful Shiba Yoshitoshi locked himself into conflict by seeking to divide his vassals, principally through vain efforts to transfer the offices of the Kai family from an older to a younger brother and to secure the censure of the shogun against the recalcitrant older brother.[6]

Overextension had consequences beyond the ranks of household vassals, since the interests of many neighboring governors and shogunal officials came to bear on the succession decisions of the Hatakeyama and the Shiba. Such interests engaged not only provincial politics but also two national offices to which the Hatakeyama had a current, and the Shiba a historical, claim: the office of *kanrei*, the chief minister or administrative officer of the shogunate; and the office of Yamashiro *shugo*, the governorship of the capital area, where the immediate military and taxation concerns of the shogunate centered.[7] And compounding the issues of power were the issues of personality. The shogunal official Ise Sadachika, for example, made mischief in the Shiba quarrel first because he loved the sister of the Kai brothers (whom he consequently favored in their joint opposition to Shiba Yoshitoshi) and later because he loved the sister of Shiba Yoshitoshi's mistress (whereupon he entered Yoshitoshi's camp).[8]

Yet by far the most important accessories to the Hatakeyama and Shiba quarrels were Hosokawa Katsumoto and Yamana Sōzen, heads of the greatest provincial houses of the time that spread into eight provinces each. Both warily allied and cordially divided, the two men committed themselves to a kind of accord when Hosokawa Katsumoto married Yamana Sōzen's daughter and, in time, adopted Yamana Sōzen's youngest son as his heir. Nonetheless, rancor colored their relations after the Hosokawa became instrumental in restoring the house of Akamatsu. (Yamana Sōzen had defeated and killed the Akamatsu head in 1441, following that head's assassination of the incumbent shogun. The Yamana had then received charge of the three provinces formerly governed by the Akamatsu, thus swelling dramatically their own provincial power.) The efforts of the Hosokawa not only to revive the Akamatsu but also to reestablish the house in its old holdings assailed the interests of the Yamana. This grudge became keener when Hosokawa Katsumoto renounced Yamana Sōzen's son as heir in favor of his own child.[9]

Hosokawa Katsumoto and Yamana Sōzen had originally united in support of Hatakeyama Masanaga in his quarrel with Hatakeyama Yoshinari. But Yamana Sōzen, in increasing antipathy to any Hosokawa favorite and increasing sympathy for the militarily brilliant Yoshinari, switched sides. The Hosokawa and the Yamana also divided over the Shiba issue. When Shiba Yoshitoshi's ill relations with his vassals provoked battle, Yamana Sōzen urged the election of Shiba Yoshikado, who subsequently became his son-in-law. Hosokawa Katsumoto took the part of Shiba Yoshitoshi.

It might have been possible, in an earlier day or with a different shogun, to resolve the quarrels of the Hatakeyama and the Shiba through shogunal mediation. But here, too, there were difficulties, some recent and particular, others inherent to the politics of faction. The conduct of Ashikaga Yoshimasa's father, the sixth shogun in the Ashikaga line, who died in 1441, had done much to discredit any shogunal role in succession controversies. He had undermined several provincial governors (and briefly heightened his own power) by arrogating to himself the right to select heirs, hence setting off lasting disputes within households. On two occasions this shogun had orchestrated assassinations of governors and, for his pains, had been assassinated (by the Akamatsu head) himself.[10] By usurping decisions conventionally left to negotiation and by wreaking havoc in provincial families, he left his son a virtually insurmountable legacy of distrust. He also left him a compelling example of what happens to unruly rulers. Ashikaga Yoshimasa himself was little disposed to explore the boundary between prudent but resolute responses to the current succession crises of his governors and the intolerable lordly autocracy of his father. He was a young shogun (born in 1436 and thus only in his teens when the Hatakeyama and Shiba quarrels began), a reluctant shogun (ready to retire before the age of twenty-eight), and, by all accounts, quite a bad shogun.[11]

Most contemporaries, like the author of the *Chronicle of Ōnin*, bristled at the ascendancy of advisers they found contemptible, particularly Ashikaga Yoshimasa's women—first his mother, later his mistress Ima Mairi no Tsubone, finally his consort Hino Tomiko. The mistress became the target of raw invective and repeated calls for censure. (She was eventually murdered for reputedly using a spell to kill Hino Tomiko's first child.)[12] Hino Tomiko proved more resourceful, and more durable. She conceived another child just as Ashikaga Yoshimi was to succeed his brother, and she promptly built a substantial faction around her newborn son, beginning with Yamana Sōzen.[13] Ashikaga Yoshimasa was also surrounded by calculating men—notably Ise Sadachika, who trifled with the Shiba and later became guardian of Hino Tomiko's infant son.[14]

Ashikaga Yoshimasa emerged in the record as a "bad shogun" not only because of his submission to putatively evil counselors (and his legendary expenditures) but also because of his retreat from crises. One indictment concerns the famine of 1461, when as many as 80,000 were said to have died and Kyoto's Kamo River washed the bones of untold abandoned corpses. Attempting no adequate policy of relief and refusing to interrupt his pleasures, the shogun found himself rebuked by the emperor himself.[15] The shogun's retreat from the crises of succession took the form of accommodation. Ashikaga Yoshimasa was prepared to intervene just as often as, and in whatever direction, his counselors advised. In the words of the *Chronicle*, "Both branches of the Hatakeyama had three times received censure and had three times been pardoned. . . . Both branches of the Shiba had been censured and pardoned twice." But the chronicler was not counting closely enough. In the case of the Hatakeyama, Ashikaga Yoshimasa made and reversed decisions five times. In these instances, he played the role of neither an autocrat nor a prudent interlocutor. He played the role of a weather vane.[16]

The revulsion over such conduct in the *Chronicle of Ōnin* suggests a vision of the shogunal role—as singular leader of the nation—that the politics of faction effectively denied. The *Chronicle* draws our attention back, however, to the particularity of medieval (or all) rule: individual men gave life to factions and bore the responsibility of their success or failure. Ashikaga Yoshimasa himself, like the principals in the Hatakeyama and the Shiba disputes, was surely an instrument of fractious parties—both within and without his own family—for the shogunate remained as much a creature of competing interests and internal negotiation as all other substantial households. Yet factions enmeshed leaders without eliminating the notion of leadership. The tension was most lively in the case of the shogun, the head of a quirky, never easily defined government that united private accommodation to a regard for rightful administration. A captive of self-interested clients, the shogun was also chief of state, custodian of appointments, and keeper of the law. The *Chronicle of Ōnin* judged him harshly not as a failed conciliator too respectful of faction but as a fatally weak ruler.

But before we assign responsibility to Ashikaga Yoshimasa, we must consider a final element in the crises of succession. The course of events was complicated by the interests of powerful vassals and allies and confused by the waffling of a shogun inclined to leave decisions to the play of competition. But the three succession quarrels finally devolved into war because violence was an acceptable recourse.

The law of the shogunate was ambiguously emphatic about violence:

Even in cases of obvious grievance, private battle must first be sanctioned by the shogunate. We have ordered time and again that parties to death and violence shall have their property confiscated. But now we forbid private battle even more sternly.

Persons who violate the law shall be executed. . . . In cases of defensive battle, we shall conduct an investigation and render judgment in accord with the circumstances.[17]

The passage resonates with trouble. It begins by acknowledging the power of unspecified grievances that, when "obvious," may be proper grounds for battle. The law also assigns the right of redress to the aggrieved party rather than an official organ or the military guard of the shogunate. While insisting that grievants receive permission for revenge, the passage accords latitude for action by making "defensive battle" a matter of investigation, not summary punishment. (The difference between offensive and defensive conduct must lie in the eye of the beholder.) This and many similar statutes were part of a distinct shogunal effort to assume jurisdiction over major issues of discipline and punishment. Nonetheless, the traditions of self-redress the shogunate tried to stem remain everywhere apparent in the presumptions and concessions of the law. Their persistence is also revealed in the necessity for periodic reiteration of the law with ever-sterner penalties.[18]

The actual conduct of the shogunate in the face of private battle was as ambiguous as the law. From the time the succession quarrels in the Hatakeyama and Shiba households began, some fifteen years before the opening of the Ōnin war, hostilities accompanied negotiation. Just as soon as the father of Hatakeyama Yoshinari had won the original permission of the shogun to appoint Yoshinari as family head, he attacked those vassals who continued to support Hatakeyama Masanaga. Fighting went on thereafter, growing particularly fierce between 1460 and 1463, when Hatakeyama Masanaga (at that point the official family head) laid siege to his cousin's fortifications with the help of an army recruited by the shogunate. The principal battle in the Shiba house occurred in 1459: commissioned by the shogun to lead a march into the eastern provinces, Shiba Yoshitoshi diverted his troops and launched a full-scale attack on his opponents in the Kai family. Another of our characters, Yamana Sōzen, was conducting an intermittent war of his own against the Akamatsu.

In response, the shogunate issued writs of censure and support. It also raised troops for disciplinary actions and retracted the appointments of some belligerents. It even secured an edict from the emperor endorsing Hatakeyama Masanaga's siege on his cousin's castles.[19] Nonetheless—and the point is fundamentally important—the acts of shogunal censure had no certain and lasting consequences. Yamana Sōzen lost neither land nor influence for his attacks on the Akamatsu. Far more telling, private battle did not preclude the reappointment of belligerents as family heads: the shogun reinstated Hatakeyama Yoshinari as head in 1466, despite shogunal and imperial writs that had sent armies out for almost three years in an unsuccessful effort to discipline him; the shogun also reinstated Shiba Yoshitoshi as head of his house in 1466, despite his treachery in diverting troops from an official march to a private reprisal.

More was at work in these instances than a shogun's weakness or a society's deference to the realities of force. The ambiguity over the right to violence that appears in both law and shogunal conduct derived from a deep ambivalence over the range of the shogunate's jurisdiction. To some degree, this ambivalence proceeded from the medieval dispersal of authority among courtly and religious proprietors, who exercised jurisdiction over their estates, and among military houses and officials, who enjoyed wide discretion in the administration of their localities. Because authority remained not only dispersed but largely undifferentiated, the rights of governance extended to armed police action and often to judgment and punishment.[20]

Yet in numerous ways the shogunate had tempered the dispersal of authority: in part, by claiming exclusive jurisdiction over a widening body of crimes that ranged from murder and treason to tampering with

0591802

harvests and night thefts; in part, by issuing an expanding number of statutory laws that fixed the limits of local discretion over the seizure of property, for example, or the collection of taxes. Far more restrictive, however, was the case law of shogunal courts, which acted on appeal when local justice failed. The shogunal courts constrained both the scope and the exercise of authority: they established a corpus of precedents; a regard for legal procedure and documentation; an attitude toward contract that mitigated capricious exercises of power; a growing habit of recourse to high tribunals; and, not least significant, a shogunal voice in the regulation of many matters (commerce, in particular) that entered official surveillance through the suits of grievants rather than executive initiative. Despite the dispersal of governing authority, which the shogunate sometimes resisted but largely accepted as the foundation of medieval politics, the courts of shogunal law fostered a convergence in governing practice. At the same time, they came to define the shogunate's most significant national function—that of interlocutor and final judge.[21]

The ambivalence of the shogunate over the range of its jurisdiction derived less from the dispersal of authority than from the limits of authority. Certain matters in medieval Japanese society, preeminently the matter of succession, stood outside the universe of statute, precedent, contract, and executive right—outside, that is, the universe of conventional expectation and duress that make the rule of law intelligible. By their very nature, succession decisions resisted the workings of law, however broadly conceived, for no review of evidence, no consultation of statutes, no invocation of past practice, no exploration of the natural order could settle them unequivocally. Each succession decision, however guided by custom and however responsive to obligations, emerged from unique negotiations (and impulses) that derived their meaning from their freedom. Any legal tradition that fixed a pattern of ascent to a family headship, that specified the relative influence any participant to the decision might exert, that precluded the reversal of an original selection—that, in short, closed the terrain of negotiation—would, of necessity, have transformed the process.

The right of the shogun to appoint family heads and grant offices brought succession decisions into the shadows of the law but no further. The resistance of great households to shogunal interference and the deference of most shogun to internal resolution combined to erode shogunal fiat. Hence, succession decisions continued to occupy the uncharted boundary between the domain of law and the domain of

134403

negotiation. These domains, the territory of medieval society, we have encountered repeatedly. They have many names, none fully apt: they are the domains of putatively public as opposed to apparently private interest; of government through legitimate institutions as opposed to factional accommodation; of leadership guided by the trust of office as opposed to the constraints of attachment. Often overlapping rather than separate, the imperatives of the two domains made the shogunate ambivalent about the use of violence. The shogunate clearly sought to regulate force as the lawful prerogative of government. Yet insofar as matters like succession fell incompletely within shogunal jurisdiction, and consequently lacked legal remedy, the shogunate retreated from any categorical statement on what remedies might be pursued. Indeed, the shogunate conceded the inevitability of "private battle," which it was prepared to endorse in the face of "obvious grievance."

Grievance was inherent in succession quarrels, with their choking entanglements of family, obligation, power, and loyalty. And perhaps because such grievance lacked the legitimacy of a violated "contract" or "right" and centered instead on violations of hope, it assumed the character of the mortal grudge: that is, in an idiosyncratic definition, a sense of personal injury that focused on another person and demanded amelioration that normal channels of restitution could not provide. Grudges are certainly inherent in the human condition, although they differ among societies in their characteristic content, the extent to which they are condoned, and the range of recourse grievants are accorded. It was one of the defining features of medieval society in Japan that the highest governing institutions in the land condoned the recourse to private battle when parties injured outside the reach of the law found cause for redress.

The Ōnin war, foreshadowed by years of armed succession quarrels, finally began in the first month of 1467. One precipitating event was the shogun's decision late in 1466 to transfer yet again the headship of the Shiba from Yoshikado to Yoshitoshi. But when Yamana Sōzen massed troops in the capital of Kyoto to support his son-in-law, Shiba Yoshikado, the shogun reversed himself once more and returned the headship to Yoshikado.[22]

The immediate provocation of the war was another shogunal decision, also taken upon the counsel of Yamana Sōzen, to transfer the Hatakeyama headship again from Masanaga to Yoshinari. On the second day of the first month in 1467, the shogun declined to exchange New

Year's visits with Hatakeyama Masanaga and stripped him of the honor of guard duty at the imperial palace. He received a New Year's call instead from Hatakeyama Yoshinari and subsequently returned the courtesy. On the sixth day of the first month, the shogun ordered Hatakeyama Masanaga to quit the mansion in Kyoto where Masanaga presided not only as Hatakeyama head but also as *kanrei*, or chief minister of the shogunal administration, a post he had received in 1464. Under shogunal order, the mansion was to be transferred to Hatakeyama Yoshinari. On the seventeenth day of the first month, Hatakeyama Masanaga burned down this mansion and moved with an army of perhaps two thousand troops to Kamigoryō-sha, a shrine in northeast Kyoto not far from the shogun's residence. The alarmed shogun then removed the imperial family from the palace to the presumed shelter of his own residence and ordered both Hosokawa Katsumoto (an ally of Hatakeyama Masanaga) and Yamana Sōzen (an ally of Hatakeyama Yoshinari) to refrain from all armed action.

Early on the morning of the eighteenth day, during a snowstorm with heavy winds, Hatakeyama Yoshinari attacked his adoptive brother with as many as three thousand horsemen. Yamana Sōzen defied the order of the shogun and dispatched troops to swell Yoshinari's army. The battle lasted one day and one night, "scattering flowers of fire everywhere and making an eerie sight." The cries of battle that filled a sky mixed with snow and flames reached the palace where, we are told, more than thirty women fainted in terror. Observers reported that the blood from as many as five hundred dead turned the waters of the Kamo River red.[23] By the morning of the nineteenth day, Hatakeyama Masanaga had been forced into retreat, ending the opening movement of what one diarist immediately called "the great upheaval of the realm" (*tenka ōran*).[24]

The word *ran*, which I translate here as upheaval, is a rare expression in Japanese records that evokes both the riot of battle and the disintegration of rebellion. Promptly elected by other diarists, the word is a prescient reading of what was to come, but a somehow disconsonant portrayal of what, so far, might be regarded as simply another clash between the Hatakeyama cousins. Yet the use of the word suggests how fully a crisis had emerged by 1467 and how clearly it found expression in the vicissitudes of the first month—when the head of government changed course for a fifth time in the Hatakeyama quarrel; when the chief minister in that government set fire to his official residence and occupied a religious sanctuary with armed men; when provincial governors massed supporting troops in the streets of the capital; when the emperor and retired emperor were compelled to flee from their palace; and when battle raged again as the chief recourse of the country's most eminent officials, this time within the environs of the country's central city. Although the aspect of "rebellion" conveyed in the word *ran* attached directly to the actions of Hatakeyama Masanaga, it also encompassed this morass of terror. Like the reproaches against the shogun in the *Chronicle of Ōnin,* which convey expectations of lofty public leadership from a man captive to private factions, the accusations of rebellion are arresting because they measure the conduct of powerful men by the standards of one domain (the domain of public interest and official trust) when the operative standards were those of another (the domain of special interest and private war). These accusations suggest how deeply, if only in rhetorical terms, the rule of law had penetrated medieval society and how imperiled it was by the rule of force.

Nor can we overlook the second aspect of the word *ran*—as riot. Although it attached directly to the episodes of battle, the word suggested a broader context of trouble: from the last months of 1466, soldiers and adventurers had been raiding the warehouses of pawnbrokers, plundering homes and mansions of valuables (especially swords and blades), and setting fires to facilitate these thefts. Soldiers of fortune attracted to Kyoto by the possibility of employment had also been demanding lodging from townspeople, and retainers of the gathering armies had been cutting trees to construct fortifications and digging up city streets to make moats.[25] Whatever we call the hostilities that focused on the Hatakeyama—whether rebellion or private battles of redress— they had consequences more terrible for most of the population than the battle itself. The gravest threat was the collapse of civil order in the presence of a government overcome by civil war.

The course of the Ōnin war following the opening engagement took two directions. First, the allies and vassals of the Hatakeyama cousins assembled in Kyoto to exchange reprisals there that continued for eleven years. Second, the battle extended to the provinces, where combatants attempted to influence the struggle in the capital by blocking the passage of troops, cutting routes of supply and reinforcement, and distracting energies from the Kyoto theater. Such tactics of diversion tended to concentrate on the provinces neighboring Kyoto and the area of the Inland Sea. But the provincial battle arose mainly from the quest for local power that had always organized the politics of faction and now resulted in open wars of conquest. The Akamatsu, for example, tried to win back their hereditary holdings in three provinces held by Yamana Sōzen; the Takeda and the Toki (both allies of Hosokawa Katsumoto and Hatakeyama Masanaga) fought against the Isshiki (an ally of Yamana Sōzen and Hatakeyama Yoshinari) over contested holdings in two provinces; the Shiba vassals in the Kai and Asakura houses sided with Yamana Sōzen in support of Shiba Yoshikado but also used the occasion to displace the Shiba entirely from local rule.[26]

In many ways, the actions in Kyoto, which provided both opportunity and license for such provincial fighting, are puzzling. How are we to answer the obvious questions: why did the capital become a crucial site of conflict and what objectives were being pursued there? It is more difficult still to grapple with the meaning of the most extraordinary development in Kyoto: armies of colossal size were gathering within the city. The *Chronicle of Ōnin* puts the combined forces of Hosokawa Katsumoto and Hatakeyama Masanaga at 160,000 men and those of Yamana Sōzen and Hatakeyama Yoshinari at 116,000. These troops came primarily from the many provinces under the direct control of the Hosokawa and the Yamana, with substantial support both from the various Hatakeyama and Shiba factions and from other provincial families—ranging from Kyushu in the west to Shinano in the east—that could not long remain neutral in a confrontation putting at risk all boundaries and all factional networks.[27]

In the ensuing narrative we shall encounter, with dismaying regularity, the huge figures that thread all contemporary (and most modern) accounts of warfare and rebellion in this period. It is easy, and seemingly prudent, to dismiss these figures, or at least to discount them. Yet I am inclined to trust the figures in a general way, not only because they recur so persistently but also because they hint at the deeper motives that helped shape, first, the Ōnin experience and, later, the culture of wartime. In effect, the huge numbers were part of a new political order in which battle was only a surface phenomenon.

Certainly the masses of men (and perhaps many women) who were assembled in the capital had little to do with the actual character of fighting there. Following the opening episode at Kamigoryō shrine, regular hostilities began in Kyoto late in the fifth month of 1467 and continued into the tenth month. Although one campaign in the southeastern hills engaged forces for almost fifteen days, battle typically took the form of brief street fighting directed against the mansions and city encampments of the principal contenders. Yamana Sōzen and his allies concentrated in the area of Horikawa, north of Ichijō (and came to be called the western camp); Hosokawa Katsumoto and his allies concentrated in the area of the shogunal mansion at Muromachi (and came to be called the eastern camp).[28] Less than one kilometer separated the headquarters of these adversaries in a well-settled section of the city with few wide streets. Diarists tell us that tens of thousands of men participated in attacks on these locations and on the various shrines, temples, and major residences scattered about the city where the combatants maintained troops. Nonetheless, most soldiers must have been squeezed into rear and largely irrelevant positions because of the urban terrain. Their utility was further diminished by the conduct of battle: assaults took place one at a time, rather than simultaneously in different locales; they usually took the form of frontal rather than pincer attacks; they hardly ever moved out to plains around the city; and, perhaps most important, they almost always concluded within a single day. After several hours of battle awarded an advantage to one side and decreed the retreat of the other, waves of reenforcements did not arrive to sustain either attacks or defenses. The engagement of the Hatakeyama cousins at Kamigoryō shrine in the first month of 1467 did last a day and a night; the first great explosion of street fighting late in the fifth month did extend into two days; and a siege in the southeastern hills (in the ninth month) ended only after two weeks of desultory fighting. Yet these were unusual events in a campaign (if we can call it that) that emphasized short raids of terror.[29]

What appears to be the most significant battle in the Kyoto theater occurred in the tenth month of 1467 when the Yamana forces succeeded in taking Shōkokuji—a major Zen temple within a block of the shogunal residence, always occupied by several thousand Hosokawa troops. The Hosokawa and their allies gave up this essential location after a few hours of fighting and did not attempt to recover it in the succeeding months. Nor did the Yamana forces press their great advantage with ensuing attacks. After the surrender of Shōkokuji, only random battles resumed in Kyoto.[30]

Yet even though the battle was limited, the physical loss to the city was profound. In a densely settled capital of wooden structures and narrow streets, the fires that inevitably attended attacks—and more often attended the looting that became one of war's commonplaces—went on long after fighting ebbed. The two days of street battle late in the fifth month desolated much of the area from Ichijō to Nijō between Abura no kōji and Ōmiya. Early in the sixth month, fires that began with arson and flew in a stiff wind burned for three days. The *Chronicle of Ōnin* describes the turmoil with characteristic poignancy (and with figures that strain credulity):

Holding aged parents in their arms, pulling along wives and children behind them, the townspeople fled the city in a roar of cries. And none was left to fight the blaze. The fires burned from Nijō in the south to Goryō in the north, from Ōdoneri in the west to Muromachi in the east—over one hundred blocks. About 30,000 residences—of nobles, military men, great and small alike—went up in flames. Everything is now ruined lots.[31]

Such images—of light giving way to darkness, heat giving way to cold, clamor giving way to quiet—fill the records of diarists who went out day after day to keep the toll of loss. Another image, of human retreat, is equally insistent: "Across our charred land, all human traces have been extinguished. For blocks on end, birds are the sole sign of life."[32] Or again, in the words of the *Chronicle of Ōnin,* "The Flower Capital of myriad ages is now a lair of foxes and wolves."[33] Many—particularly nobles, members of religious communities, and skilled craftspeople in the textile and metal-working trades—simply abandoned Kyoto, mostly for the nearby towns of Uji, Sakamoto, Nara, Sakai, and Ōtsu. Some of the more affluent residents dispatched their families and their treasures to the countryside but remained in the city themselves, in the company of household guards and servants, to protect mansions that they fortified with moats and gates of bamboo spears.[34] But most of the capital's residents could only retreat from their ruined homes to the shanty towns that spread through the streets and back lots of temporarily safe neighborhoods. Safe lodging of any type was rare: the fires of Ōnin finally destroyed over one half of the capital, including as many as seven thousand residences of military men and two hundred mansions of the court nobility.[35]

But what did the men who laid waste to this great city really want? In part, I think, they wanted the waste—not so much the waste of an abstract phenomenon called "the capital," where buildings signified an enduring past or a universal government or a common cultural legacy or any other "idea" of general and transcendent import, but the waste of the particular places that signified a particular enemy's hold on authority. The geography of battle followed the geography of personal power as soldiers assailed mansions and encampments (often at religious sanctuaries) that, whatever their larger associations with impersonal institutions of rule, conveyed more immediately the ambitions of the adversary who resided there. The burning appears to be an act of rage and an act of humiliation fired by a grudge. It may also have been a form of purgation inspired by the same concern over defilement that led, under the terms of medieval justice, to the torching of homes once occupied by criminals.[36] As I likened the beheading of battleground enemies to the mutilation of criminals, so I am inclined to view the burning of mansions as a rite of punishment and exorcism derived from criminal law. And like the military leaders under attack who committed suicide and entrusted their heads to vassals to preclude violation at the hand of an enemy, so Hatakeyama Masanaga set fire to his own residence to preclude its violation at the hand of a rival.

A desire to injure—to ravage the physical sites in Kyoto held by the adversary—helps explain hostilities directed not toward the capture of the city through a sustained campaign but toward the ferocious insult of an enemy never finally beaten back or even deprived of sustenance. (The Yamana forces who took Shōkokuji without pressing the attack also took all but one of the entry points to the city without imposing an embargo on food.[37]) Yet the interest in injury does little to explain the gathering of huge forces in Kyoto. A garrison might retain a formidable presence, but it could neither facilitate nor fend off the arson that lay at the heart of battle. The notion of presence, however, may be essential to the Ōnin experience. A conflict I have thus far, and perhaps mistakenly, described in the language of "battle" and "armies" might better be described in the language of "demonstration" and "witness."

The great assembly of people in Kyoto may have been just that—a great assembly of people. Assembly seems, in short, a new attempt at government: a substitute for negotiations that had failed, for shogunal decisions that had only exacerbated discord, and for battles that had achieved no resolution to succession quarrels now fifteen years old. Hence, to return to my earlier question (for what purposes were such large armies gathered in Japan's capital city?), let me suggest that the eastern and western camps were engaged in two related but somewhat different acts. They were showing their strength in the most literal terms possible, thus using the demonstration as a form of coercion. Yet they were also bearing testimony to their cause in the nation's central city, thus using the power of witness as a statement of legitimacy and superior purpose.

While issues of local control were being fought out in the provinces, Kyoto was becoming the site of basically political rather than military action. The apparent objectives were old ones: the capitulation of opponents and the ascendancy of one factional network. And these objectives presumed some return to the old framework of rule—one that allowed for the survival of the shogunate and the resumption of negotiations over power. The eastern and western camps stopped short not only of total war in the capital but even of the determined escalation of battle that might have eliminated all possibility of a conventional settlement. Nonetheless, their need for spectacle as a tool of power indicated the essential failure of the institutional polity. And their resort to mass assembly opened opportunities for a politics of the street, which had a life of its own and could move in unforeseen directions.

I call demonstration and witness a new attempt at government insofar as they were part of a body of strategies—what we might think of as protocols—that men used to manage violence.[38] On one hand, these protocols represented versatile efforts to stem disaster by interposing a substitute mode of control between the failing rule of law and the emerging rule of force. Some protocols, such as the great assembly of partisans or the burning of a significant place, functioned as alternatives to battle—as efforts to subdue the enemy by intimidation rather than arms. Other protocols limited bloodshed and destruction once a battle occurred. They ranged from the practice we have noted already (a reliance on brief engagements usually conducted during daylight, which concluded in retreat and little pursuit of the fleeing adversary) to attempts to limit atrocities against civilians and to leave farmland undisturbed. Still other protocols became efforts to terminate hostilities and to prevent their reoccurrence: the surrender of surrogates or hostages, for example, by adversaries seeking accord; the election of symbolic death, in the form of exile or retirement to a monastery, by adversaries ready to surrender.[39]

Together, these protocols constituted a retreat from endless bloodletting. If as many as five hundred men died when the Hatakeyama cousins met at Kamigoryō shrine in the first month of 1467, the slaughter was unusual. We more often encounter battles putatively involving ten thousand or more men that ended in a few score deaths. Even in the *Chronicle of Ōnin*—otherwise so ready with tallies of combatants and the havoc they raised—we find few and typically small totals for casualties. The threshold of bearable human sacrifice seems low; the disjunctions between the size of the armies and the duration of the battles, and between the size of the armies and the extent of the carnage, point to agreements about the conduct of war.

Yet while these protocols may have managed violence, they were also part of an inherently violent order of existence. The protocols emerged as a code of conflict—or, in effect, rules of war—that presumed a right to force and an attendant necessity to shape hostility to one's own advantage. Brutal instruments themselves, they took their efficacy from the threat of accelerating brutality if they failed.

It is curious that protocols designed to limit damage should have attended conflict rooted in the grudge. Why, given the personal hatreds between the Ōnin antagonists, did confrontation stop short of the cruelest bloodletting? Some suggestion of an answer lies in the dual purposes of the succession quarrels. Because most participants were motivated by the search for local power, the contests did not admit of decisive resolution through battle. The ruin of the land would have put the very prize of victory at risk. And the accompanying casualties would have threatened equally critical human resources. Neither ruthless campaigns nor singular conquests could reorganize the dense patterns and loyalties of everyday land management. Effective local takeover came slowly and followed many routes—the occasional emblematic victory, persuasive displays of superior numbers, cunning ties to significant men, the recruitment with suitable reward of an enemy's retainers, the gradual penetration of important fortifications. In the end, the protocols of war did not so much define conflict as they were themselves defined by the exigencies of a tortuous struggle that advanced, village by village, district by district.

The personal enmity accompanying the quest for power dictated a second purpose of conflict—retribution. This goal accounts for the similarities between adversaries and criminals, and, accordingly, for some of the more disquieting conventions of wartime conduct. The exorcism of enemy mansions by fire, the mutilation of dead soldiers on the battlefield, the exaction of symbolic deaths and hostage sacrifices from defeated opponents, the occasional slaughter of an enemy's household, the public humiliation of the vanquished by displaying heads or parading captured leaders—all find equivalents in the criminal justice of the medieval period.[40] Retribution accounts, too, for the spectacular insults—using an opponent's lacquered skull as a drinking cup, taking an enemy's consorts and daughters as concubines.[41] There are doubtless many tendencies at work here. But the overtones of rancor and the echoes of criminal punishment suggest the properties of the grudge, which required personal redress. The conventions of conflict, then, accommodated the realities of local politics without denying the power of the grievance.

But after eleven years of occupation in the capital, the politics of demonstration had failed either to alleviate grievances or to inspire a political solution to the contests in the provinces. Fire raids on the residences of the military and the sanctuaries of partisans offered the principal structure to an increasingly structureless debacle. The litany of ruin in and around the city measured the "progress" of conflict: Gion, Yoshida, Tōji, Saihōji, Shōren'in, Kenninji, Kiyomizu, Kōryūji, Daigoji, Seiganji, Hōshōji, Shōgōin, Kōzanji, Kurama, Nanzenji, Ninnaji, Tenryūji, Sennyūji. . . . [42] Change was marked by the watchtowers that rose while pagodas fell, the moats that defined boundaries formerly fixed by avenues or garden walls, the rudimentary fortresses that supplanted great religious enclaves.[43] Movement was sufficiently obscure to provoke rumors that peace, or at least a truce, was imminent and to prompt a number of commanders to leave Kyoto.

Some of the most consequential events of the Ōnin war occurred without human agency in 1473 when, within two months, both Yamana Sōzen and Hosokawa Katsumoto died of natural causes. The conflict between their two houses abated then as the Hosokawa heir abandoned the western camp and withdrew his troops from the capital. Yet this fracturing of the "sides" and the "structure" of battle was hardly novel: within the first year of the hostilities, the partisans of the two shogunal pretenders had switched loyalties when the western camp embraced Ashikaga Yoshimi and the eastern camp embraced Ashikaga Yoshihisa. Other rifts moved the incumbent shogun (Ashikaga Yoshimasa) to transfer support from Yamana Sōzen to Hosokawa Katsumoto even as he seemed still ambivalently linked to the Yamana. The head of the Ōuchi house, a crucial supporter of Hatakeyama Yoshinari, quarreled regularly with Yoshinari and finally aligned with his cousin.[44]

None of these events terminated the hostilities in the capital; each opened new grievances and fresh upheavals over land. Demonstration and injury brought stalemate. What resolution did occur—primarily the elevation of Ashikaga Yoshihisa as shogun shortly after the deaths of Yamana Sōzen and Hosokawa Katsumoto—seemed barely relevant to conflicts increasingly cut off from the original succession quarrels and now fueled by emerging troubles. The issue of the Shiba succession receded in Kyoto as provincial deputies and rivals of the Shiba house (the Asakura in Echizen, the Imagawa in Tōtōmi, the Oda in Owari) simply eliminated both of the contending Shiba factions in local battles. The Hatakeyama quarrel did continue to organize the fighting in the capital. But not only did partisans move back and forth between sides; they found themselves consumed by more immediate challenges. The Ōuchi faced provincial attacks from the Ōtomo and the Shōni; the Yamana were preoccupied with the Akamatsu.

Where, then, shall we find an "ending" to the Ōnin war? Like beginnings, endings are a matter of perspective. The armed occupation of the capital, which had steadily diminished from 1473, came to an apparent close late in 1477. In the ninth month Hatakeyama Yoshinari removed his armies to Kawachi, now the major theater of his battles against his cousin. And in the eleventh month the last combatants in the Ōuchi and Toki houses burned down their Kyoto mansions and returned home to repel invasions and confront rebellions there.

After Ōnin

The Ōnin war was inconclusive on a grand scale: it effected no settlement, identified no group of victors, established no durable alliances. We might find a renunciation of the shogunal institution, at least as it had been known. Private battle appeared to deny the principles of final assent to shogunal authority, some consonance between office and power, and general compliance with shogunal statutes and judicial decisions. Nonetheless, renunciation is too categorical a term, for throughout their cumulatively momentous but discretely focused quarrels, the contenders still identified with the old military elite and still fought for prizes within the old political order. Nor does it accurately represent the shadowy visions of men who had yet to struggle toward alternative governing structures or rival notions of legitimacy and political purpose. Although upheaval had surely occurred, the consequences were not sure; and different men saw them, or anticipated them, in different ways.

On the one hand, a priestly diarist of Nara pronounced the shogunate dead. Writing in the eleventh month of 1477, a day before the last combatants of Ōnin burned down their camps and departed the capital, he passed this judgment on his times:

In all the affairs of the realm, there are no felicitous tidings. There is no obedience to shogunal commands in any of the nearby provinces—not in Ōmi, Mino, Owari, Tōtōmi, Mikawa, Hida, Noto, Kaga, Echizen, Yamato, or Kawachi. Nor are land rents paid in any of these provinces. And beyond these places, land rents are also being withheld in Kii and Settsu and Etchū and Izumi because of the deep confusion in these provinces. The provinces that receive the shogun's commands are only Harima, Bizen, Mimasaka, Bitchū, Bingo, Ise, Iga, Awaji, and the provinces of Shikoku. But even these are not obedient. Ordered to comply with shogunal commands in accord with the law and in keeping with their official appointments, the military governors there pay respect to the shogun. However, their deputies and other men of the land entirely withhold obedience. Thus, in effect, all of Japan is beyond the reach of the shogun's commands.[45]

In its finality, this entry insists on rupture. If we look to the city of Kyoto, we find evidence of rupture there in the exodus that cast the capital to the side of national politics (assailing the very notions of "capital" and "national" politics). Military governors, once resident in the city, returned to the provinces. Even Hatakeyama Masanaga, as *kanrei* and governor of Yamashiro the nominally most important shogunal deputy, carried his battles with his cousin to Yamato and Kawachi. Masanaga issued no official documents and preserved no official presence in Kyoto.[46] His patrons in the capital, moreover, were dissolving again into black quarrels. The retired shogun Ashikaga Yoshimasa supported Hatakeyama Masanaga, but both his son (now the incumbent shogun Ashikaga Yoshihisa) and his wife (the redoubtable Hino Tomiko) embraced the cause of the cousin, Hatakeyama Yoshinari. The fissure between the two Ashikaga provoked rumors that all Kyoto would be destroyed by battles between them. Actual battle was forestalled, but not before fortifications went up and sides were drawn: the shogunal guardsmen (*hōkōshū*) aligned with Ashikaga Yoshihisa, the officials of the Administrative Board (the *bugyōnin* of the *mandokoro*) aligned with Ashikaga Yoshimasa.[47]

On the other hand, rupture gave way to images of restoration in the years following Ōnin. Projecting a vision of recovery onto the landscape of Kyoto, officials began filling in the moats and trenches of wartime; they turned to rebuilding the imperial palace and the shogunal mansion; they summoned home the nobles and the priests who had sought refuge in other, more hospitable places.[48] Despite animosities within the shogunal household, members of the shogunal administration resumed routine city governance by making judicial decisions and issuing directives on taxes, loans, currency exchange, and proprietary privileges. To replenish the shogunal coffers and assert control over the home province, they imposed a levy in Yamashiro, demanding one-fifth of the taxes normally due to private proprietors.[49] And in 1482, in one of the more dramatic gestures of the day, Ashikaga Yoshimasa opened construction of a marvelous Buddhist temple and retreat known as the Silver Pavilion.[50] For the priestly diarist of Nara, as for historians burdened by hindsight, the complex may have signified vainglory or imperviousness to trouble. It may also have conveyed embittered withdrawal from contention with Yoshihisa, since Yoshimasa's move there had brought an end to the public confrontation between father and son. Or the Silver Pavilion may have connoted a repossessed shogunal dignity at a time when building signaled hope and Yoshimasa's retreat promised some concord in rule.

The tension between perceptions of rupture and expectations of restoration after Ōnin appears often but obliquely in documents. An edict concerning salt taxes issued in 1507, long after the Ōnin war, states: "It is the imperial will that the violations of recent years be stopped and that the laws from the time before Ōnin be protected."[51] Here, the idea of rupture strikes more deeply—because it is expressed more incidentally—than it does in the verdict of our priestly diarist: the edict simply takes Ōnin for granted as a divide in human experience. It separates the time "before upheaval" from the time "after upheaval" when "laws" survive in memory but are measured in "violations." But although rupture has lasted long enough to be embedded in the language of chronology, it is not conceded any power over future events. The edict insists on, imagines the possibility of, return. Or again, an aristocratic diarist began his entry for the fourth day of the eighth month of 1520 with these words: "I hear the imperial enthronement ceremony is to be postponed once more."[52] That enthronement ceremony had not occurred in the nineteen years since the current emperor succeeded his father. Imperial penury, the disdain of some shogunal officials toward the throne, continuing battles in Kyoto—all conspired against this most basic rite of renewal and political coherence. Rupture is implicit in the diarist's words. Nonetheless, he speaks of "postponement." The ceremony is deferred, not dead.

The tension between rupture and restoration also appeared in the military events that followed the Ōnin war. And, indeed, it was the confused messages of these events that helped sustain the ambivalence in the documents. One strange episode began in 1487 when the shogun Ashikaga Yoshihisa marched with eight thousand troops against the head of the Rokkaku house, a military governor (*shugo*) with a shogunal appointment in Ōmi province. This campaign grew not out of a personal quarrel, but out of repeated violations in the Rokkaku domain of the estate rights of absentee aristocratic and religious proprietors. It was a disciplinary act of state in defense of shogunal and estate law and the fiduciary character of a governor's office. The campaign denied, in effect, the prerogative seized by governors and other would-be magnates in their quest for consolidated local power: the authority to distribute and confirm landholdings independently. The march was interesting for its size and the participation of other governors putatively united with the shogun in affirming the old order. It was more interesting yet for the personal leadership of Ashikaga Yoshihisa, since no shogun had led troops into battle for almost a century.

The campaign stalled and Ashikaga Yoshihisa died in camp in 1489. Two years later his cousin and successor as shogun, Ashikaga Yoshitane, resumed the march at the head of an army raised from the houses of Hosokawa, Hatakeyama, Shiba, Yamana, Akamatsu, Takeda, Isshiki, Kyōgoku, Niki, and Ōuchi. When this campaign was equally unsuccessful, Yoshitane returned to Kyoto.[53]

How should we read this episode? Should we emphasize the rupture signified by Rokkaku's lawless conduct, the resurrection of shogun as generals, and the failure of a campaign that consumed four years, two administrations, and the resources of fifteen provinces? Should we emphasize the restoration signified by a shogun committed to support lawful proprietors and a martial community ready to halt a movement that could still be called—and thus labeled deviant—a "rebellion"?

But if irresolution characterized the post-Ōnin years, stasis did not. For the residents of Kyoto, movement derived from two sequences of events: first, the resumption of hostilities in Yamashiro and the emergence there of a "provincial uprising" between 1485 and 1493; second, the usurpation of shogunal power by successive members of the Hosokawa family in the decades after 1491.

The Yamashiro Story

War between the Hatakeyama cousins concentrated, in the years after Ōnin, in the provinces of Kawachi and Yamato, although sporadic battles occurred in the home province of Yamashiro. From the beginning of their conflict, Yamashiro had been the great prize—its revenues, its men, its access to the transportation arteries leading from Kyoto, its identification with the historic power of the capital. Toward the close of 1485, the cousins assembled sizable armies there for a fight each side expected to win decisively. They engaged this time not in the politics of demonstration but in a wasting battle that continued for sixty-three days in winter cold and rain. Fighting came to a close in the twelfth month, when a wide assembly of local people made three demands: that combatants from both sides withdraw from the province; that powers of governance be restored to the courtly and religious proprietors who held most local land as estates; and that recently established toll barriers be removed. The assembly, drawn mainly from three districts in southern Yamashiro, constituted an apparently horizontal alliance of male residents between the ages of fifteen and sixty; it embraced common farmers as well as the armed land managers who functioned as minor military leaders in the area.[54]

In the days following the assembly, the Hatakeyama cousins withdrew their armies—perhaps because battle had exhausted them, perhaps because the assembly had threatened to fight against them, perhaps because the assembly included former supporters whose defection made a continuing struggle all but impossible. Fortified by this success, the farmers and land managers convened again in the second month of 1486, this time on the grounds of Byōdōin, an eleventh-century temple founded by the Fujiwara family in the town of Uji. In this place still alive with courtly associations, the assembly asserted control over the province and selected thirty-six men as representatives. Each month, in rotation, three of them were to act as magistrates of Yamashiro. The magistrates seized practical power in the fifth month of that year by announcing that residents would withhold half of the taxes due to estate proprietors (excepting three shrines) in order to support the costs of provincial administration and defense.[55]

These developments presented the shogunate with both an opportunity and a challenge. The opportunity arose with the retreat of the Hatakeyama cousins from Yamashiro, an area that the financially weakened administration had turned to increasingly for revenue.[56] The challenge arose with the rebellion of a seemingly united community of local men who appeared resolved to govern themselves; for the confiscation of the half-tax (*hanzei*) mirrored, or mocked, the prerogatives claimed by the shogun and his governors. The challenge was somewhat mitigated, however, by the assembly's call for the restoration of proprietary authority, which was answered by aristocrats and abbots who sent out inspectors to survey their estates.

Ready to reclaim Yamashiro for himself, the shogun appointed a new military governor of the province toward the close of the fifth month of 1486. (The appointee was Ise Sadaroku, an official of the shogunate's Board of Administration.) Rejecting this appointment, the assembly continued to meet and withhold taxes.[57] The monthly magistrates also assumed judicial powers by presiding, for example, over a disputed land sale and by executing a merchant who had killed and robbed a local man. For the next eight years, until the eighth month of 1493, the shogunate claimed nominal authority over a province in which local magistrates and a local assembly were successfully defying shogunal administration.[58]

The Yamashiro events were described, in the parlance of the times, as a *kuni ikki*. The word *ikki* had at least two faces. It denoted a form of organization that might be translated as *league,* insofar as it brought persons of common purpose into sometimes long-term and often horizontal associations governed by written or unwritten codes. The word also denoted a form of action that is normally translated as *uprising,* insofar as individual or collective leagues exploded into forceful and often armed movements against authorities. The word *kuni* means province, indicating in this context both the geographical spread of the *ikki* and its purpose: some degree of power over a province by league members.[59] On several occasions before the Yamashiro action, similar but lesser *kuni ikki* had occurred.[60] The Yamashiro uprising was nonetheless remarkable in its duration, its direct rebuke to the shogunate, and its capacity to generate an alternative form of local government. It was notable, too, as part of a wider pattern of agitation in the home province, which began in 1482 and continued until 1511. Almost annually during these three decades, Yamashiro and surrounding areas generated uprisings of another kind—*tokusei ikki,* or organized marches into Kyoto by grievants demanding the cancellation of debts owed to the moneylending establishments of the capital. Accompanied by arson and sometimes by murder, these marches were carefully orchestrated demonstrations that brought forms of popular resistance to the center of Kyoto's life.

What are we to make of the Yamashiro uprising? Why did it happen, and what did it signify?

In large part, the uprising was a reaction by local people against two months of punishing warfare in their communities. It was an act of rage over brutal injury. Yet in its rejection of warlord leadership and its election of an alternative government, the uprising also bore an agenda, which historians have associated with its presumptive organizers, the *jizamurai* (literally, "soldiers of the land").[61] Holders of various property rights, they typically occupied one or more managerial posts on the estates of absentee proprietors, and they typically aspired to direct control over the land and villagers they administered for others. Armed themselves, they commanded small bands of fighters from their villages and neighboring areas where their fame or infamy had spread. Some held one or more "castles," usually crude towers with outlying fortifications. These were the men who constituted the most important element in the warlords' armies, and, indeed, many of Yamashiro's "soldiers of the land" had fought for one or the other of the Hatakeyama cousins since the outbreak of the Ōnin war.

They fought for prizes in land, although precisely what this meant is hard to say. A more direct control of property might entail autonomous power, or some version of enfeoffment, or simply enhanced privileges within the structure of estate holding that legally dominated Yamashiro. The demand by the Yamashiro assembly in 1485 that local authority be restored to civil proprietors suggests some accommodation with the old order. At the same time, the selection of local magistrates and the withholding of taxes suggest a movement toward autonomy that was simply camouflaged by the deference to estate holders. Clear enough, however, was a resolve in Yamashiro to separate land management from the Hatakeyama warlords. They had brought ruin, not prizes, to the soldiers of the land, and their battles showed no evidence of conclusion; conclusion, if it did come, would identify only one victor and thus only one side eligible for the spoils. And that victorious side would include not just men of Yamashiro but powerful rivals as well, for perhaps the most troubling, if unsurprising, dimension of the battle for Yamashiro in 1485 was the participation of Hatakeyama vassals from Kawachi and Yamato provinces.[62] Allies in war, these outsiders would be competitors with local soldiers for the gains of conquest.

The men of Yamashiro turned, then, to themselves, with some overtures to the proprietary community. Their seemingly horizontal union was encouraged by several anomalous features of the province: no great military house had been able to establish a dominant presence there (largely as a result of the frequent rotation of military governors in the home province);[63] and no local managers had emerged as leading magnates able to subordinate their peers (largely as a result of the development and close surveillance of many small estates in the home province).[64] But while the formation of the Yamashiro league was facilitated by the absence of a military hierarchy, the league could not withstand renewed struggles for local advantage. After 1486, fighting resumed between Yamashiro's soldiers of the land. Once more, they sought assistance from outside warlords (again, the Hatakeyama cousins, the Hosokawa, and the Ōuchi), on whose behalf they also fought in other provinces. The uprising finally concluded in 1493, following a campaign instigated by the shogunate, when the soldiers of Yamashiro accepted a military governor sent from the capital.[65]

The collapse of the league tends to encourage a cynical reading of the Yamashiro story—one that emphasizes the opportunism of local warriors who used solidarity as a front for personal ambition and then called for renewed proprietary authority only to substitute weak aristocrats for overlords in the mold of the Hatakeyama. Yet this reading presumes a clarity of purpose among the soldiers of the land. I suspect, rather, that the motives of the soldiers were both varied and incompletely formed and that the uprising signaled a process of political testing instead of a movement toward any single goal. Hence, the significance of the Yamashiro events emerges less from either their purposes or their conclusion (which might be interpreted in many different ways) than from their very occurrence. Three aspects of the uprising are noteworthy: the prominence of rather humble military men in spreading the rebellion after Ōnin; the radical vision of political organization implicit in the formation of the league; and the reappearance of demonstration as a mode of coercion and appeal.

Initially striking is the heightened visibility and independence of soldiers of the land—not just the great deputies of provincial governors (*shugo-dai*) who had long shaped local politics but lesser managers and holders of property rights with paltry claims to lordship themselves. The men of Yamashiro rose up as new players in wartime action, breaking open a conflict that had previously centered on a military elite. Although uncommon in its length, the Yamashiro challenge was part of a wider movement that provoked roughly contemporary uprisings in neighboring Izumi (1473), Settsu (1477–82), the Nishioka district of Yamashiro (1487), and Tanba (1489–93) as well as later uprisings in more distant areas of the country. All of these actions involved soldiers of the land. All opposed not just military governors (in each of these cases, governors from the Hosokawa family) but also their deputies (in these cases Hosokawa vassals from Shikoku who had been awarded local posts in preference to soldiers of the land). And all combined martial aggression with efforts to usurp rights of governance—to appropriate taxes, for example, or control estate properties.[66]

The uprising of local soldiers illumined the spread of violence as the dynamic of force took over. Provoked by ambition and old injuries, these men responded to particular opportunities and oppressions brought by Ōnin: the damage of local battles, the instability in rule, the increase in wartime taxation, the absence of governors on distant campaigns, the insult conveyed by the surrogate administration of deputies from outside provinces. Disturbing in itself, this spread of violence was all the more important for its exposure of basic cleavages between warlords and shogunal officials, their privileged deputies, and the men who made up their armies. The cleavages were hardly new, but now open rebellion was dividing the martial houses that were also at war with one another.

Rebellion was expanding, moreover, from internecine conflict into break-away movements. *Ikki* represented forms of alliance antithetical to the prevailing structures of lordship. The new alliances tended to be horizontal rather than vertical and, more important, to center on groups of common interest rather than individual parties bound by personally advantageous exchanges. However volatile or manipulative those alliances, the leagues reenvisioned politics as corporate action— not as discrete accommodations between particular men with limited purposes. They did have prewar models: organized marches (again called *ikki*) of debtors with tax grievances or tradespeople opposed to toll barriers; and, more important, *sō,* village organizations, particularly in Yamato and Yamashiro, that claimed control over internal matters (water, commons, entry into the community, lending practices) and created administrative bodies and codes to regulate them.[67] With the advent of Ōnin and the spread of provincial battle, such alliances and actions multiplied, and *ikki* became a staple of the language.

Ikki never became a dominant form of political organization during the war years, nor were many individual movements durable. Some of them, preeminently the marches, involved specific protests against (more or less) specific grievances and were ephemeral in conception. Others, preeminently provincial uprisings like the one in Yamashiro, fomented internal competition if they escaped suppression by the very warlords they rejected. Still others, preeminently the religious leagues, were destroyed by the violent reprisals of warlords and rival sectarians alike. But the striking violence of these reprisals was a measure of the challenge to late medieval society presented by the *ikki*—as was the alternative response, which was otherwise uncharacteristic of warlord politics, of appeasement and cooptation. These responses grew out of fear, for only in retrospect is it possible to determine that the *ikki* movement was neither ascendant nor durable. At the time, it not only challenged the vertical and particular formation of power; it also kept springing up in new places and new contexts—in villages and provinces, in religious communities and urban neighborhoods, in quarrels over debts and trade and taxes.

In some contexts, moreover, the *ikki* movement did prove durable. It survived best in the *sō* or the *do ikki,* which united small (*not* district- or provincewide) village assemblies against proprietary control. But some aspects also survived in Yamashiro itself. There the provincial uprising came to a nominal end in 1493 when most soldiers of the land submitted themselves to the reappointed governor (Ise Sadaroku) and the rest were crushed in an attack that "made [the last outpost of the *ikki*] a dead place in an instant."[68] Yet Yamashiro was not subsequently tamed by any military overlord: no daimyo consolidated his power and no substantial military taxes were collected there. Yamashiro remained a breeding ground for uprisings against brokers and toll barriers. Its soldiers continued to feed several rival armies. And its estate structure survived.

Implicit in these two issues—the heightened activism and the challenging organization of the soldiers of the land—is a third point, which returns us to the themes of the Ōnin war. This is the reappearance of demonstration and witness in some of the most dramatic events of the Yamashiro uprising: the public gathering on two occasions of male residents between the ages of fifteen and sixty; the proclamation on the first occasion of ultimata to their military overlords; the formation on the second occasion of "province laws" and a representative assembly; the subsequent declaration of a new taxation policy. These acts of demonstration and witness occurred, moreover, in theatrical spaces. The ultimata were issued from the Hachiman shrine, a sanctuary dedicated to an ancient emperor who was venerated as the tutelary deity of Japan's most eminent martial family (the Minamoto); the laws and the assembly were formed, over the course of a ten-day occupation, at the aristocratic temple of Byōdōin.

Appropriating the politics of demonstration, the soldiers of the land massed numbers and occupied significant places in exercises of private power that purported to stem violence but contained threats of escalating violence should demonstration fail. They based their actions on the imperatives of *jiriki* (the power of the self). Much as the phrase *private war* defined the redress of the Ōnin contenders, *jiriki* signaled mobilization within the communities of village and urban neighborhood. Ex-

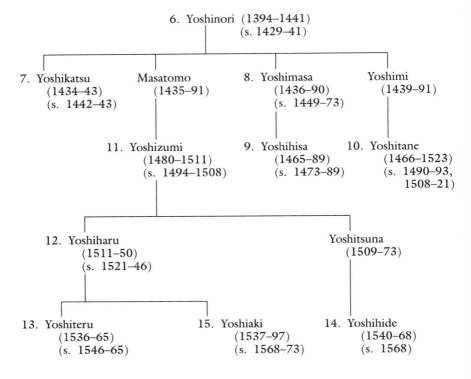

Figure 1. The Ashikaga Shogunal Line, 1429–1573

ercised outside the bounds of law and in a context of force, the power of the self (or a body of selves) renounced the power of the other (*ta-riki*)—the power of office, order, overlord.

The apparent end to the Yamashiro uprising in 1493 was a kind of victory for the shogunate insofar as it deferred any deep resolution to the crises in the home province. But that uprising exposed again the spread of force and the readiness of local soldiers to explore alternative models of political organization.

The Hosokawa Story

The shogunal campaign in Yamashiro during 1493 was part of a larger convulsion within the shogunate, which ended in a coup.

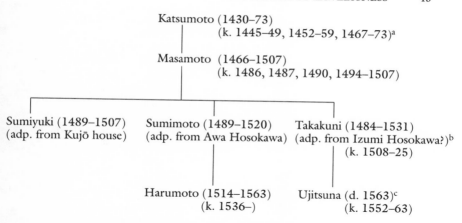

Figure 2. The *Kanrei* Line of the Hosokawa House, 1445–1563

NOTES. Descended from the Ashikaga house (and ultimately from the Seiwa Genji), the main line of the Hosokawa moved from Mikawa to establish bases, through *shugo* appointments, in Settsu, Tanba, Sanuki, and Tosa. Branch lines established themselves in Awa, Awaji, Bitchū, and Izumi. The Hosokawa house retained a fair degre of cohesion until the Ōnin war, but subsequent strife led to deep rifts, evinced in the battles between Masamoto's adopted heirs during 1507–8. Throughout the Era of Warring States, the provincial power of the Hosokawa was an uncertain matter, dependent on wavering alliances with deputies and branch heads.

[a]Sources disagree about which Hosokawa heads formally held the *kanrei* title, and during which years. This list was put together on the basis of information provided in Takayanagi Kōji and Takeuchi Rizō, eds., *Kadokawa Nihon-shi jiten,* and Kokushi Daijiten Henshū Iinkai, ed., *Kokushi daijiten.* Contemporary documents frequently refer to the Hosokawa heads as *ukyō daibu,* or Ministers of the Right [eastern] Sector of the Capital—an old courtly title, monopolized by the Hosokawa, that came to indicate primary jurisdiction over Kyoto.

[b]Sources also disagree concerning whether Takakuni was formally adopted by Masamoto.

[c]After the death of his own son (who may briefly have served as *kanrei* in 1525), Takakuni adopted a cousin's son (Ujitsuna) to succeed him as Hosokawa family head.

Its leader was Hosokawa Masamoto, the *kanrei,* or chief administrative officer of the shogunate. Its target was Ashikaga Yoshitane, the incumbent shogun.

The trouble had its origins in the Ōnin war, and to describe it is to return to the numbing genealogy of quarrels. The succession problem in the Ashikaga house that figured in Ōnin was resolved (in a manner) when Ashikaga Yoshihisa succeeded his father (the eighth shogun,

Figure 3. The Principal Transitions in Kyoto's Government, 1467–1568

1. The Ōnin
   War,
   1467–77

   War was provoked by succession quarrels in the Ashikaga, Hatakeyama, and Shiba families and driven by conflicts throughout the great martial houses. Although Ashikaga Yoshihisa was eventually installed as 9th shogun (against the claims of his uncle, Yoshimi), and Hatakeyama Masanaga installed as *kanrei* and Yamashiro *shugo* (against the claims of his cousin, Yoshinari), these decisions had little impact on escalating contests that moved from Kyoto to the provinces without resolution.

2. The coup of
   Hosokawa
   Masamoto,
   1493–94

   Hosokawa Masamoto secured his hold over the shogunal administration (and the office of *kanrei*) by forcibly ousting the 10th shogun, Ashikaga Yoshitane, and arranging the elevation of his own favorite, Ashikaga Yoshizumi, as 11th shogun. Masamoto's troops enhanced his power by defeating Hatakeyama Masanaga in battle (thus precipitating the suicide of this old rival and supporter of Yoshitane) and quelling a lengthy uprising in Yamashiro.

3. The battles
   of the
   Hosokawa
   heirs,
   1507–8

   Continuing dissension among Hosokawa Masamoto's adopted heirs and their supporters provoked three successive attempts at a coup. Masamoto was killed and Hosokawa Sumiyuki installed as successor and family head in 1507, 7th month; Sumiyuki committed suicide under attack and was succeeded by Hosokawa Sumimoto in 1507, 8th month; Sumimoto fled Kyoto under attack and was succeeded as *kanrei* by Hosokawa Takakuni in 1508, 7th month. Ashikaga Yoshizumi was also ousted as shogun at this point, and Ashikaga Yoshitane recovered his office. (Takakuni faced repeated challenges from Sumimoto's partisans after 1508, as well as increasing opposition from Ashikaga Yoshitane.)

4. The rivalry
   of two
   shogunates;
   the rise of
   the Lotus,
   1527–36

   The *kanrei* Hosokawa Takakuni and Ashikaga Yoshiharu (installed as 12th shogun in 1521, after Yoshitane split with Takakuni) fled Kyoto under attack from partisans of Hosokawa Harumoto (son of Sumimoto) and Ashikaga Yoshitsuna (adopted heir of Yoshitane). Two rival, and absentee, administrations—one under Yoshiharu in Ōmi, the other under Yoshitsuna in Sakai—competed for power between 1527 and 1532. Although Hosokawa Harumoto (who became *kanrei*) and Ashikaga Yoshiharu (who survived as the titled

Figure 3, *continued*

	shogun) reached an accord in 1532, the reconstituted shogunate did not fully reassemble in Kyoto until 1536. Under the banner of the Lotus sect, the commoners of Kyoto were ascendant in the city from 1532 until the suppression of their uprising in 1536.
5. The challenge of Miyoshi Chōkei, 1549–53	After a decade of fissure, Hosokawa Harumoto and Ashikaga Yoshiteru (who succeeded his father as 13th shogun when Yoshiharu split with Harumoto) fled Kyoto under attack from Miyoshi Chōkei, scion of a deputy house long implicated in Hosokawa fortunes. Chōkei dominated Kyoto after 1549, but conclusively established his rule there only in 1553—following almost five more years of battle with partisans of Hosokawa Harumoto and, intermittently, Ashikaga Yoshiteru. Chōkei governed Kyoto autocratically from 1553 until 1558, dispensing with any shogunal mascot. (Ashikaga Yoshiteru remained in exile.) Hosokawa Ujitsuna, adopted son of Takakuni, served nominally as *kanrei*.
6. Assassination and interregnum, 1565–68	A sort of shogunal restoration was achieved after 1558, when Ashikaga Yoshiteru returned to Kyoto as a result of armed action and compromise with Miyoshi Chōkei. But the death of Chōkei (1563) and the aggressive posture of Yoshiteru provoked another coup in 1565. Matsunaga Hisahide and three other powerful deputies of Chōkei attacked the shogun directly, forced his suicide, and slaughtered his retainers. The ensuing turmoil left Matsunaga Hisahide ascendant in Kyoto, yet delayed the induction of a shogunal successor (Ashikaga Yoshihide, the 14th shogun) for three years, until 1568, 2d month.
7. The invasion of Oda Nobunaga, 1568	Following a series of important conquests and alliances in the east-central provinces, Oda Nobunaga made a bid for national hegemony by entering Kyoto as the champion of yet another shogunal pretender—Ashikaga Yoshiaki (brother of the slain 13th shogun and cousin of the incumbent 14th shogun). Yoshiaki was installed as the 15th (and last) Ashikaga shogun in 1568, 10th month, but conflict between him and Nobunaga opened soon thereafter.

Yoshimasa) in 1473 and so prevailed over the rival claimant, Ashikaga Yoshimi (Yoshimasa's brother, Yoshihisa's uncle). But the succession problem arose again in 1489, when the childless Yoshihisa died. Yoshihisa had adopted as his heir Ashikaga Yoshitane, who was the son of Yoshimi. Hosokawa Masamoto and others opposed the choice of Yoshitane and championed Ashikaga Yoshizumi—a nephew and adopted son of the eighth shogun who had not been implicated in the Ōnin conflicts.[69] Despite such opposition, Ashikaga Yoshitane was elevated as the tenth shogun in 1490. His installation posed problems for Hosokawa Masamoto, not only because Masamoto had supported a rival for shogunal office but also because Ashikaga Yoshitane was strongly allied to Hatakeyama Masanaga.

This alliance was threatening because Hatakeyama Masanaga and Hosokawa Masamoto were rivals for the office of *kanrei,* which had alternated between their two houses for much of the Muromachi period. Hosokawa Masamoto's father (Katsumoto) occupied the office during the first half of the Ōnin war, to be succeeded after his death by Hatakeyama Masanaga. The office returned to Hosokawa hands in 1486, when Masamoto received his first appointment, only to revert briefly back to Hatakeyama Masanaga. Hosokawa Masamoto soon recovered the *kanrei* position but, estranged from the shogun Ashikaga Yoshitane, he faced the possibility that the office of *kanrei* would soon be restored to the Hatakeyama.[70]

Numbing as these personal histories are, they must not be trivialized, for they reveal several now-familiar forces crucial in sustaining warfare. One was emotion—the feelings of pride and anger that spawned mortal grudges in a society preoccupied with honor. The power of emotion was amplified by the wide-spread understanding of it in late medieval Japan. Jurists sometimes condoned the grudge; chroniclers and diarists made it a narrative frame to interpret conflict; and warlords and soldiers did battle in its service. Sanctioned or not, the grudge satisfactorily organized ideas and actions that required no translation into other terms—of law or religion, of ideology or economics—before they made good sense. Because family injuries could rationalize conflict, they often became a guise for opportunistic campaigns. Still, motives in even the most callous initiatives are hard to dissect. A guise fits best if the actor makes it a second skin.

Another force that influenced many of the personal histories of wartime was the attraction of traditional office. For men like Hosokawa Masamoto, titles such as *kanrei* touched vitally on matters of identity. Hence the possibility of dishonor, and vengeance, were the title withheld. But they also touched vitally on awards of land and thus on an official's power to hold his retainers. As *kanrei,* and also as military governor of up to seven provinces (an achievement directly tied to *kanrei* office), Hosokawa Masamoto could reward his supporters with tax exemptions or taxation privileges; with appointments as deputy governors and attendant administrative and fiscal rights; with posts on surviving estates that were extracted from civil proprietors under duress. Office and power retained a cogent association. With an irony common to the period, Masamoto acted lawlessly to hold on to his lawful position.

He moved in two directions. First, throughout much of 1493, he attacked the soldiers of Yamashiro with armies raised from Hosokawa strongholds in Settsu, Tanba, and Yamato. The campaign was intended to demonstrate Masamoto's authority as *kanrei* and expand the resources available to his deputies. Second, he went to war against the shogun. In the fourth month of 1493, Hosokawa Masamoto sent troops into Kawachi province where Ashikaga Yoshitane was fighting on behalf of Hatakeyama Masanaga in Masanaga's continuing battles against his cousin (at this point, against the now-deceased cousin's son). The Hosokawa troops reversed the tide of battle in Kawachi, precipitated the suicide of Hatakeyama Masanaga, and took Ashikaga Yoshitane prisoner. This campaign was intended both to eliminate Masanaga as a rival for *kanrei* office and undo the shogun himself.

On the second day of the fifth month of 1493, an aristocratic diarist described the events of the previous day:

In the early evening, [Hosokawa Masamoto's commander in Kawachi] entered the capital holding the lord of Imadegawa, the shogun Yoshitane, as his prisoner. The Great Tree [*taiju,* a reference to the shogun] rode in a crudely constructed palanquin guarded on either side by [Hosokawa deputies]. There were also military police in attendance. Troops bearing the shogunal robes led [the procession]. Following them were two mounted horsemen. After them came the lord of Imadegawa and, behind him, [Hosokawa's commander] with additional horsemen numbering over fifty. They proceeded to the north of the capital along Higashi no tōin street. The world of men is disordered; the state of our upheaval cannot be contained in words. [The exposure of] the shogunal robes troubles the spirit. Thronging the sides of the street, the spectators crouched down, under order to do so. The shogun was taken to the temple of Ryōanji in the northern hills. The members of the shogun's personal guard who accompanied him back to Kyoto from the engagement [in Kawachi] have all renounced the world and entered holy orders, I hear. I shall list their names. [A list of more than thirty names follows.][71]

After this spectacle of humiliation, Hosokawa retainers burned down the Kyoto residences of Masamoto's opponents. Ashikaga Yoshitane remained imprisoned for a time in Ryōanji, a family temple and mortuary ground of the Hosokawa house, but was then permitted to escape into exile. Hosokawa Masamoto subsequently arranged for the initiation ceremonies and the formal induction as shogun of Ashikaga Yoshizumi, now a youth of fourteen, whom Masamoto had earlier supported against Ashikaga Yoshitane and harbored as a ward in his own house for several years.[72]

Here again, a private war was played out in the interests of a strong-man's ambition. The victim on this occasion was the incumbent shogun, and its leader was the ranking shogunal deputy. For almost sixty years after the coup of 1493, the fiercely contending heads of the Hosokawa house tried to subject shogunal puppets like Ashikaga Yoshizumi to their own dominion. To take the measure of the accompanying upheaval, let us survey one more sequence in the Hosokawa history.

A homosexual who took no wives and had no children, Hosokawa Masamoto originally provided for his succession by adopting a younger son from the aristocratic house of Kujō. When this bizarre choice of a nobleman caused opposition among the senior Hosokawa retainers, Masamoto adopted a second son from a branch Hosokawa house in the province of Awa on the island of Shikoku. The original heir, known as Hosokawa Sumiyuki, was appointed military governor (*shugo*) of Tanba; the newer heir, known as Hosokawa Sumimoto, was appointed military governor of Settsu.[73] Ambitious retainers grouped around each of the heirs. The interests of these retainers emerged as paramount in the succession quarrels that soon engulfed the Hosokawa, for both adoptive sons were children when appointed to their posts as governors and adolescents when rebellion overpowered them. (Sumimoto was born in 1489, Sumiyuki probably around the same time.[74])

One of the retainers was Yakushiji Motoichi, deputy governor of Settsu, who went to war against the *kanrei*, Hosokawa Masamoto, in 1504 to replace him with his adoptive son Sumimoto. The account of the campaign in Nakamikado Nobutane's diary began this book. Although seemingly concluded by the suicide of Yakushiji and the parade through Kyoto of heads from fallen partisans, the rebellion was not over.

Two years later, in 1506, another army of Sumimoto's supporters marched from Settsu toward the capital, this time led by the retainer Miyoshi Yukinaga (whose military base was in the Hosokawa province of Awa.) Hosokawa Masamoto fled the capital for a time, but his retainer Kōzai Motonaga (deputy governor of Yamashiro) fought an inconclusive battle in the streets with Hosokawa Sumimoto's men.

Kōzai Motonaga was, however, increasingly aligned with Hosokawa Sumiyuki and estranged from Hosokawa Masamoto—for the *kanrei* had intervened against brutal efforts by Kōzai to extract revenues in Yamashiro for himself. In 1507 Hosokawa Sumiyuki, Kōzai Motonaga, and their men attacked Hosokawa Masamoto as he sat naked in the bath of his Kyoto residence and then cut off his head. They also burned the Kyoto residences of both Hosokawa Sumimoto and his protector Miyoshi Yukinaga, who abandoned the capital. In the seventh month of 1507, within two weeks of these events, the dazed shogun originally installed in office by Hosokawa Masamoto was forced to recognize Masamoto's assassin Sumiyuki as head of the Hosokawa.[75]

Hosokawa Sumiyuki survived in Kyoto for less than a month. After adherents of Hosokawa Sumimoto launched attacks against Sumiyuki in Settsu and Yamashiro, Sumimoto entered Kyoto with troops of his allies (including Miyoshi Yukinaga and the son of Yakushiji Motoichi). Sumiyuki committed suicide, and Kōzai Motonaga was killed. One day later, the shogun appointed Hosokawa Sumimoto as successor.[76]

Hosokawa Sumimoto survived in Kyoto for less than nine months. His nemesis was Hosokawa Takakuni, scion of another branch of the Hosokawa, whose head served as military governor of Izumi. Takakuni had originally supported Sumimoto yet came to resent the ascendancy of other favorites and his own apparent exclusion from the line of *kanrei* succession. Takakuni found a patron in Ōuchi Yoshioki, governor of two provinces in western Japan and long an opponent of Hosokawa Masamoto. In the fourth month of 1508, Kyoto was again invaded by a sizable army, raised by Takakuni and Ōuchi Yoshioki. In the face of this onslaught, Hosokawa Sumimoto burned down his Kyoto mansion and fled the capital with Miyoshi Yukinaga. Within a week they were joined in exile by the incumbent shogun, Ashikaga Yoshizumi. This departure cleared the way for a sort of "restoration" that Ōuchi Yoshioki had planned from the onset of his entry into the conflict. The former shogun Ashikaga Yoshitane, ousted from office in Hosokawa Masamoto's coup of 1493, had taken refuge with the sympathetic Ōuchi and now returned to authority under their protection. He reentered the capital in the sixth month of 1508, resumed shogunal office in the seventh month, and promptly appointed Hosokawa Takakuni as *kanrei* and Ōuchi Yoshioki as governor of Yamashiro.[77]

Over the course of a year, then, two Hosokawa heads had died (Masamoto through murder, Sumiyuki through suicide), one had been forced into exile (Sumimoto), and a fourth had succeeded to office after yet another change of shogun. Hosokawa Takakuni presided over Kyoto for almost two decades, until 1527. Few years went by, however, without violent reprisals against him. Miyoshi Yukinaga (in support of Hosokawa Sumimoto) provoked almost constant provincial agitation until 1511, when he succeeded for a time in occupying Kyoto and pushing Takakuni into temporary exile. Takakuni rallied but fled Kyoto again in 1520 under attack by Sumimoto and Miyoshi Yukinaga. Finally victorious against Yukinaga (who committed suicide in 1520), Takakuni then endured public censure from the shogun Ashikaga Yoshitane, who renounced his *kanrei*'s administration by abandoning the capital (this time permanently) in 1521. The intermittent warfare climaxed in 1527 when Takakuni fell victim, at length, to old grudges: he and his men were defeated just outside Kyoto by an army raised by Hosokawa Harumoto (the son of Hosokawa Sumimoto) and Miyoshi Motonaga (the son of Miyoshi Yukinaga). And thus, slowly and painfully, another transition.[78]

What distances have we traveled from the opening stages of Ōnin? By many standards, they are not great. Decades after huge armies first gathered in Kyoto, the shogunate still survived as an institution, the province of Yamashiro remained under official jurisdiction, and the internecine conflicts of the Hosokawa continued to focus on the conventional titles and prizes of the old order. Like the diarist Nakamikado Nobutane, the historian of early wartime might well regard the troubles of the period as discrete contests without transformative significance. They fitted into an old vocabulary of grievance, and they could be perceived as ephemeral challenges to a polity that would outlive them.

Yet by other standards, the distance between Ōnin and the early sixteenth century is very great indeed. Shogunal authority was reduced geographically to provinces where allies, family members, or vassals of the Hosokawa used the title of *shugo* (provincial military governor) and rendered some form of military service to the shogun and *kanrei*. The number of such provinces probably hovered between ten and twenty during the years 1493–1508 but shifted constantly as governors (like the Ōuchi) opposed and aligned with different Hosokawa rivals, as branch houses (like the Awa Hosokawa) fought against their relations, and as allies (like the Asakura or the Isshiki) moved into open rebellion or deliberate withdrawal from Hosokawa battles.[79]

Not only was shogunal authority in the provinces both limited and conditional, it remained just one variable in power struggles that were ultimately shaped by a man's relationships with his vassals. Kōzai Motonaga, Miyoshi Yukinaga, and their kind took leading roles in contests for high office when they alternately turned on warlords who inadequately rewarded them and embraced lords from whom greater spoils might be expected. Their Hosokawa lords were not quite puppets, but they were caught in a snarl of attachments. Perhaps the most ironic aspect of the Hosokawa story, however, is the looseness of the snarl: nothing reliably held men together.

The Hosokawa coups seemed to deny, first, the obligations and hierarchical relations of office (the *kanrei* Masamoto renounced the shogun Yoshitane, and the *shugo* Ōuchi Yoshioki renounced both an incumbent shogun and the *kanrei*). They also assailed the ties of family (Hosokawa Takakuni supplanted his kinsman Sumimoto, and the Yakushiji house split three ways among the claimants to Masamoto's title). They violated, too, the loyalty associated with vassalage (Masamoto's men went over to Sumimoto, and Sumimoto's men went over to Takakuni). In a particularly striking fashion, they exposed the insufficiency of all rewards among men alert to new opportunities (Hosokawa Masamoto's promotion of Kōzai Motonaga as a deputy governor, or of his two adoptive sons as *shugo,* only increased the appetites of these officials and their supporters). And as this catalog implies, the coups indicated the volatility of military advantage (for the balance of force was repeatedly altered by the entry of new players like Ōuchi Yoshioki or the defections of old allies like Takakuni from Sumimoto). In effect, the men who were seemingly pursuing institutional authority were also cutting themselves loose from the constraints of office, household, service, patronage, and martial alliance. The shogunate did survive. But to emphasize its continuity is to ignore both the dramatic constriction in its sphere of influence and the fragmenting relations among officials who were committed, preeminently, to their own interests.

The extent of upheaval appears even clearer in Yamashiro. There the soldiers of the land began to reject the shogunal institution altogether—its *kanrei,* its provincial governor, its administration of justice and taxes—to explore a version of self-rule. Despite the apparent opportunism of these soldiers and the final divisions among them, their uprising constituted a radical experiment in power that lasted for eight years in the home province itself.

Thus, a war that had emerged from a sequence of succession quarrels brought forth not ephemeral but fundamental challenges. Like the

Ōnin war itself, many of these challenges turned, superficially at least, on questions of "who": just which rival should hold or succeed to office (or a family headship, an estate title, a military post)? We find a seeming continuity in institutional structures, for questions about succession presume the integrity of systems. But like the Yamashiro uprising, most of these challenges also exposed questions of "where": did power lie in the capital or in the provinces, among putative leaders or the subordinates who propelled them, in hierarchical organizations or self-governing communities? Questions about the locus of power involved the further question of "how": was power exercised through lawful office or customary privilege, the force of the self, tentative compromises between warlords and their subordinates? And questions of agency raised the ultimate question of "why": what purposes did power serve? These questions did not presume the integrity of existing systems. They exhibited an essential skepticism about all political and social attachments, which marked the greatest distance between the world before and the world after Ōnin.

Although these questions swept aside all assumptions, they did not elicit clear answers. The soldiers of Yamashiro moved in one direction, the contentious partisans of the Hosokawa in another, the warlords who broke away from the shogunate to struggle for provincial hegemony in yet another. This disparity of interests helps account for the irresolution that also marked the world after Ōnin, when practical divisions in force and purpose led to stalemates or to cycles of aggression, resistance, and retreat. The final obscurity of interest among such contenders contributed to irresolution as well; for the participants in each contest we have examined hesitated before making ultimate decisions about the fate of the shogunate, for example, or (in the case of Yamashiro) committing themselves to a new order. Instead of new settlements, we discover the politics of demonstration. Mass spectacle emerged as a testing ground where demonstrators could dramatize their grievances; signal their opposition to a particular enemy or a general state of being; explore their internal resolve and direction; and appraise the character of resistance surrounding them. An alternative to open battle, demonstration served as a brake on violence. A substitute for failing institutions, demonstration served as a declaration of crisis.

2

Dancing Is Forbidden: The Structures of Urban Conflict

In 1506, the courtier Sanjōnishi Sanetaka copied into his diary a set of regulations for Kyoto which, he noted with approval, "are just as they should be." The orders appeared on wooden placards, posted at intersections, in strokes of thick black ink:[1]

Forbidden—

Violations of Coinage Exchange Laws

Theft

Arson

Armed Assault

Quarrels

Sumō Wrestling

Gambling

Dancing

some years later another diarist copied out similar prohibitions against "gambling, bathing in bathhouses, pleasure boating, nighttime outings, and discharging arrows."[2] And another: "Today all communal dancing in Kyoto, even that of children, has been forbidden. Also forbidden are excursions with lanterns."[3]

Something odd, something *not* "just as it should be," ripples often in the laws that military officials circulated in the capital during the Age of Warring States. We find it, for example, in regulations for temple precincts that begin with conventional warnings against felling bamboo and consuming meat and making love on sacred ground but go on to condemn "raising rebellion" and "breaking up and stealing away with ritual objects" (to sell their jewels and golden parts).[4] We find it in a shogun's demand to Kyoto's "men of wealth" for loans to finance the coming-of-age ceremonies of his son: a dignified statement on procedure closes with the promise that "we will punish anyone who, when funds are to be collected, responds by raising violent havoc."[5] And we find it in stipulations that pawned articles must be redeemed "peacefully by women during the daylight hours."[6]

The oddness in some of these orders comes from strange conjunctions. In what sort of world is taking baths the criminal cousin of discharging arrows? What links arson to wrestling in a short list of eight urban problems? Did readers of the placards feel a vaulting rise in tone when cautioned first against eating meat and then against treason? The warnings against rebellion (and assault and stealing icons) also appear odd in their obviousness. In what sort of world must a government instruct the public that arson is a crime? Did Sanjōnishi Sanetaka approve of the placards (and fastidiously transcribe their message) because he found in them some consoling evidence that officials had discovered the will to restrain disorder? Or was he simply gratified that actions ubiquitous enough to have become part of the normal order of things were resolutely being labeled deviant?

The mentality of vigilance suggested by the regulations is a particular sign of trouble. The statute concerning loans makes an axiomatic connection between a shogunal command and the possibility (likelihood?) of violent resistance—a connection more telling insofar as it involves not a faceless urban mob but the community of affluent townsmen who have been exhorted to underwrite one of the rites of shogunal power. The stipulations concerning the recovery of pawned goods presume that already flinty transactions might blaze if entrusted to men or conducted under the cover of night. Indeed, darkness emerges as a peril in much warring states law. One of the lists of prohibitions condemns nighttime excursions in a disconcerting catalog that includes boating and bathing. Do these activities, too, provide occasions for unexpected (or expected) trouble? With the stroke of an official brush, do forms of play become forms of crime because experience has made dancing frightening? And are the laws against this now-criminal play the weirdly logical laws of a world about to explode?

In the following pages, I move away from individual episodes of war to examine the Kyoto scene itself and the ways in which city people experienced, and thought about, the upheaval after Ōnin. My subject is not the explosive event but the mundane patterns of wartime disturbance that generated the climate of fear pervading virtually all documents of the time. These documents take us into a world where the "oddness" of the laws was hardly discernible. In the thin and hallucinatory air of apprehension, statutes forbidding the dancing of children might well have seemed "just as they should be." The diarists of the capital sometimes voiced this apprehension with straightforward eloquence: "We are in extremity and our neighborhood is in commotion, looking toward a heaven that has lost its poles."[7] Yet more often, the search for the mind of war must be oblique—pursued through the sorts of conjunctions found routinely in the diaries of Kyoto's nobles.

24th day.   The monks of Myōkakuji and Myōrenji had a formal debate today on matters of doctrine. Because the Myōkakuji people prevailed on points of the Buddhist law, the Myōrenji people battered the Myōkakuji abbot. Since he is an old man, this will surely lead to outrageous reprisals.

27th day.   Last evening the monks of Myōkakuji and Myōrenji did battle. When there were rumors this morning of further attacks, the military officials issued a decree and the two sides were reconciled.[8]

And again,

Kōzai Mataroku [or Motonaga, deputy governor of Yamashiro] set out for the Kamo shrine and demanded men to assist him in the forthcoming campaign. Shrine officials refused on the basis of their formal exemption from surveillance and taxation by the shogunate. People say this will lead to outrageous reprisals.

   Later, there was a fire in the north of the capital, which I heard was at the Kamo shrine. It has been incinerated, not one inch spared.[9]

Here, once more, is the axiomatic connection between conflict and reprisal, although in these cases the possibility of havoc is swiftly realized. Here, also, is the dry and secretarial tone linking the images of doctrinal debate and physical assault, tax resistance and shrine incineration, although in these cases a shadow of dismay is cast by the fierce economy of the narratives and the interjection of the word *outrageous* (*motte no hoka*) before the inevitable *reprisal*.

As the quotations above suggest, uneasiness in the capital had many sources. They ranged from strife among military men to intemperate rule by the victors, from sectarian conflict to invasion of the city by rural debtors, from the ascendancy of self-redress to the ascendancy of out-right outlaws. Uneasiness also flowed from less tangible threats: from the slipperiness of language and meaning (in a world where boating could slide into crime, wealthy townsmen into presumptive felons, and yesterday's shogun into today's traitor); and from the slipperiness, too, of boundaries (in a world where a sanctuary could be trespassed, a palace converted into a shantytown, a vagrant transformed into a general, and an aristocrat hired as a scribe). All these threats derived additional power from the specter of the unknown. What could happen next?

To trace this uneasiness, I have constructed, in a fashion native to scholarship but alien to experience, a taxonomy of suffering in Kyoto—first disentangling and lining up the forms of trouble faced by residents after the outbreak of Ōnin and then examining their relationships to expose the dynamic of force in everyday life. The artificiality of the exercise is constantly reproached by the documents. Everything neat, static, and bleak in my analysis is challenged, for example, by the following diary entry:

In the morning, [the current military strongmen in the city] attacked a small residence at Ichijō-Karasuma, because the occupant was said to be a relative of one of their enemies. However, the people of the neighborhood gathered quickly around and the invaders withdrew without incident. In the afternoon, I visited the Yakushi Kannon temple and then called at Yanagihara's residence. . . . In early evening [the strongmen] conducted another raid at the home of [an aristocrat], which eventuated in violence. Thereupon, the townspeople of both the northern and the southern sectors of the capital, several hundred of them, rushed to assemble; shouting, they surrounded and attacked the invaders on four sides. Their shouts sounded again and again, as if from an army. An amazing situation. Night fell without incident. The two sides were pacified.[10]

Crowded into this narrative is not a neat taxonomy of trouble but a number of merging elements: a background of fights for control of Kyoto by two rival armies, one of them occupying the capital with difficulty; a wave of purges in the city directed against enemies and their sympathizers; a denial of the authority of current overlords called, here and elsewhere, "invaders," "villains," and "thieves"[11]; a capacity among the townspeople for collective resistance; and an implication that residents bore arms. But just as the passage frustrates this sort of dissection by the rush and integrity of its development, so it warns us, too, that things changed quickly. Although alarm was a daily companion, perils advanced and then receded ("the invaders withdrew," "Night fell without incident"); personal rhythms marked the hours ("I visited the Ya-kushi Kannon temple and then called at Yanagihara's residence"); the familiar note of surprise belied the predictability of events ("An amazing situation"). Across the days and weeks of trouble, no less than across the decades, the trouble remained intermittent. And bad as it was, trouble was not always, perhaps not even usually, the mother of despair. The description of invasions by Kyoto's strongmen does not close in a black tone. And the passage itself suggests some of the resources that fortified Kyoto's residents: the ability to conceive of their overlords as illegitimate, the will to protest, the occasional standoff (surely a victory of sorts) in their contests.

Like the diarist, I pursue several themes in this chapter. While alert to the limits of taxonomic analysis, I nonetheless take a long view of the many decades to war to abstract from contemporary records a catalog of the recurrent problems facing Kyoto's civilians: physical destruction and predation by soldiers; purge and emergency taxation by successive overlords; agrarian uprisings, improvised justice in a society of self-redress, and spreading criminality. This approach combines pattern and detail to suggest the consequences of war in daily life and the logic of their connections. Once more we encounter the injury and the unleashing of interest that were part of the culture of lawlessness, though this time as routine aspects of the urban experience. Violence was not confined to the battlefield, nor did the suspension of political and social constants cease when individual campaigns ended.

Yet the patterns of trouble in Kyoto illuminate more than injury and self-interest. They also indicate the resourcefulness of townspeople who did not surrender to wartime crises. In urban trouble itself (in purges, for example, in agrarian uprisings, and in improvised justice) a political structure is visible. Demonstration moved into the popular life of the city, as it had moved into martial contests, both to expose and to organize conflict. In this case, "lawless" conduct involved a series of experiments in the distribution of power outside institutional frameworks.

Urban Geography, Urban Mayhem

On the twelfth day of the seventh month of the first year of Ōnin, one courtly diarist took stock of the results of recent fighting in the streets of the capital:

Of late, Kyoto has extensively fallen to fire . . . [Our losses] extend:

1. from Takatsukasa-Higashi no tōin to Nijō; from Takatsukasa-Karasuma to Nijō; from Goryō no tsuji to Konoe; from there to Kasuga;
2. from Ogawa-Kita ōji to Nishi no tōin and Kasuga; from Tsuchimikado-kōji to Nakamikado;
3. from Ichijō and the great sanctuaries of the north toward Uchino, everything has been leveled by fire. The mansions of Lords Konoe and Takatsukasa are burned down.[12]

Although individual battles ended in Kyoto, the havoc they wreaked did not. For all residents, the physical destruction of the city was among the most daunting consequences of war. As the above quotation intimates, Ōnin caused the greatest losses. More than half the city burned, including thousands of elite mansions and temple buildings. (See Map 3.) The Lotus uprising of 1536 brought about similar levels of destruction, when military men and estate proprietors united to suppress a rebellion of townspeople: "They set fire to the twenty-one temples of the Lotus sectarians and, beyond this, to all of southern Kyoto. More than half of northern Kyoto has also burned."[13] Other campaigns in the capital were less devastating, but each instance of violent political transition and each of the invasions that punctuated the intervening years resulted in conflagrations that maps can hardly describe. Absent in such representations is a sense of the always-uncertain progress of devastation, the juxtaposition of ruin and temporarily safe abode, the tumult of fortification and refuge-seeking in places of presumed security. The courtly diarists caught this unnerving pace as they went out, day by day, to prepare their accounts. Counting the city blocks lost to fire, tracing boundaries, estimating the number of fallen buildings—they looked and measured with uncanny discipline as their city became a target of attack. And then they dissolved in grief: "Our world is a dark place, dark for all infinity."[14]

Such cries may have echoed the general sentiments of townspeople under siege, but they expressed quite particularly the despair of courtiers and their intimates. "The Citadel of Peace and Tranquillity, known from the time of Emperor Kanmu [Kyoto's founder, d. 806], is now dead," wrote one aristocrat in 1527.[15] A year earlier the poet Sōchō had written in much the same mood:

Crossing the mountain pass, I came to the entry station at Awata without encountering a single person. Once the road through this pass was so lively that people jostled one another's hats and brushed shoulders while horses and carriages passed constantly. Now looking over Kyoto, at the homes of high and low alike, I saw but one building where once there had been ten. The dwellings of the common people are given over to farming. The palace is a tangle of summer grasses. It is too much for words.[16]

For Sōchō, and for most diarists who wrote of the city, Kyoto was a human-centered world—extraordinary not because of its beautiful site and exquisite birds but because of the marks men and women had made on the landscape. The ebbing of the crowds of his memory, and the attrition of the peerless buildings of his memory, revealed no pleasing natural vista. The encroaching fields were a sign of calamity. And animals were symbols of human retreat from a once-civilized place. As we have heard from another observer: "The Flower Capital of myriad ages is now a lair of foxes and wolves." Yet another observed that men had brutalized the work of other men as thoughtlessly as they subdued the natural creation: "Like hornets' nests, the sanctuaries of the eastern and western hills have all been burned and crushed."[17]

The destruction of Kyoto signified to these writers the destruction of civility and, one suspects, of identity itself. Buildings representing order also represented secure social places and coherent lives. Thus the despair of the writers, although inspired by a ravaged cityscape, surely derived most acutely from fears of their own physical and social effacement. Such concerns proved well placed, for urban geography underwent two major changes in wartime—an erosion of the elite presence and a withdrawal of residents into two fortified sectors.

The erosion of the courtly presence resulted primarily from failures to reconstruct or repair the palace and noble mansions. Despite rebuilding efforts immediately after Ōnin, the work was limited or abandoned in succeeding decades.[18] The imperial palace was partially restored around 1479, but we have no later records of substantial repair when the complex was damaged by wind and floods, the spreading fire of battle, the arson of thieves, and the influx of refugees who built shantytowns on its grounds.[19] Attention focused not on the condition of the buildings but on the poor defenses of the grounds, particularly the moats (which were never finished and only erratically guarded by recruits from noble and commoner households). The very need for such defenses shocked contemporary diarists, who found in them a "judgment of heaven" and a warning of "the end of the world,"[20] even as they railed against "the comings and goings of peddlers and beggars" that provided ample evidence of the palace's vulnerability.[21] The Portuguese Jesuit João Rodrigues (who came to Japan in 1577) reported:

The walls surrounding the King's palace were made of wood covered by reeds and clay, and were old and dilapidated. Everything was left open and abandoned without any guards, and anyone who desired could enter the courtyard right up to the royal palace without anyone stopping him, as we ourselves did to look around.[22]

The palace buildings themselves appeared "indistinguishable from common dwellings in the neighborhood."[23]

The palace was exposed not only by its poor defenses but by the withdrawal of aristocrats from areas to its north and east that, burned out during Ōnin, became a new wilderness. Nobles either declined to rebuild there or, like the Nakamikado family, never returned to partially restored mansions, where they felt unsafe. Some aristocrats (like the Sanjōnishi, the Kajūji, and the Takakura) did maintain dignified new residences, usually south and west of the palace.[24] Nonetheless, many courtiers took rented lodgings (some on back streets), found shelter in temples or provincial estates, or hid their financial embarrassment behind brave fronts. The imperial treasurer, Yamashina Tokitsugu, kept up his walls and gates but concealed his leaking roofs by borrowing the homes of friends for formal meetings.[25]

Economic problems lay at the heart of most such difficulties. The imperial house, which had received income from as many as 250 landholdings before the war, collected occasional revenue from no more than 34 holdings after Ōnin.[26] Aristocrats faced similar constriction and their diaries abound in references to the expedients they used to make do. Yamashina Tokitsugu pawned not just fine swords but mosquito nets as well. Nobles loaned out precious manuscripts for copying; sometimes they sold the texts (like Sanjōnishi Sanetaka's medieval copy of *The Tale of Genji*). They suspended major and minor ceremonies; they even postponed interments.[27]

Yet as grave as the financial distress of the nobility was the decline in military support it signified. Provincial warriors drained income from courtly estates that surviving officials in the shogunate would neither secure nor replace. Indicating a certain shogunal indifference to the court's plight, the *kanrei* Hosokawa Masamoto dismissed pleas for enthronement funds by archly observing that "even if the enthronement ceremony is held, the common people will not know the emperor is emperor; and even if it is not held, I will know the emperor is emperor."[28] When it came to clearly urgent matters, such as the palace defenses, officials were more cooperative; but then, too, action was sporadic and subject to tense negotiations with the townspeople recruited as laborers. In effect, the nobility lacked committed protectors. The shabby palace—open to thieves, peddlers, and refugees—became a statement of this vulnerability. The relationship between physical settings and identities is conveyed again in one courtier's description of an emperor still waiting, after seventeen years, for the enthronement ritual: "Because the ceremony has not yet occurred, the emperor will not go out [to participate in New Year's events]. I hear he simply sits behind his blinds."[29] The blinds not only conceal; they represent impotence.

The erosion of the elite presence in Kyoto was not confined to the court. The shogunal presence was diminished first by the fires of Ōnin and then by the mass exodus of the shogun's military governors. The shogun's personal guard (*hōkōshū*) also disappeared from Kyoto, where it had occupied a large quarter north of the palace. Never rebuilt after Ōnin, the quarter became irrelevant to shogunal life after 1493 when a Hosokawa coup largely eliminated the guardsmen themselves.[30] There is pictorial evidence that the Hosokawa *kanrei* and their major deputies kept great mansions in the capital, but the documentary record concentrates on the periodic raids at such sites without sustaining the image of opulent display.[31] We do know that the shogunal residence itself (the Hana no gosho) was restored around 1479 and that construction of new mansions was undertaken around 1515, 1525, 1542, and 1564. Here the record is so thin, however, that even the locations of some of the complexes are unknown.[32]

If the shogun (and his *kanrei*) could project a powerful presence on occasion, the image competed with others: of flight into prolonged exile (Ashikaga Yoshiharu was away from Kyoto from 1528 until 1534, and Ashikaga Yoshiteru rarely entered Kyoto between 1549 and 1558); of flight into fortified temples (where Yoshiharu lived for eight years from 1534 to 1542).[33] Whatever shogunal mansions remained standing during these absences were prey to theft and waste. Neither of the two exiled shogun was able to return to a habitable residence in Kyoto. From the mid-1540s, moreover, the construction of castles in Kyoto's hills preoccupied the shogun. But these were crude affairs, hastily built and easily captured, rather than princely edifices.[34] They belonged not to the late medieval world of shogunal dignity—where the mansions of shogun and military governors signified cultivation and affluence—but to a world of forcibly barracked soldiers and street battle.

More profound than these changes in the elite's presence was the second major development in urban geography: the contraction and fortification of the capital. Residents retreated into two urban "islands," one in northern and one in southern Kyoto, which together covered about two square kilometers—roughly one-quarter of the pre-Ōnin city. (Compare Map 2 and Map 4.) The islands ringed the commercial centers of upper and lower Kyoto (at the intersection of Muromachi and Tachiuri in the north, and Shijō and Karasuma in the south) where the principal defenses of the Ōnin period had been erected and where subsequent extensions of walls and moats created rudimentary stockades. Muromachi avenue was the only significant artery connecting them.[35]

The clearest portrait of this redistribution of the population emerges in documents rather late in date, which indicate the outer reaches of Kyoto's reconstruction during wartime. Compiled in 1570 and 1571, the records list all neighborhoods compelled to participate in a citywide scheme to support the imperial house financially. Map 4 shows the location of these neighborhoods as well as additional urban settlements described in other documents.[36] The map omits certain groups that are hard to track: cultivators who moved into deserted areas, populations still resident around several major temples and shrines, and marginal communities (whose members worked, for example, as gardeners, sweepers, or leather tanners) dispersed around the city. Beyond these groups, there is no evidence of commercial or residential development of the capital outside locales hatched on the map. Here we find all identified guilds and markets, bathhouses, brewers and brokers, and sponsors of the Gion festival. Here we find all organized neighborhoods, all residents who might be mobilized for a civic program of taxation.[37] Even as late as 1583, a Kyoto magistrate was offering tax concessions to persons who would develop the presumably attractive but vacant site indicated by an X on the map. Later census data shows that residents began to move into the area indicated by a Y only in the 1550s.[38] Almost a century after Ōnin, great stretches of Kyoto remained abandoned.

The Ōnin defenses had originally attracted residents, but the two islands developed through purposeful reconstruction. Kyoto people undertook building efforts that sometimes took dramatic form (in the sixteen Nichiren temples erected after 1544, for example) yet more often involved the methodical recovery of neighborhoods destroyed by invasions and fire storms. Such efforts apparently re-created pleasing cityscapes, which the very missionaries who chronicled the wartime devastation judged as exceptionally clean, prosperous, and favored by nature. (The first missionaries arrived in Japan during the 1540s.) The people who were capable of such recovery nonetheless chose to live in

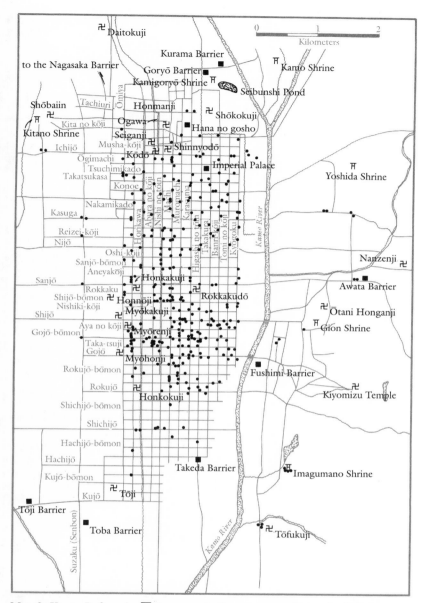

Map 2. Kyoto Before the Ōnin war. • indicates prewar firms of *sake* brewers, pawnbrokers, and oil dealers. Unlike their postwar successors, these firms spread throughout the urban grid east of Ōmiya street. Major sites mentioned in the text of this book are also identified. Based on an insert to *Kyōto no rekishi,* vol. 3. Courtesy of Kyōto-shi Rekishi Shiryō-kan.

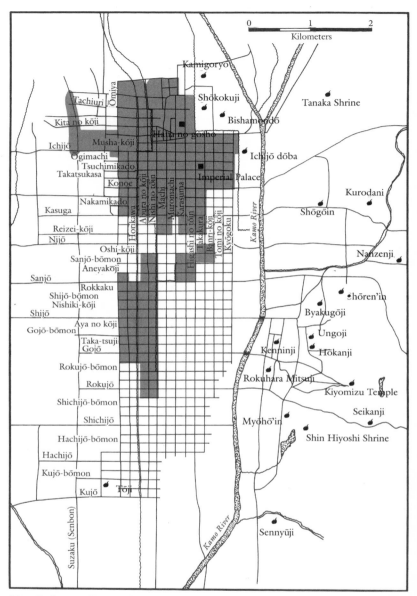

Map 3. Areas of Kyoto burned during the Ōnin war. The shading and the fire symbols indicate the principal areas within Kyoto and on the city's outskirts where significant damage occurred during the Ōnin war. The representation of damage to the streets of the southern sector of the capital is somewhat conjectural because surviving records concerning this area are more suggestive than detailed. Based on *Kyōto no rekishi* 3:348 and Imatani Akira, *Ōnin no ran: Shūkan Asahi hyakka Nihon no rekishi* 18, *Chūsei* 2, no. 7, p. 5-219.

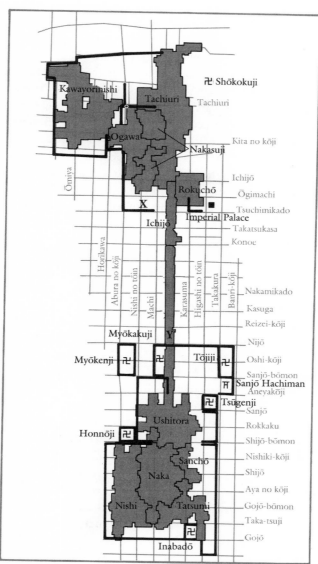

Map 4. Kyoto during the Age of Warring States: fortification and neighborhood federation. The heavy line indicates the moats and earthen walls constructed around Kyoto for defense during the Age of Warring States. The shaded areas indicate the neighborhood federations (*machi-gumi*) that embraced virtually all of residential Kyoto during wartime. X is a lot still vacant as late at 1583; Y is an area settled only in the 1550s. The redevelopment of Kyoto in wartime was a protracted process. Based on *Kyōto no rekishi* 4:109–11; Takahashi Yasuo, *Kyōto chūsei toshi-shi kenkyū*, between pp. 372 and 373; and Imatani Akira, *Ōnin no ran: Shūkan Asahi hyakka Nihon no rekishi* 18, *Chūsei* 2, no. 2, p. 5-221. Courtesy of Kyōto-shi Rekishi Shiryō-kan.

these two small islands and, in the pursuit of security, even abandoned other areas left untouched by Ōnin. (Compare Map 3 and Map 4.)[39]

Security took the form of outer moats and earthen walls partially reinforced with stone. Although the work was probably routine, it concentrated in the Ōnin years, in the period of large debtors' uprisings around 1484, and in the decade between 1527 and 1536 when Kyoto was embroiled first in the wars between two rival shogunates and then in the Lotus uprising. In 1534, for example, the shogunate ordered the construction of comprehensive new moats.[40] Security also took the form of gates and fences both at intersections and at important buildings within the islands. These were timber structures, joined by ropes and fortified with palings of bamboo sharpened into spikes.[41] Whatever physical protection these defenses offered, I suspect that security in Kyoto was more deeply associated with the symbolic resistance they declared and the close proximity of neighbors they enforced. In the end, the defenses did little more than impede attacks even as they created vital targets where fires, once started, had catastrophic effects.

When Kyoto's residents elected the security of the fortified islands, they created settlement patterns denser than any they had known before, though similar to those that prevailed after wartime. Cadastres from the later sixteenth century describe building frontages of two to four meters (very few were wider), lined up twenty and more to a street with negligible spaces between.[42] Very early in wartime, moreover, back lots within the urban islands were given over to additional domestic construction and new alleys were cut between older avenues.[43] The density implied by such evidence is difficult to confirm with the population figures, which are highly conjectural. But if we take a conservative estimate of 100,000 (the standard population estimate for the year 1500 is 150,000), we might very tentatively conclude that the urban islands accorded each resident only twenty square meters of space.[44]

In building their fortified islands, residents of Kyoto abandoned one city—"The Citadel of Peace and Tranquillity," which had been defined by expanse, symmetry, and the gracious compounds of the elite, to shape a new one defined by the crowding of a stockade. This new city signified resilience and calculation. But it also embodied the anxiety we observed in the urban laws cited at the beginning of this chapter. Fortresses rise in memory and anticipation of violence:

There is talk that the world will explode in chaos. Lately in Tanba province some deputies of the Hosokawa have twice provoked battles. . . . At night people here [in Kyoto] are stealing away with their belongings. Soon there will be a conflagration. This is the work of demons. Kyoto will go through yet another transformation. We must be cautious.[45]

Here news, or rumor, of distant battles prompted expectations of local turmoil. And again, as we saw in the diary entries that opened this book, expectations of turmoil prompted flight—not just by unencumbered persons looking for temporary shelter but by residents preparing for the destruction of their homes. They carried household goods—furnishings, even mats and portable walls, rather than irreplaceable objects alone. Such fear did not preclude astonishing acts of recovery. Yet wartime geography continued to reflect a complex movement between injury and renewal.

Coupled with the physical destruction of battle was the general mayhem that accompanied the movement of troops. The laws of military officials in Kyoto testify to the problem:

Because this area is close to a battle encampment, troops must be present in Kyoto. Should there be violent havoc raised by them—lawless disturbances or the like—you are to respond immediately to terminate the havoc and need not inform us prior to your actions. [Addressed to townsmen leaders in individual neighborhoods.][46]

Arresting both in its presumption of trouble and in its delegation of police power over military men to townsmen (a confession of official helplessness?), the document stirs worry in its blanket reference to "violent havoc." Other laws describe the trouble in greater detail:

Item: There is to be absolutely no forcible seizure by our men of valuables entrusted by our enemies to current residents of the city. If there is any violation of this order, you are to report it to us and there will be swift punishment. . . .

Item: We are not now concerned with those who took bribes from the neighborhoods and households and claimed they would ensure their safety at the time of our enemy's defeat. However, we will absolutely not countenance anyone who currently makes inappropriate demands.[47]

In these orders, trouble is associated with "my troops" or "our men" —the insiders in service to Kyoto's current overlords who are being held to some standard of good conduct. Outsiders also make an appearance: in this case as "enemy" soldiers hostile to "our men," but in other cases as anonymous *rōnin* who become the object of additional laws:

Should anyone harbor *rōnin*, we will immediately carry out punishments, even if the offense occurred in the past.[48]

Although we have come to associate *rōnin* with the "masterless samurai" of a later era, when ill fortune cast adrift men with claims to military status, the *rōnin* of wartime were more likely to be adventurers seeking employment as mercenaries. Even these already-imprecise categories—adherents, adversaries, adventurers—were invented by the authorities in the capital. In the diary literature, the categories conflate in a richer vocabulary that includes "villains," "thieves," "bad men," "official bad men," "white soldiers" (or "naked" soldiers of fortune equipped only with loin cloths and swords), inexperienced "green soldiers," "gangs of fleet foot" (prepared to rush in and out of opportunity), and "foot soldiers" (a generic and often pejorative term for the martial mob).[49] These terms resonate with the commotion fighting men brought to the city and draw attention to the varied composition of fighting bands. During the Ōnin war the vagabond Honekawa Kōken became a "foot-soldier general" charged by the head of the eastern army to lead the "bad men of Kyoto" (*Kyōchū akutō*) in blocking the supply routes of the western army, a service he rendered in part by setting fires throughout the southern capital. A certain Mizushi led another band of "bad men" under the direction of the western army.[50]

The status of these unwelcome guests had negligible significance for Kyoto residents who were the target of abuse by insider and outsider alike. As the laws I cited suggest, theft in various forms was the chief problem: confiscation of goods from enemies and suspected enemies; appropriation of blades and horses throughout the city; extortion of bribes and protection money; looting of pawnbrokers; squatting in deserted buildings; indiscriminate felling of trees and bamboo for shelter and fortification.[51] An illustrated scroll depicting the history of the Kyoto temple of Shinnyodō portrays soldiers, under the direction of a mounted commander, stripping a temple building of flooring, walls, beams, and balustrades during the Ōnin war.[52] Expectations of similar raids frightened not only the townspeople who fled the capital bearing their furnishings but also the aristocrats and defeated generals who departed Kyoto only after entrusting their *tatami* (woven straw mats) and sliding doors to influential friends. (After the suicide of a shogun in 1565, guards secured his valuables and took them to the imperial palace for safekeeping.)[53] In one of the most direct comments on these affairs, a monk concluded, "No justice at all is executed. High and low alike simply do as they please."[54]

It is hard to know whether crimes against persons occurred with the frequency of crimes against property. Urban laws intimate difficulties by proscribing *tsujikiri,* armed assault on the streets, and aristocratic diarists recorded a few such incidents within their own experience.[55] More often we find brief references to unspecified "quarrels" between soldiers and townspeople, some eventuating in large melees and death, which may have arisen from assaults.[56] Because the references typically involve either individuals close to the diarists or episodes that provoked sizable retaliation, the low incidence of recorded personal attack may be a distortion of the sources.

Or were the white and green troops who assailed property somehow constrained from attacking people? This point deserves reflection, since a variety of incidents raise questions about the limits to violence in this period. We have noted already that death and wounding often appear problematically low among combatants in battle. (Diarists can mention an invasion of 25,000 troops and the death of fewer than 10 men.) Further, the death and wounding of civilians close to battle appear unusual. *Kenbutsu,* or sightseeing, at martial engagements remained popular among aristocrats until firearms made their first appearance in a Kyoto battle of 1550 and one onlooker was struck by a bullet.[57] More significant, I know of no raids on Kyoto's citizens by soldiers flushed with victory or defeat.

Let me introduce three rather startling pieces of evidence that also involve restrained conduct, or expectations of restrained conduct, by fighting men. These examples range widely in circumstance, but all focus attention on the boundaries between expected (permissible?) and unexpected (impermissible?) actions. I pursue the point since our understanding of war's calamities must include some tentative sense of war's codes. I am concerned here neither with "honor" nor with an implicitly contractual understanding of the warrior's role. I am interested, rather, in the fuzzy boundary between atrocities and the unexceptional (however pathological) burdens of violence.

No. 1.   *Go-Hōkōin-ki.* 1498, 12th month.

> 4th day.   I received the following report. Kōzai Mataroku [the deputy governor of Yamashiro], while returning from a hawking expedition in Yamashina, seized a local man, whereupon everyone in the district rose up and took Mataroku prisoner. At this, Mataroku's remaining entourage in Kitahata rode out [on a rescue mission] but returned without recovering him.

> 8th day.   I hear that, because of a directive from [Hosokawa Masamoto, the *kanrei*], a force of six or seven thousand men raised [by

his allies] rode out to Yamashina to combine forces with those of Kōzai Mataroku.

10th day.   Yesterday the various troops dispatched to Yamashina returned in the evening. I hear they burned down the districts there.

11th day.   Kōzai Mataroku returned to Kyoto from Yamashina early this morning.[58]

No. 2.   *Rokuen nichiroku.* 1499, 10th month.
1st day.   Members of a league of the land [*do ikki*] [demanding cancellation of land rents] have camped at Kitsune-zaka in the north of the city. Hosokawa's army has attacked them.

5th day.   Early today Akazawa Sōeki [a deputy of Hosokawa Masamoto] directly entered Kitsune-zaka in the north . . . leading more than five hundred horsemen. They defeated the league as if cutting through bamboo. The league members dispersed. Because people of Matsuzaki Fukue had sympathized with the league, the troops wanted to level it. Akazawa stopped his men from attacking the people of Fukue. It is a blessing of heaven that they did not do this injury.[59]

No. 3.   *Nisui-ki.* 1532, 8th month.
23d day.   Today, they say, the Kyoto forces assembled and headed for Yamashina Honganji [the headquarters of the Ikkō sect]. I hear the great majority were Nichiren believers; regular warriors made up the smaller part [of the army]. Then they surrounded Honganji on four sides with archers. They say the encounter has not yet eventuated in battle.

24th day.   There was a battle early in the day. By midmorning [the Kyoto forces] attacked and took Honganji. Several dozen [Honganji] people died under attack and then the temple was burned. In a short period the [Kyoto forces] also torched surrounding structures and houses so that not one remains standing. Smoke replaced the sky. . . . For four and five generations, Honganji had boasted of glory in wealth and honor. They say the temple precincts were great beyond measure and as impressive as a veritable Buddhist paradise. Even the homes there were not surpassed by those of the capital. The people residing there were all prosperous and distinguished, and accordingly their residences displayed great beauty. The quick destruction of all this today must be the work of heaven. So we must conclude. So we must conclude. The Kyoto forces returned this evening, every one laden with treasure.[60]

In example No. 1, local people of Yamashina (*"everyone"* in the district") succeeded in taking captive a shogunal official and holding him for a week, until an army of some size ravaged the area and sprang the prisoner. Their immediate provocation was Kōzai's apprehension of a neighbor (perhaps intended as a hostage to coerce his community into paying taxes or bribes or settling some other score),[61] but a long history of troubled relations between the Hosokawa regime and the people of Yamashina surely figured as well.[62] Crucial to our discussion is the fact confirmed by the report's final line: *the Yamashina men did not kill Kōzai Mataroku*. What constrained them? Regard for a man of rank and status who was nonetheless their enemy? Fear of official vengeance more devastating than an attack by six thousand soldiers and extensive burning? A code that allowed arrest, counterarrest, mass demonstration, and even reprisal through fire, but that checked the murder of a prisoner?

Example No. 2, which concerns a battle between shogunal troops and (again) men from Yamashina demanding tax relief, portrays reprisals against sympathizers in surrounding villages as unacceptable. Its language is powerful: the march on Fukue would have been an "injury" and restraint was "a blessing of heaven." A landed proprietor, the noble chronicler had no reason to identify with league members and good reason to condemn their armed demonstrations. He records the defeat at Kitsune-zaka in a dispassionate voice. But strikes against noncombatants provoke his censure.

The third example reports the fall of Yamashina Honganji, the great headquarters of the Jōdo Shinshū sect, after years of warfare with the Nichiren sect of Kyoto. The account speaks of the mercilessly thorough destruction of the temple and its town, as well as the subsequent looting of treasure. But again, battle casualties are low and the fighting is confined to a few daylight hours, for the victors are en route home by evening. Despite ideological bitterness and a history of exceptionally violent attacks, the fury unleashed against this "veritable Buddhist paradise" did not result in a bloodbath. Men and women were not hunted and trapped, beaten and stabbed.

The evidence of constraint I have offered here is not only limited; it is also diverse in a fashion that is alternately helpful (in suggesting the range of an ethic discouraging the violation of persons) and unhelpful (in frustrating attention to comparable rather than discrete events).

Equally critical, evidence of constraint can sometimes be rebutted with evidence of brutal assaults against people—evidence we have particular occasion to note in Chapter 4. Yet I am searching here less for an articulate and unassailed principle than for hints of probably inchoate assumptions about what war permitted and what it did not, about distinctions between the horribly commonplace and the uncommonly horrible. Our limited and diverse evidence hints at a code of conflict that may have helped protect life off the immediate field of battle. It also reveals a society compelled to expect arson and destruction, flight and homelessness, theft and plunder, and the terror of huge martial demonstrations.

The Rule (and Misrule) of the Victors

The battle that brought physical destruction and general mayhem to Kyoto also brought new rulers. All of them worked, though variously, within the institutional structure of the shogunate, and most of them maintained forms of conventional urban governance. But the image of continuity that was mocked by repeated coups was assailed as well by the spectacles that successive warlords mounted in the capital to establish their rule and by the demands for wartime taxes that pitched them into conflict with Kyoto's civil proprietors and townspeople.

THE PURGE

Government in Kyoto changed hands violently seven times during the Age of Warring States. The purge that effected change on each occasion became the most dramatic act of wartime rule by the capital's successive conquerors. Or rather, purge emerged as a sequence of acts in a play revived by every new overlord from Hosokawa Masamoto in 1493 to Oda Nobunaga in 1568. To bring the structure of purge into focus, let me briefly review three of these upheavals in power—two of them already familiar to us.

The *kanrei* Hosokawa Masamoto gathered shogunal authority into his own hands by mounting a coup against Ashikaga Yoshitane, the incumbent shogun, in 1493. Masamoto first sent an army to Kawachi province to ensure the defeat there of the shogun and his allies. Soldiers then escorted Ashikaga Yoshitane back to Kyoto and paraded him through the streets of the capital in a humiliating show of defeat. Ashikaga Yoshitane was imprisoned in a family temple of the Hosokawa; his guard was forced to take the tonsure in a form of symbolic death; and Masamoto burned down the mansions of old enemies in a rite of purgation. A new party of Masamoto's deputies took over Kyoto's offices, and the fourteen-year-old Ashikaga Yoshizumi, Masamoto's ward, became the eleventh shogun in the Ashikaga line.[63]

The next transfer, from Hosokawa Masamoto to Hosokawa Takakuni, occurred between 1507 and 1508 as first one and then another of Masamoto's adoptive sons mounted a patricidal and fratricidal contest for power. Hosokawa Sumiyuki killed Masamoto in his bath, took his head, torched enemy mansions, assumed headship of the Hosokawa house with shogunal consent, and made a round of new political appointments. Within six weeks, his adoptive-brother Hosokawa Sumimoto led an army into Kyoto and forced his suicide, killed Sumiyuki's allies in street battles, assumed the headship of the Hosokawa house with shogunal consent, and made a round of new political appointments. Eight months later, Sumimoto's adoptive-brother Hosokawa Takakuni forced Sumimoto and his deputies into exile, processed into the capital with a force raised in three provinces, torched enemy mansions, and compelled the incumbent shogun Ashikaga Yoshizumi to flee the city (and his terrified wife to hide with sympathizers). Finally, two months thereafter, Takakuni oversaw the return to Kyoto of Ashikaga Yoshitane (the shogun usurped by Yoshizumi through the machinations of Hosokawa Masamoto), who entered the capital, again in a widely observed parade, under the escort of thousands of soldiers. Reinstalled as shogun, Yoshitane confirmed Takakuni as head of the Hosokawa house and chief administrative officer of the shogunate (*kanrei*).[64]

Let us consider just one more transition. Early in 1527, after years of intermittent attack, Hosokawa Takakuni faced a decisive challenge from his nephew, Hosokawa Harumoto, and a broader coalition of opponents. Takakuni's small army was defeated by a far superior force at the battle of the Katsura River, just west of the capital. Hosokawa Takakuni, the incumbent shogun, and the magistrates of the Board of Administration were forced into flight by the victors, who subsequently marched ten thousand soldiers into Kyoto in a parade that included seventy mounted commanders and twenty palanquins. Hosokawa Harumoto arranged a transfer of official titles to his party and a promotion of Ashikaga Yoshitsuna that promised his imminent appointment as shogun.[65]

These and other incidents contained a remarkable combination of elements: purge began with a violent and theatrical act of conquest; it continued with expurgation of the old guard through fire, flight, exile, arrest, and monastic retreat—all associated with humiliation and impotence; it advanced to a statement on the contrasting power of the conqueror—who marched columns of armed men through the capital in a mass display of force; and it concluded with the installation of new men in office, typically under the aegis of a puppet shogun. Transition was partly a matter of brute martial superiority. It was also partly a matter of inducting the new conquerors into office. But neither singly nor in combination were these elements sufficient. Transition further required a demonstration of the sort we witnessed in Ōnin and the Yamashiro uprising. Demonstration consisted, again, of parade and witness, as well as a ritual debasement of the coup victims.

Purge clearly belonged to the new politics that associated power with a process of coercion and appeal enacted on the streets. This was an inherently incongruous politics, for while demonstration seemed to dramatize conviction and sureness of purpose, it was really an exploration of the unknown. Because there were no maps for change, the demonstration of purge had to chart strange territory: the limits of tolerance within the political system for violent transfers of authority; the extent of the support victors could marshall and sustain; the deepest motives that drove the victors and their partisans; the boundaries between private battle and anarchy. And this exploration assumed the critical engagement of its audience.

The chief audience of purge was the members of the new regime themselves. Demonstration might build resolve and internal cohesion by reassuring uneasy victors of their ascendancy. Certainly addressed, too, was the audience of military adversaries and uncommitted soldiers, who would know of the purge through spies and rumors and who might be intimidated by the flamboyantly methodical takeover of the capital. And demonstration addressed the residents of the capital as well: the merchants, who provided essential tax revenues;[66] the general population, which could undercut victory through insurrection or quiet treason (harboring enemies, withholding supplies); the noble and religious proprietors, who might stir up both urban and provincial opposition; the imperial house, which still confirmed shogunal appointments and approved extraordinary taxation. Unless they would undo the structures of city governance and political legitimation, the leaders of coup required some consent from these constituencies.

Perilously at issue in the conduct of a purge was just this problem of legitimacy and consent to a new leadership. On one level, the process seemed to insist that the shogunal institution was indispensable to rightful government, thus affirming continuity and reconciliation. To rationalize a coup, the accompanying purge included the debasement of old officials and the elevation of unsullied mascots. Debasement was crucial. In every case, the conquerors were linked to their victims by ties of family or vassalage that exacerbated the aspects of treachery in their coup. In almost every case, moreover, the conquerors numbered the incumbent shogun among their victims. Extremely rare in the first three hundred years of martial governance, when the person of the shogun appeared inviolable even if his administration did not, direct attacks on the shogun brought a new lawlessness to rule after 1493. To return themselves to the shadows of the law, the conquerors elevated new Ashikaga heirs to office and took titles from them. But as if conceding the fragility of this gesture before the enormity of their actions, they had to transform their shogunal adversaries into prisoners exposed like criminals, or into felons on the run, or into hapless generals unfit for military office.

The choice of a new shogun was dramatically calculated as well. The Ashikaga scions brought by leaders of coups to the capital for new shogunal appointments were usually obscure relatives of the incumbent raised outside Kyoto, who possessed some aura of innocence. Typically, they were children.[67] The only weathered insider elevated to the shogunate after a coup was Ashikaga Yoshitane, the man ousted from office by Hosokawa Masamoto in 1493 and then returned to office by Hosokawa Takakuni in 1508 as a symbol of restoration. But Hosokawa Masamoto's own choice of shogun was a fourteen-year old boy, and two later nominees were each ten years old on succession. A courtly diarist describes the arrival of one of these boys in language that suggests the perhaps-spontaneous response elicited by beautiful youths caught up in surprising fates:

The young lord is now ten years old. He entered Kyoto this morning. The blinds of his palanquin were drawn up. His face is very beautiful. . . . His unexpected destiny is truly auspicious.[68]

This sort of quotation reinforces the images of continuity and reconciliation in the process of purge even as it implies the successful manipulation of at least the courtly audience. Thus, most stages of the coups passed without recorded public incident. The diarists did write with shock of shogunal exiles ("everyone is amazed," "this is unbearable")[69] but then confessed their powerlessness ("there is nothing we can do") and accorded the new shogun and the new *kanrei* the courtesy of their titles, which were duly granted by the emperor.[70] Indeed, the shock over the exiles partly explains why the purges seemed to succeed: civil proprietors resolutely identified with the shogunal institution and hence were disposed to countenance transitions that preserved the regime.[71] When the shogun Ashikaga Yoshitane survived an attack in 1509 that left him wounded in eight places, the courtier Sanjōnishi Sanetaka observed:

26th day.   . . . The shogun himself showed great valor, thus escaping grave harm, and he forced the villains into retreat. This is an unprecedented affair and an inspiring tale for future generations. I cannot adequately write of these things. . . . A [shogunal envoy] went to the palace to convey the details and then came here to speak with me. . . . I went to the [shogunal] residence soon thereafter with Reizei Dainagon, Higashi Bōjō, and Anegakōji to convey our shock. There were a great many people already gathered. . . .

27th day.   Early in the morning I dispatched letters to various places about last night's affair. Many people also came here to inquire. This is all utterly intolerable. But it is remarkable that the shogun is safe. The workings of heaven preserved him.[72]

In his horror over this attack, Sanetaka reveals deep, essentially ideological loyalties to both an individual shogun and the shogunal institution itself. Such loyalties posed a threat to leaders of coups, since their assaults on the shogun might inspire revulsion and counter-coups. But if skillfully manipulated, such loyalties also provided invaluable assistance to leaders of coups. By transferring nominal shogunal authority from a debased incumbent to an appealing successor, they could exploit the institutional loyalties to rationalize the overthrow of the particular man.

And this exploitation was the essence of purge. In the end, the purges were not about continuity and reconciliation within a legitimate institution. They were about the appearance of continuity, the utility of gestures of reconciliation, and the fiction of legitimacy. Coups declared that power was contingent on force. Purges suggested that power might be translated into official authority through the orchestration of meaning by a conqueror (who acted out debasement and renewal) and the passive collusion of audiences (who kept the right titles in use and otherwise kept quiet). Hence, authority was released from institutions or laws to reside in ambiguous performances and tentative agreements among the many parties to spectacle who chose to live with an uncertainty they could not yet resolve.

But these agreements were tentative at best. Some coups failed immediately at the hands of rival warlords; all faced continuing challenges—not only from rivals but from residents of Kyoto as well. When a coup of 1565 provoked the suicide of the shogun, for example, as many as eighty thousand persons were said to have assembled at the funeral in protest.[73] The ensuing three-year interregnum effectively crippled the would-be victors.[74] Yet even less dire circumstances created substantial risks: dissension within the victor's own ranks; attacks from forces loyal to his predecessor or from other adversaries; guerrilla actions in the city. So purge had to become routine. Following the opening spectacles of transition, purges took the form of enemy hunts.

Item: If our enemies mingle with Kyoto's population, or if they conceal themselves here, you must swiftly cast them out. Should there be any concealed person, when we discover the fact it shall be a crime held against everyone in the particular place and everyone who knew of it.

Item: There will be stern punishment for anyone who consorts with the enemy. There shall be a reward for anyone who reveals such a crime.

Item: No blame will attach to those who, while not themselves associates of the enemy, nonetheless consorted opportunistically with them in the past. From now on, however, consorting is another matter.[75]

Another city law responded more radically to the problem.

Item: Leaving or entering Kyoto, by persons of whatever status, is to cease. Therefore, you are to apprehend anyone leaving or entering, otherwise violating the law, or raising havoc. Then report them immediately.[76]

Enemy is a fearfully imprecise word, especially since the more obvious adversaries of Kyoto's victors—the vanquished leaders, their men, and conspicuous sympathizers—either fled town after coups or became objects of the opening rites of purge. Who, then, *was* the remaining enemy? Just how far the term carried and how aggressively an uneasy regime could interpret it become clear in a series of attacks launched in Kyoto during the late months of 1527.[77] These attacks belong to the history of Hosokawa Harumoto's coup, which produced two rival shogunal administrations. The apparent victors, sustained by troops from Awa province, attempted to complete the transition to their rule by purging "enemies" from the capital during the eleventh month.[78] Yamashina Tokitsugu reports:

11th month, 29th day.
This morning about ten men from the gang of Awa invaded the house of the *tatami* maker of this neighborhood. The people of northern Kyoto, all the way from Nijō avenue, rose up and surrounded them with two or three thousand persons. . . .

Again, in late afternoon, they invaded [a courtier's] house on Musha-kōji. And again, the people of the various blocks rose up and surrounded them, shouting and crying. They say there were about ten invaders, five or six of whom were struck by arrows. . . .

12th month, 1st day.
Because of the disturbance [at the *tatami* maker's place], they say the invaders are coming back to this neighborhood. People here are building fortified gates for the block and hence asked me for bamboo. I gave them ten stalks. They erected a gate at the entrance to the alley nearby. I also sent over *sake* to the people of the block.[79]

The next report is from Sanjōnishi Sanetaka.

There are rumors that the villains are going to break into this neighborhood, so we are erecting a fortified fence at my gate. This is outrageous. This is outrageous. In front of the spiked gate at the northern part of the neighborhood they are digging a ditch and building a fence of bamboo. People from the Gon-chūnagon's house have asked for fifty bamboo stalks for this purpose.[80]

At the same time, Yamashina Tokitsugu reported defensive actions at the imperial palace, where "everybody" was gathering to help.[81] Later he added that "there are orders to build guard huts at the palace and to bring tools over there and *tatami* and so forth. . . ." As a result of this fortification, "the palace has a weird appearance." The same presumption of danger to the throne moved the *Nisui* diarist to conclude, "This is the end of the world, the upheaval of the world."[82]

These raids apparently had some particular targets—the *tatami* maker, the courtier living on Musha-kōji, for example. A document quoted earlier in this chapter, which concerns the same sequence of events, identifies another victim as someone "said to be a relative of one of [the invaders'] enemies." But the diarists linger briefly over these particular targets, hardly noting the particular reasons why they might be targets at all. Instead, they focus on the whole neighborhood as the victim of the attack. Composed of sudden raids by small gangs on horseback, purges seem to have moved across the social and physical geography of the capital less as instruments of reprisal against obvious "enemies" and more as an instrument of terror against all doubters—including, at least in the minds of high-ranking courtiers, the emperor himself.

Such enemy hunts tended to be sporadic and exemplary, rather like the parades that opened the sequence of a purge. But they were different in their brute intrusion into civilian life, which provoked determined opposition. The resistance, like the raids, crossed class lines to gather *tatami* makers and nobles into a common front. It extended from mass gatherings of armed defenders to the construction of fortifications to declarations of the invaders' illegitimacy (explicit in the language of the diarists, implicit in the act of fortification). Here we discover the familiar spiral of violence as attack inspired counterattack. We also discover an ongoing exchange of demonstration and counterdemonstration, as parties to the new politics continued to test one another. The testing at this stage exposed clearly adversarial relations, which the opening stages of the purge had deflected onto vanquished leaders. And thus it exposed the limits of acquiescence among Kyoto's residents following violent transitions in power.

The adversarial relations between conquerors and townspeople created lasting problems of security for both groups. Let me conclude this section with one more suggestion about the dynamic of conflict and its complicated results. To guard their own safety, as we have seen, successive warlords attempted to purge Kyoto of *rōnin* and enemies by engaging townspeople in networks of corporate responsibility. (Harboring adversaries "shall be a crime held against everyone in the particular place and everyone who knew of it.") Warnings that the community shared the guilt of the offender spilled over into laws concerning such volatile affairs as religious affiliation, coinage exchange, and taxation. Statutes governing the value of coins and the mix of disparate coins acceptable in commercial transactions (*erizeni-rei*) closed in this fashion:

These items are strictly established. If there are violators, men will have their heads cut off and women will have their fingers cut off. If anyone willfully and selfishly exchanges coins [in violation of these items], the act is to be reported by the townspeople. Anyone concealing such a crime shall bear the same guilt [as the offender].[83]

Statutes outlawing the practice of the Nichiren faith in Kyoto included these directives:

Item: . . . Anyone who conceals a Nichiren priest is guilty of a crime.

Item: If there is any household that displays a Nichiren amulet or devotional oaths, that house, the two adjoining houses, and the three facing houses will be confiscated.[84]

Further stipulations that informants would be rewarded brought worry over spies to the center of daily life. And since neighbors stood and fell together, they had to know each other. Strangers, loners, persons of obscure background or questionable loyalties—all posed a threat to the communities.

Not surprisingly, then, neighborhood associations insisted that sales of property be limited to insiders ("land in one neighborhood is not to be sold to persons from outside the neighborhood") and that renters come with guarantees and guarantors.[85] Guild laws display vigilance over "outsiders" not only to protect commercial monopolies but also to prevent "quarrels," "disagreements," "direct complaints" to the authorities, and anything impeding "unanimity in all things."[86] A league of farmers near Tōji, a temple in southern Kyoto, composed a "joint pledge" that members "shall assemble together if anyone seeks to enter our group and consider each case on its merits with no negligence." Outsiders of the league become "enemies" to whom "no one shall disclose our official deliberations."[87]

Although intense self-scrutiny could forge groups solid in their resistance to the authorities, it could just as well accommodate the purposes of those authorities: by merging the identities of individuals and their associations in a fashion that legitimated the principle of corporate responsibility; by excluding from these associations the very persons most likely to provoke trouble; by engaging neighbors as a kind of moral police; by discouraging association and identification beyond the security of the group. These measures have psychological as well as practical consequences. And it may be the most malign effect of surveillance that apparently suitable responses to terror contain within themselves new terrors.

EXPLOITING THE RESOURCES OF THE CAPITAL

Warlords who survived coups and purges to assume jurisdiction over Kyoto promptly laid claim to the capital's resources. Some of these were historical perquisites of shogunal office—certain proprietary taxes and guild fees, and, more important, the monthly business taxes on brewers and pawnbrokers.[88] Claims upon these resources were sources of contention, for even in the realm of what we might consider "normal" governance, the conventions of the past provided only a general guide to wartime conduct. But my concern here is the specific burden on the city that derived from "extraordinary" (*hibun*) impositions related to battle. Conquerors tried to exploit Kyoto in unfamiliar ways that exacerbated the adversarial relations opened by the purges.

At least three "extraordinary" impositions became more or less routine: demands for local barracking of soldiers (*jintori, kishuku*); corvée levies for military construction; and claims of eminent domain over trees and bamboo growing in the city. Although these exactions are the subject of occasional laws, quarrels, and hardships noted by the diarists, they appear more often as specific exemptions in the decrees that military officials sometimes addressed to individual neighborhoods. In 1558, for example, the neighborhood of Takatsukasa-Seiwain was officially excused, probably for a year's time, from barracking duty. In 1561, one neighborhood on Muromachi was excused from tree felling.[89] Such formal exemption assumes official access to the homes, labor, and lumber of Kyoto's residents.

The toll of these exactions remains hard to measure because our best informants, the courtly diarists, belonged to the class that most successfully negotiated exemptions from them. They and their servants were impressed to dig city moats during the Ōnin war, but labor duties fell essentially on the townspeople who cut major trenches in 1484, 1534, and 1563[90]; maintained these and other defenses by annual contributions of labor; and helped erect both shogunal headquarters in the city and castles in the hills nearby. Records, generally fragmentary, trace the construction of at least nineteen of these castles during wartime, and their references to labor indicate recruitment from the capital and its environs—Yamashina and areas close to Tōji.[91] Deforestation was a consequence not only of this building but also of fortification and reconstruction after fires in the city itself. Hence the demands for trees and bamboo from urban neighborhoods, which reflect a substantial violation of Kyoto's hills.[92] Barracking duty was probably substantial as well. If we assume an intermittent need to house, say, 10,000 soldiers, and hypothetically assign half of them to camps outside the city, we are left with 5,000 men to be distributed among something like 15,000 city dwellings. In this scenario, one in three Kyoto homes provided shelter and food, on occasion, for provincial troops.[93]

The wartime rulers of Kyoto tried to appropriate local resources more directly through extraordinary taxes in cash which, though variously named (as "arrow" or "commissariat" or "half" levies), revealed a single critical need for revenue. The *hanzei*, or "half-tax," levy (the claim by military governors to half of the annual land dues owed to proprietors) had long helped to sustain military administrations outside the capital.

Thus, Kyoto's strongmen impressed this levy in Yamashiro, the province embracing the capital and its environs, but with disappointing results. Here are several entries from the diary of Sanjōnishi Sanetaka:

1497, 10th month.
11th day.   My estate agent has sent me official directives from the military deputy of Yamashiro [demanding surrender to him of half of our tax revenues]. I ordered him to respond that our property has been, from of old, immune to official intrusion and exactions. Ours is a world without the Way (*mudō no yo*). There is too much grief.

12th day.   I sent further instructions to my agent that he show to the military magistrates the age-old documents concerning the areas of Ikeda and Imayamazaki in our estate of Toba, . . . and that he insist there be no disturbance in them since they are exempt properties.

18th day.   I received a letter from the emperor inquiring about sending orders through an imperial ambassador to Hosokawa Masamoto [the *kanrei*] stating that the conduct of his deputy in Yamashiro is inappropriate. I assented to this plan.

21st day.   Today three nobles . . . all went at imperial command to make a statement to the shogun concerning affairs in Yamashiro. I hear they saw Hosokawa Ukyō Daifu Masamoto. I shall inquire about and record the details.

11th month, 2d day.   Tonight the shogun replied that there is to be no further violation by the military governor Bitchū no kami Sadamichi in the administration of Yamashiro. A fortuitous resolution.[94]

Obdurate before a challenge to the "old" and "age-old" privileges of proprietorship, Sanetaka associates the half-tax not with lawful rule but with the loss of "the Way." He resorts first to rebuttals of the military deputy on the Yamashiro scene and then to intervention by the throne with the shogun's highest official. Complaints that "the conduct of his deputy in Yamashiro is inappropriate" elicit the concession that a "violation" has occurred and is not to be repeated. Again in 1504, courtiers opposed demands for a half-tax in Yamashiro with "conferences" and appeals ("conveying our distress as noblemen") to the emperor. This levy, too, was "withdrawn."[95] When yet another half-tax was imposed three years later, in 1507, the emperor despatched two more ambassadors to the shogun condemning such efforts once again. Again, a retraction of the half-tax.[96]

But retraction in fact, rather than in word, required the cooperation of shogunal deputies in Yamashiro. Despite the withdrawal of the half-tax in 1504, for example, a diarist tells us of continuing impositions:

9th month.

10th day.   Kōzai Mataroku marched out to Ichijōji and Takano [villages just north of Kyoto] because of their defiance of the half-tax. He quickly burned the villages down.

11th day.   Today Kōzai again marched out against Yamashiro, but he was stopped by men of the area. Later Hosokawa Masamoto [the *kanrei*] returned to the capital from Tanba province. Because Kōzai had defied Masamoto's orders [in continuing to enforce the half-tax and in assailing the villages], Masamoto himself marched out to Yamashina to punish Kōzai. But Kōzai had fled to Saga. From today, the Yamashiro half-tax is to cease.

21st day.   Kōzai has not ceased the half-tax.[97]

These passages reveal something of the conflict at work in Yamashiro. On one level, the conflict arrayed civil proprietors against shogunal officials, preeminently the *kanrei,* who found in the half-tax both a potential revenue and an occasion to announce control over the home province. It is no accident that half-tax levies tended to follow transition and purge as demonstrations of hegemony. But the competition over Yamashiro also entangled both the ambitious deputies of the *kanrei* and the still-belligerent "men of the land." Although the provincewide uprising of their leagues had ended by 1493, the men of the land alternately aligned with and resisted overlords who were ultimately incapable of subordinating them. The appeals of courtly proprietors may have moved Hosokawa Masamoto to withdraw a half-tax levy in 1504. The intervention of "men of the area" actually "stopped" the march of Kōzai Mataroku.

Half-tax levies in Yamashiro occurred periodically after 1507, only to fail repeatedly. Never did military officials in the home province succeed there with this most basic expression of martial rule.[98] Yet victories in tax battles were never simple. They remained, most obviously, transitory: one retraction did not preclude renewed levies. They also precipitated reprisals: Kōzai Mataroku burned down the villages of Ichijōji and Takano. We noted a similar act of retribution in the opening pages of this chapter: frustrated in his demand for "men to assist him in the forthcoming campaign," Kōzai burned down the Kamo shrine—"it has been incinerated, not one inch spared." And finally, opposition to the "half-tax" moved military officials to impose alternative levies: commissariat taxes (*hyōrōmai*), "arrow" taxes (*yasen*), and "roof" taxes (*munabetsusen*). Here is a description from Yamashina Tokitsugu of an attempt to collect a commissariat tax:

1529, 1st month.

10th day.   From midafternoon, the bell at Kōdō temple began pealing out an alarm. Asserting that they were to collect a commissariat tax, two [military deputies] burst into the property of Lord Ichijō and, we heard, took his wife and children hostage. My father went over to Ichijō's residence. This is an extraordinary calamity. . . .

11th day.   . . . Because the road to Ichijō's residence was blocked in the front, I entered from Toriya, a house on Muromachi avenue. Again the Kōdō bell sounded. People of the blocks rose up and surrounded [Lord Ichijō's residence]. When the townsman Takaya Yōsuke attacked from the north, [the military deputies] struck seven or eight of Takaya's group with arrows and three died. The deputies also clashed to the south with people of the neighborhoods. The arrows finally stopped after mediation efforts by representatives of Ise no kami [a military administrator] and Ogawa Yamashiro no kami, from Niki Jirō's household [a courtier]. There had also been arrows discharged from Ichijō's residence itself. . . . The courtiers who had gone out to Ichijō's residence [to render assistance] numbered about 200. In addition, all the people of Muromachi neighborhood had charged over there. Because of the mediation, all of us returned home at night by the same road. [The military deputies] numbered about 200 yesterday, I think, and about 120 or 130 today, they say. . . .[99]

Evocative of the neighborhood purges in 1527 that inspired popular resistance, this raid set determined soldiers (up to 200 of them, armed with arrows, prepared to take courtly hostages and to fire on courtly and commoner defenders) against equally determined residents.

Such confrontations typically stopped short of extreme resolutions. They revealed the antagonistic relations already seen in the neighborhood purges as they proceeded according to increasingly clear protocols: mass assembly was followed by limited violence and bloodshed and then by mediation and dispersal. Here, again, both sides explored unknown territory through calculated steps as demonstration was restrained by counterdemonstration. The capacity of military officials to alternate aggression with retreat suggests not only the volatility of Kyoto's politics but a cunning that forestalled chaos as well. Warlords pushed hard—and often successfully—on Kyoto. Yet warlords also canceled the half-tax,[100] granted discrete exemptions to individual neighborhoods, and pulled away from armed encounters with townspeople.

The officials' cunning in the face of resistance may help explain the seeming absence of a plan for military conscription in Kyoto. The diary entries that open this book—Nakamikado Nobutane's account of the rebellion against Hosokawa Masamoto in 1504—assert that the Hosokawa party "deployed the people of southern Kyoto by excusing them of their land rents." We find later references to "townspeople from the

southern sector of the capital" who entered the service of the Sakai shogun after 1529.[101] The evidence of conscription is no more than tantalizing, however. The chief instance of mobilization involved the Nichiren sectarians of Kyoto who, between 1532 and 1536, joined the
campaigns of their military overlords in numbers reputedly as large as
20,000. Yet the circumstances of those campaigns were singular. Commoners fought in alliance with overlords, not under duress. Instead of
conscription, the wartime record reveals selective calls for help, such as
this shogunal order to Nanzenji temple in 1495:

> Word has leaked out that a gang of bad men is conspiring to raise an uprising
> in the name of demanding a cancellation of debts. Despite firm orders forbid-
> ding this in the past, we hear they are planning another insurrection. This can-
> not be anything other than a grave crime. Hence, without wasting a day or an
> hour, you are to apprehend the ringleaders, execute them, and bring their heads
> to us. We order you to send directives to all your affiliates that, should anyone
> resist compliance, his lands will be confiscated.[102]

Or again, a shogunal order to Honmanji in 1533:

> We hear that an uprising of provincials is forming. We order you to assemble
> your strength and render loyal service to us. There is to be no negligence.[103]

In such cases, Kyoto's military officials avoided open conscription in
the city by requiring the leaders of religious establishments to engage
in police actions. The religious leaders had to recruit their own men and
affiliates, not in voluntary civic service but in urgent ("without wasting
a day or an hour"), brutal ("execute them and bring their heads to us"),
and compulsory ("should anyone resist compliance his lands will be
confiscated") deeds of war.

These demands for service were far outnumbered by occasions that
compelled townspeople to rise in self-defense without any shogunal initiative. As the passages above suggest, the uprisings (*ikki*) of rural debtors and agrarian leagues posed a particularly acute threat—sometimes
annually, sometimes several times in a single year. And seldom was the
shogunate ready to meet these emergencies.[104] Even in lesser crises—
when waves of theft and arson washed Kyoto, or when mundane quarrels led to confrontations—the *ad hoc* police actions of courtiers or abbots or townspeople often proved more consequential than the actions
of shogunal officials. The limits of official resources in the city appear
vividly in a lengthy correspondence between Hosokawa deputies and
the Kitano shrine over a local priest who had turned traitor: incapable

of apprehending the priest themselves despite repeated pleas from the Hosokawa, managers of the shrine received help only when the Hosokawa appealed to thirteen provincial allies to form an arrest party. No adequate local soldiery, no standing police force, existed to meet this challenge.[105] In short, in one of the great ironies of wartime history, Kyoto was occupied by military rulers unable to provide military protection for the city.

This situation derived partly from institutional change. The Board of Retainers (*samurai-dokoro*), the shogunal organ that exercised police jurisdiction in the capital, fractured after the Ōnin war and the creation by Hosokawa overlords of personal regimes largely impervious to old institutional structures. The Board of Retainers all but disappears from the record in 1485.[106] The guard of the shogun himself (the *hōkōshū*), once an efficient force of several hundred men, also withered after Hosokawa Masamoto effected his coup against Ashikaga Yoshitane in 1493.[107] The Hosokawa relied, instead, on provincial military networks distributed throughout, and generally headquartered in, Awa, Settsu, Izumi, Tanba, and (erratically) Yamashiro. Although assembled in the capital for marches led by the Hosokawa, members of the network did not maintain a permanent garrison in Kyoto. Indeed, soldiers there may rarely have surpassed the several hundred men mentioned in tax raids and the like, although the sources are too patchy on this subject to sustain a conclusion.[108] If the number of soldiers in Kyoto was modest, the situation both accords with the vulnerability of regimes distracted by campaigns elsewhere and illuminates their conduct in the capital itself. Forced to compensate for meager forces in Kyoto, the warlords governed through a combination of initial swagger (purge, terrifying raids, ensuing conciliation) and consistent deflection of police duty to residents. In short, their cunning treatment of Kyoto's people seems a mixture of adroit politics and strained martial resources.

This mixture of strength and weakness exposed the people of Kyoto to the injuries of two worlds. They were subject to coups and the spectacles that followed them; continuing hunts for "the enemy" in a society bifurcated into insiders and outsiders; levies on the resources of shelter, labor, lumber, and cash; and induction into the defense and police forces of their city. They were also subject to urban rioting that their overlords could not contain and, as we see shortly, almost surely helped to provoke. The nobleman Kanrōji Chikanaga gives us a taste of the riots in a diary account of an uprising of 1484.

Bearing torches, a gang of thieves [or debtors seeking the cancellation of debts] invaded a pawnbroker's shop on the northern corner of Ichijō-Karasuma. People of the neighborhood marched out against them armed with bows and arrows. The head of the firm marched out as well and I hear that he and his wife were killed, their child wounded. An evil wind carried the fire set at the brokerage across a full block of Muromachi destroying everything. The residence of Lord Hino completely burned down. We are in extremity and our neighborhood in commotion, looking toward a heaven that has lost its poles. Still, the homes before my residence are yet safe. In recent years the numbers of thieves have swollen terribly. In a world without a *kanrei,* without a Board of Retainers, without a city magistrate, without a police chief, without any inquiry into or investigation of crime, we have such calamities all about us. It is unbearable.[109]

Uprisings in the City

The attack on the pawnbroker that Kanrōji Chikanaga describes was one episode in a long chronology of specific troubles that people of the day called *ikki,* which denoted, as we have seen, both uprisings and the leagues that organized them.[110] For the people of Kyoto, *ikki* figured most importantly in the guise of uprising and most frequently in the form of demands for the cancellation of debts. Leagues of the land did act in opposition to the political authority of absentee lords in both the military and aristocratic communities.[111] Leagues of Buddhist sectarians also acted against other religious communities and their political patrons. But urban uprising, or, really, urban invasion, most often occurred in pursuit of *tokusei*—an act of "virtuous government" that became a euphemism for debt cancellation. The ultimate audience of these uprisings was the shogun or his deputies who, since the late thirteenth century, had exercised the authority to declare moratoria or amnesties on debts owed to a variety of moneylenders; the immediate targets of violent action were individual firms, typically Kyoto's *sake* brewers and pawnbrokers, that made the majority of substantial loans. Most participants came from the leagues of the land in rural Yamashiro province. Diarists noted with care, however, the presence in these raids of "retainers of military lords in Kyoto, other samurai, and various bad men." Some commoners in Kyoto, indebted to their more affluent neighbors, may have joined the uprisings as well. Penurious aristocrats living in hock offered at least quiet support for the decrees cancelling their debts, if not for the armed marchers demanding them. In the matter of debtors' uprisings, then, the lines between insiders and outsiders, partisans and adversaries, were not well drawn.[112]

Such uprisings were not new to the age of civil war. *Ikki* had terrorized Kyoto as early as 1428 as one expression of economic change: in the more advanced economy of the home provinces, increasingly dominated by market forces and transactions in cash, loans had become crucial to a more specialized, commercial agriculture. And although much lending activity remained in the hands of local headmen and land managers, much more had moved into the sphere of professional brokers in Kyoto, where lending rates of 5–6 percent per month, payable in advance, prevailed.[113] But even though the uprisings were not new, their number increased during the decade preceding Ōnin until, during the thirty long years between 1482 and 1511, they became a nearly annual scourge.[114] The rate of riot accelerated in "a world without a *kanrei*, without a Board of Retainers, without a city magistrate, without a police chief, without any inquiry into or investigation of crime." (Kanrōji Chikanaga's portrayal of a dead or lost government is the more arresting for its literal inaccuracy: in name, the offices he lists were all filled in 1484.) Other observers also noticed the connection between one crisis and another, between political turmoil and subsequent uprising:

A cancellation of debts will be carried out throughout the realm. They are now posting the announcements. Because the Kyoto party lost the advantage in the latest battle in Tanba, nothing can be done about the riot in Kyoto. Following the government's defeat in Tanba, the leagues rose up demanding debt cancellation and, accordingly, there is no recourse but to post the said announcements.[115]

The actual conduct of uprisings belonged to the politics of demonstration. Debtors' rebellions began, often "at night" or "in the dead of night" or "at dusk," as league members assembled in separate parties "at the entrances to the capital." These were official barriers set up for the collection of tolls and the surveillance of travelers, which stood outside the city, mostly in the hills, where rural highways met the roads of Kyoto. There league members set "torches and campfires burning in all directions through the hills" and "raised shouts and cries of war." The opening displays might go on for days as the men of the land dispersed into the forests at sunrise only to reassemble with their torches and shouts when night fell. Finally, they descended into Kyoto, again "yelling the cries of war," to attack specific brokers. Some raids occurred in darkness. Most fell in early morning when the terror of the nighttime fires in the hills was fresh and the rhythms of the day had yet to assert themselves, but when daylight could reveal the force of the invaders' numbers.[116]

Early this morning the leagues of the land raised war cries in the west and opened attack. When the brokers and their men retaliated, one broker named Takaya was executed, I hear. About ten other men in the group of defenders were killed as well.[117]

This particular raid, in the tenth month of 1495, went on for at least three days as firms in different parts of the city faced arson and the murder of their owners. The only defense of the city came from men recruited by the brokers themselves and the "people of the neighborhoods," who succeeded in "killing scores of members of the league."[118]

These uprisings combined theatrical elements with limited recourse to violence: targets were selective, indiscriminate assaults apparently contained, and casualties few. Fire emerged as the primary tool of the uprising, in part to inspire terror and perhaps to expurgate the brokers' "crime," but more to facilitate the theft and destruction of loan records and the looting of pawned goods. The individual acts achieved a kind of debt cancellation, for the brokers under attack lost both the receipts and the collateral essential to the recovery of their loans. Yet the spectacle of the uprising projected itself higher, toward the military officials capable of rescinding debts across the city. It served as a type of negotiation through mass action.

The response of military officials was a mixture of opportunism, intransigence, and concession that probably encouraged the uprisings. The early raids moved officials to regulate lending practices more elaborately: they tried to keep rates at 4–6 percent per month, stipulated the duration of loans, intervened against the forfeiture of some real property rights, inveighed against schemes to compound interest or collect it in advance, and protected borrowers from paying interest that was three or four times larger than the original loan.[119] But the impulse toward reform (and the implicit rebuke to lenders, which may have legitimated demonstration) was compromised by both the limited efficacy of the regulation and the concessions that were made to the lenders—preeminently a retreat from protecting real property against foreclosure.[120]

When officials took the drastic step of cancelling debts, they revealed a more unsettling ambivalence in attitude and confusion in policy. A decree of 1441 rescinded numerous contracts between lenders and borrowers. Although it did not affect loans made at low rates of interest (typically at 2 percent and primarily by religious establishments) and loans secured by certain categories of real property, the decree permitted most borrowers to terminate payment and recover their collateral.[121] The decrees of later years, however, made debt policy contingent on the payment of bounties to the shogunate. In decrees of 1454, 1457, and 1480, officials declared that they would confirm loan contracts if *lenders* paid to the shogunate, within a stipulated period, a sum equal to 10 (or sometimes 20) percent of each outstanding loan held by the lenders; otherwise, officials declared that they would cancel loan contracts and rescind debts if *borrowers* paid to the shogunate, within a stipulated period, a sum equal to 10 (or 20) percent of their outstanding loans.[122]

These actions accorded some advantages to lenders—who were protected from a summary cancellation of debts such as that of 1441 and permitted to enforce their loan contracts on the delivery of fees. But the actions carried clear disadvantages as well: enforcement of the loan contract not only required a substantial payoff; it also depended on the faltering resolve of a shogunate vulnerable to intimidation by debtors and alert to opportunities to enrich itself. The decrees offered a similarly mixed message to borrowers: they refused to cancel debts outright and defended the interests of brokers even as they revealed deep worries over debtors' uprisings, a disposition to accommodate borrowers (again, at a price), and an official interest in profiting from loan policies.

Indeed, the only unambiguous message in the decrees governing loans concerned official self-interest. Fees collected from lenders and borrowers after the decree of 1480, for example, came to a total of 2,032 *kan.* This figure acquires significance if we consider that the major income available to the shogunate in Kyoto, from business taxes levied on brewers and brokers, amounted to about 22 *kan* per month during this period. The fees collected after the 1480 decree represented roughly eight years' worth of conventional business taxes.[123] This kind of payoff gave the shogunate ample incentive to intervene in the loan process. Opportunism was particularly clear in the decree of 1480, for this order appeared spontaneously, *in the absence* of any precipitating uprising, and could not be interpreted as a direct response to agitation. It suggests a form of official collusion with opponents of the brokers or, at the very least, a declaration that brokers were fair game.

Thus, the increase in uprisings after 1480 was encouraged by the disarray in government, the general ascendancy of the politics of demonstration, *and* the willingness of officials to tamper adventurously with the brokerage establishment. Subsequent decrees on loans—those of

1504, 1520, and 1526 (which followed uprisings)—abandoned even the guise of preferential treatment for lenders to accommodate whoever came first: any broker who arrived promptly before officials with a 10 percent fee would find his loan contracts confirmed, but any borrower who arrived more promptly with the 10 percent would find his loan contract canceled.[124] Such terms acknowledged the overriding shogunal concern with revenue, yet they also gave a new prominence to the interests of the debtors. Equally or more to the point, such terms accommodated borrowers from the elite community whose debts had mounted during wartime. One inventory of debts canceled after borrowers paid their fees of 10 percent during 1504 contains fifty-two important names. Nobles, abbots, and shogunal officials had as much as humbler borrowers—and more—to gain from the decrees on loans.[125] One final encouragement to uprising, then, was the very breadth of common cause.

The effects of uprisings on the lending establishment of Kyoto appear limited; for neither rural nor urban borrowers could tolerate the collapse of credit, and the shogunal decrees, however disruptive when they occurred, remained uncommon. Further, the thirty-year peak of uprisings between 1482 and 1511 gradually leveled off, perhaps as a result of improving rice prices after a period of deflation and the easing of famines, which affected large parts of the country between 1490 and 1500.[126] Yet the long ascendancy of the *ikki* indicated once again the movement of politics into the streets, where exemplary violence was licensed as an instrument of mass appeal and coercion. The rules of collision still seemed to be working: demonstrators discouraged horrific reprisals by orchestrating their attacks with care; shogunal officials made limited and oblique concessions to debtors whose interests could be manipulated to advantage, but whose power could compromise their own authority in the city. The ultimate results of the collision remained obscure, however, since both the limits of uprisings and the flexibility of military officials were matters of constant renegotiation.

The Society of Self-Redress

Throughout 1516 the two Buddhist temples of Tōji and Tōjiin were locked in a dispute over access to river water in the southwestern area of Kyoto. The following document, issued to the administrative office of Tōji by shogunal magistrates, traces the opening scenes in the troubles.

> No. 1.   Administrators of Tōjiin have brought suit to us over the recent dispute with Tōji concerning water use at Suzaku. Tōjiin asserts not only that invaders from Tōji struck a neighborhood child at the water's source, but also that a certain Tsutsumi Saburō Yuemonnosuke gathered troops on behalf of Tōji and led them into that place. When the people of Tōjiin struck back, one of their men, the farmer Jirōkyūrō, was struck and killed. This is an outrage. Since the law is clear regarding [the crime of] private battle, the death penalty is to be carried out [against Tsutsumi]. Furthermore, because an official of Tōji, a man named Mikawa, as well as all his relatives, were of the same mind as Tsutsumi and thus joined him in violating the law, we order you [the Tōji administrators] to issue your own stern orders [insisting upon the punishment of these people] as well.

Three months later, as the quarrel intensified, shogunal magistrates issued the following inquiry to farmers who worked land in the surrounding villages.

> In the matter of the recent dispute over water use in the area of Shichijō and Suzaku: Administrators of Tōjiin assert that, since the time of the original quarrel at the water source, Tōji has again gathered forces and sent them there. When we raised questions with administrators of Tōji, they asserted the following: "Matters did come to violence during the dispute over water. But when we attacked the residents of Suzaku, people from the surrounding areas joined forces with both sides, faced off against each other, and joined the battle. This in turn led to wounding, and some people were struck and killed." The differences in the statements of Tōji and Tōjiin are not without points of doubt. Thus we order you farmers to abandon all partiality and inform us fully about what really occurred. There is to be no delay.[127]

We find in these episodes a familiar configuration: a "quarrel" arises; one contestant gathers supporters and takes armed action; the defenders respond with armed action; interested parties from the area join in the fracas; further wounding and even death occurs; reprisals continue. We also find in the documents that describe the episodes a familiar vocabulary: "invaders," "troops," "battle," "violence," "joined forces." These are the patterns and the words of *jiriki kyūsai*, the self-redress of grievances. Here, we meet it across the spectrum of civic troubles and across the boundaries of class and community. The civilian residents of Kyoto, our focus in the following pages, took armed action against military men and invading leagues of the land, and also against their proprietors, their religious enemies, their criminal assailants, and their neighbors.[128]

Like the uprisings of leagues of the land, the self-redress of grievances was not new to wartime Kyoto. But the narratives of these incidents after Ōnin point to several singular features that both locate them in the larger context of upheaval and assign them a disturbing prominence. Let me tease out these features from a sequence of examples, some of them darkly comic, that take us into the everyday world of self-redress.

No. 2.   *Sanetaka kō-ki.* 1506, 7th month, 16th day.

In Tachibana alley, children were parading with lanterns for the Ceremony of Myriad Lamps when retainers of a military official [*kaikō*] stopped them, declaring that prohibitions against such activity had been issued. Thereupon, an argument broke out. When the retainers smashed the lanterns, someone from the house of Kada Jirōzaemon wrested away the wooden sword of one of the retainers and beat him with it. Rumors followed that, because of the beating, the official himself would attack and destroy the whole neighborhood.

In a discussion of this matter with Tokimoto Sukune [another aristocrat], I urged that he immediately meet with [military officials]. I also wrote him a letter to this effect. But difficulties arose [and negotiations failed]. Finally, Saitō Tōtōmi no kami made a plan. Tokimoto, taking along Kada Jirōzaemon, was to go and seek forgiveness from Matsuda Buzen no kami [a shogunal magistrate]. I included some words of support, and the affair ended without further incident. As for these recent events, my brush is inadequate [to describe them]. They are outrageous.[129]

No. 3.   *Chikatoshi nikki.* 1539, 8th month, 3d day.

Yesterday some retainers of Ōdachi Hyōgo-dono went out to Muromachi-Tsuchimikado to demand from Sanpukuji temple the payment of the land taxes which were in arrears. Since the lawful rate is 60 *sen* per unit, the retainers said they would collect a total tax of 1 *kan* 200 *mon*. The people of Sanpukuji responded that this claim was unimaginable and would not acknowledge the debt. Although the retainers again demanded payment, the Sanpukuji simply hurled insults at them and then, armed with furniture and household tools, attacked the retainers. Subsequently other people in the neighborhood joined in to beat up the retainers.

The shogun heard about this affair and rendered the judgment that, according to the law, I must punish Tsutsui Saburōbei, one of my own deputies, who also holds a post at Sanpukuji [and was therefore culpable for the attack on the tax collectors]. I responded that, according to precedents established by previous *kanrei*, I was not obliged to punish my own deputy on the order of the shogun.

[From the diary of an official of the shogunal Board of Administration, Ninagawa Chikatoshi.][130]

No. 4.   *Sanetaka kō-ki*. 1533, 2d month.

14th day.   At nightfall I had a letter from Nijō's wife saying that the son of her husband's wet nurse—a priest of the Ikkō sect from Saihōji in Fushimi—was apprehended today on the road. People from a temple of the Nichiren sect did this. Nijō's wife asks that we dispatch a letter from the Ōi house imploring that the priest's life be spared. . . .

15th day.   When I returned home, there was another letter from Nijō. Last night the prisoner was killed. How awful. How awful.[131]

No. 5.   *Tokitsugu kyō-ki*. 1533, 2d month, 18th day.

I hear that members of the Nichiren sect have apprehended several arsonists. Because there was to be a formal assembly of the community [to decide their fate], Sanjō Aso and Jimyōin and I went out together to view the proceedings. They brought forward the three arsonists and immediately executed them.[132]

No. 6.   *Tokitsugu kyō-ki*. 1549, 9th month, 7th day.

In order to enforce judgment and apprehend the two foot soldiers who had pillaged the fields of Shōgoin in eastern Kawara, about 5,000 people of northern Kyoto set out for an attack. They apprehended both men, I hear, and put them to death.[133]

No. 7.   *Tokitsugu kyō-ki*. 1550, 5th month, 2d day.

There was a quarrel at Nijō-Muromachi . . . and, from about noon until late afternoon, the opponents confronted each other. I sent Ōzawa Kamon Kanimori to deliver word to Lord Nijō and to Sanuki no kami Tadamune. I hear that one hundred persons, on both sides of the quarrel, were wounded. The commoner elders of northern and southern Kyoto intervened. Lord Nijō also went out to the scene, I understand.[134]

No. 8.   *Tokitsugu kyō-ki.* 1551, 1st month, 24th day.

There was a quarrel between Muromachi and our neighborhood. One person from here, as well as the priest Obata, who had acted as a mediator, were struck and killed. Hence, people of our neighborhood said they were going to attack Muromachi and this promised to eventuate in large-scale mayhem. So I went to consult Anzenji, and then Hirohashi. I also went to consult Karasumaru and Nakamikado and shared a cup of *sake* with them. Then I went to Lord Ichijō and drank *sake* again. I heard that the elders of northern Kyoto had mediated the quarrel.[135]

No. 9.   *Tokitsugu kyō-ki.* 1554, 5th month, 21st day.

Early in the morning, there were rumors that villagers of Yoshida would invade the village of Shirakawa [in connection with a quarrel over cutting grass]. Hence, I rushed out to the area. Together with me on the same road [seeking to halt the invasion] were Karasumaru, Hirohashi, Nakamikado, Tominokōji father and son. . . . My own retinue included Ōzawa Izumo no kami, Sawaji Chikugo no kami . . . and three lower retainers. We wore light armor. Those mentioned above [all from aristocratic households] numbered over eighty. Five hundred men from northern Kyoto also joined forces with us. The mediation was successful.[136]

Although these narratives are diverse, they all turn on the appearance of *jiriki*, a term I have translated as "self" in the phrase self-redress (*jiriki kyūsai*) but that more literally and more revealingly means "the power of the I." A word of Buddhist origins, it contrasts with *tariki*— the "power of the other," or the power of the Buddha and Bodhisattvas on whom, in the Mahayana message, we must rely. *Tariki* evokes the world of dependency through faith, the majesty and authority of the other, the transfer of initiative and responsibility. *Jiriki* evokes the world of autonomy through action, the centrality of the self (or a body of selves), the seizing of initiative. In the passages I have cited, the power of the I is sometimes manifested in offensive action by Kyoto's residents, more commonly in defensive actions, occasionally in the enforcing of judgment (if, in fact, these things can be so easily disentangled).

Most of the narratives begin with a quarrel—over water or a street parade or taxes or religion or grass cutting or (Nos. 7 and 8) unspecified troubles. The sources remain silent on the rights and wrongs of these quarrels (who *did* have rightful access to the water or the grass? were the Sanpukuji taxpayers really in arrears?), as if conceding the divergent perspectives that define a quarrel in the first place. The narratives continue then with *jiriki*—the actions of contestants who rely on the power of the self to redress their grievances. *Redress* is a usefully imprecise word here, for it finesses the problem of just what is happening. The actors are variously dramatizing the quarrel, venting rage against the opponent, punishing that opponent for injuries received, and seeking a resolution through displays of strength. There are certainly aspects of demonstration in some of the incidents, particularly in the massing of supporters, the hurling of insults, and the manipulating of rumor. Yet we also find spontaneity and loss of control. Wounding and death appear calculated on certain occasions, the product of the moment on others.

Most of the narratives move from the quarrel and its redress to a third stage of development: outside efforts to settle the accumulated grievances. Redress itself routinely failed as a form of resolution. In No. 1 (and to some extent in No. 3), justice is the preserve of an official world. Members of the shogunate's administration receive Tōjiin's suit, pass judgment on Tsutsumi, instruct Tōji to discipline collaborators, command local farmers to give testimony. Although the shogunate never fully disappeared from the workings of wartime justice, our additional examples mention a variety of mediators and judges. Nobles, for example, act several times as interlocutors and, in No. 9, as a sort of posse leading as many as six hundred persons in a mission of peacekeeping.[137] Townspeople appear in No. 6 in stunningly large numbers, as enforcers of a "judgment" actually rendered by the shogunate but spontaneously executed by a mob.[138] They reappear elsewhere in a semiofficial and autonomous capacity: in No. 5 as members of a "formal assembly" of the Nichiren sect that publicly tries and kills criminals; in Nos. 7 and 8 as "elders of the northern and southern city" who mediate successfully among quarreling neighborhoods.

Our narratives raise tough questions concerning perceptions of self-redress: was it lawless? and in whose eyes? Officials of the shogunate assigned Tōji's attack to the realm of illegal "private battle" and found its ringleader guilty of a capital crime (No. 1). They responded in a similar fashion to the defenders of Sanpukuji by ordering the punishment of a temple official (No. 3). Our documents represent Tōji's administrators, however, as recalcitrant: they appear to acknowledge the violence but not the illegality of the attack, and they defend themselves by recriminating their adversaries. In No. 3, the lord of Tsutsui Saburōbei—

an important shogunal administrator, Ninagawa Chikatoshi—simply invokes a jurisdictional issue, denying the relevance of shogunal judgment to the relations between man and vassal.[139] In No. 2, attention moves away from the children and their defender to focus on the official thugs who cite alleged laws to stop street play, smash the children's lanterns while wielding swords, and inspire fear of neighborhoodwide reprisal for the humiliation dealt to them. Whereupon neighborhood nobles exhaust themselves in strategies to apologize. The incident is so riddled with disproportionate reactions that the comment "outrageous" is hardly adequate.

In effect, we encounter in these three examples no shared perception of self-redress. The silence of the sources on the rights and wrongs of the precipitating quarrels descends, as well, upon the rights and wrongs of violent reprisals. Although reprisals may be "awful," the issue of lawfulness is raised by the shogunate alone—not by a great temple, a high-ranking aristocrat, or a military lord. What we do encounter in these three examples is reproach of the shogunate—reproach of officials who can be argued down, denied jurisdiction, and implicitly accused of lawless action themselves. What we encounter in the additional examples is a preoccupation with the settlement of grudges outside official structures. I abuse my sources by asking them a question they do not address, for the authors—if asked directly whether they found self-redress rightful—might well condemn it. But I think we discover in their narratives a society in which asking such questions had become a kind of luxury, and answering them an irrelevance. The lively issue was a practical one—the issue of intervention.

Thus, the self-redress of wartime appears distinctive not only because *jiriki* was being taken for granted as a new norm but also because the shogunate was being discredited as the custodian of order. Intelligible boundaries between public justice and private battle had been eroded. The officials of governments created through coups were themselves fair game now for popular reprisals (by the Sanpukuji people, by the resisters to neighborhood purges or commissariat taxes or lantern smashing). And these same officials were being circumvented by attempts at alternate governance—most notably the assemblies of the Nichiren sect and councils of elders in the neighborhoods.[140] Just as the spectacles of purge had relegated legitimacy to the realm of performance, and just as the uprisings of debtors had subjected official policy to negotiation on the street, so the ascendancy of self-redress at all levels was removing justice to emergency forums.

The justice actually meted out by extralegal bodies is not extensively documented. In the examples cited, we note the summary execution of the arsonists (No. 5); the murder of the imprisoned priest (No. 4); the dispatching of six hundred men, some in armor, to punish the grass cutters (No. 9); the departure of five thousand men to kill the pillagers (No. 6). In another instance, a group of neighborhood elders enforced justice against a murderer, who had already fled the city, by burning down his house in the presence of five hundred guards.[141] Once more the elements of demonstration are striking—public spectacle, the massing of witnesses, efforts at coercion and appeal.

In these cases, demonstration appears necessary to give weight to improvised justice. The various judges we encounter—the elders, counselors, posses, and courtly mediators—acted not as regular tribunals but as personal agents attempting to halt violence and continuing armed reprisals. Hence, the efficacy of their actions could not derive from their institutional character or the privileges conceded to established authorities. Rather, it had to derive from the potency of the acts themselves—from qualities of terror or size or finality so great that they forced an end to the cycle of redress.[142] Still, the extralegal administration of justice was itself part of the cycle of redress as well as an extension of the politics of demonstration. And both redress and demonstration were acts with open endings.

Outright Outlawry

Go-Hōkōin-ki. 1494, 8th month.

4th day.   There was a fire to the west of us tonight. It broke out at the monastery of Rozanji. Several hundred structures went up in flames. They say it was arson. This fury of fire is the work of demons.

9th day.   Today there was fire at two locations. Remarkable.

17th day.   Today there was a fire near the palace at Nishi-ōji, alarmingly close to us. But thank heaven nothing untoward happened there. . . .

19th day.   Today they apprehended the woman who has been setting fires in this area. Following a forcible interrogation of her today, they also apprehended four or five male members of her gang.[143]

The conflagrations that this diarist found "remarkable" were nothing of the kind in 1494. One month earlier an act of arson in the southern sector of the city, at Shijō and Muromachi, had spread wildly to level fifty-four blocks of Kyoto. One month later fires would fan out from the temple of Tōji after an uprising by a league of the land.[144] Not at all "the work of demons" of any preternatural sort, on most occasions "this fury of fire" was the work of thieves, who used the cover of flames for robbery and worked together in at least semiprofessional bands that kept up their raids for days at a time. If a single gang was responsible for the damage described in the Go-Hōkōin report, it plundered successfully in this campaign for two weeks or more. Other campaigns, by this or other bands, advanced across the top of aristocratic society in 1494. Nakamikado Nobutane was robbed and wounded in his mansion during the sixth month. Yamashina Tokikuni was robbed in the seventh month by thieves who also killed his son.[145] The only startling disclosure of the Go-Hōkōin report concerns the sex of the gang leader. But nothing in the words of the diarist suggests he was astonished at female crime.

The crimes of arson and theft were pervasive in Kyoto during the age of war. They afflicted great nobles and great monasteries, and they afflicted single households repeatedly. This, from the diary of Nakamikado Nobutane in 1502:

Nobutane kyō-ki. 1502, 4th month, 6th day.
People came early this morning to report that last night several scores of thieves broke into my retreat at Kaguragaoka and stole clothing and various other things. My manager mortally struck one of them and he died in the hills, I hear. How awful. Such a thing happening on top of our current distress! What will become of us! . . . They say the thieves entered the retreat by felling trees from the surrounding hills and filling in the moat with them. Last year, on the night of the ninth day of the first month, thieves broke into my Kyoto place. On the twenty-eighth day of the seventh month, I lost everything to fire. What misfortune. But this is not all. I also endured a theft on the third day of the sixth month of 1494. This, then, is the third occasion of theft.[146]

In all, Nakamikado Nobutane was robbed six times. On at least four occasions thieves also penetrated the imperial palace. (Tokitsugu kyō-ki, 1534, 1st month, 28th day: "Tonight a large gang of thieves came to Madenokōji's place. They even entered the palace and stole most of what was at hand, I hear.") Looking for prizes like courtly robes and gilded icons, criminal bands resorted to elaborate tactics (like felling trees and bridging moats) and they carried weapons that they were prepared to use ("The thieves wounded one person at Madenokōji's place").[147] Typically the work of night, robbery touched not only its immediate victims but all Kyoto households that could be terrified by rumor and anticipation:

Nisui-ki. 1527, 5th month, 6th day.
People are talking about the several score thieves from various places who have gathered in the southern sector of the capital and night after night breed havoc. There is talk that they will soon invade this neighborhood. Everybody is apprehensive. There is no guard at the eastern gate to the palace. Fear dominates. What will become of us? It is altogether like the collapse of the realm.[148]

Here again we find force, large numbers of thieves presumably organized into gangs, spreading havoc over the course of days, and the assumption that every place is vulnerable. We also find a significant date. This round of theft occurred after the unfinished coup of the "Sakai shogun" while two rival administrations and their armies were struggling for control of Kyoto. The woman's arsonous attacks in 1494, described at the beginning of this section, occurred in the months following Hosokawa Masamoto's coup against Ashikaga Yoshitane before Masamoto's puppet, the boy Ashikaga Yoshizumi, was formally installed as shogun. Although crime remained endemic during the age of war, particularly heinous outbreaks accompanied political turmoil—when the threat of social breakdown was most severe and common outlawry seemed hardly distinguishable from the arson of overlords and the pillaging of soldiers. Indeed, the language describing criminal assaults blurs into the language of all calamities: the assaults "breed havoc"; they are "invasions" and the "work of demons"; they inspire "fear" and "apprehension," suggesting the "collapse of the realm." Moreover, the assailants are not all marginal men and women:

Tokitsugu kyō-ki. 1527, 5th month, 29th day.
The keeper of the shogunal storehouse, Arami Magosaburō, has recently committed crimes. Following forcible night thefts in various locations, he was wounded and fled. Tonight he returned to Kyoto, whereupon Takaya Yōsuke arrived with an entourage and killed him. Arami's father has fled to Yamashiro [expecting reprisals] but will probably return. They have sealed the doors to the house of [Arami's older brother] because of Arami's crime.[149]

Is it only coincidental that this military official, just like "several score thieves from various locations," found the troubled months of 1527 an attractive time for crime? And was that crime, for him, a clear departure from the actions of the purge?

While political turmoil provided the occasion for outlawry, the retreat of the shogunate from urban policing made defense against crime the business of Kyoto's residents. The reports of Nakamikado Nobutane and others speak of household managers and guards, probably armed, who wounded and sometimes killed their assailants.[150] The need for self-defense extended to the palace which, although formerly protected by soldiers from the shogunate's Board of Retainers, now received only erratic policing from aristocrats and their servants (who stood guard in rotation) and from neighborhood associations in the vicinity.[151] The apprehension and punishment of criminals also fell, repeatedly if not always, to residents. While the "forcible interrogation" of the female arsonist may have been undertaken by the shogunate (the details are not specified), it was the townsman Takaya Yōsuke and his entourage who took and killed the keeper of the shogunal warehouse and then sealed his brother's house.[152] On some occasions, noble proprietors made and enforced judgments:

Go-Hōkōin-ki. 1503, 10th month.
18th day.   The person responsible for the night theft last month has been identified. He is a neighborhood person. They say the villain has fled. Because he resided on land under my jurisdiction, I shall confiscate his small house. They say, however, that the villain was a retainer of Hosokawa Masamoto's deputy Ishida. In the evening I sent an envoy [to Ishida] asking what was to be done. [In effect, who should enforce justice—the lord of the criminal vassal or the proprietor of the criminal's land?]

20th day.   I had a letter from Ishida saying that the hut of the thief should be at my disposition. So I destroyed it.[153]

The punishments in these cases belonged to the world of private justice. They were summary and harsh, perhaps in an exemplary fashion: assailants were killed if apprehended, their property was destroyed, and their relatives were in jeopardy.

Reprise

By concluding this long chapter with a discussion of crime, I may seem to emphasize the junglelike qualities of Kyoto during wartime. Certainly, the violent expression of interest and its spread across ever-enlarging groups are among my major concerns. To use a more apt image, Kyoto resembled a bundle of exposed nerves, each so raw as to respond in extremity to impulse. Thus, once the force of the self had been released, we find monks battering abbots after religious debates, townspeople pummeling tax collectors with furniture, shogunal deputies torching the shrines of uncooperative priests, rivals for office assassinating their brothers. Such acts confuse the seeming clarity of my taxonomy. It appears capricious to assign mortal quarrels over water to one category of travail, for example, while reserving the arson of thieves for another. All these acts may belong to an undifferentiated culture of lawlessness in which sensible people quite properly had to worry about the dancing of children.

Yet more was at work in Kyoto than random nervous explosions. Beneath the individual injuries and the nearly identical violence they provoked were systemic problems and divergent responses to them. The clearest problems concerned the nature of political legitimacy; the authority of rulers over the ruled in areas such as taxation and justice; the role of popular agitation in constraining or directing official conduct; and the movement from self-redress into nascent efforts at self-rule. Another problem, which we confront in greater detail later, has surfaced here briefly—the place of the court and civil proprietors in urban governance. These issues are somewhat different from those we encountered in Chapter 1, but they turn on the same fundamental questions about the locus and the agency of power: where did power lie, and how was it to be exercised?

The answers remain as unclear at the urban level as they did at the national level. It is the questioning itself and the convulsion it reflected that are the defining attributes of wartime. Two partial answers are nonetheless emerging. First, there appeared a strong presumption that power was dispersed among many actors—warlords and their deputies, leagues engaged in uprisings, particular groups of townspeople and their forums—who variously chose to act in aggression, resistance, and pursuit of alternative modes of association. Further, there appeared a working agreement that relations between these actors had to be negotiated through the new politics of demonstration. The mediation of institutions continue to matter. The use of brute force regularly intruded as well. Still and all, the spectacles of mass assembly repeatedly organized and expressed conflicts over issues as basic as legitimacy, taxation, justice, and debt policy.

The politics of demonstration was not a series of random explosions, however prominently such acts figured in wartime; it was a politics of ambiguity. It required calculated steps and then flexible retreats, a relationship with its audiences that mixed coercion with adroit appeal. It flaunted strength but existed only in the absence of a hegemonic authority. It expressed resolve but was premised on an internal and external testing of commitment that invited counterdemonstration. In short, demonstration was both a structure of political action and a medium of social reconfiguration.

3

Word Wars:
The Refuge of the Past

On occasion, men of Kyoto wrote of what consoled them in time of trouble. "I must count it fortunate," noted a wry Nakamikado Nobutane after messengers informed him of a third robbery at his mansion in little over a year's time, "that I am here [in a temple retreat], and not there."[1] Comfort on this occasion came partly, as it often did for wartime diarists, from comparison: something bad could have been something worse. Other writers in other moments described the ruin of shrines, or the raids of assassins, only to close their accounts with expressions of relief: "The head priest is unharmed. What good fortune!" "The shogun is safe. The workings of heaven preserved him!" "Still, the homes before my residence are safe."[2]

The last remark suggests another aspect of consolation in the words of Nakamikado Nobutane: a perception of space and time that made motion a refuge. If some places were, for a while, threatened, others remained, for a while, secure. Passage held the possibility of respite. And so all men and women waited for the passing of time, and many of them moved. Some moved in and out of Kyoto; others, like Nakamikado, moved from place to place within the city; still others moved without moving by altering through fortification or imagination the places where they lived. Some experienced, too, small and unexpected movements of spirit or memory. The poet Sōchō, dismayed by the look of wartorn Kyoto, found his mood suddenly broken.

[A poem composed] at the home of an old acquaintance on Musha-kōji after a long trip by palanquin:

Stretching out my aging back
twisted from the palanquin,
I was brushed by breezes of the Capital of Flowers
that bloom in all seasons.
And in an instant, this word—*Capital*—captures peace.[3]

Here the motion of the mind begins with a talismanic word. And like *capital* (*miyako*), many words from the past used in the documents of wartime held the power of names to transfigure: the shogun was neither puppet nor captive but the "Great Tree"; the ravaged palace was always the "Deep Interior." Even when used habitually, without reflection (or perhaps, especially when used habitually, without reflection), such words could mitigate trouble by making it strange. But sometimes, as for an old poet refreshed less by a scented breeze than by a pungent phrase, words pierced the casings of habit to recover, for a moment, their original grace.

The men whose voices we still hear today were writers, and hence words loomed large for them. The consolations of routine or denial or escape or play that also figure in their diaries surely loomed far larger than language for most of their contemporaries. Still, for writers, words acted to hold or recover memory, to build private histories of opposition. (Decades after the shogun Yoshitane fell to the 1493 coup of Hosokawa Masamoto, for example, courtiers and their friends were still passing around manuscript copies of poems decrying the event.[4]) For men of many stations throughout the war years, words also became part of the public arsenal of resistance.

This is a chapter about words—about the consolations they provided, the protests they conveyed, the realities they constructed. Although documents have figured throughout the discussion thus far, I have been most concerned with action. Tracing a history of battles and coups, uprisings and self-redress, I have returned again and again to the politics of demonstration, which dramatized conflict and sought melioration in spectacles of movement on the street. But now I turn to the politics of words which also remained important in Kyoto across the decades of upheaval. This was a politics of litigation and petition. It used the forms and the language of medieval justice to express grievances and seek relief through shogunal offices. The participants in this verbal politics covered the spectrum of Kyoto's civilian population. They included the throne itself, courtly and religious proprietors, and the commoner elite in enterprises such as brewing and weaving; yet they also included a wide variety of licensed tradespeople who purveyed vegetables, for example, or cakes or baskets. Their word wars did not replace the politics of demonstration. Rather, the two types of politics were routinely practiced, sometimes alternately and sometimes simultaneously, by the same players.

This paradox lies at the heart of my analysis. I have previously described the near collapse of medieval institutions: the provincial rebellion against the shogunate, the exploration of alternative governance through *ikki* and improvised justice, the negotiation of legitimacy through coups and purges, the supplanting of law by the force of the self. These developments were indeterminate. A new polity was not clearly forming, nor was the old polity fully destroyed. The old polity has tended to appear in my discussion, however, as a shell of titles that survived because of a persisting disparity of interest and an obscurity of ultimate purpose among many competing groups. In the following pages I suggest that the medieval order endured in Kyoto as more than a shell of titles, and for reasons deeper than divided interest or limited vision.

The paradoxical coexistence of demonstration (which presumed the debility of institutions) with the word wars (which presumed the efficacy of shogunal judicature) might seem just one more indication of the confusing oscillation, perhaps the ambivalence, of the age. Yet we find in wartime less ambivalence, with its implication of a mixed or wavering mind, than a kind of schizophrenia, a mind split between mutually compelling poles. Demonstration illustrates the movement toward political and social reinvention. The word wars illustrate a movement toward the past. The word wars help explain the indeterminacy of wartime change, for they pulled Kyoto's residents away from commitment to radical action. But in their own way, however, they too revealed substantial reserves of courage.

The suits and petitions we examine here employed various levels of meaning. Most obviously, they attempted to recover old privileges. Civil proprietors sought the restoration of manorial rights, ranging from taxation to judicial autonomy, that were under assault by warlords and tenants. Tradespeople sought the enforcement of commercial licenses that were under assault by new urban and agrarian competitors alike. As deeply conservative responses to urgently practical needs, the suits belonged to the politics of interest—pursued through institutional channels rather than on the streets because the interests derived their cogency from the institutional order of estate and guild. Yet on another level, the suits were a resourceful instrument of protest and remonstration—not only against particular violators of interest but against the shogunate itself. While invoking the support of the shogunate, litigants were also attempting to define the official agenda and organize the conduct of their military overlords. Although such remonstrations were different from street battles against soldiers hunting enemies or collecting martial taxes, they were equally charged with a resolve to shape urban rule. On still another level, moreover, the suits of wartime sought to construct a reality beyond the machinations of power. They spoke insistently, in morally inflected language, of "things as they should be." Petitioners transformed themselves into judges of, and their interests into measures of, the order that "should" prevail.

But in another resemblance to demonstration, the word wars seemed to convey certainty even as they searched for it. "Things as they should be" were invariably the things of the "past," though less a historical past of mixed meanings than an invented past of coherent institutions and stable identities. That past was a rampart against confusion, where names, titles, privileges, offices, and attachments constructed a sanctuary. It permitted desire to obscure turmoil; it provided a vantage from which mundane troubles could still be labeled departures from a putative norm.

Premises and Petitioners

In 1515 the woodcutters of Onoyama presented a long document to officials in the shogunate:

Because of the order to cut wood from this imperially protected mountain for use in the construction of the new shogunal mansion on Sanjō avenue, the official carpenter came down [for an inspection] only to find everything—even small trees—already felled. Why has this mountain been cleared? Because all of our trees have been steadily used for the emperor's everyday torches, for his charcoal, for the illumination of his nighttime theatricals, and for the monthly sweepings. Even when the Hana no gosho was built, we sent no wood from this mountain [since routine burdens were already so heavy]. And similarly, when the Higashiyama residence was built, there was no shogunal command for our lumber. Our gratitude would know no bounds if you would rescind the present order [for lumber for the Sanjō mansion], thus conforming to these precedents and decreeing what is fitting. The laborers of this area have all worked diligently on the mountain since, from of old, they have had no fields to cultivate. If you should cut and take our trees on this occasion, we would fail in our obligations to provide the imperial torches and charcoal and such. And we should definitely not fail in these obligations. If we receive orders rescinding the request [for lumber for the Sanjō mansion], we shall all know profound respect.[5]

This document is full of marvels, not the least of which is an exemplary formal language provided, perhaps, by a scribe at court—for the Onoyama woodcutters and their mountain were protected by the throne. The obligation of imperial service emerges at the center of the argument: the workers of Onoyama cannot render lumber to the shogun since their primary duty is to a court that is already straining their resources. Evoking the scene of a barren hillside, they move on to a litany of their contributions—a litany rich in ceremonial imagery that exalts the throne and its servants while putting an importunate shogunate in its place. The argument about imperial service is made twice, for the dull or intransigent reader, capped after the reprise with something of a warning: "we should definitely not fail in these obligations."

Lest one argument prove insufficient, the document represents the petitioners as faithful laborers set apart from the customary work of farming. They are loyal to their patrons, deferential toward the shogun; surely it is unseemly to push them further. And this line of defense is linked to one more: the shogunal order for lumber breaks with tradition. The two greatest construction projects of earlier Ashikaga shogun took no Onoyama trees. Hence, current military officials are instructed by these artisans to replace their order with a new and "fitting" decree that acknowledges the practices of the past. Decorum survives in the document, at least rhetorically, for "gratitude" and "respect" are extended to the shogunal institution. But here again, the aspect of negotiation matters: the respect remains conditional, implicitly dependent upon a suitable response.

I begin with this mundane dispute, in part, because disputes that find their way into words tend to be mundane. However grave their contexts or their deepest motivations, these quarrels are articulated in terms of manageable propositions about taxes or water access or the like. It is possible that the Onoyama woodcutters stood proxy in this encounter for a court intent on rebuking a shogunate that, though it could neither keep order nor finance an enthronement ceremony for the emperor, was constructing a new headquarters for itself. Thus, the document may touch on issues of legitimacy, control over symbolically important buildings, and the role of the throne in enforcing public morality. Yet on its surface the document is a punctilious appeal that posits the existence of two honorable parties engaged in negotiations, which, in turn, are part of an intelligible process of civil governance.

This is an important point: the acknowledgment of the institutional dignity of the shogunate. In this and many similar documents we find at least a nominal consent to the notion projected by successive usurpers that the shogunate retained vitality. But there is another important point: the woodcutters insist on participating in definitions of the shogunal role. Specifically, they hold military officials to the standards of past practice. Claims to legitimate historical offices carry obligations that cannot be erased. Through their word wars, petitioners joined a political dynamic, conceding to warlords their place in a shogunal tradition yet demanding that continuity be more than a convenient fiction.

What did it mean, though, to hold military officials to the standards of past practice? The woodcutters are clear about two assumptions. First, they assume that the separate authority of multiple proprietors is to be preserved. The survival of independent jurisdictions not only buffers men like our woodcutters from the demands of a shogunate constrained by law and tradition; it also inspires political remonstration. However humble an extension of the imperial court, the woodcutters have a fixed social place and just expectations that sanction this challenge to the shogunate. Second, they assume that precedents matter. By citing shogunal conduct during the construction of the Hana no gosho and the Higashiyama residence, the petitioners subordinate the current administration to the power of record and historical witness.

Two further assumptions are inextricable from those above. The first is that no "emergency," such as a state of war or a thorough-going martial law, has put the shogunate on a new footing. Military government is not accorded new, absolutist powers that eradicate older traditions of diffused authority; and Kyoto is not, at least in the eyes of petitioners, part of a war machine in the control of a dictatorship. The second is that the shogunate is not a unitary, monolithic institution. Capable of "rescinding" an order, it is seen as a body of parts capable of internal debate and revision. Taken together, these assumptions served as one foundation for urban politics in wartime.

They underlie the word wars of the two constituencies most deeply invested in the old order: courtly and religious estate proprietors on the one hand, and licensed specialists and tradespeople on the other. And these word wars lodge two characteristic types of complaint: against impositions and intrusions by the shogunate on the one hand, and against instances of social disorder to be stemmed by the shogunate on the other.

The petition of the woodcutters illustrates the first type of complaint, although we most often find such objections in the documents of the proprietary elite. Here, an excerpt from the diary of an official at Kitano shrine:

Item: On the evening of the twenty-sixth day of the tenth month of 1509, there was a night attack upon the shogun. The shogun sustained many injuries.

Item: On the twenty-seventh day of the same month, the shogunal police magistrate Inō no Ōmi no kami descended on the place of [the attacker,] Tani Shojirō. Shojirō had fled. In his residential compound are Shojirō's house, the house of his elder sister, and the house of his younger sister, all of which were sealed by the magistrate.

Item: The administrative office [Shōbaiin] of this shrine reported [to Man-jūin, the temple with which Kitano was affiliated] concerning the affair of Sho-jirō's house. The office asked how the disposal of the property [kessho] held by the assailant of the shogun should be handled. The answer came: "Because, from of old, this shrine has been a place guaranteed asylum against military intrusion [shugo funyū no zaisho], the disposal of property is a matter for the shrine office of investigation [the Shōbaiin kumonjo]. It is ordered that the dis-posal of property be carried out as shrine business by the shrine, and that this judgment be conveyed to the shogunate."[6]

In this case, officials of Kitano shrine turn to their administrative su-periors at the temple of Manjūin following the entry of a shogunal force into their precincts. An independent jurisdiction—confirmed in law un-der the rubric shugo funyū, centered on property and judicial rights like kessho, and exercised in practice through organs like the Shōbaiin ku-monjo—is affirmed by the superior in a ruling directed at the shogunate. Affirming independence in almost shockingly unusual circumstances, Manjūin denies military officers the conventional rights of punishment and redress against a would-be assassin of the shogun.

At issue throughout such quarrels between proprietary and shogunal authorities were manorial boundaries, which the civil elite tried continu-ally to defend against trespass or dissolution. Using historical guaran-tees of private jurisdiction over their holdings, proprietors resisted not only the police intervention of the military but also, as we have seen, the shogunal determination to tax their property and marshall its human resources. Thus, shugo funyū became the rallying cry that was heard when courtiers denied recurrent shogunal claims to a half-tax in Ya-mashiro, when the Kamo shrine refused to recruit corvée labor for battle, when Lord Ichijō withheld a commissariat levy. Attacks on the abuse of military authority spread to the highest levels when the throne itself objected to general levies of roof taxes and field taxes in Kyoto and the home provinces.[7]

The word wars of this age moved in two directions, however. The larger body of wartime suits and petitions cast military officials as allies of complainants with grievances against other parties. Again the complainants were estate proprietors and licensed tradespeople, although in these cases the commoners were as well represented as the members of the civil elite.

The essential problem for proprietors came from the universal erosion of the estate structure and the resulting contraction, extreme in most cases, of land revenue. Though largely helpless to recover their holdings from warlords and local magnates in more distant provinces, proprietors continued to struggle over the home province of Yamashiro—where their interests were contested not only by shogunal deputies but also by soldiers of the land and villagers withholding taxes. In perhaps an ironic move, proprietors enlisted help against villagers from the very shogunate that was otherwise a competitor for Yamashiro's wealth.

Claiming a half-tax reduction in the capital and its environs, the farmers of Yamashiro are withholding land taxes. This is intolerable. . . . Taxes are to be rendered as in the past.[8]

Yet the elite found no easing of the economic crisis in Yamashiro, even in the best of times. Its members turned, then, to Kyoto itself, where they invoked shogunal help to collect land rents and taxes from the commoners living on their holdings in the capital:

1539, 5th month, 11th day.
In the matter of the suit concerning the domestic site (ten *jō* wide and twenty *jō* deep, now being used as dry field) at Rokkaku–Higashi no tōin that has been brought by [the noble] Kameyama [house]: Inasmuch as this is a [Kameyama] holding, we issued a document of guarantee four years ago. Nonetheless, we understand that the land taxes are still not being paid, as [tenants offer] various excuses. This is intolerable. You are ordered immediately to render the taxes to [the Kameyama house].
[Addressed to the residents of the holding by two shogunal magistrates.][9]

Another example:

Kanrei narabi ni mandokoro kabegaki. 1540, 7th month.
In the matter of the suit brought once again by [the noble] Nagahara Echizen

no kami Shigetaka: In past years the land taxes of southern Kyoto have not been paid, and the residents have made one excuse or another. The various proprietors made an appeal through a joint-signature petition, and a writ [demanding payment] was issued.[10]

Chikatoshi nikki. 1542, 7th month, 14th day.
Nagahara Echizen no kami Shigetaka brought suit in past years concerning the land taxes due to the temples and shrines and courtly proprietors from southern Kyoto. But even though writs [ordering payment] were issued, there is continuing disobedience.[11]

These samples illuminate several characteristic features of the substantial record of proprietary suits over urban land taxes: incidences of both discrete and sustained tax delinquency among Kyoto's commoners; and a proprietary resolve to appeal to the shogunate, both individually and corporately (through "joint-signature petitions"), even when such appeals proved futile over the course of years and involved marginal holdings (the Kameyama suit involved less than half an acre of land, outside the settled urban islands, which was probably used, perhaps erratically, as a kitchen garden).

We find a similar pattern of recalcitrance among taxpayers and obdurateness among proprietors in commercial relations:

1508, 9th month, 27th day.
In the matter of the [retail] rice taxes from Kyoto and its environs due to the Bureau of the Palace Kitchen, which was brought by [Funahashi Nobuyoshi]: Inasmuch as [these retail taxes] are your vestiture, we are issuing a writ of guarantee. The retail rice sellers are to render you taxes as in the past. It is ordered that if there is delinquency, there will be unusual punishment.
[From two shogunal magistrates.][12]

1540, 12th month, 6th day.
In the matter of guild fees that are at issue between the gold and silver foil guild and Lord Konoe: . . . Inasmuch as this guild has no writ of tax exemption, a writ will be issued to the Konoe house that business fees are to be rendered, as in the past.
[A memorandum of the shogunal magistrates.][13]

1517, 8th month, 30th day.
In the matter of the *sake* malt taxes: In accord with the [shogunal] judgment of last year, there was some payment for a time. Then, however, there was delinquency as before. This is an offense. [Tax payment] should be ordered again, as the will of the shogun, to the minister [Lord Shirakawa].
[Letter from Hirohashi Morimitsu to Lord Shirakawa.][14]

Both the organization of trade in Kyoto and its crises appear in detail in Chapter 5. Here I wish only to indicate yet another source of grievance for proprietors (in their roles as commercial patrons) and their reliance on the shogunate for restitution. Cut off from most estate revenues, the civil elite tried to feed on Kyoto—where a combination of urban retreat into the two fortified islands and chronic tax delinquency constricted their land rents; and where a combination of trade crises and unpaid business fees constricted their commercial income. And just as proprietors sought alliances with the shogunate against Kyoto's commoners, so they sought help in their quarrels with each other. One of the most remarkable of these quarrels involved the imperial regent and the imperial treasurer who, for thirty years, bickered over fish. At stake were the business fees of Kyoto dealers in salted products (protected by the regent), whose trade was threatened by dealers from the Awazu area of Lake Biwa (protected by the treasurer). A taste of the debate:

Response by the imperial treasurer to the accusations of cheating [lodged against him by the imperial regent]:

Item: [The regent] alleges that trade in various fish products throughout the capital by the Awazu guild [protected by the throne and hence governed by the treasurer] did not occur in the past. He demands that we immediately produce documentation [to support claims that Awazu does have rights to the Kyoto trade]. The Awazu people became licensed imperial traders in the time of Emperor Tenji [r. 668–671], and thereafter, in 1316, were appointed to the imperial treasury; they have lawful writs from the Naishidokoro, the Hiyoshi shrine, and the imperial court. Continuing business without change to the present day, the Awazu people do not at all represent a lawless disturbance [to the Kyoto fish trade]. . . . [This rebuttal of the regent includes four more items and includes citations of five documents guaranteeing the Awazu trade.][15]

Quarrels over commerce and commercial rights equally engaged Kyoto's commoners, whose word wars largely focused on trade. Their suits came from the commoner elite (brewers and brokers, rice wholesalers, major weavers), but they also came from humble purveyors and minor guildsmen, pack horse drivers and turnip sellers; for Kyoto's market was a densely organized one that enveloped most workers in networks of patronage. Their suits took aim at threatening outsiders (smugglers, unlicensed rivals, new associations), but they also took aim at patrons and fellow guildsmen; for Kyoto's market was riven by internal as well as external crises.

A suit brought to [the shogunal administration in 1545] by the *sake* brewers of northern and southern Kyoto, in regard to the making of malt throughout the capital:

It is intolerable that the malt makers of western Kyoto have recently flouted documents to the effect that [malt making by them] is strictly forbidden. Herewith our reasoning: In the past there were over one hundred [licensed] firms involved in the malt enterprise in Kyoto proper. There has been no change [in this number]. But the original recognition of these firms, all in eastern Kyoto and all licensed by the shogunate, was opposed by the malt makers of western Kyoto.

They attacked various brewers, perpetrated violence, and then barricaded themselves [in defiance] at Kitano shrine. Consulted over these events by officials from Mount Hiei [a former patron of the brewers], the shogunate subjugated the several scores of men barricaded at the shrine in 1444 and then burned down the shrine completely. This event, known as the malt melee, was familiar to all the realm.

The shrine destroyed at that time, though unsurpassed in richness of ornamentation and deeply revered, faced such demolition solely because of the profound malfeasance of the western malt makers. And *now* they have selfishly lodged a false suit [claiming licensing privileges]! What sort of loyalty is this! Have they no fear of the shogun, of public principles?

Although they have produced old documents [licensing their enterprises], these date from before the melee of 1444. How could these be honored?[16]

This document goes on at commendable length before concluding: "We would be grateful if you would attend to our meaning and just throw out the false suit of the western malt makers." Quite as full of marvels as the woodcutters' petition, it combines invective and vexation with a richly embroidered retelling of events now more than one hundred years old. The bloody resolution of the "malt melee" of 1444 must be remembered by a shogunate inveighed to protect the monopoly of the eastern brewers against the ever-renewed offensives (false suits, presentations of immaterial documents, floutings) of their western competitors.

The suits of both proprietors and tradespeople (which we sample more extensively in Chapter 5) are full of tensions that, inherent in medieval rule, became overt in wartime. Estate holders who protested the shogunal violation of proprietary autonomy also demanded shogunal enforcement of the taxation privileges they could not enforce themselves. And the licensed tradespeople who operated within the zealously guarded spheres of individual patrons also invoked shogunal authority to protect the commercial privileges those patrons could not protect themselves. In effect, petitioners cast the shogunate as the universal and public guarantor of privileges that derived from particular and private corporations. (And so we find the intriguing language of the righteous malt makers: "Have [those western people] no fear of the shogun, of public principles?")

Petitioners tended to address the shogunate, moreover, in terms that transformed complaint into remonstration. Shogunal taxes, say, or the actions of competitors were "not as they should be," a condition associated with the "unprecedented," the "arbitrary," the "libertine," the "selfish." What petitioners sought was a return to "things as they should be," a condition associated with "the past," "prior times," "things as they have come down to us." Expressing a moral calculus, this lexicon made petitioners into counselors. They became the custodians of memory who could advise a shogunate that had "lost the Way."[17]

The "Way" was a construction of interest and artful remembrance and plots about the past. But just what did these plots say about the present and why did litigants create them? In positing continuous norms, the suits were so disconsonant with a culture driven by violence and demonstration as to seem conceptually naive and politically irrelevant. Were they, then, simply an exercise in denial?

Divisions and Divided Minds
Within the Shogunate

To a fair degree, I think, the suits and petitions reflected perceptions that the shogunate might actually work well on behalf of litigants—that it was not only a fixture of the capital but still a potential source of order. And such perceptions were sustained by a premise that appears in the woodcutters' document: that the shogunate was not a monolithic institution but a body of parts capable of internal debate and revision. We have encountered ample evidence already of the personal divisions, often enough mortal divisions, between individual *kanrei* and their subordinates on the one hand and their rivals on the other. Here I want to consider three different divisions—between the shogun and his deputies, between the different arms of the shogunal administration, between the two minds of the *kanrei* themselves—that offered space for the wedge of verbal politics. This politics was neither naive nor irrelevant; it exploited genuine confusion over the polity to keep (some) medieval practices alive.

Late in 1493, officials of the Kitano shrine confiscated the house of a blacksmith who had resided on Kitano property. These officials then faced repeated demands from Miyoshi, one of the *kanrei*'s men, that the house be restored to the blacksmith's son, one of Miyoshi's retainers. Kitano turned for a ruling to the temple of Manjūin, its administrative superior. Manjūin decreed:

> There must absolutely *not* be any pardon [that is, any cession of property to the blacksmith's son] because the criminal [the blacksmith himself] committed one of the "three great crimes of state." He burned down the shrine of the tutelary deity at the imperial palace. While it is difficult to refuse the demand of Miyoshi, it is also difficult to rescind the confiscation and thus effect a pardon. If we were to do so, the news would travel to Sanjō [a shogunal residence] and would even enter the shogun's ears. Whereupon things would not be as they should be for Manjūin and Kitano.[18]

Like the Kitano document concerned with a would-be shogunal assassin, this one too turns on a shocking crime of wartime—the burning of an imperial shrine, presumably by a thief (who occupied the honorable station of Kitano blacksmith and managed to place a son in shogunal service). This document also contains assumptions about separate jurisdictions and the power of the past to give meaning to notions like "three great crimes of state." But unlike the document quoted earlier, it invokes the person of the shogun (the Kubō-sama), who stands above the machinations of his men and will, should he hear of any complicity by Kitano in the pardon of a criminal house, right the wrong. The shogunal official Miyoshi becomes, here, a traitor to the shogun.

This separation of a good shogun from his bad deputies allowed opposition to particular officials without rejection of the shogunal institution itself. Always rhetorically possible, the separation was all the easier because direct shogunal pronouncements (*migyōsho*) had disappeared from a system of symbolic leadership by the time of Ōnin.[19] A veiled shogun, even a "puppet" shogun, could be invented to suit the taste of an audience. And the youth and obscurity of most wartime shogun enhanced their image of innocence. (Of the six who occupied office between 1473 and 1568, one acceded at the age of eight, two at the age of ten, and one at the age of fourteen. See the brief biographical sketches in Figure 4.) The very detachment of these boys that made them appealing to leaders of coups freed them not just from association with violent purges but also from intimate association with the later politics of their handlers.

But separations between shogun and their deputies did not have to be imagined. One shogun was assassinated; three were forcibly removed from office. Ashikaga Yoshitane reproached an ungovernable *kanrei* by abandoning the capital. (Prompting the *Nisui* diarist to wonder, "Did he flee because there were many occasions when the shogun could not concur in the decisions [of the *kanrei*]? . . . Did he flee because [the *kanrei*] acted with no restraint? This is a grievous situation.")[20] And Ashikaga Yoshiharu and Ashikaga Yoshihide actually went to battle against their *kanrei*.

As they entered into war, these shogun entangled their institution even more tightly in violence. These were not innocent actors. But my point is that in disparate roles—as symbols, puppets, victims, rebels—the shogun of wartime could be dissociated from their deputies, even portrayed as rightful critics of those deputies. The agitation among courtiers over attacks on the shogun, the extraordinary attendance at the funeral of the assassinated shogun, the ejaculations of sympathy for shogun forced to the battlefield—all indicate a certain readiness to identify with an institution that transcended its officials.

If petitioners gained a sort of moral or psychological leverage from the separation of the shogun from his officials, they could retain some confidence in military government by dissociating lawless from righteous officials. Broadly speaking, the wartime shogunate had two arms: the administrative council of magistrates (or *bugyō-nin*), with its functionaries, and the personal retinue of the *kanrei* (made up of generally untitled deputies known generically as *kanrei-dai*).

The magistrates were professional and largely hereditary bureaucrats who undertook almost all conventional operations of civil governance in wartime. Many of them were associated with the Board of Administration (*mandokoro*), the only formal bureau of the shogunate that long survived the Ōnin war; and some of them bore titles derived from this and other prewar bureaus of shogunal rule. Yet the distinctions of office and title that implied bureaucratic divisions in authority had little significance during the Era of Warring States (and may never have had much). The magistrates were able technicians—skilled in law, precedents, and procedure—who made up a kind of general administrative council or secretariat. They heard and ruled on judicial appeals, including commercial cases; issued laws concerning debt cancellations and coinage exchange; supervised routine shogunal financial interests (business taxes, loans); arbitrated most quarrels that came to the shogunate for mediation; and oversaw some civic functions like the Gion festival and some general concerns like the city baths.[21] Throughout the extant rulings of the magistrates, particularly the commercial rulings, there is a formidable preoccupation with documentation and systematic inquiry, which was not only urged by various petitioners but also embedded in the medieval judicial tradition to which they were heir.[22]

Figure 4. Biographical Sketches of the Wartime Shogun

No. 9.   ASHIKAGA YOSHIHISA (1465–89, s. 1473–89, age 8 at accession, age 24 at death). Installed during the Ōnin war. Died in a campaign against the Rokkaku of Ōmi. Was away from Kyoto for much of the last eighteen months of his tenure because of the campaign.

No. 10.   ASHIKAGA YOSHITANE (1466–1523, s. 1490–93, age 24 at accession, age 57 at death). Adopted by Ashikaga Yoshimasa (No. 8) and installed with the support of Hatakeyama Masanaga, despite opposition to the elevation of this natural son of Ashikaga Yoshimi (who had been embroiled in the succession quarrel with Yoshihisa that helped provoke the Ōnin war). Removed from office and exiled as a result of a coup by the *kanrei* Hosokawa Masamoto. Was away from Kyoto almost two years, first in the Rokkaku campaign, then in the Hatakeyama campaign.

No. 11.   ASHIKAGA YOSHIZUMI (1480–1511, s. 1494–1508, age 14 at accession, age 31 at death). Established in office through the coup of Masamoto. Fled Kyoto and was then removed from office and exiled as a result of a coup by Hosokawa Takakuni.

No. 10.   ASHIKAGA YOSHITANE (s. 1508–21). Restored to office by Takakuni's coup but then broke with Takakuni and fled into exile. Adopted Yoshitsuna as heir and attempted to install him as shogun against the will of Hosokawa Takakuni.

No. 12.   ASHIKAGA YOSHIHARU (1511–1550, s. 1521–46, age 10 at accession, age 39 at death). Elevated to office through machinations of Takakuni. Fled Kyoto and remained in exile from 1527 until 1534, during the ascendancy of the rival "Sakai shogunate" and the Hokke uprising. Returned to Kyoto under the influence of Hosokawa Harumoto. In 1546, the shogun left Kyoto after a split with Harumoto, waged war against him, and resigned office in favor of his son, Yoshiteru. Was away from Kyoto for seven years, 1527–34.

No. 13.   ASHIKAGA YOSHITERU (1536–1565, s. 1546–65, age 10 at accession, age 29 at death). Succeeded to office when his father resigned in defiance of Harumoto. Joined his father's battles against Harumoto, then made peace with Harumoto. Between 1548 and 1553, the shogun alternately aligned with Harumoto and Harumoto's rival, Miyoshi Chōkei, in a series of battles for control of the capital. Chōkei conclusively defeated the shogun in 1553 and began a five-year rule of Kyoto, while the shogun remained in exile. The shogun returned to Kyoto in 1558 and made peace with Chōkei but helped provoke continuing assaults against him. Chōkei died in 1564; he was succeeded by his rival

Figure 4, *continued*

and subordinate Matsunaga Hisahide. Hisahide's men forced the suicide of the shogun in 1565. Was away from Kyoto intermittently between 1546 and 1553, and continuously from 1553 to 1558.

No. 14.   ASHIKAGA YOSHIHIDE (1540–1568, s. 1568, age 28 at accession, age 28 at death). Succeeded to office, after a three-year hiatus in shogunal appointment, through the machinations of Hisahide's deputies. Remained in office less than ten months before being unseated through the coup of Oda Nobunaga. Fled to Settsu and died there of illness.

Beyond the administrative council of magistrates, a variety of "other officials" shared the exercise of shogunal authority. These were deputies of the *kanrei,* who principally served the military interests of themselves and their masters. They imposed (or tried to impose) special military taxes (*hanzei, tansen, munabetsusen*); they issued summons for labor and martial help; they supervised the defenses of the capital; they sometimes assumed judicial and other functions normally exercised by the administrative council. In some respects, these deputies might be regarded as successors to the prewar Board of Retainers, once the major police arm of the shogunate. They acted, however, as essentially private clients of their *kanrei* warlords. These men conducted the rites of purge and exploited the resources of the capital on behalf of Hosokawa Masamoto and his successors.[23]

This depiction of the magistrates and the constellation of *kanrei* deputies suggests several divisions: between civil and martial functions, between public and private interests, between institutional and ad hoc governance. Although such discriminations are imperfect, I suspect that they illuminate the somewhat looser distinction that petitioners made between the "normal" and the "deviant" and, in turn, between the acceptable and the problematic. When referring to the shogunate, writers often used generic terms like "the military house" (*buke*), which may imply that they perceived it in some ways as a unitary institution. The responses of diarists and litigants to the shogunate nonetheless suggest that in practice, if not always in an articulate or fully conscious fashion, they associated the civil functions of the magistrates with normal (even indispensable) governance and the martial impositions of the *kanrei* and his deputies with extraordinary and problematic governance. The former were part of a comprehensible order, rooted in the past and protective of "things as they should be." The latter were almost invariably "not as they should be." In the language of the shogunate itself, the martial taxes of wartime, the demands for lumber or for labor or for barrack-ing soldiers were all *hibun kayaku*—nonstandard or extraordinary imposts.[24]

The decrees of shogunal administrators frequently accommodated the interests of proprietors and licensed tradespeople and thus encouraged appeals. These decrees reveal much of the history of wartime suits for despite the loss of many original complaints, the shogunal judgments recapitulate their details. Although we have seen some such decrees already, let me offer a wider sample of documents to expose a shogunal face I have barely shown before.

Nanzenji monjo. 1535, 10th month, 26th day.

> The shogunal official has made his investigation [of a stabbing incident on temple grounds] and you are to know, in accord with the directive sent to you in the twelfth month of last year, that this temple itself retains the privileges of justice and punishment [throughout its own proprietorship]. . . .
>
> [Addressed to Nanzenji temple by nine shogunal officials.][25]

Tokitsugu kyō-ki. 1534, 4th month, 29th day.

> We [officials in the shogunate] understand that [the order to several neighborhoods adjacent to the imperial palace to dig moats around the palace] has caused hardship. . . . Hence, although work on the general [city] moats will consequently be delayed, you are first to attend exclusively to the imperial orders [and are thus excused from the labor on the general moat].
>
> [Addressed by the shogunal deputy Ibaragi Nagataka to the said neighborhoods.][26]

Naginata boko-chō monjo. 1549.

> The following actions are strictly forbidden in the neighborhood of Shijō-Abura no kōji: lawless violence by soldiers, the felling of trees and bamboo, the imposition of arrow and commissariat taxes.[27]

Kanrei narabi ni mandokoro kabegaki. 1500, 9th month.

> Regulations for the *Sake* Brewers and Pawnbrokers of Kyoto and Its Environs.
>
> Item: Firms that have suffered in the recent fire are excused from all payment of fees for six months, excluding the month of the fire.

Item: New firms are excused from fees for five months but must assiduously pay fees after that time.[28]

Tanaka Mitsuharu-shi shozō monjo. 1544, 12th month, 18th day.
In the matter of the headship of the *obi* [silk] guild, which has been brought to suit by Yoshida Munetada: . . . Although Nakayama Kamonnosuke presented us with a document [which named himself as the guild head], claiming that the document represented the will of the guild patron, we dismissed his claim as false. Inasmuch as we now decree that Munetada is to be guild head, in conformity with a writ of guaranty [issued three years ago], you are swiftly to carry out these instructions.

[Addressed to members of the *obi* guild by the shogunal deputy Ibaragi Nagataka.])[29]

Kuga-ke komonjo. 1517, 8th month, 19th day.
In the matter of the fees from the leather workers of Kyoto and its environs, which are part of your house vesticure: Although these fees are part of your vesticure [literally, your "fief," *tōchigyō*], we hear that certain individuals are not paying the exactions and are acting willfully. This is entirely without reason. Hence inasmuch as Tarōzaemon and Heiemon have been appointed guild heads, it is ordered that the fees be fully rendered to you as your proper vesticure, as in the past.

[Addressed to the house administrator of the former Minister of the Right by two shogunal magistrates.][30]

In these and similar cases, shogunal magistrates confirmed proprietary claims (to independent jurisdictions, land and commercial taxes), granted exemptions from extraordinary military imposts, and variously served the mercantile community (by confirming privileges, resolving disputes over guild headships and the like, offering tax concessions). Is this the shogunate of coups and purges, of misrule and aggrandizement?

Before I reflect further on such tendencies toward moderation, let me consider, finally, the disparate tendencies in the minds of the *kanrei* themselves. By portraying a divided administration in which shogun might be dissociated from their officials, and administrative magistrates from *kanrei* deputies, I have seemingly placed the burden of misrule on the successive Hosokawa warlords who governed Kyoto. The charge is often well placed, for they and their subordinates brought violence and

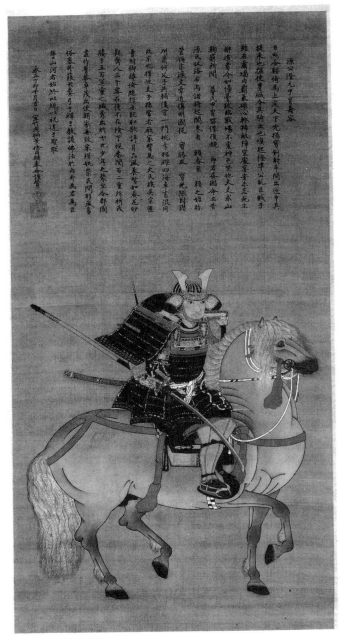

Portrait of Hosokawa Sumimoto.
Inscription by Keijo Shūrin, 1507. 119.5 cm. × 59.5 cm.; color
on silk. Registered as an Important Cultural Property. Courtesy
of Eisei Bunko, Tokyo.

its reverberating consequences to the center of post-Ōnin governance in the capital. Yet the charge is difficult to lodge unequivocally—as such charges always are—not only because a number of players and problems made for a culture of lawlessness but also because *kanrei* behavior vacillated. The *kanrei* moved, or were pushed, in two directions that, however incompatible in the end, they generally tried to reconcile: they wavered between what we might call in retrospect a past and a future order, between protection of the estate system and the creation of military lordships, between affiliation with the courtly elite and with their local retainers.

Thus, we find, on the one hand, the patterns of trouble examined in the previous chapter: coups and purges, havoc surrounding repeated battle, complicity in debtors' uprisings, impositions of war taxes, violations of manorial boundaries. We also find efforts to undermine the entire estate structure by transferring control from proprietors to military deputies and by selectively granting tax privileges and tax exemptions to these deputies.[31] Kyoto's warlords made inroads into the commercial world as well. They levied their own import duties at new barriers around the capital, and they moved certain guilds into their own sphere of influence.

We find, on the other hand, both discrete and broad endorsements of the old regime. On occasion, the *kanrei* and their deputies retracted extraordinary tax demands, confirmed manorial rights, removed lawless officials from Yamashiro, and resisted calls for debt cancellations.[32] More generally, they refrained from fundamental changes in the polity: from disestablishing the Board of Administration and dismissing the magistrates; from confiscating wholesale the estates of Yamashiro; from reorganizing Kyoto's trade to their own advantage. Kyoto and Yamashiro remained anomalous in a Japan where provincial warlords were denying estate rights and transforming commerce through the suspension of market fees and guild monopolies.[33] These areas remained anomalous, too, in their freedom from embargoes on food and military supplies, and from demands for popular conscription. The successive *kanrei* did not tamper systematically with the proprietary and commercial elite, and they pulled back, once a purge was accomplished, from the conversion of Kyoto into a war machine. The actions of *kanrei* Hosokawa Masamoto even suggest an impulse toward the reconciliation and integration of the military and courtly elites: he took the remarkable step of adopting a courtier as his heir (a decision that provoked new crises).[34]

Thus, the suits and petitions of Kyoto's old guard did not address an implacable administration fully opposed to old interests. But why the bifurcation in the conduct of the *kanrei*? In good measure, the *kanrei* were repeating the practices of the pre-Ōnin period, when military men exploited the opportunities of office to build private power. Although enhanced by forcible seizure and by battle, the land holdings of medieval officials grew primarily from quasi-legal incursions against estates and public properties.[35] And for wartime *kanrei* and their deputies, no less than for their predecessors, power remained associated with shogunal titles that could be parlayed into receiverships over manors, access to the half-tax and other imposts, control over police duties and the disposition of confiscated property, and limited discretion over conscripts and corvée laborers. The contradictions in such behavior were very deep and very old: military officials thrived on a manorial system that they were devouring; they sought prestige from a shogunate, and ultimately a throne, whose authority they were eviscerating.

One of the synoptic stories of wartime concerns the final abandonment of these contradictions, as warlords and local magnates severed most ties to central institutions and seized direct power over land through force. But these contradictions survived in Kyoto for a very long time. True, they collapsed slowly, tortuously, in a number of provinces. Still, they lasted in the Kyoto area until the end—until the so-called "unifiers" of the nation blasted into the capital after 1568, destroyed a shogunate preoccupied for generations in internecine bloodletting, and brought to the home provinces a version of military rule that had come to maturity in outside domains.[36] The survival in Kyoto of the old order, or remnants of it, bears particular reflection, since immense pressures were working there, as in more distant provinces, against continuity. Momentum alone cannot account for the Hosokawa polity.

It was endangered, most obviously, by the gravely reduced geographical reach of the shogunate and the consequent paucity of rewards for the retainers who alternately made and broke *kanrei* power. Those rewards were jeopardized, moreover, by attacks from rivals, rebellions by local soldiers, and the wavering of the *kanrei* themselves. And such conflict led to splits with the *kanrei* as supporters tried to build independent lordships; to coalitions against the *kanrei;* to revolts of the kind that plagued Hosokawa Masamoto throughout his tenure; and finally to coups, as warriors regrouped around new claimants to the *kanrei* office from whom they might expect more.[37] Pushed by the ambition of their retainers, the *kanrei* imposed military taxes and assailed estates (some of them, primarily Hosokawa Harumoto and later Miyoshi Chōkei, more actively than others).[38] Yet they continued to live within the proprietary structures of the past.

We might find compelling explanations for the survival of the old order in a number of single or combined factors: in the moderating influences on the *kanrei* exercised by the shogun and the administrative magistrates (and occasionally even by deputies);[39] in the residual esteem for the shogunal institution and its historical role that is implicit in the struggle for high office; in the basic weakness of *kanrei* who—faced with contentious vassals and rivals—needed the resources of old titles, and the business taxes of brewers and brokers; in the murky objectives of rule that worked in favor of compromise rather than risky new visions. Yet here I would like to pursue a somewhat different explanation, which returns us to the dynamic of politics. If their deputies pushed the *kanrei* in one direction, the civil and commercial elite of Kyoto pushed them in another. The word wars of the capital's petitioners created serious pressures of their own.

To understand the influence of the word wars we must recall the exceptional features of the capital where they took place. Kyoto was a city of immense population (and had been since the ninth century) in a country of very limited urban development.[40] At the core of Kyoto's population were the aristocratic and religious communities—for five hundred years and more the nation's great absentee proprietors. And around this core gathered the large majority of the nation's professional artisans and traders, who depended on the patronage and the consumption of the proprietary class. Hence we find concentrated in a single remarkable center the constituencies most profoundly invested in the manorial order. Nor were they just quietly symbolic custodians of a lost past. They were avid litigants who used a morally charged language to influence the shogunate's agenda. Singularly important was the remonstration of the throne itself. A sample of documents:

Sanetaka kō-ki. 1507, 9th month, 3d day.
> Today an imperial ambassador was dispatched to the shogunate to order [a cessation of] the half-tax in Yamashiro.[41]

Oyudono no ue no nikki. 1538, 3d month, 3d day.
> [The courtier] Kajūji Chūnagon came from the shogunate, saying that a roof tax throughout Kyoto is to be ordered to fund the *gosen-*

> *bōkō* [a major Buddhist ceremony]. The court responded that this
> should absolutely not happen.[42]

Nisui-ki. 1519, 10th month, 10th day.

> [Shogunal officials] declared that there must be a postponement [of
> the imperial enthronement ceremonies]. The emperor responded
> that there have been repeated postponements and that now, because
> the twenty-first day [when the ceremonies were to have taken place]
> draws close, there must not be a further postponement. Whatever
> the difficulties, insofar as the imperial orders have gone forth the em-
> peror declares that there should only be delight [in complying with
> them]. . . . The emperor is not pleased [with the shogunal insistence
> on postponement]. It is an outrage.[43]

The throne is the judge in these matters, not the grievant; it is implicitly the source of rightful authority and not simply a contestant against
a peer institution. Although its complaints were circumspect and sporadic, I suspect they nonetheless legitimated the word wars of others.
And these word wars, in turn, generated political tensions unique to
the capital. Provincial warlords struggled with the specters of distant
proprietors, but their principal challenges were local and military: they
could seize estates and dispatch an occasional gift to the throne be-
tokening a kind of homage. The shogunal officials of Kyoto, however,
endured a routine barrage of suits and visits from imperial ambassadors.
The old order and its most luminous supporters were part of their daily
reality (one that even the "unifiers" transformed cautiously).[44] Compelled to deal with the imperatives of two worlds, those of their deputies
and those of the capital's elites, the *kanrei* moved in irreconcilable directions.

But we are not through with my questions. What story about the
present were petitioners constructing through their word wars? Why, in
a culture of violence and demonstration that exposed both cleavages
among themselves and some will toward social reinvention, did petitioners insist on the putative norms of the past? Divisions within the
shogunate may have given them leverage for complaint, and the occasional responsiveness of officials may have given them hope for success.
And as their remonstrations encouraged both the divisions and the responsiveness, the petitioners may have been caught in a sustaining political exchange. Yet such observations place too much emphasis on the
process of politics and too little on the passions that must sustain it.

Needs, Habits, Identities

Let me return to the notion that responsive decrees from the shogunate gave petitioners hope of success in their word wars. I have no doubt that grievants sought amelioration through the process of official complaint. But to talk of success is to enter unnavigable space. Did a decree confirming a tax right signify more than the continued delinquency of taxpayers? Did an attempted retraction of a half-tax signify more than the imposition of new levies? And did evidence of responsible shogunal governance mitigate the continuing experiences of lawlessness: were purges offset by careful regulation of the rice market, the burning of two villages offset by decrees protecting manorial boundaries? I raise these questions not to deprecate the importance of small victories in word wars or the will to victory that helped propel them. Rather, I suggest that in an often-tormented society, where success was fragile and hard to measure convincingly, we must seek more widely for the motives of word wars and define more broadly the meanings of victory.

The strongest motive behind many petitions, surely, was desperation. Penurious aristocrats and crisis-ridden tradespeople with little other recourse turned—in documents that often have ragged edges and shrill tones—to official complaints, which were better than nothing. Since petitioners were so frequently and so painfully at odds with fellow residents of Kyoto, recourse to the shogunate at least had the merit of deflecting rancor otherwise likely to provoke endless self-redress. Yet even though petitioners acted out of desperation, I stress less the aspect of despair (which ill accounts for the thirty-year quarrel between aristocrats over fish, for example) than the aspect of compulsion. I think grievants waged their word wars because they couldn't help but wage them: they acted almost instinctively, in response to the passion of routine.

A courtier made the following entry in his diary in the seventh month of 1496:

The Kajūji Chūnagon dispatched an envoy [to the former minister Ōtsuki Tokimitsu] to enquire about the following matter. After a repeated illness, the Chūnagon's father died on the eleventh day of this month. One of the deceased's three daughters is pregnant, and the Chūnagon asked whether she should participate in the funeral service. When the former minister met Kajūji Chūnagon before his gate, the minister said that he could not personally survey all the precedents and hence resolve the problem regarding a pregnant woman's participation in a funeral. However, he did not know of any law or precedent that specified that she should not participate. As a general matter, since it is her father [who died], there seems no need to make a problem of her attendance. Thus he responded.[45]

In part, this quotation is about the rhythms in actual lives that prevail over most crises. As the *Nisui*-diarist interrupted his report of neighborhood purges to note that he "visited the Yakushi Kannon temple and called at Yanagihara's residence," so the imperial treasurer punctuated accounts of grievous financial trouble with details about his medical practice. (Once, over the course of six days, he prescribed seven medicines for "the female servant of a carpenter in the neighborhood who was burned by boiling water from a tub she was carrying." He also kept careful notations about her appetite and bowel movements.)[46] As the poet Sōchō turned from bitter comments on the capital's warlords to observations on the tea ceremonies he attended (the gate before one tea house was constructed of "large cedar and pine logs," the garden was "very clean" and strewn with "five or six leaves of fallen ivy"),[47] so Yamashina Tokitsugu turned from records of battle to observations on cock fights ("This morning I went to the palace for a cock fight. . . . There were seventeen or eighteen birds. My bird came, as usual, from Nomura village. He lost. Grief. Grief.").[48] That is, for the Kajūji Chūnagon as for his fellows, the preoccupations of attachment and interest and station kept conduct in the grooves of the familiar and the habitual.

But our Chūnagon is not just caught in the drama of a family death. He is fastidiously attentive to decorum and the possibility of ritual pollution (an interest apparently shared by the diarist who preserved this vignette). Summoning a courtly savant who can offer advice on the precedents, Kajūji meets the man at his gate (lest the savant himself be polluted by entering a household touched by death) to discuss the propriety of his pregnant sister's attendance at the funeral rites.

Governed by practical rhythms, residents of Kyoto were governed, too, by decorum (things as they should be). Noble diarists worried about the gifts they gave, the leaking roofs that precluded the dignified reception of guests, the purchase of seasonal robes, the number of bamboo stalks contributed for the New Year's fires at court.[49] The townspeople we glimpse obliquely in diaries and documents worried about ground-breaking ceremonies, the nomenclature and language of their suits, the details of the Gion festival.[50] The habits and obligations that shaped daily life, as well as the punctiliousness that both embellished and gave meaning to it, could not constitute a sphere of the "private" or the "quotidian" that was separable from politics. The pressure of routine that we observe in a noble's preoccupation with a correct funeral is equally clear in the following suit of 1523:

> The master of the lathe Uchiki Shōtarō Munemori brings suit: Because I was vested with the privileges of the imperial carpenter [*kinri-sama ondaiku-shiki*], I have produced honorable objects every year without fail. Although the privileges of the shogunal carpenter [*kubō-sama ondaiku-shiki*] were transmitted of old to Yuyama Ichiyubei, the privileges were withdrawn from him in the time of [Ashikaga Yoshimasa] because of the inadequacy of the honorable objects. Henceforth I was vested with these privileges and I complied in discharging them. A shogunal writ to this effect was handed down to me in 1519. However, while I have been pursuing my business in the capital, the man Suketarō has infringed upon my trade. This is unspeakable. I would be grateful if [the shogunate] would conduct a searching investigation into this matter and render stern judgment [against Suketarō].[51]

Munemori's suit was surely born of grievance (even desperation), and it was probably encouraged by the receipt of a previous shogunal writ and some presumption of "success." But I suspect that the actual enforcement of privileges—which the previous writ obviously failed to achieve—was only partly at stake. The suit reads essentially as a declaration of identity: the well-named Uchiki Shōtarō Munemori is a "master of the lathe" who bears the privileges both of the imperial carpenter (literally, the honorable carpenter of the august forbidden interior) and the shogunal carpenter (the honorable carpenter of the august public ruler); he produces honorable objects without failure and in a fashion superior to Yuyama Ichiyubei; he holds official documents and refuses to tolerate in silence the infringement of the man Suketarō, who lacks surname, title, affiliation, and writs of confirmation. Munemori locates himself in the richly decorous world of master artisans producing fine objects for august patrons, where names and acts transcend sterile functions to define social place and the lively dimensions of livelihood. And thus locating him, the suit seems less a pursuit or defense of "normal" relations than a restoration or articulation of them (regardless of the outcome). Not incidentally, the suit also locates and defines the shogunate itself: it is headed by the august public ruler descended from Ashikaga Yoshimasa, who consumes honorable objects made by a lathe master who serves the throne as well; it is the author of honorable writs, searching investigations, and stern judgments; it is the source of justice, the righter of wrongs, the object of gratitude. Such suits attempted to shape the exercise of shogunal power; they just as surely helped exalt that power.

What I have called the passion of routine, then, had to do with the mundane urgency of maintaining one's identity, a fitting identity. It had to do with interring a father properly, noticing the number of fallen ivy leaves in a tea garden, wearing winter robes after the ninth month, and blessing the ground of a new house. It had to do with upbraiding an upstart artisan, seizing the property of a criminal blacksmith, retaining jurisdiction over one's own proprietary holdings, and denouncing a new version of the malt melee. It had to do with defending Onoyama from trespass—who would those woodcutters be without their imperially protected organization, their imperially protected mountain, their well-defined work and well-defined market, their access to distinguished interlocutors, and their ability to imagine their world?

Like the document of the Onoyama woodcutters, the suits and petitions of wartime are all, to my knowledge, about "manageable propositions." They are almost startling in their concern with practical issues of taxation, trade licenses, and the like. Violence did not produce a public literature of invective against assassination and urban havoc. But this is not to say that the deepest issues were not at stake in the manageable propositions. On one level they engaged daily needs that might be successfully relieved by the shogunate. On this level they sustained, and were sustained by, a set of useful political assumptions (about the survival of multiple jurisdictions, the role of precedent) and important political realities (the divisions within the shogunate, the sometime pattern of temperate administration) that abated change. On a more serious level the petitions engaged problems of identity, centered in work and station, that were alleviated by an insistence on continuity. On this level they were sustained by the compulsions of habit, which were much stronger than political calculations. On yet another level, the petitions reflected inchoate desires for something that might have been called the "past" but was, instead, anything other than the present. "Things as they should be" were things as they were not. In their concern with old privileges and stable identities, the suits construct a model for the present, inspired by a normative past, that includes a confident vision of

restoration. They contain too much evidence of past and present contention, however, to offer any prescription for harmony. Thus, they tell
a story that resembles the story of demonstration, filled with profound
disturbance and groping for resolution. Yet the suits tell this story in a
consoling language of principle that evokes the promise of (or reveals
the need for) transcendence: there *is* a way things *could* be.

4

Popular Insurrection

Though the cherries too have bloomed,
in the capital it is the spring
of a single pale Willow.

Since the winter, Kyoto has been a place of uproar. It is beyond belief. There
was battle around Shichijō avenue on the twelfth and thirteenth days of the
second month of 1527. . . . But none is left [now] to fight [Yanagimoto Kata-
haru]. He is nothing but a woodcutter from the mountains of Tanba.[1]

Here once more the poet Sōchō, author of the passage, uses the word
capital, although neither that image nor the flowering of the cherries
brings consolation. Spring can barely stir the wintry place that belongs
now to the willow (*yanagi*), that is, to the warlord *Yanagi*moto Kataharu. Words on this occasion are weapons: Yanagimoto of Tanba, the
feller of great trees, is the enemy.

The word wars of concern to us in the preceding chapter helped
maintain notions of continuity and shape the exercise of power within a
structure of civil governance that men and women could hold together,
if only in their minds. Yet this verbal politics always coexisted with the
politics of demonstration, in a society pushing more deliberately toward
reconfiguration than toward restoration. Kyoto's residents turned as often to force and mass witness as to suits. As we have observed them thus
far, the street actions of townspeople were most often explosive gestures
of protest that discredited the warlord regimes without indicating an
alternative polity. But now we examine a period of sustained rather than

explosive uprisings, when demonstration gave way to vision. It occurred during the greatest upheaval since Ōnin, in a time impervious to the fictions of word wars.

This period began in the wintry spring of 1527, Sōchō's year of the willow, and lasted until the late months of 1536. Its opening phases saw stunning military confusion and the loss of whatever stability had encouraged the quest for a normal politics. Its unfolding saw a dramatic popular movement with an increasingly radical agenda, as commoners responded to the upheaval by moving to the forefront of a new urban order. Their word wars became blood wars. By 1532 the politics of demonstration, also of martial alliance and martial aggression, became ascendant among townspeople who met the chaos with an extraordinary vision. The vision shattered in fire storms and massacre.

Stage One: The Snarls in the Shogunate, 1526–1532

Cast of Characters

The Ōmi Shogunate	*The Sakai Shogunate*
Ashikaga Yoshiharu	Ashikaga Yoshitsuna
Hosokawa Takakuni	Hosokawa Harumoto
	Miyoshi Motonaga
Yanagimoto Kataharu	

There was nothing new about the first episode in Kyoto's new troubles. It began with a quarrel. In 1526, the *kanrei* Hosokawa Takakuni sent one of his Kyoto deputies and a large party of laborers to the province of Settsu, where they were to assist in constructing a castle for the *kanrei's* younger brother. When brawls broke out between the visiting and the resident labor teams (provoking the visitors at one point to dump tiles and rubble on the donjon site), the *kanrei's* brother leveled charges against the deputy in charge. The *kanrei* then compelled his deputy, Kōzai Motomori, to commit suicide. And very swiftly, this death divided the shogunate.[2]

Redress was initiated by two of Kōzai's relatives: his brother Yanagimoto Kataharu, a minor local magnate of Tanba; and his brother-in-law, a minor castellan and district official of the same province. Uniting

Figure 5. Chronology of Events, 1526–1532

1526	the quarrel at the castle site in Settsu, Kōzai Motomori dies
	Yanagimoto Kataharu raises rebellion
1527/2	the battle of Katsura River (Hosokawa Takakuni versus Yanagimoto)
	Ashikaga Yoshiharu and Hosokawa Takakuni flee to Ōmi
	the rival shogunate assembles in Sakai
1527/10–12	battle in Kyoto between the rival shogunates
	neighborhood purges and fortification
	tax withholding begins
1528/1	open battle begins between Yanagimoto Kataharu and Miyoshi Motonaga
1530	Hosokawa Takakuni defeats Yanagimoto Kataharu in Harima (Kataharu dies)
	extensive street fighting in Kyoto, continuing in 1531
1531/6	Miyoshi Motonaga defeats Hosokawa Takakuni in Settsu (Takakuni dies)
	Miyoshi Motonaga allies with Ashikaga Yoshitsuna against Hosokawa Harumoto, Ibaragi Nagataka, Kizawa Nagamasa, and Miyoshi Masanaga
1532/6	Miyoshi Motonaga is defeated by Hosokawa Harumoto in alliance with the Ikkō sect (Motonaga dies)
	Ashikaga Yoshitsuna flees into exile
	Ashikaga Yoshiharu and Hosokawa Harumoto make peace

small forces of their own, these men found several local allies who joined them in raids against Hosokawa fortifications first in Tanba and then in the home province of Yamashiro. Apprehension in the capital encouraged an uprising of debtors, which, within hours, moved the intimidated shogunate to cancel debts. Early in 1527 the shogun himself took shelter in fortified quarters at the temple of Honkokuji and the *kanrei* began construction of a new castle in the eastern hills. The *kanrei* also sought help from several great provincial houses (the Takeda of Wakasa, the Asakura of Echizen, the Akamatsu of Harima, and the Rokkaku of Ōmi).[3]

From the outside, much in this sequence of events seems disproportionate—the furor at the construction site, the campaign of Kōzai's brothers, the advent of uprisings and the capitulation by officials to debtors, the apparent preparations for war by a shogunate unable to quell a small-time vendetta. But disproportion is the measure of instability. In this case, one vendetta drew strength from another to break shogunal composure, for Kōzai's brothers also made a successful alliance with Hosokawa Harumoto, Miyoshi Motonaga, and Ashikaga Yoshitsuna.

We are now at a familiar juncture in a familiar story, though one that will move in unfamiliar directions. The story turns again on competition for shogunal offices—in this case the offices of both shogun and *kanrei*—which continued to involve members of the Ashikaga and Hosokawa houses and to replay old quarrels among them. The story also turns again on the deputies of the Hosokawa, who used family vendettas for their own purposes.

To locate the problem of competition and old quarrels, let me move backward for a moment. In what I have called the third transition in Kyoto's wartime government, the *kanrei* Hosokawa Takakuni had risen to power in 1508 by ousting from office his kinsman Hosokawa Sumimoto. Sumimoto assailed Takakuni in and out of the capital until his own death in 1520, whereupon the burden of vengeance fell to his young son, Hosokawa Harumoto. Harumoto's branch of the Hosokawa house made its headquarters in the Shikoku province of Awa. And there Harumoto was surrounded by major retainers in the Miyoshi house, preeminently Miyoshi Motonaga (who was the grandson of Miyoshi Yukinaga, the chief support of Hosokawa Sumimoto) and by a claimant to shogunal office, Ashikaga Yoshitsuna.

And so, for a moment, we return to the shogunal begats. Ashikaga Yoshitsuna was the brother of the incumbent shogun, Ashikaga Yoshiharu; both men were sons of Ashikaga Yoshizumi, the much abused eleventh shogun installed in office through one Hosokawa coup (in 1493) and deposed from office through another (Takakuni's coup of 1508). Yoshizumi was succeeded by Ashikaga Yoshitane, the shogun who had been deposed by the coup of 1493 but reinstalled through the coup of 1508. Yoshitane eventually adopted Ashikaga Yoshitsuna as his heir and presumptive successor, but this succession pattern was disturbed in 1521 when Yoshitane broke with his *kanrei*, Hosokawa Taka-kuni, and fled to Awa. Takakuni subsequently oversaw the elevation as shogun of Ashikaga Yoshiharu (who had been raised apart from his brother in the province of Harima). Although Yoshitane attempted to reverse this decision through rebellion, Yoshiharu survived in shogunal office and Yoshitsuna remained an exile in Awa.[4]

Thus, in 1526 and 1527 the shogunate—in the persons of Ashikaga Yoshiharu and his *kanrei*, Hosokawa Takakuni—faced an immediate challenge from Yanagimoto Kataharu (the avenger of his brother Kōzai Motomori). It faced a broader challenge, one clearly aimed at coup and a redistribution of shogunal offices, from Yanagimoto's new allies: Hosokawa Harumoto, Miyoshi Motonaga, and Ashikaga Yoshitsuna (the avengers of Hosokawa Sumimoto, Miyoshi Yukinaga, and Ashikaga Yoshitane). We are swept again into the dizzying genealogies of quarrels.

But having located those quarrels, the powerful surface text of the rebellion, let me also locate the deputies and retainers who finally transformed them into open warfare. Ashikaga Yoshitsuna was only fifteen years old and Hosokawa Harumoto only twelve in 1526. In effect, they were mascots of Yanagimoto Kataharu and Miyoshi Motonaga, and of the many other men who led soldiers to battle. Like Miyoshi, some of these men were the highly placed deputies of provincial governors whose appointments as district officials, castellans, and estate managers had provided foundations for petty lordships. (Branches of the Miyoshi house had thrived both in Awa and in Settsu under local Hosokawa governors in those two provinces.) Like Yanagimoto, some of these men were minor local magnates who had extended their influence through military affiliation with peers, local officials, and aspiring warlords. The important participants in this shogunal quarrel came, in effect, from different strata of the complex world of local military power. Their influence emerged from lateral as well as vertical alliances with one another and, most important, from connections with the disparate and armed peasants who made up their armies. These alliances and connections were fractious (as we have seen already in the Yamashiro uprising and the earlier trials of the Hosokawa *kanrei*), but they were exceedingly potent as long as they lasted.

In the crisis that developed after 1526, the ambitions of the provincial commanders continued to focus, apparently, on old stakes: the elevation of sympathetic leaders to the offices of shogun and *kanrei,* and the consequent award to themselves of official appointments useful in raising additional men and income. The resources of Kyoto itself, and of a still-fragmented Yamashiro, provided a significant incentive for war. For men like Yanagimoto, animus toward the incumbent *kanrei* provided an incentive as well. Sometimes this animus grew from personal injury. More often it derived from the old and inherent contradictions in a shogunate that excited the appetites of supporters looking for lordships but frustrated them with concessions to established property holders.[5] In a continuing paradox, the rebels of 1526 fought within rather than against these contradictions. Except for the mystifying Miyoshi Motonaga.

By the thirteenth day of the second month, 1527, the troops raised by Yanagimoto Kataharu and Miyoshi Motonaga had assembled at a temple by the Katsura River, southwest of Kyoto. There they met in battle a force recruited by the *kanrei,* Hosokawa Takakuni. This force had been contributed principally by the Takeda house of Wakasa, the only ally to respond to the *kanrei*'s pleas for military assistance. The courtier Yamashina Tokitsugu, one of many observers of the "bustle" preceding the battle and then of the fighting itself, estimated the "enemy" army of the Yanagimoto and the Miyoshi at 12,000 men, and the army of the "Kyoto party" at 2,000.[6] Some courtiers joined the battle.

Yanagimoto achieved a quick victory, and by the afternoon of the thirteenth the first "procession" marking a transition and purge filled the streets of the capital with fleeing and wounded soldiers from the "Kyoto party" who, in fact, were largely young men from the countryside of Wakasa. During the night of the fourteenth day, courtiers were roused from sleep to gather on a hill near the palace and watch a second procession: the departure from Kyoto of the shogun, Ashikaga Yoshiharu; the *kanrei,* Hosokawa Takakuni; and officials of the Board of Administration. The third procession took place on the sixteenth day of the second month, when Yanagimoto Kataharu entered the capital accompanied by 70 or more mounted commanders, 20 palanquins, and 10,000 foot soldiers.[7] And so began what I have called the fourth transition in Kyoto's wartime government.

But there was nothing clean and final about it. The incumbent administration set up a government in exile in the province of Ōmi, where its members both planned continuing military operations and issued the "routine" documents (confirmations of land rights, tax rulings, various prohibitions) meant to convey unbroken shogunal authority. A parallel, rival administration emerged in the city of Sakai, where Ashikaga Yoshitsuna, Hosokawa Harumoto, and Miyoshi Motonaga took up residence. Envoys of Yoshitsuna approached the throne with gifts of a gold-emblazoned sword and a white horse, seeking an official title that was finally bestowed by the emperor in the seventh month: Ashikaga Yoshitsuna was made "Head of the Bureau of Horses, Left Division" at the fifth rank, the promotion customarily preceding appointment as shogun. Even earlier, the Sakai deputies had begun to issue the "routine" documents of public rule (mimicking the language and the content of those dispatched from Ōmi), which were meant to convey the transfer of shogunal authority to Ashikaga Yoshitsuna. Hosokawa Harumoto, the would-be *kanrei,* assumed headship of the Hosokawa house and the governorship of three provinces: Yamashiro, Settsu, and Tanba. Miyoshi Motonaga served, in effect, as the deputy governor of Yamashiro, and a further series of appointments—as magistrates, deputy governors, and district chiefs—went out to the men of Awa, Settsu, and Tanba who had sustained the coup.[8]

We are now at a juncture in a somewhat new story. The two rival shogunates, neither of them resident in Kyoto, continued to struggle for ascendancy over the course of five years. That struggle was complicated first by internal cleavages in the Sakai party, which exposed the dominant roles in the crisis of men like Miyoshi Motonaga, and then by the surrender of what government existed to provincial commanders at war with each other.

The contest between the two shogunates moved between the provinces and Kyoto itself. When efforts by the Miyoshi army to pacify Settsu remained inconclusive, Ashikaga Yoshiharu (the "Ōmi shogun") reentered Kyoto in the tenth month of 1527. In the eleventh month the Miyoshi pursued him there, bringing regular street fighting to a head by attacking some of Ashikaga Yoshiharu's champions at Saiin. More than two hundred soldiers lost their lives. Sporadic battles occurred through the twelfth month, leaving Kyoto neighborhoods burned and pillaged.

At this point fissures opened in the Sakai party between Yanagimoto Kataharu, who had claimed practical military control of Kyoto since the battle of Katsura River, and Miyoshi Motonaga, who wanted that control for himself. The two men and their troops fought in the center of Kyoto, near the intersection of Muromachi and Tachiuri, in the first month of 1528. (Briefly, in one of the more curious reversals in a treacherous age, Miyoshi Motonaga and Hosokawa Takakuni made a fragile alliance against Yanagimoto.)[9]

After 1528 the battles between and within the shogunates continued in tandem. The Ōmi *kanrei*, Hosokawa Takakuni, began a personal odyssey through the provinces in quest of support, which he finally obtained from the Urakami house in Bizen. This alliance led him into campaigns against Sakai partisans in Harima. During 1530 Takakuni defeated an army there led by Yanagimoto Kataharu, who died in battle. Takakuni then moved into Settsu and Kyoto, where street fighting between Ōmi and Sakai forces resumed toward the close of 1530. But the rally of Hosokawa Takakuni and the Ōmi forces ended in Settsu in the sixth month of 1531, when Miyoshi Motonaga defeated them in battle and precipitated the suicide of Takakuni.[10]

Let me see the military sequence through. Miyoshi Motonaga's victory against Hosokawa Takakuni and the collapse of the Ōmi party did not heal the rifts in Sakai. A rivalry that had once focused on Yanagimoto Kataharu now opened between Miyoshi Motonaga and three other powerful opponents (Ibaragi Nagataka, a castellan of Settsu who had served the Sakai shogun since 1527; Kizawa Nagamasa, a deputy governor of Kawachi who had succeeded Yanagimoto as effective commander of Kyoto; and Miyoshi Masanaga, the uncle of Miyoshi Motonaga.) The "Sakai shogun," Ashikaga Yoshitsuna, now a man of twenty, supported Miyoshi Motonaga. The "Sakai *kanrei*," Hosokawa Harumoto, now a man of eighteen, supported Motonaga's enemies. After several military engagements demonstrated Miyoshi Motonaga's advantage, the desperate Hosokawa Harumoto turned for assistance to an improbable ally—the army of religious sectarians loyal to the Ikkō temple of Honganji. These sectarians, reportedly 210,000 strong, attacked Miyoshi Motonaga in Sakai in the sixth month of 1532. Motonaga took his own life. Ashikaga Yoshitsuna failed in an attempt to kill himself and fled to exile in Awa. The Sakai *kanrei*, Hosokawa Harumoto, then made peace with the Ōmi shogun, Ashikaga Yoshiharu.[11]

Like most narratives of the warring states era, this one moved from vengeance to changing alignments and death. By 1532 most of the principals in the battles begun in 1526 were gone: Yanagimoto Kataharu, Miyoshi Motonaga, and Hosokawa Takakuni were dead; Ashikaga Yoshitsuna was in flight. A new shogunal administration, stitched together of once-inimical pieces, seemed to be forming—but still outside Kyoto and still under assault. And again, like most narratives of the warring states era, this one turned on issues of gain and advantage—not on the attachments of blood or vassalage, the restraints of law or office holding, the logic of numerical strength or geographical position, the compulsions of vendetta.

Nonetheless, several elements warn of change. One is the conduct of Miyoshi Motonaga who, though he died too early to reveal his political course, might be associated with departures from familiar shogunal directions. By keeping the rival shogunate in Sakai, for example, he may have been declaring independence from Kyoto and the old elites that constrained military autocracy. Further, Miyoshi's differences with important Sakai partisans (preeminently Ibaragi Nagataka) appear to have been founded on his resolve to disestablish the manorial system and thus to break the pattern of compromise with the old order. Although he found Ashikaga Yoshitsuna a useful prop to his ambitions, Miyoshi may also have been ready to topple the shogunal institution as it had been known. In short, there are intimations that Miyoshi's vision of the coup was new, not old; it may have derived from a program, rather than from grudges and appetite alone, and aimed at direct military lordship over the domain of the capital.[12]

But clearer than a change in mind after 1526 was a change in leading participants: local warrior bands fully replaced the "great houses" in directing shogunal coups. Neither the Hosokawa nor the surviving provincial governors determined the course of battle, but an elastic group of ambitious castellans and deputies like Yanagimoto, Miyoshi, Urakami, Ibaragi, Kizawa.[13] Their struggles replayed the old themes of private war. They bore, however, new tonalities of discord. Hosokawa Takakuni's futile calls for help before the battle of Katsura River, his strange trek through the provinces in pursuit of support, the regular disarray in Sakai, the fateful alliance between Hosokawa Harumoto and the Ikkō sectarians—these and similar episodes over the period of six years revealed a fracturing of interest and an impoverishment of shogunal resources that had been barely apparent in the Ōnin war, or even in the internecine coups of 1493 and 1507–8. The factions that formed around the rival shogunates, moreover, failed to hold the capital. Yanagimoto's procession after the battle of Katsura was an ironic prelude to recurrent street fighting that peaked in six major battles in Kyoto, including almost-uninterrupted warfare in the first three months of 1531.[14] While the contending shogun remained out of town except for forays into well-defended temples, Kyoto stood as an unwilling host to the warrior bands of Awa, Settsu, and Kawachi that, like Sōchō's "woodcutter from the mountains of Tanba," the residents regarded as the enemy.

And thus to one more change of great importance. Kyoto's towns-people responded to the uncommon upheaval after 1526 in forceful ways. Their conduct was dramatic, if yet unclear in meaning and direction. We must explore it briefly now, in anticipation of the storm that broke in 1532.

The resumed battle brought reverberating troubles to Kyoto: the debtors' uprising, the looting and confiscation of "enemy property," attempts at military recruitment,[15] a spate of suspicious fires and the gratuitous burning of temples like Daitokuji,[16] opportunistic thievery, and the suspension of the Gion festival.[17] The "force of the self" manifested itself, too, in local quarrels over land. In the eighth month of 1527, some two thousand men raised by the noble Konoe house attacked a similar number of men from the Seibunshi village not far from the imperial palace. The Seibunshi, diviners and healers with a marginal status, were cultivating fields claimed by the Konoe.[18]

The most significant events of this period, however, occurred in the eleventh and twelfth months of 1527, when Miyoshi Motonaga was attempting to purge all loyalists to the Ōmi adminstration from Kyoto and, with exemplary displays of force, to terrorize the city into submission. Here, part of a report from Yamashina Tokitsugu that we have seen before:

11th month, 29th day.   This morning about ten men from the gang of Awa invaded the house of the *tatami* maker of this neighborhood. The people of northern Kyoto, all the way from Nijō avenue, rose up and surrounded them with two or three thousand persons.[19]

For several weeks townspeople gathered in resistance to troops described as "thieves" and "invaders," and they constructed barriers against assault—gates and fences fortified with spikes, bamboo palings, and moats. As we noted previously, the fortification extended to the imperial palace, where moats dug in response to the threat of criminal bands were amplified with "guard huts" and fences.[20]

Perhaps because of such actions, the neighborhood purges subsided in 1528. But townspeople rose again in defiance of military taxation imposed by Kyoto's new overlords. A report from Yamashina Tokitsugu we have seen before:

The bell at Kōdō temple began pealing out an alarm. Asserting that they were to collect a commissariat tax, two [military deputies] burst into the property of Lord Ichijō and, we heard, took his wife and children hostage. . . .

[Next day.]   Again the Kōdō bell sounded. People of the blocks rose up and surrounded [Lord Ichijō's residence]. When the townsman Takaya Yōsuke attacked from the north, [the military deputies] struck seven or eight of Takaya's group with arrows and three died. The deputies also clashed to the south with people of the neighborhoods. . . . The courtiers who had gone out to Ichijō's residence [to render assistance] numbered about 200. In addition, all the people of Muromachi neighborhood had charged over there.[21]

Tax defiance may have been endemic, in part because of the "extraordinary" martial levies that Yanigimoto tried to impose throughout Yamashiro despite imperial orders to desist.[22] On one occasion, villagers of Mimaki attacked deputies trying to collect a roof tax.[23] But a report from the courtier Sanjōnishi Sanetaka, from the second month of 1528, complains of more general withholding:

The people throughout Kyoto and its environs are claiming an exemption from half their taxes [hanzei]. We are suffering gravely in this matter. Even my small property revenues from southern Kyoto have been cut in half. This is grievous.[24]

In 1528, 1529, and 1530, officials representing both the Sakai and the Ōmi administrations had to issue and reissue orders to Kyoto's townspeople to render their standard, but apparently delinquent, land rents:

Konoe Hisamichi kō-ki. 1529, 7th month.
13th day.   Yanagimoto's decree has arrived. He demands that the land rents of the various places, which have been withheld, be paid.

14th day.   Yanagimoto and [his deputy] Matsui have sternly demanded the land rents of the various places. As of old, they are to be rendered to the proper proprietors.[25]

In sum, street fights and fortification and tax battles moved Kyoto's townspeople into grave confrontation with their military overlords after 1526. Acting sometimes in alliance with noble and religious proprietors, they also broke with the old elite through their tax delinquency. In these years of peril, high and low alike attempted the sort of accommodation to military rulers that I have associated with word wars: from the rival administrations they sought and received confirmations of land and commercial rights, for example, and decisions about transfers of a guild headship.[26] Nonetheless, they also met violence with violence. They attacked and wounded their assailants; they armed themselves with bows and arrows; they raised razor-sharp palings. Further, they engaged in the politics of demonstration. The sounding of bells, the raising of shouts and cries, the assembly of persons, the encircling of targets—all of these actions played on themes we have observed before in debtors' and provincial uprisings, military parades and battles. The force of numbers remains the critical element, for demonstration drew its power from mass witness. Two or three thousand townspeople, we are told, gathered in defense of the *tatami* maker. Two hundred courtiers and "all" the people of Muromachi, we are told, gathered in defense of Lord Ichijō.

But just what was demonstration about or against. To some extent, it may have been a political statement about the illegitimacy of the "villains" from Sakai, a statement given force by the endurance of the Ōmi regime.[27] This proposition, however, assigns to the townspeople undivided loyalties as well as a conscious political agenda. More simply, the demonstrations may have been a familiar response to emergency military intrusions that became singularly egregious when accompanied by local purges. This proposition, however, flattens difference by equating the uprising of "people from northern Kyoto, all the way from Nijō avenue," with the pummeling of tax collectors or the beating of the lantern smasher. Finally, the demonstrations may have been inchoate expressions of independence. This proposition, vague enough to cover many meanings, begins at least to account for the ensuing tax defiance—against traditional proprietors no less than upstart warlords—which recalls the withholding of a half-tax by participants in the Yamashiro uprising. In both Yamashiro and Kyoto, tax withholding followed locally traumatic and unresolved warfare as a reaction against all conventional governance.[28] Bloody contests over power created vacuums of power.

In this phase of trouble, Kyoto's townspeople used the devices of demonstration, fortification, and tax battle to make an obscure statement of resistance. This statement took radical shape in 1532 and succeeding years. Its evolution was inextricable from the spectacle of chaos among the provincial commanders fighting for Kyoto.

Stage Two: "The Uprising of the Realm Under Heaven," 1532–1536

Gion shugyō nikki. 1532.
7th month, 28th day.   Because there have been rumors that the Ikkō sectarians would attack the Hokke sectarians [of Kyoto], people are saying that the Hokke people are planning an insurrection and will make common cause with

[Hosokawa Harumoto] to attack [the local Ikkō sanctuary of] Yamashina. . . .
A man called Yamamura, who was a retainer of the Yanagimoto, will command
them. . . .

8th month, 7th day.   Yamamura assembled the [participants in the Hokke]
uprising [*ikki*] of northern and southern Kyoto, and they conducted a circular
procession [*uchimawari*].

8th month, 10th day.   Today Yamamura led a circular procession and then
burned down several temples of the Ikkō sectarians. They say [the Hokke sectar-
ians] conducted another circular procession in Yamashina.

8th month, 11th day.   Yamamura assembled the Hokke townspeople of northern and southern Kyoto, and they conducted a circular procession in the eastern
hills [of Kyoto].

8th month, 12th day.   The Hokke warriors of northern and southern Kyoto
conducted a circular procession, rousing their spirits.[29]

Abruptly, dazzlingly breaking into the documents of wartime were
new words (*uchimawari*, "circular procession") and fierce old words in
new contexts (*muhon* and *ikki*, "insurrection" and "uprising," now
linked to the Hokke sectarians).[30] For ten months—from the eighth
month of 1532 through the sixth month of 1533—this vocabulary
dominated accounts of Kyoto's battles, and for four years it dominated
accounts of Kyoto's politics.

The emphasis in the passages above falls on *uchimawari*, an almost
daily activity left mainly undescribed except for the images conveyed by
the characters: *mawari* is a circling, *uchi* is an interior. "Procession,"
then, with its image of linear movement from a starting point to a destination, distorts what is more aptly a flowing ring around a center, which
might be either an inside guarded by a human cordon or a target cut
off by a contracting noose. "Procession," with its image of completion
(when the destination is reached) or periodicy (when a progress is ritu-
ally repeated), also distorts what is more aptly an unbroken revolution—
a continuum suggested by the resumption (rather than the repetition)
of the *uchimawari* day after day.

Nisui-ki. 1532, 8th month, 7th day.
I invited Madenokōji out again and we went sightseeing [*kenbutsu*] at the
[Hokke] temple of Honkokuji on Rokujō avenue. The retainers of Yanagimoto
are joining the townspeople of all Kyoto in an *uchimawari*. I understand there
are three or four thousand participants. There are rumors that the Ikkō sectarians will next attack the Hokke sectarians. So now at the fortress of Honkokuji
they are gathering for a [preparatory] feast. It is all deeply strange.[31]

Here our vision of the *uchimawari* expands somewhat to include considerable size—three or four thousand participants in this account, as many as ten or twenty thousand as time advances. It takes on, too, a festive quality, implied by the feasting and the magnetic attraction of sightseers. But it also includes something ominous, implied by the rumors of attack that have precipitated the assembly and the deep strangeness perceived by a noble voyeur. This strangeness may be intensified for the modern reader by conjunctions seemingly taken for granted by the diarist: between temple and fortress, religious sectarians and combatants. Before we examine those connections, let me infer several additional features of the *uchimawari* from the identification of its participants as Hokke believers.

As they circled the capital in swelling numbers, the marchers probably chanted in sonorous voices the mantra of Hokke congregations: *Namu myōhō Renge-kyō,* "All praise to the marvelous law of the Lotus Sutra." The refrain, like the march itself, would have been paced by the sounds of drums and bells, the cries of flutes. Astride horses or on foot, participants may have borne long white banners mounted on bamboo poles, inscribed in black with either the mantra or an individual character. They may have carried torches as well, perhaps lit from sacred fire. And it is likely that the visual display was embellished by the robes of the marching priests and the matching coats and headbands of different temple congregations.

My inferences about the conduct of the *uchimawari*, though theatrical, are broadly faithful to the images of spectacle evoked by diary references to size, frequency, and vaguely weird movement. Further inferences, about causality and meaning, are more perilous, for our reserved and possibly baffled diarists locate the *uchimawari* across a spectrum of associations. Its participants are responding, we are told, to rumors of attack and thus may be cast in a role of self-defense; but they are also "planning an insurrection," which leads to assaults on "several temples of the Ikkō sectarians," and thus assume a role of aggression. They ally with Hosokawa Harumoto and apparently accept the command of a retainer of the Yanagimoto; but they also constitute a movement (*ikki*), anterior to military alliance, that embraces "northern and southern Kyoto." They are defined repeatedly in sectarian terms that imply specifically religious battles; but they are also characterized as "the townspeople of all Kyoto," whose motivations are unstated. They are commoners; but they are warriors. They are feast-makers; but they are arsonists. They are fellow Kyotoites; but they are objects of observation.

Martial and political and social and religious meanings swirl around them and their processions, but in a haze that occludes clear readings.

Let us move then, for a moment, to the shelter of chronology and context. Just before the *uchimawari*, Hosokawa Harumoto's men and the Ikkō sectarians had formed the alliance that, on the twentieth day of the sixth month of 1532, resulted in the defeat and suicide of Miyoshi Motonaga. This battle concluded a horrific series of engagements, lasting six days, in which masses of Ikkō combatants descended on the fortifications of the Miyoshi in Kawachi and Settsu. Diarists and chroniclers estimated Ikkō strength in various engagements at 30,000, 100,000, and more than 200,000 men. They reported uncommonly high casualty figures: 3,000 members of the Miyoshi party died in a battle of the fifteenth day, according to Yamashina Tokitsugu.[32] After Miyoshi's defeat, Tokitsugu found "the realm under heaven, all of it, a realm of uprising [*ikki*]. I lament. I lament."[33] These events were extraordinary, in part because of the immensity of the (even heavily discounted) troop numbers—numbers matched previously only in the Ōnin war, and then only in the aggregate strength of provincial armies assembled by hereditary military governors. They were all the more extraordinary because the troops came from sectarian communities of commoners and because they had aligned with a would-be shogunal overlord.

Ikkō (literally, "single-minded") had emerged as the popular designation of adherents of the True Pure Land school of Buddhism, a sect founded on the teachings of the thirteenth-century monk Shinran. Too simply stated, Shinran preached a message of universal salvation for those who accepted the gift of faith from the Buddha Amida. Offspring of a degenerate age long separated from the original revelation of the Buddhist law, men and women in their abject weakness were deemed incapable of redemption through piety, good works, and religious discipline. Such practices became in Shinran's eyes statements of arrogance, for they presumed that mortals might save themselves and hence renounce the saving power of Amida. For Shinran, salvation could proceed only from faith—a faith neither elected nor generated by men and women, who had themselves no strength to elect or to generate it, but a faith given by Amida and then accepted.

This galvanizing message attracted both a mass—largely rural—following and a sustained attack from other sects (preeminently the Tendai establishment of Enryakuji). It also acquired political resonances. The religious tenets of universal salvation and equality under the Buddhist law inspired a basically lay movement free from hierarchical clerical control; Ikkō believers assembled in generally autonomous communities centered on a local teacher and a local chapel. And such organizations fed, and were fed by, convictions about political self-rule and a more localized, egalitarian distribution of power. From the time of the Ōnin war, armed Ikkō adherents challenged the rule of daimyo overlords on behalf of either their own associations or sympathetic local warriors. After decades of havoc in the province of Kaga, Ikkō sectarians there established control by 1531. The success of this protracted uprising (again, *ikki*) and a mounting incidence of other Ikkō actions cast the sectarians as agrarian rebels alarmingly different in two respects from participants in other *ikki:* first, their uprisings had a clearer ideological dimension and hence, perhaps, greater tenacity and imperviousness to internal collapse; second, their members shared allegiance to a national religious movement and hence might draw support for a local, seemingly discrete action from fellow sectarians in distant parts.[34]

The possibilities for corporate action increased significantly in the later fifteenth century as the patriarch Rennyo imposed a degree of union on the disparate Ikkō brethren, establishing as a sectarian headquarters the temple of Honganji in Yamashina, just outside Kyoto. Directives from Honganji helped shape the Ikkō victory in Kaga and, in 1532, marshaled Ikkō support for Hosokawa Harumoto's campaign against Miyoshi Motonaga.[35] Our sources, though, remain only suggestive about why Ikkō armies joined Hosokawa Harumoto and how such awful numbers of men were actually brought to battle. We know that the original connection between the Hosokawa and Honganji was established through family relations of the Hosokawa general Ibaragi.[36] And we are told something of the Ikkō structure by a court woman, writing on the fifth day of the sixth month of 1532, who described a system of command that placed Honganji over its own "direct adherents, over the adherents of temples led by relatives of the abbot, and over the adherents of branch temples."[37] Given reports about the size and efficiency of Ikkō armies, this sketch of a simple and absolute system of command acquires a certain persuasive force. But even if we credit Honganji with such unprecedented power to mobilize adherents, *who* mobilized them—an adolescent abbot, sixteen years old at the time? And why did they fight for the very sort of overlord so long attacked by fellow sectarians in Kaga?

Something of an answer may be suggested by Ikkō actions following the fall of Miyoshi Motonaga on the twentieth day of the sixth month. By the seventeenth day of the next month, Ikkō armies had risen up again, this time in Nara, where they attacked both the Kasuga shrine and Kōfukuji temple. They burned down nearly a score of monasteries. In numbers estimated by diarists at one to two hundred thousand, Ikkō adherents then fanned out over Settsu, Kawachi, and Izumi, where they burned minor fortresses, rival temples, and estate offices. On the second day of the eighth month, they attacked Hosokawa Harumoto in Sakai. The Hosokawa general Ibaragi described the rampage as "an explosion of selfish interests" and wondered if it "would crush all other interests." The *Nisui* diarist concluded: "The realm under heaven is a world of uprising. This is the end of the world. It is grievous. It is grievous."[38]

The brief and quickly sundered alliance of Ikkō armies with Hosokawa Harumoto may have emerged from many things: a web of personal connections; a joint antipathy to Miyoshi Motonaga—perceived by Honganji, perhaps, as a far more serious threat than Harumoto's failing supporters; an Ikkō desire to demonstrate to Harumoto his dependency on a sectarian army now in line for substantial reward. But the spread of the uprising suggests an unleashing of force that, even if controlled at the onset, had escaped its leaders and a particular direction to find multiple, seemingly universal targets among military and courtly and religious proprietors. The fragmentation of authority in the provinces around the capital surely emboldened Ikkō armies. The recent ascendancy of Ikkō adherents in Kaga and the convincing victory against Miyoshi Motonaga, who had withstood other challengers, may have given rage and ambition a new sense of invincibility.

Although courtly diarists turned repeatedly to apocalyptic language, the alarm in Kyoto over Ikkō uprisings belonged to a new order of hysteria. The size attributed to Ikkō armies, the scope of their six-week offensive, the variety of their targets, the incendiary mix of religion and politics in their movement—all such features located this series of *ikki* beyond the categories of struggle familiar to residents of the capital. It quickly became apparent that the uprising would engulf them, too. By the end of the seventh month, still some days before the Ikkō adherents marched on Hosokawa Harumoto in Sakai, the Gion diarist was recording "rumors" of an impending Ikkō assault upon the "Hokke sectarians" of Kyoto. There followed, then, the alliance between Hokke sectarians and Hosokawa Harumoto, the appointment of the man Yamamura to command a Hokke army, and the daily round of *uchimawari*.

And then there followed a series of strikes by Hokke armies against Ikkō sanctuaries. By the tenth day of the eighth month, they had "burned down several temples" in Yamashina. On the seventeenth day they fought with Ikkō adherents at the Shirudani barrier, and on the nineteenth they attacked an Ikkō army from Settsu in the Nishioka district of Yamashiro. On the twenty-fourth day, joined by troops of Hosokawa Harumoto and the Rokkaku house of Ōmi, they attacked and burned down the Honganji headquarters in Yamashina, where the abbot himself was in residence. In succeeding months they attacked Ikkō strongholds in Yamazaki, Amagasaki, throughout Settsu, and Sakai.[39]

The diary accounts of the early encounters clearly identify the combatants from Kyoto as "Hokke adherents" and ascribe to them both numerical power and martial efficiency.

The Kyoto force was about ten thousand strong. The Honganji people numbered four thousand or five thousand. The greater part of the Kyoto force was composed of Hokke adherents. This is very interesting. At Shirudani they attacked and killed some numbers of the Ikkō adherents and defeated them.[40]

Conducting an *uchimawari* from Yamashina around the eastern hills, the Kyoto people met the Ikkō people and, mounting a battle on Hanayama, demolished the Ikkō adherents of Yamashina. One hundred twenty or thirty [Ikkō adherents] were killed.[41]

Yanagimoto's men, relying upon the Hokke adherents of Kyoto, went to meet [the Ikkō adherents] at Tōji. More than three hundred of the Honganji adherents died under attack and the rest scattered in various directions, discarding all their belongings as they fled.[42]

The crucially important battle occurred on the twenty-fourth day of the eighth month when the Kyoto party succeeded in taking Yamashina Honganji. One description of that event we have seen already in Chapter 2. Here, another:

23d day.   The Hokke adherents throughout Kyoto, every one of them, set out from the various places for the capital barriers to march on Yamashina Honganji. The Hokke adherents of northern and southern Kyoto had gathered first at the temples to which they belonged. . . . The Rokkaku men from Ōtsu gathered at the eastern barrier, the Yanagimoto men gathered at the Shirudani barrier, and, in addition, the people of more than fifty local districts gathered on the eastern Iwakura hills. They set fire to the Hanayama district, the Otowa district, and Tsushi no oka in Yamashina. The theft of crops and other goods is beyond description. Tonight they set camp at various places.

24th day.   From early morning there were battles several times at stations on the four sides of Honganji, and [Honganji] was closed off by fire from the Nomura district. In early afternoon, a fierce group of attackers broke into [the temple compound] from Honganji's fortified gates. Heisuke and other defenders surrendered to Rokkaku. I do not know the number of the [Honganji] rebels. The attackers burned down the inner and outer precincts of the temple, leaving behind not a single house.[43]

The *Nisui* diarist provides a grisly epitaph:

25th day.   I hear the theft of treasure from the Honganji rubble continues even today, without exhaustion.

26th day.   Today as yesterday they were still searching through the rubble. Finally, I hear, they dug up several hundred gold coins. They say several score provincials died [struggling over the booty]. It is laughable.[44]

What are we to make of these events? Simply, common-sensically, we might discover the townspeople of Kyoto making an urgent alliance with warlords to save the city from an incalculable threat. The element of common cause is unmistakable. Kyoto's people acted not alone but in concert with, and apparently under the leadership of, military men in the houses of Hosokawa (and Rokkaku, Yanagimoto, Yakushiji, Ibaragi). Armed monks from the Tendai temple of Enryakuji entered the assault against Honganji as well.[45] This coalition of often-hostile elements was one measure of the peril associated with the spreading Ikkō challenge. We are nonetheless left with puzzles: the size and readiness of the commoner army, which permitted the coalition successfully to take the offensive against Ikkō sanctuaries; the meanings of the characterization of this army as a force of Hokke sectarians; and the complex of motives, beyond urban self-defense, that either moved the sectarians in the first place or emerged as they demonstrated their value to Hosokawa Harumoto.

We find intimations of martial resources among Kyoto's commoners before the onset of *uchimawari*. In 1504 and again in 1511 they joined in the battles surrounding the Hosokawa struggles for the *kanrei* title;[46] they mounted defenses against various invasions of debtors; they engaged in group actions of self-redress. Most recently and collectively, they used the resources of demonstration, fortification, and tax resistance against military officials in the capital from 1527. Yet nowhere in the record up to 1532 do we find huge figures for commoner combatants or allusions to "more than four hundred men on horseback" and "martial equipment that dazzles the eye."[47] Nowhere do we find repeated *uchimawari*. Nowhere do we find extra-urban campaigns against seasoned troops. The leap from a defense of a *tatami* maker by two or three thousand townspeople to a march against an Ikkō army by ten thousand Hokke adherents is not unimaginable. But it is a leap, one almost surely produced by the difference between "townspeople" and "Hokke adherents."

Hokke ("lotus," or "flower of the law") had emerged as the popular designation of adherents of the Nichiren school of Buddhism, a sect founded on the teachings of the thirteenth-century monk Nichiren. Nichiren preached a message of universal salvation for those who honored, and lived by the precepts of, the Lotus Sutra. A contemporary of Shinran, Nichiren decried the "single-minded" emphasis placed by True Pure Land teachers on faith in Amida and invocation of that Buddha's name. Rather, he found in the Lotus Sutra—in its complex portrayal of the Buddha nature, its definition of virtuous conduct that must amplify ejaculations of faith, and its exaltation of the "Superb Action" of propagating the truth of the law to outsiders—a path to, not a formula for, salvation. Single-minded himself, Nichiren denounced rival sects with an ardor that his followers captured in two slogans: *fuju fuse*, "do not give, do not take"—or, in effect, remain inviolate from other sects and nonbelievers; and *shakubuku guzū*, "break what is bent, widen the path"—or, in effect, destroy heterodoxy and spread the truth. His message attracted a substantial, largely urban following and a sustained attack from other sects (preeminently the Tendai establishment of Enryakuji). It also acquired economic resonances. The religious tenet of *sokushin jōbutsu*, "become a Buddha in this very body," came to be associated not only with enlightenment in the course of mortal life but also with the worldly prosperity significant of membership among the elect. Wealth was not quite sacralized, but it became consistent with, or a manifestation of, piety. And sectarian enthusiasm spread throughout the population of townspeople.[48]

Around the time of the Ōnin war, one official claimed that "over half of Kyoto is made up of Hokke adherents."[49] Whatever the fraction, the equation in later diaries between "townspeople" and "Hokke sectarians" suggests a pronounced Hokke presence in the city—either because a commoner majority was actually affiliated with Lotus temples or because a commoner majority might be expected to move in the direction chosen by the sectarians. Somewhat clearer evidence of Lotus influence appears in the sect's appeal to the commoner elite and in its remarkable buildings. The Gotō, goldsmiths and swordsmiths patronized by the Ashikaga, were long-time supporters of the Lotus temple of Myōkakuji, who wrote in their family code:

As this house cherishes the Nichiren sect, [our descendants] will make Myōka-kuji our memorial temple for continuing generations. Allegiance to other sects is strictly forbidden.[50]

The Kanō (fan makers and painters), the Hon'ami (swordmakers, and later artists and ceramicists), the Suminokura (warehousers and traders), the Chaya (purveyors of dry goods)—all belonged to Lotus temples in Kyoto and often received posthumous names bearing the character "Nichi," a mark of devotion to the sect's founder.[51] Records of the benefactions that made temple construction possible, moreover, attribute large contributions to the leading weavers, *sake* brewers, and salt merchants of the capital.[52]

Conversion extended into the ranks of courtiers and military men as well,[53] but noble diarists tended to convey a certain suspicion toward the sect.

It is said that the Minister of the Center Nijō is converting to the Nichiren sect. At court they say this is not as it should be and that someone should remonstrate with him.[54]

The son of the former imperial regent Takatsukasa entered Buddhist orders at the Hokke temple of Myōhonji. This is very strange. There is no precedent for a son of the regental lineages entering orders at a Hokke temple.[55]

We have been discussing the clerical promotion in the Nichiren sect. [The priest Nissu of Honkokuji was to be appointed Sōjō, the second highest clerical rank bestowed by the throne.] This is something I disapprove of.[56]

It is tempting to read class antagonism into these remarks, although it is just as easy to read religious prejudice or political unease—for Nichiren priests continued to play the Savonarola-like role of their founder in criticizing shogunal politics, and their congregations continued to provoke martial attacks from Enryakuji.[57] In 1465 shogunal officials had to order Enryakuji to desist from an assault with a warning:

Because over half of Kyoto is made up of Hokke adherents, the whole city will be cast into unparalled upheaval when the pious Hokke elders, sacrificing their own lives, lead a war of defense [against Enryakuji].[58]

Even when Japan entered the Age of Warring States, then, the Lotus sect was associated with volatile enmities, with a group of "elders" (*danna*), and with potential citywide upheaval.

For most of Kyoto's residents, the temples of the sect illustrated quite literally the local power of the Lotus. In 1532 there were twenty-one of them. But more impressive than their number was their location (for they stood in and around the urban settlements where no other concentration of sanctuaries existed), and their formidable facades and excellent condition (for they had been rebuilt and fortified after Ōnin while many other religious compounds remained wasted). The temples also had exceptionally bold dimensions: Honkokuji, the Lotus headquarters in Kyoto, occupied twelve square blocks; Myōkenji, eight; Honnōji, four; and other Hokke temples up to three. Honnōji alone was twice the size of the imperial palace and roughly equivalent to the largest shogunal mansion. Outwardly, the temples resembled stockades, since they were surrounded by moats, watchtowers, and stout walls against the sort of attacks that Enryakuji had launched in the fourteenth and fifteenth centuries. Their interiors may well have been lavish, although we know only of the Hokke temples reconstructed later in the century, which stirred the envy of warlords and the incredulity of Portuguese missionaries. But for aristocrats consigned to rented lodgings, for shogun dependent on loans from *sake* brewers, for monks in impoverished monasteries, and for any number of humble passersby, the size and strength of the Lotus temples must have amply signified the resources of their patrons.[59]

Let us reflect again, then, on the position of the Hokke sectarians in the face of the Ikkō challenge. Resources of manpower and money were presumably available (if at considerable sacrifice) to congregations that could sustain a high order of temple construction. But the organization and mobilization of those resources is less clear. We can infer the existence of at least a rudimentary organization from scarce but significant references to "elders," sectarian "assemblies" (*shūkai*), and the gathering of troops before battle at the temples to which they avowed allegiance.[60] References to the Hokke movement as an *ikki*, with its implication that forming a "league" made it possible to escalate activity into an "uprising," contribute to the impression of an organization; so does the fortification of Hokke sanctuaries, with its implication that martial planning guided construction. Finally, of course, we come to the evidence of the *uchimawari*. This sort of procession conveys rallying powers, even as it suggests an emerging process of mobilization. A way of "rousing spirits," the *uchimawari* recruited men to a body simultaneously demonstrating terrible force, custodianship of the city, and the resolve of the Lotus.

The centering of demonstration on Lotus believers suggests that the Hokke sect had emerged as the most formidable institution of Kyoto's townspeople. Although previous displays of defense or redress had engaged substantial numbers and evinced a potential for unified movement, only the tax delinquency after 1527 revealed a growing self-consciousness among otherwise ephemeral acts of commoner resistance. The rise of Lotus adherents in 1532, then, may primarily reflect their superior institutional resources: the urgent task of self-defense that could not be undertaken by unorganized townspeople was spearheaded by their largest, most coherent body. Yet it is likely that the genius of the Lotus uprising derived from an openness of meaning. The heady mix of politics, class war, and ideology discoverable in the Ikkō movement found a counterpart in the Hokke movement.[61] Participants defending Kyoto against aggression could variously focus on the confrontation between city and country, commercial and agrarian interests, Amida and the Lotus. If most of them acted on behalf of work and neighborhood, believers could also protect their temples, fight the heterodox, break the bent, and widen the path. Their principal targets were not forts and villages but Ikkō mausoleums and sanctuaries, which they torched so that "smoke replaced the sky" and then desecrated so that no icon survived in the rubble.

After its opening episodes and the devastation of Yamashina Honganji, the campaign against the Ikkō sectarians moved with greater difficulty. Ikkō troops defeated the Kyoto party in Yamazaki in the fall of 1532, fought successfully in the streets of the capital, and ousted Hosokawa Harumoto from Sakai early in 1533—an event misunderstood in Kyoto as the end of Harumoto. ("Sakai has fallen. The Ikkō uprising has taken it. Harumoto and his retainers are dead. This is unbearable.") But Harumoto and the Hokke sectarians resumed their offensive in the third month and recovered Sakai in the fourth. In the fifth month they marched on Ishiyama Honganji, in Settsu, which the Ikkō forces and their abbot now made their headquarters. Yamashina Tokitsugu estimated the Hokke force at ten thousand men, including hundreds of horsemen, who repeated the *uchimawari* before each attack.[62] The events at Ishiyama Honganji were the last in a ten-month campaign against the Ikkō establishment. Several weeks into an inconclusive siege of the Ishiyama fortress, Hosokawa Harumoto concluded a truce with the abbot and withdrew his troops. The Hokke army withdrew as well. Kyoto's wars of religion between Amida and the Lotus—if this is what they were—ended in stalemate.[63] As religious meanings receded, new campaigns and new meanings emerged.

These campaigns were not really new at all. Let us remember Hosokawa Takakuni, Miyoshi Motonaga, and the debtors' uprisings. Their ghosts and their avengers, absent from the Ikkō-Hokke narrative, were not absent from Kyoto. Takakuni's brother Hosokawa Harukuni (and later his adopted son Ujitsuna) used the distraction of the Ikkō campaign to stage sorties in the capital in the winter of 1532 and to invade it in the fifth and sixth months of 1533, when, in the words of the *Gion* diarist, "Kyoto was empty of troops."[64] Harukuni made camp in the northwestern hills, defeated near Ninnaji a small Hokke party left to defend Kyoto during the Ishiyama march, and then penetrated the inner city to Nijō–Nishi no tōin. At this juncture Hosokawa Harumoto made the truce at Ishiyama and sent the sectarians home to the capital. Compounding the threat of Hosokawa Harukuni was the renewed activity of agrarian leagues around the capital. In the twelfth month of 1532, leagues demanding the cancellation of debts rioted in the capital; and in the summer and fall of 1533 leagues demanding the cancellation of taxes rioted throughout the capital's environs.[65] Caught in violence on all sides, Kyoto's defenders abandoned their unfinished reprisals against the Ikkō army to defend their own urban boundaries.

The Hokke armies now played the role against Hosokawa Harukuni's troops and agrarian rebels that they had played against the Ikkō sectarians. The *Nisui* diarist tells us that twenty thousand Hokke adherents battled debtors in 1532, burning their camps throughout the northern and eastern hills of Kyoto. From the seventh through the tenth months of 1533, the adherents repulsed leagues claiming tax cancellations and local governing rights in exchange for the service they had rendered during the Ikkō campaign.[66] In both cases, the Hokke armies responded to orders from Hosokawa Harumoto:

We dispatch these orders because we hear that leagues of the land are rising. It is ordered that you [the adherents of Honmanji and other Hokke temples] assemble your strength and render loyal service. There is to be no negligence.[67]

In the tenth and twelfth months of 1533, Hokke adherents repulsed the troops of Hosokawa Harukuni in a series of engagements concentrated in the northwest of Kyoto. This action responded to a directive from Hosokawa Harumoto's deputies:

We are informed that the enemy [Harukuni] is on the march from Tanba. It is ordered that the Hokke sectarians of the various temples immediately defend Kyoto vigorously and excel in loyal service.[68]

Although Kyoto was "in a state of extraordinary disorder," diarists reported the success of the Hokke troops: "Everything finally quieted. How fortunate. How fortunate."[69] They also reported devastating raids by Hokke troops on villages that had harbored Hosokawa Harukuni's men:

This morning the Nichiren adherents burned down eleven villages—including Saihendo, Saiin, Yamanouchi, Kori, Umezu, Kawabata, and others. It is unbearable.[70]

By 1534, Kyoto's defenders—still and persistently described as Hokke sectarians—had restored a semblance of peace to the capital. Hosokawa Harumoto entered the city, and the shogun, Ashikaga Yoshiharu, resumed residence there after an exile of seven years.[71]

Kyoto's military and political life had altered profoundly, however, since this shogun had fled the capital in the wake of the troubles of 1527. In what I have called stage one of the crisis, the calamitous rule first of two rival shogunates and then of an internally divided Sakai regime had moved Kyoto's townspeople to demonstration, fortification, and tax delinquency. In stage two, or what we have seen of it thus far, the assaults on the Sakai regime first by Ikkō adherents, and then by warlord avengers and agrarian rebels, had moved Kyoto's Hokke sectarians to ally with Harumoto and conduct martial campaigns both in and out of the capital. Following the truce at Ishiyama, Harumoto—mindful of his debts—addressed the Hokke community: "My pleasure is extreme for, throughout this long encampment and its hardships, you have fully excelled in martial achievement and ardor."[72] And indeed, Harumoto's survival appears to have been critically linked to the assistance of Hokke armies: they entered an Ikkō war his own deputies had not been able to win, constituted "the better part" of the force marshalled against Yamashina, joined him in recovering Sakai after the rout of his own troops, sustained a siege at Ishiyama sufficient to earn a truce, and successfully pushed Harukuni out of Kyoto.

The change in the military situation involved more than the rise of an indispensable commoner army, however. The change also involved a commoner-military alliance that lasted beyond the challenge of the Ikkō uprising with its immediate appeals to self-interest. The alliance survived as the commoner army made the warlord and agrarian enemies of Hosokawa Harumoto into its own enemies, in an unprecedented action that surpassed considerations of martial defense to suggest a political course. Let us note one further change in the military situation: the possible delegation of urban defense, by 1533, to the "Hokke sectarians." The various Hosokawa generals who "led" earlier marches of the commoner army disappear from accounts of the urban battles of 1533 and 1534. Hosokawa Harumoto's direct orders to the sectarians for "loyal service" in the defense of Kyoto may have acknowledged the absence of an intermediate command and the emergence of a once-subordinate force of townspeople as the capital's primary guard.[73]

The durability of this alliance across the transition of 1533 and the new prominence of the Hokke army are best interpreted as seminal political changes. The documentation is not large, but it is arresting. Here, a sample of the principal texts.

No. 1.   *Sanetaka kō-ki*. 1533, 2d month.

14th day.   At nightfall I had a letter from Nijō's wife saying that the son of her husband's wet nurse—a priest of the Ikkō sect from Saihōji temple in Fushimi—was apprehended today on the road. People from a temple of the Nichiren sect did this. . . .

15th day.   When I returned home there was another letter from Nijō. Last night the prisoner was killed. How awful. How awful.[74]

No. 2.   *Tokitsugu kyō-ki*. 1533, 2d month, 18th day.

I hear that members of the Nichiren sect have apprehended several arsonists. Because there was to be a formal assembly of the community [to decide their fate], Sanjō Asō and Jimyōin and I went out together to view the proceedings. They brought forward the three arsonists and immediately executed them.[75]

No. 3.   *Tsuchimikado monjo*. 1533, 12th month, 5th day.

Tsuchimikado Shūri Daibu Ariharu Ason has brought suit in the matter of the revenues from the barrier taxes in Kyoto and its environs, which are properly the vestiture of the Ogawa Bōjō house. We have dispatched a confirmation, conforming to the documents presented by the Bōjō house, that these revenues are, in full, its proper vestiture. It is ordered that, in the event of any violation [of their rights], you are to combine forces with Tsuchimikado [to end the violation].

[Signed by two shogunal magistrates and addressed to Hokke sectarians (*sho Hokke-shūchū*.)][76]

No. 4.   *Tsuchimikado monjo*. 1534, 11th month, 25th day.

Tsuchimikado Shūri Daibu Ariharu Ason has brought suit in the matter of the revenues from the barrier taxes in Kyoto and its environs. . . . Inasmuch as there was a judgment on this case in the twelfth month of the past year, it is ordered again to the sectarians that there is to be no violation [of the revenue rights].

[Signed by two shogunal magistrates and addressed to the temples of the Hokke sectarians [(*sho Hokke-shū shojichū*.)][77]

No. 5.   *Tokitsugu kyō-ki.* 1534, 3d month, 16th day.

I hear that the Nichiren sectarians have asked [Hosokawa Harumoto's deputy] Kizawa, through the agency of the Rokkaku house, for [proprietorship of] eleven districts in Uji, seven districts in Yamashina, and ten districts in Higashiyama. I hear that the request for the Yamashina districts will be supported [by the shogunate]. This is outrageous.[78]

No. 6.   *Gensuke onen-ki.* 1534, 11th month.

Kizawa Ukyō ordered the eleven districts [in Uji] and the seven districts in Yamashina [vested in the Hokke sectarians] and sent out directives on this matter. In response, the imperial court ordered excluded [from the vestiture] the holdings of the Yamashina house in Yamashina. The court answered the shogunate that Yamashina will be managed as in the past.[79]

No. 7.   *Chōfukuji monjo.* 1535, 9th month, 27th day.

The administrator of Chōfukuji temple in Umezu brings suit in the matter of various wet and dry fields that are the property of the temple and its submonasteries. We order that, conforming to the rights of [Chōfukuji's] vestiture, you are to expel all persons causing offense and to carry out fully all related business.

[Signed by two shogunal magistrates and addressed to the Hokke sectarians of the five temples.][80]

No. 8.   *Zachū Tenbun monogatari.*

The Hokke sectarians have taken power in Kyoto. The government of Kyoto and its environs, which underlies the control of the shogun and the *kanrei,* is entirely an affair of the Hokke sectarians. . . . Among the elders of the Hokke sectarians are those who have taken power in the form of an assembly.[81]

No. 9.   *Rokuon'in monjo.*

[D]uring the time of the Nichiren sectarians, the land rents of Kyoto were not paid. . . . Because this situation obtained for all land rents, our revenues were likewise affected. But since 1537, the various proprietors have had their vestitures restored as they were originally.[82]

An interpretation of these texts must be influenced by two facts about the shogunate: it remained largely an absentee administration until the end of 1536; and its documents tended to be confirmatory decrees about property or rulings in property suits rather than urban laws or criminal judgments.[83] Although the shogun was lodged in Kyoto temples from 1534, Hosokawa Harumoto (the effective *kanrei*), his retainers, and his magistrates traveled from Sakai to Awaji to Settsu to Ōmi. Harumoto visited Kyoto but briefly (in the eighth month of 1534 and the first month of 1535). The chief seat of his administration after the siege of Ishiyama Honganji was Karashigawa castle in Settsu, where he and his men oversaw the continuing military operations. (They also carried on something of a ceremonial life. Yamashina Tokitsugu writes of banquets and lavish exchanges of gifts during discussions of his manifold property problems.)[84]

What, then, of the texts? They hint, first, at the rise of popular justice—whether in the form of vigilante attacks on sectarian enemies (No. 1) or "proceedings" by an "assembly" against alleged criminals (No. 2). Text No. 8 refers again to that assembly (the *shūkai no shū*), peopling it, though still anonymously, with certain of the "elders" (patrons or leaders, *danna*) of the Hokke sect. Normally descriptive of lay benefactors, the word *danna* probably refers to prosperous townsmen, not clerics. The reports make no allusion to "official" police or judicial privileges and hence may suggest the sort of independent initiative apparent in the raid by Hokke troops on the eleven villages linked with Hosokawa Harukuni. In Nos. 3, 4, and 7, however, we find shogunal deputies empowering the Hokke adherents to conduct official business: they are charged to eliminate violations at the capital's barriers (to close illegal toll stations, to collect and properly channel fees) and to suppress lawless conduct at a temple in Umezu. The blanket forms of address in these documents, mystifying any effort to identify a Hokke leadership or structure of authority, sustain the portrayal of the sectarians as an undifferentiated horde, which we have encountered with troubling consistency. (The point is all the more vivid when we pause over the elaborate designation of the aristocratic plaintiff in No. 3 as "Tsuchimikado Shūri Daibu Ariharu Ason.") The ambiguity in the documents about "violations" also raises the possibility that it is the sectarians themselves who are preying upon toll revenues and fields. In Nos. 5 and 6, we discover that the popular assumption of police and judicial power has led to demands for proprietary power. Reputedly seeking control of twenty-eight agrarian districts around the city, the Hokke sectarians encounter vehement opposition from courtiers but (reputedly) some concessions from military officials. These would-be entrants into the proprietary class are also dealing insults to the old proprietary elite by withholding land rents in the capital (No. 9).

It is possible to place a soft interpretation on these texts, which emphasizes the ambiguity of the situation the texts describe and thus resists any radical characterization of the Hokke years. This interpretation would find nothing new in popular justice and tax delinquency; it would account for the police powers of the townspeople in the distractions of an absentee shogunate. It would also raise doubts about the size and representativeness of any Lotus "movement." If it advanced an argument on the basis of the texts, that argument would be guarded: in the vacuum of power created by shogunal wars, some (limited) body of townspeople took on (limited) functions of urban rule under the aegis of military officials, and this experience of a police role led (some) commoners to pursue rewards in the form of agrarian revenues. The pursuit of such rewards, combined with the general mobilization of townspeople and their emergency police powers, may suggest a new activism among commoners. Still, these commoners remained subordinate to military men, and dramatic change in political relations remains undemonstrable.

The hard interpretation of the texts, the only one that seems in accord with the unfolding events of the Lotus uprising, would find political relations profoundly and demonstrably changed. It would begin with the *Tenbun monogatari* (No. 8)—with the perception, there and elsewhere, that "the government of Kyoto . . . is entirely an affair of the Hokke sectarians"[85] and that the period after 1532 was "the time of the Nichiren believers." This interpretation would emphasize not just the opportunistic entry of commoners into a government deserted by its embattled officials but also the calculated efforts of commoners to join the governing elite as part of a new structure of power. The interpretation would find in Hosokawa Harumoto's otherwise baffling absence from the capital a sign of intimidation by the townspeople. And it would find in commoner demands for proprietary control (over as many as twenty-eight districts in the home province!) a demonstration of radical ambitions.[86]

Let me begin with an inferential argument. Between 1526 and 1532, the shogunate was rent by trouble: the trouble lasted a long time, without promise of a successful transition to a new regime; it kept major claimants to power out of Kyoto but returned brutal fighting to the city; it revealed the dependency of shogunal contenders on lesser provincial castellans who were divided among themselves and unable to achieve a military settlement; it forced Hosokawa Harumoto into an alliance with

Ikkō armies; and it resulted in war between Harumoto and these Ikkō armies. During these years, the townspeople of Kyoto had engaged in acts of protest (street battles, fortification, tax delinquency) that heightened their awareness of their resources and opened the possibility of bolder acts. Then in midyear of 1532 those townspeople allied with Harumoto to battle the Ikkō movement—in large measure to defend the city, in significant measure to suppress rival sectarians, and in some measure to fill a military role in which Harumoto's provincial deputies had failed. Although frequently opposed to Harumoto, the townspeople found occasion in their mutual peril to reforge political relations by turning from protest to alliance. In effect, the pursuit of political gain, typically the stuff of martial unions, influenced this compact as well. And ten months later, after often-victorious military service, the issue of gain was ready for negotiation. The issue had acquired a certain urgency, moreover, because the townspeople were now waging fresh campaigns for Harumoto in Kyoto—campaigns that did not respond to visceral sectarian feeling or cataclysmic threats to the capital and, hence, operated more purely according to the calculus of reward.

The actions of the townspeople in 1533 against "leagues of the land" deserve attention since the agrarian uprisings also engaged the problem of reward. The armed farmers of Yamashiro had joined in marches against Ikkō armies in 1532–33 and, from 1532, had withheld half of their taxes as a price for service.[87] When shogunal officials judged the price "intolerable" and ordered that "taxes be promptly rendered as of old,"[88] the leagues organized attacks on the capital and its proprietors to extort concessions through force. They were repulsed, then, by armies of townspeople. The alliance of the townspeople with Hosokawa Harumoto, and against the farmers with whom they might have found a common cause, probably reflected a variety of historical enmities—provoked by the raids of agrarian debtors on Kyoto's brokers, the rivalries between urban and provincial guilds, and the forfeiture of land rights by rural borrowers to city lenders. But let me suggest, too, that by 1533 the townspeople had chosen to identify with warlords rather than rebel farmers both because they had assumed an official governing role and because they envisioned, for themselves, a proprietary claim to rural tax revenues.

The role they were playing was that of the *samurai-dokoro* (the shogunal Board of Retainers), which had defended the home province until the Ōnin war much weakened it and personal retainers of the *kanrei* replaced it. As the new "retainers" of the *kanrei* Hosokawa Harumoto, the townspeople moved from the Ikkō campaign to the Harukuni campaign to the campaign against men of the land—all at official behest. Seeming confirmation of the responsibilities, and the privileges, of their role in defense came with the jurisdiction granted the "Hokke sectarians" over the capital's toll barriers. Like the powers described in document No. 7, this charge evoked the duties of the Board of Retainers[89] and must have appeared as a reward made to important allies by the shogunate. It may have been convenient for the shogunate to delegate this police work, and the delegation may have been anticipated by similar overtures to civil proprietors in the past. Nonetheless, the deputizing of commoners indicates a consequential renegotiation of power, which was also implied by the shogunate's withdrawal from criminal litigation in this period and by Hosokawa Harumoto's continued absence from the capital. That withdrawal suggests either a surrender of Kyoto to a new retainer guard of townspeople or a watchful posture of retreat as the consequences of commoner militance revealed themselves.

By 1534, and perhaps earlier, the ante had been upped again. The concession of an official role to the townspeople brought demands for greater power—the tax rights in twenty-eight districts that retainers of the shogunate, or de facto members of the Board of Retainers, might expect. Here again, at least initially and tentatively, there appeared some flexibility in the shogunal response (Nos. 5 and 6). Yet in the end, shogunal officials supported the old elite: they met individual complaints about tax violations by issuing confirmatory documents of vestiture to proprietors such as Tōji and the Hino house.[90] The confirmations of old interests effectively precluded the entry of the commoners into the proprietary class. The townspeople reacted this time with passive but full-scale disobedience. The observations of document No. 9, variously repeated in the suits of other temples and noble families, describe a return to the sort of mass tax delinquency practiced after 1528.[91] Now withholding not just a half but a full tax on their city lots, commoners took from one purse what they were denied from another. And as if anticipating a violent response, they began renewing the defenses around their neighborhoods.[92]

The response to these events came over the course of six days in the seventh month of 1536.

Rokuon nichiroku. 1536, 7th month, 22d day.

> Before dawn, the Hokke sectarians conducted an *uchimawari.* Later in the morning their fortress at Matsugasaki fell [to the troops of Enryakuji on Mount Hiei]. Because Yamamoto of Iwakura and Wa-

tanabe of Tanaka had turned traitor against the sectarians, the Hokke adherents attacked and burned down the village of Tanaka after midday. There were rumors that they would then attack this temple [Rokuonji].[93]

Hisamichi kō-ki. 1536, 7th month, 22d day.

This morning we watched the procession of the Hokke sectarians at Kaguraoka. They burned down Tanaka, the Mirokudō, and the Kawasaki Kannondō. Their force numbered about thirty thousand men, I hear. This morning, after completely burning down Matsugasaki, the troops of the Sanmon [Enryakuji on Mount Hiei] also carried out a brief procession.[94]

Rokuon nichiroku. 1536, 7th month, 23d day.

Before dawn, the Hokke troops from Ryūhonji were positioned at a fortress outside Ise's mansion. The [Hokke] troops from Myōkenji went to the Goryō barrier. At night the Hiei troops descended the mountain, filling the hills with their torches.[95]

Yuen kishō. 1536, 7th month, 23d day.

There is an altercation brewing between the Sanmon [Enryakuji on Mount Hiei] and the Hokke sectarians of Kyoto. The monasteries of the Sanmon, allying with the temples of Echizen [Ikkō forces?] and all of Ōmi, constitute a force of some tens of thousands, they say. They say they will exterminate the Hokke sectarians of Kyoto.

Is the reason for this the events of last spring? At that time a priest of [Enryakuji] lectured in Kyoto on the Lotus Sutra. Somebody calling himself a Hokke sectarian interjected a number of responses into the lecture, making it into a dispute; whereupon the lecturer was at something of a loss to respond and lost face. The lecture consequently ended in confusion. Because [Enryakuji] itself lost face, people say [the monastery] was determined to punish the Hokke sectarians of Kyoto.[96]

Rokuon nichiroku. 1536, 7th month, 25th day.

The Hokke and the [Enryakuji] troops fought. The [Enryakuji] troops took about ten heads from the Hokke sectarians. People say Gengorō and a horseman from the Hokke side were taken captive. We do not know the truth of the matter.[97]

Gensuke onen-ki. 1536, 7th month, 27th day.

The forces of [Enryakuji] cut into Kyoto. They set fire to the twenty-one temples of the Hokke sectarians and, beyond this, all of southern

Kyoto. More than half of northern Kyoto has also burned. They have attacked and killed Nichiren adherents and various others. I do not know the number of the dead. I think it is about three thousand. I do not know the extent of death beyond this. The Seiganji hall, Hyakumanben, and other sanctuaries have also burned down.[98]

Although joined by troops from the Rokkaku and Hosokawa houses, the assault on the Hokke sectarians was led by armies from Mount Hiei.[99] The doctrinal rivalries discussed in a report of the twenty-third day, and lively throughout Kyoto's medieval history, surely played a role in the debacle. Yet the monks of Hiei offered a broader rationale for their action in an indictment of the Hokke sectarians that accused them of four offenses: digging up private property in Kyoto for their moats; inciting hostility toward believers outside the Hokke fold; freely executing their own judicial decisions; and exacting their own taxes.[100] Here we find an echo of the *Tenbun monogatari*: "The Hokke sectarians have taken power in Kyoto. The government of Kyoto . . . is entirely an affair of the Hokke sectarians." Fueling sectarian feeling was political and social antipathy to commoners who had assumed the governing privileges of the old elite, who had presumed to exact for military service the rewards reserved for a military and proprietary class. If the weak Hosokawa administration was disposed to bend toward forms of commoner rule, the larger community of elite interests exploded.[101]

The devastation of this explosion—the slaughter of thousands ("men and women alike"),[102] the systematic torching of temples, the ruin of over half of the capital—demands a hard rather than a soft interpretation of the political change that preceded and provoked it.[103] The only counterpart to the events of the twenty-seventh day of the seventh month was the annihilation of Yamashina Honganji. And even that did not take so horrible a toll of dead or cut so wide a swath of destruction. This ending to the Hokke story reveals the gravity of a movement that escalated from protest to alliance to the reconception of urban authority, thus exposing fundamental conflicts of class and power. The old elite clearly saw in that movement not a familiar pattern of agitation or self-redress but a revolutionary challenge to its own polity, economy, and social definition. It responded not with the compromises and retreats familiar to wartime politics but with consummate rage.

Just over two months later, shogunal officials posted the following order:

Item: Should any Nichiren priests or members of the assembly (*shūkai no yakara*) remain in Kyoto or its environs, it is the shogun's will that they be brought to judgment. If the priests reenter lay life or mingle into other sects, they are equally culpable. Anyone who sympathizes with them is guilty of a crime.

Item: If there is any household that displays a Nichiren amulet or devotional oaths, that house, the two adjoining houses, and the three facing houses will be confiscated.

Item: Any revival of the sect or its practices is to cease.[104]

An administration whose survival had been tied to Hokke support resolved to banish the Lotus sect from the capital and its hinterlands—by exiling its lay as well as its religious leadership, by using corporate surveillance and corporate punishment to purge all traces of belief, by proscribing all religious functions. In its injunction against laicization or conversion to other sects by Nichiren priests (practices desirable if a change in religious climate was the principal objective of the order), a political motive seems paramount. Here is a commitment to remove physically all powerful persons associated not just with a creed they might have been persuaded to abandon, but with a movement.

This observation returns us to a problem I have continued to finesse: the identity of the Hokke uprising. Was it a general movement of townspeople that, though organized around the city's primary religious institution, transcended religious interest to promote a collective political agenda? Was it a specifically sectarian movement that, though resonant with collective concerns over defense and governance, subordinated political interest to advance a militantly religious agenda? To what extent did antagonisms of class animate political or religious agendas?

In Substitution for a Conclusion

One implicit subject of my discussion and one absorbing problem in the events of these years is the nature of, and the movement between, inside and outside. For the authors of our documents, all members of what I have labeled and frozen as "the elite," the categories of inside and outside mattered profoundly. They too labeled and froze, homogenized and objectified, by casting the many players in this drama as "Hokke sectarians" who formed "leagues" and fomented "uprisings." Differences, personalities, affinities, and complexities were subsumed in a language that allowed "elders" and "assemblies" but otherwise insisted on the sort of leveling and abstraction that everywhere dominates the lexicon of trouble from commoners. The trouble was always "*ikki*"; its makers were "men of the land" or "Ikkō sectarians" or "seekers of debt cancellations"; their numbers, too large for realistic imagining, were "tens of thousands" or "tens of ten thousands." These words, defining an outside, held together an inside. The outside was watched (*kenbutsu*), judged (the attack on the villages was "unbearable"), and subjected to disputes between courtiers and shogunal officials. Observed but not encountered, that outside too was held together.

The identity of the "Hokke movement," its members and their uprising, becomes, then, the more vexing. Did the players in this drama, who remain silent, recognize themselves in the characterization of "Hokke sectarians"? And did the users of the label really intend meanings any deeper than "outsider?"

I have surrendered to the categories of the documents by portraying the events after 1532 as an attempt by commoners to move from the outside to an inside peculiarly vulnerable to opening and redefinition. As the "woodcutter from the mountains of Tanba" laid claim to the capital, agrarian and sectarian turmoil in many quarters responded to a shogunal crisis that invited new configurations of power. In my rendering, the Hokke solution had a conservative dimension insofar as it was founded on a military alliance against shogunal enemies, the enforcement of proprietary privileges over the countryside, and the deputizing of commoner allies as urban officials subordinate to the *kanrei*. Yet in its presumption that the inside was supple enough to bear substantial reconception, the solution also breached the boundaries of class, political hierarchy, and possibly the role accorded religious institutions. The breach proved intolerable to an "elite" that could absorb provincial castellans but not the horde perceived as "Hokke sectarians." Insiders who were unprepared for a radical redefinition of their membership ferociously defended the boundaries.

Where did the will to assail these boundaries come from? In large measure, the Hokke movement was a combination of momentum and self-conscious daring. Like the Yamashiro uprising, the Hokke experience proceeded in logical stages: remarkable military confusion led to protest and demonstration; popular agitation provoked new visions of the possible; efforts at self-rule expanded in the face of retreat or seeming compliance by military officials; devastating reprisals from an ultimately intransigent elite followed. In effect, injury and opportunity and ambition shaped the will to rebel. And these factors may have been sufficient.

Yet let me also—finally—account for the religious passion that I have dodged. I take my lead from the shogunal officials who predicted in 1465 that "the whole city will be cast into unparalled upheaval when the pious Hokke elders, sacrificing their own lives, lead a war of defense [against Enryakuji]." What concerns me here is less the piety or the sectarian philosophy that led to rebellion than the quality of absolute conviction—mortal conviction—conveyed in the document. The sense of unalterable right also apparent in the Hokke slogans ("do not give, do not take"; "break what is bent, widen the path"), fueled by the certainty of zealots, helped fire a movement that spread beyond religious interests (and beyond the sectarian community). The Lotus attitude may have been more crucial than the Lotus beliefs, the ardor of the minority as important as the commitment of the majority.

The religious element that lent zeal to what was also, irreducibly, a class politics set the Hokke movement apart from all other conflicts in Kyoto's wartime history. The difference was accentuated by the extent of commoner participation (townspeople marshalled armies as large as twenty thousand; they were seemingly able to stop the flow of urban taxes to proprietors) and by the ascendancy, for a time, of a military-commoner alliance. Unlike the soldiers of the land from Yamashiro, Kyoto's townspeople did not seek autonomy but entry into a redrawn elite—a vision ironically more radical than autonomy, insofar as it posited an equality between, rather than a separation of, the commoners and their masters. Thus, an inchoate notion that had arisen from the politics of demonstration developed into a new and clear political idea. Suspension and indeterminacy had yielded to purpose. And then to massacre.

One last, bleak note. The categories of inside and outside have also played, if loosely, in my allusions to mimicry. As townspeople forcibly occupied the political arena, they engaged in the politics of force. They demonstrated their power by mass assembly, procession, fortification, and brute violence—such as the murder of the Ikkō priest, the summary execution of the arsonists, and the incineration of eleven villages. They resorted to devastating battle in the ten-month campaign against the Ikkō sectarians and the six-month campaign against Hosokawa Harukuni and the leagues of the land. They sought reward by demanding proprietary rights and withholding land rents. In sum, the townspeople played by rules of war that licensed the force of the self. They employed the protocols of witness, which work through terror; the conventions of military alliance, which require enemies; and the negotiations for gain, which substitute one overlord for another. Moving from outside to inside, the townspeople mimicked the strategies of the warlords who were already there. I do not want to slight the potentially transforming visions of Kyoto's townspeople. Nor do I want to ignore the pathologies they brought with them.

5

Work: The Structures of Daily Life

As the fires died in Kyoto's Hokke temples, the movement of commoners associated with those temples appeared to die as well. In the years after Hiei's raid of 1536, neither armed mobilizations nor guerrilla insurgency revived the battle between the city's commoners and the now-diverse groups—of Ikkō sectarians, agrarian leagues, landed proprietors, and military strongmen—who might be represented as their enemies. The alliance of commoner armies with warlords or other constituencies also failed to recur. Indeed, gone from the Kyoto scene were almost all hallmarks of popular militance. Thus, diarists came to refer in a comfortable past tense to the "age of the Nichiren sectarians," which ended, by their count, toward the end of 1536, "when the various proprietors had their vestitures restored as they were originally."[1] Another symbol of apparent restoration was the return to Kyoto of the *kanrei*, Hosokawa Harumoto, after an eight-year absence.

But is it really possible that the Lotus uprising, the multifaceted emergence over four years of a mass commoner movement, did die in 1536? And, if so, how did the most sensational development in Kyoto's wartime history come to such an end?

Perhaps an explanation for the seeming death of the movement lies in the cataclysm the Lotus uprising unleashed. Within hours on a summer day, a coalition of forces burned the temples of Kyoto's commoners, as well as half the city, and killed thousands of Lotus adherents. Already embattled by agrarian leagues, the townspeople found themselves vanquished by their erstwhile patrons and allies. And if the goal of their movement had been a governing role in Kyoto and a proprietary authority in Yamashiro (a goal that posited both a union of interest with their overlords and some parity between military service and reward), this too foundered completely, leaving supporters bereft of purpose.

Yet the very cataclysm that might explain the death of the uprising might more compellingly explain the birth of a full-scale rebellion, or at least a new insurrection. One recourse open to the commoners was sabotage—arson, the withholding of goods and foodstuffs, night attacks. Amplifying the resources for sabotage available to any urban population were the weapons, money, organization, and martial experience of the sectarians who, though horribly assaulted, were not disarmed or placed under military surveillance. The record, at any rate, reveals no additional policing beyond the requirement of self-scrutiny. ("If there is any household that displays a Nichiren amulet . . . , that house, the two adjoining houses, and the three facing houses will be confiscated."[2]) And further amplifying the resources of the townspeople was the weakness of the opposition. Even though their opponents had gathered together for one invasion, a sustained campaign, especially against guerrilla forces, must have seemed unlikely: Hiei had as often fought against warlords as for them; internal divisions continued to assail Hosokawa Harumoto's armies; realliance of the kanrei with Ikkō sectarians would only invite a replaying of old treacheries; and alliance with agrarian leagues would invite the very negotiations over rewards that had broken the ties between the kanrei and the Hokke adherents. The critical question after 1536 was not whether the townspeople could mount counterreprisals but whether Hosokawa Harumoto could hold the capital without their help.

Nonetheless, a sullen calm descended on Kyoto. To understand this development, we must think again not so much about armed force and its calculations as about normal routines and the constraints they placed on the lives and imaginations of ordinary people. In particular, we must move away from the mass of Lotus adherents (and their corporate opportunities and purposes) to reflect on groups and individuals within the population of townspeople, as well as the price they would have paid for rebellion. We know these groups and individuals best, however imperfectly, as workers. And as workers, Kyoto's townspeople faced mundane imperatives that all but precluded, I think, the choice of resumed insurrection after the Hokke uprising. This chapter focuses, therefore, on the everyday world of labor—which existed throughout and across the divide of Hokke—and the structures that continued to hold together the otherwise-divided communities of Kyoto.

In some respects, this inquiry leads us back into the realm of word wars. The suits brought by Kyoto's residents had enabled them to frame a critique of misrule; they had also protected litigants from some of the specific violations of wartime and larger assaults on traditional identities. Word wars as I have characterized them provided a sort of rampart against trouble. But ramparts can also be prisons. Facing economic crises and dissension among themselves, Kyoto's workers increasingly reveal in their suits a symbiotic relationship with patrons and shogunal officials from which escape was profoundly difficult. The needs of work pushed tradespeople into an accommodation with the elite.

Yet accommodation is not the same thing as closure. Explosions, especially those of the magnitude of Hokke, cannot leave the landscape unaltered. The fissures concealed by compromise or retreat remained open. Hence, here and in the final chapters of this book I examine the slow and often-devious alteration of the political landscape under the pressure of violent confrontation. Change in Kyoto was not a matter of dramatic social reconfiguration after crises. It occurred, rather, as the fissures left by war both bent institutions into new shapes (without breaking them entirely) and diverted conflict into new directions.

In the domain of work, we see the bending—the defiance and manipulation of patrons by their clients, an increasing autonomy among workers, a movement toward new patterns of organization, a changed tone in commercial relationships. Still, my discussion focuses on the tenacity of the traditional commercial order, which finally contravened rebellion among the commoners. But the rebellious energy most apparent in Hokke was deflected into other channels, not extinguished. In the following chapter, concerning neighborhood organizations, I explore an extraordinary metamorphosis in politics that emerged from the Lotus uprising to take form in institutions seemingly compatible with "normal" governance. My last chapter treats changes in the imagination of commoners as they created, in play, a space to redefine themselves in society.

I begin my discussion of work with a general description of workers—how they were named and perceived and organized, what sorts of things they did. I turn then to the dislocations—in importing, produc-

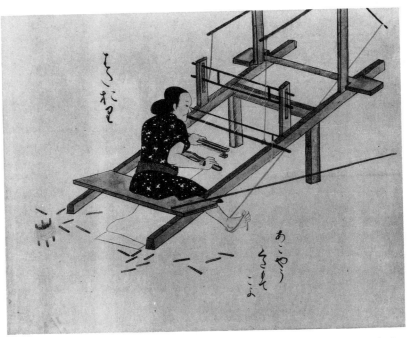

"People of skill." One woman weaving cloth on a loom, another dyeing cloth in indigo.
Detail from the first scroll of *Nanajū ichiban shokunin uta-awase* (The poem contest between seventy-one pairs of people of skill). Copy by Kanō Seisen and Kanō Shōsen of an original work attributed to Tosa Mitsunobu (d. 1527?). Color on paper. Courtesy of the Tokyo National Museum.

tion, and distribution—that help explain their continuing alliance with their patrons. Finally, I consider the skein of cultural issues that caught workers, ever more contentiously, in habits of dependency.

The "People of Skill"

Most of Kyoto's commoners were *shokunin*, a word that later designated craftspeople but, in the parlance of the time, referred more inclusively to "people of skill." The word belongs to the great texts about work—the illustrated scrolls, the lists of regional products and manufactures, the urban directories—that provided panoramic statements on the world of skill for the elite audience that first consumed

them in the medieval period, and for the popular audience of travelers and shoppers and seekers of knowledge that purchased them after the mid-seventeenth century. A supple term, *shokunin* embraced carpenters, metal casters, wig makers, gardeners, stonecutters, all manner of sellers; it also embraced gamblers, lion dancers, breeders of bush warblers, chanters of stories, and shamanesses. The term tended to exclude farmers, or at least those engaged solely in cultivation, although it did cover the peddlers of countless farm products. It also excluded most members of the elite—nobles, warriors, priests—whose skills were not so easy to capture. The emperor, for example, did not belong to the band of the skilled, whereas the more accessible specialists at the fringes of high society (diviners, sutra copiers, physicians) did. In general, then, *shokunin* described workers engaged in the market, who sold goods and services.[3]

No mundane rendering of the word transmits the color of the texts. The pictorial and literary accounts of work drew attention not only to its variety, by juxtaposing mendicant bell ringers with fan folders or palanquin bearers with lute carvers, but also to its many environments. They illustrated the characteristic tools and shops, the costumes and

furnishings, of scores of workers. And they went on to marvelous cata-
logs of the goods streaming from workers' hands: silk figured with peo-
nies or Chinese grasses, gold-flecked lacquer, sharkskin sword sheaths,
persimmon-tinted crepe papers. Such lists were not so much inventories
as litanies of pleasure that evoked an expanding commercial economy
where people of skill became subjects of intense interest and their products objects of spreading desire. At the center of curiosity lay Japan's
economic heartland. By 1635 one list of products and manufactures
identified roughly seven hundred items produced in Kyoto and the
home provinces.[4]

The term *shokunin* had two resonances. Like other homogenizing
words of the time ("Lotus sectarians," "men of the land"), it grouped
and flattened to make workers part of a single, somewhat-curious universe where swordsmiths and vegetable peddlers, silk merchants and
monkey trainers, shared an identity. In folding screens that represent
Kyoto in the sixteenth century, the neighborhoods of commoners are
dense arenas of motion that the near eye makes out as discrete employments but the more distant eye—removed only a few feet from the
screen—makes out as a blur of undifferentiated activity in a field of almost identical shops.[5] Alternatively, the term *shokunin* framed the very
general to focus on the completely specific. It meant workers, but it also
meant the individual holder of a closely defined skill. *Shokunin* designated the drum teacher or the player of the horizontal flute, not the
generic musician. It designated the embroiderer or the dyer, not the
generic textile worker. In the handscrolls representing "people of skill"
engaged in imaginary poetry contests, each subject is a solitary practitioner of a singular trade, removed from social context.[6]

But in practice, the workers of Kyoto constituted neither an unsorted
mass nor a host of solitary practitioners. As represented in suits and petitions, in the decrees of officials, in internal regulations, these workers
made up many particular groups that were defined not only by employment but by organization, the geography of the market, and the attachments of patronage. They were, for example, "members of the citrus
fruit guild serving as purveyors to the Gion shrine." They were "the blue
ash wholesalers of the Nagasaka barrier." They were "members of the
rice guild of southern Kyoto, honorary palanquin bearers to the court."[7]

Distinctively named and placed, these workers belonged, at least in
conception, to an ordered commercial sphere that had developed within
the frames of the late classical and medieval economies. Although the
frames of the past had loosened by the Era of Warring States, trade re-

mained governed by certain durable presumptions: that the goods of
the land fell under the jurisdiction of proprietary authorities; that the
production and circulation of goods required proper licenses from proprietors and due compensation to these patrons from producers and
traders (in cash or kind or services); that relations between proprietors
and subordinates entailed a further exchange of protection for deference.[8] Like the society and the polity that had produced it, this economy was a creature of privilege, control, and vertical organization.

The commercial documents of wartime speak insistently of licenses—"documents of proof," "shogunal decrees," "imperial decrees"—which identified rightful groups of workers. They divide the
world between the insiders with licenses and patrons, and the outsiders
without them who violate "things as they should be." The latter are
"villains" who "plot new and devious schemes"; they behave "selfishly";
they inflict "grave trouble" in a manner "unseen and unheard in the
past." The structures of patronage, the exchanges of deference for protection, emerge as bulwarks of "the Way," creating "permanent and
peaceful good relations."[9]

As the contention apparent in this language indicates, Kyoto's commercial sphere was something less than orderly. Not only did insiders
and outsiders confront each other; insiders too struggled among themselves and with their patrons, bending the structures of trade into new
configurations. Workers once bound to their patrons as servants were
achieving greater parity in increasingly contractual relationships
through which business fees (rather than tribute) bought specific trade
rights. Workers began writing internal codes to regulate their own conduct, narrowing the control of their patrons, and even changing patrons. The exchange of deference for protection was accompanied by
mutual suspicion and anger. Nonetheless, the striking feature of surviving commercial documents is the tenacity of old structures and presumptions. Thus, a sample of documents from the years after the
Hokke uprising:

1540, 12th month.

> The six members of the guild of salt wholesalers bring suit [to the
> shogunal administration]: From of old, the six men of this guild have
> conducted business. But recently Hasegawa Yoji, though not a mem-
> ber of this guild, has unscrupulously stolen shogunal decrees and
> likewise the pronouncements of [the *kanrei*], and so engaged in the
> salt trade. Plotting new and devious schemes, [he has behaved] out-

rageously. We would know the profoundest respect if, inasmuch as [Hasegawa] is not in our guild, you would hear our suit and, conforming to our many documents of proof, reissue a decree like those of the past concerning the rightfulness of our guild trade from of old.[10]

1548, 8th month, 22d day.

The members of the rice guild of southern Kyoto, honorary palanquin bearers to the court, bring suit [to the shogunal administration]: The exemption of our guild members from various taxes, by imperial favor, has not changed. However, because our documents of proof were lost in the disturbances of last year, we would know the profoundest respect if you would reissue a decree and order that the rice trade should proceed as of old and that, conforming to guild law, illicit peddling is to cease.[11]

1539, 12th month, 30th day.

The following has been ordered in accord with the wish of twenty residents of Kyoto, conveyed in a jointly signed petition, that they be newly added to the group collecting taxes from the *sake* brewers and pawnbrokers (*nōsengata*):

In the matter of tax collection from the brewers and brokers of Kyoto and its environs: Inasmuch as the twenty men submitted a joint-signature petition, it is ordered that they be appointed as collecting agents. A shogunal decree will be issued to the effect that they are to hand over the taxes, every month, to the shogunal treasury official for the shogun's use.

In gratitude for their appointment as tax collectors, the men [each?] conveyed 300 *hiki*. Sano, Nakayama, and Yasui came here [as representatives of the group to deliver the gift]. They also gave 500 *hiki* to [the shogunal official Masuda]. I understand they will continue to offer 100 *hiki* each month. Another 100 *hiki* will go to [the shogunal official] Dōun.
[From the diary of Ninagawa Chikatoshi, of the shogunate's Board of Administration.][12]

The last document is the most arresting. Collectors of taxes from Kyoto's brewers and pawnbrokers, the *nōsengata* were brewers and brokers themselves, who received official appointments from the shogunate to collect monthly business fees from their peers. The brewers and brokers of Kyoto made up the city's largest and most affluent commercial group, constituting what was most likely a commoner elite. The docu-

ment cited above suggests that their organization did not crack notice-
ably after 1536. Twenty new men were willing to pay, and to pay well,
for the apparent privilege of appointment by the warlord regime that
served as patron to the brewer-brokers.

What made for this continuing alliance? Why did the structures of
patronage hold after the Hokke uprising?

In considering these questions, I look at the groups of workers who
dominated Kyoto's economic life: those who brought goods into the
capital, processed or finished items there, and distributed products both
within Kyoto and beyond. Although these categories are foreign to contemporary documents, they usefully organize our understanding of the
commercial scene and its challenges. I exclude from my discussion three
other categories of workers who infrequently enter the record. The
smallest group included the providers of myriad services—mediums,
dance teachers, hair dressers, prostitutes—who plied trades in such defining urban spheres as entertainment, instruction, and healing. More
numerous were the servants, including temporary or day laborers as well
as regular retainers, who were attached to households and institutions
in a range of menial and more prestigious positions: sweepers, porters,
grooms, preparers of food, wet nurses, guards. Finally, a large number
of farmers worked land held, at least nominally, by noble and religious
proprietors outside the fortified urban "islands" in northern and southern Kyoto. Some of these farmers were squatters; others held cultivation
rights. Some ran marginal kitchen gardens; others produced crops like
turnips or tea or indigo for the market. Confined to a relatively small
area within the city boundaries and small in number compared to their
rural neighbors, these farmers may not have been a critical element in
Kyoto's economy.[13]

Once more, then, my questions: what made for the continuing alliance between workers and patrons in wartime? why did the structures
of patronage hold after the Hokke uprising?

The Crises in Supply, Production, and Distribution

Part of the answer, perhaps its most compelling part, lies
in the enduring crisis in the world of work. In the face of multiple challenges, workers found in protected organizations a barrier against com-

petition and a changing market. Within the import sector, crisis turned on the struggle between city people and provincials for control over, and profit from, goods entering Kyoto from the countryside. It turned too, though they appear less frequently in the documentary record, on struggles between city people.

The imports at stake in these contests covered a great range. Food-stuffs dominated, beginning with rice, salt, and salted or fresh fish, and including (only to begin the list) soy beans, barley, citrus fruits, persimmons, eggplants, radishes, turnips, leeks, bamboo shoots, birds, crustaceans, seaweeds and kelps, chestnuts, lotus roots, and tea. Some of these items were processed before shipment. Other major imports were the raw and partially finished materials needed by Kyoto's industries. Kyoto's textile workers used provincial silk thread and undyed silk cloth, cotton stuffs, ramie (hemp), and dyeing and fixing agents such as madder, indigo, lavender root, and blue ash. Other craftspeople used imported iron, tin, copper, gold, silver, mercury, mica, mother of pearl, lacquer juice, paper mulberry, bamboo, many types of lumber, stone, animal pelts, clay, and carbon. Finally, a number of finished manufactures entered Kyoto. Some of them supplied what the city did not produce itself, at least in significant volume. These items included sedge products, bamboo or reed blinds, and charcoal. Others duplicated goods produced in Kyoto, although they were generally judged "inferior." These items included paper, silk and brocade, pottery, metal pots, and kettles.[14]

One control on import traffic was the levying of tolls (as a fixed percentage of value) on goods carried through the barriers at the principal entries to the capital. These were erected, for the most part in the fourteenth century, to benefit the imperial court and the nobility, although on occasion the shogunate and various religious institutions put up (usually temporary) toll stations of their own.[15] The barriers were not a conduit for any trader content to pay a toll and thus break into the urban market, however. They served, rather, as a first check on commerce, which was then controlled by licensed purveyors, import guilds, and monopsonist enterprises. Let me briefly survey the organization of these groups before I turn to their troubles.

Remote descendants of the peasants who once delivered tribute and services to their proprietors, the purveyors paid business taxes in cash or in kind to individual patrons for the right to transport goods into the capital and peddle them there—sometimes in a specific geographical area, sometimes from shelves in rudimentary shops. They typically acquired exemptions from barrier tolls and, to varying degrees, exemptions from retail taxes in the city. Most purveyors of record served the imperial court and dealt in seasonal farm products such as vegetables and fruits, which they probably moved to the capital in rather small loads. Other purveyors served noble households, the shogunate, temples, and shrines; they went by various titles depending on the identity of their patrons. (*Kugonin* served the court and the nobility, for example, *jinnin* served Shintō shrines, and *yoriudo* the Buddhist temples.) Their numbers were not fixed, nor was their trade insulated from competition; a particular item might be handled by several purveyors associated with several patrons. Although the distinction is too fine for a disparate group, we might think of purveyors more as country people, or as occasional residents of the capital, who combined farming with the transport and circulation of cash crops.[16]

Beyond the licensed purveyors, though rarely fully separate from them either in title or operation, were the *za,* or guilds, which also handled imports and sales (often wholesales). Again to draw perhaps too fine a set of distinctions, the guilds tended to be fairly stable organizations of several members, typically resident in the capital, who operated from regular shops that depended on separate purchase agents and transporters from the countryside. The guilds, too, paid business taxes to patrons in exchange for a variety of privileges, which tended to be defined through suits and negotiation. They might acquire exclusive rights to purchase a certain item in specified country places, toll exemptions for their transporters, exemptions from urban sales taxes for themselves, and fair control over distribution in the city of specific products. Thus, for example, members of the Awazu guild received, and ran the wholesale market in, all fresh fish coming to Kyoto through the port of Awazu on Lake Biwa. They were licensed by the imperial treasurer.[17] Members of the citrus fruit guild received and marketed citrus fruit produced in Yamashiro province under license from the Gion shrine.[18]

Monopsonist or monopolist enterprises went frequently by the name of guild (*za*), and their members by the title of purveyor (*kugonin*), although they were also called *ton'ya* (or *toiya*). The word describes businesses involved in the storage and wholesale of goods and, particularly later, businesses involved in the transport of goods—activities that could be combined in a single, multistage enterprise but more commonly remained separate. They can be distinguished from import guilds less by their functions, however, than by their greater success in acquiring exclusive purchase rights to the provincial goods that they then distributed as wholesalers. Full monopsony (or, more properly in most cases, oligopsony) management was rare in wartime Kyoto. Nonetheless, a number of *ton'ya* acquired a strong hold either over specific imported items (like blue ash, iron, mica) or over a range of items from a specific province. Many of these goods were precious and unusual products from particular locales (which were more susceptible to control than common cash crops), although *ton'ya* handled a number of foodstuffs as well.[19]

For example, a group of rice merchants purchased all (or most) rice carried into Kyoto and sold it from two wholesale markets on Sanjō and Shichijō avenues. This enterprise was licensed by the imperial court. Six wholesalers, licensed by the imperial regent, had exclusive purchase rights to all salt carried in from the Yodo market. The Mibu house protected eight or more purchasers of copper from Settsu, Bizen, Bitchū, and Mimasaka. The imperial treasurer protected purchasers of woven silk from Kaga. And the Gion shrine protected the cotton oligopsony as well as the purchasers of the lumber that was carried from Tanba via the Hozu River.[20]

The import trade was organized to afford urban guilds and monopsonies an upper hand over the country producers, buyers, and transporters who worked as their suppliers. Although rural purveyors with suitable patrons might gain fairly easy access to the market in a number of (more perishable?) foodstuffs, other country people faced barrier tolls (unless exempted through their relations with licensed traders), a closed system of distribution, and the control on prices that monopsony purchase brought with it. There were differences, however, between the organization and the actual workings of trade. In practice, city people faced trouble.

Perennial trouble came from smugglers and illicit peddlers. The smuggling of goods into Kyoto, either by slipping through erratically guarded barriers or avoiding the principal entries altogether, hurt the elite proprietors who lost toll revenue. Illicit peddling—or what was called "engaging in direct sales," a phrase that posits a norm of indirect sales to wholesalers—hurt the import guilds and monopsonists as well.[21] Their suits and petitions ring with complaints against "country traders" and "new traders" and "alley vendors" who were bypassing licensed buyers to sell imports on the street. The peddlers ran a kind of black market not only in rice, salt, fruit, and other foodstuffs but also in items like blue ash, bamboo, and cotton.[22]

The volume of this illicit trade is impossible to measure. Its inducements are clear, though, and their unusual strength in wartime suggests that the volume may have been considerable. One of the principal inducements to smuggling and direct sales was turmoil within a transport "industry" caught in the transition between medieval and early modern patterns of trade. As in the medieval period, transport in wartime remained largely a farm by-employment among a range of part-time shippers, porters, carters, and pack-horse drivers with rudimentary organizations. But although medieval transporters had often retailed their own goods, the acceleration in wartime of monopsony both curtailed the functions and constrained the profits of transporters. Very gradually, transporters took the lead of import *ton'ya* to develop the specialized and licensed operations that became commonplace in the seventeenth century. In 1543, for example, a group of pack-horse drivers successfully petitioned the shogunate for exclusive rights to carry and to store all salted products moving on the road from Ōtsu to Yamashina and through the Shirudani barrier into Kyoto. But wartime shippers more typically found themselves bound disadvantageously to licensed buyers. Anger sometimes took the form of attacks on toll barriers. It also took the form of the once-routine peddling that was now forbidden.[23]

Peddling was invited, moreover, by weak policing in a commercial world that relied on consent rather than force to operate. Licensed traders under siege railed against the interlopers and asked for new decrees in formulaic complaints oddly lacking in references to punishment: "[Our competitors] have been conducting business again with exceeding selfishness and our business suffers. . . . Accordingly, we would know the profoundest respect if you would issue another decree . . . that lawless commerce is to cease. . . ."[24] The resulting decrees condemned the interlopers and demanded that they desist in equally formulaic judgments lacking in references to punishment: "We hear of late that, violating previous policy, the pack-horse drivers are selling rice directly to small retailers. This is entirely not as it should be. . . . Such new practices are to cease."[25]

Surely concealed here are official and vigilante acts of reprisal—the confiscation of peddlers' goods and carts and animals, and perhaps even the beating of the vendors. But the dominant image in the documents is of a porous market protected by respect for patrons and their licenses—a respect, even if instrumental in peacetime, that wavered in a culture of lawlessness. The respect of insiders for the system that protected them was, itself, a problem. What, then, of outsiders, many of them producers and transporters from the home provinces who were heirs of, or parties to, the Yamashiro provincial uprisings, the debtors' marches, and the leagues of men of the land? The major official activity of Kyoto's commoners during the years of Hokke ascendancy was the policing of the barriers. An admission of the shogunate's inability to do this job, the deputizing of commoners also acknowledged an acute need to enforce control on the import market and a powerful community of interest among the patrons and the city people who suffered from its absence.

More important influences on illicit peddling were the increasing production of cash crops in the home provinces and mounting competition among rural suppliers for the urban trade. Kyoto's commercial problems did not arise from a scarcity of goods; the documents describe struggles for profit and market access, not for expanded supply.[26] Surviving figures from one barrier, for example, show a fourfold growth in toll revenue during wartime.[27] Much of the increased traffic was associated with "new traders"—generally, country merchants without patrons who simply paid their tolls and then broke into the city markets as mavericks. But alliances were also arising between farmers producing cash crops and courtiers looking for the business taxes of new purveyors to sustain themselves. Soon after the Ōnin war the imperial treasurer collected fees from more than 250 peasants who were permitted to enter Kyoto without paying barrier tolls on their goods.[28] Similar alliances developed between "new traders" and the patrons of guilds and monopsonies. Again to increase business taxes, patrons enlarged the membership of certain wholesale enterprises (in cotton and bamboo, for example) to accommodate country merchants.[29] But whether they were absorbed into patronage networks or consigned to the sphere of mavericks, these traders appear part of a swelling commercial economy that put unusual pressure on Kyoto's import organizations.

Thus, even though the volume of the illicit trade cannot be measured, we can still take account of the separate and combined problems—the grievances of transporters, the permeability of an ill-policed market, the increases in trade goods and country merchants—that altered the balance of control between city people and provincials. And smuggling and peddling were by no means the only indications of trouble. Import control was strained when the country suppliers of guilds diverted goods to the periodic markets outside large towns and when producers broke monopsonies altogether by refusing to sell to them. (Indigo producers just south of Kyoto, for example, succeeded in breaking the indigo *ton'ya*.)[30]

A further challenge to Kyoto's wholesalers came from a new breed of traders: the *goyō shōnin,* or privileged merchants in the service of daimyo houses, who were emerging in some domains by the late fifteenth century and becoming fixtures of domainal governance by the mid-sixteenth. The eclipse of Kyoto people by these new men is best documented in the case of the ramie (or raw hemp) trade between Echigo, where ramie was mainly produced, and the capital. Exclusive rights to buy, transport, and sell Echigo ramie had once been held by an urban guild (which operated out of Tennōji as well as Kyoto) licensed by the noble Sanjōnishi family. The Tennōji branch of the guild collapsed after 1497 when the Uesugi, daimyo of Echigo, canceled the guild's tax exemptions at toll barriers within this province. In succeeding years, the Uesugi replaced the Kyoto branch with an "Echigo guild," headed by a local merchant, which took over all aspects of the hemp trade in Kyoto and other towns. The Echigo guild paid fees to the Sanjōnishi house for sales rights in the capital, but control over this trade effectively shifted from Kyoto to the provinces.[31] Similarly, the Imagawa daimyo of Suruga organized the trade in locally produced madder under a Suruga merchant.[32] And other challenges (to the copper market in Tanba, the gold market in Kai, the silk market in Kaga, the iron market in Bitchū) accompanied the consolidation of daimyo power throughout the provinces. In effect, Kyoto's wholesalers faced not just the injury to licensed trade caused by an increasing and unpoliced supply but also the potential transfer of control to domainal lords and their privileged merchants.[33]

Kyoto people could survive the transfer only as subordinates of daimyo patrons and their organizations. Indeed, they already had experience of outside control. The most famous commercial organization of medieval and early modern Japan was the Ōyamazaki oil guild, which was operated from, and licensed by, the Iwashimizu Hachiman shrine, a few hours' journey southeast of Kyoto. Members of the guild purchased sesame seeds in western Japan, processed the oil at Iwashimizu, transported it to affiliated wholesalers in Kyoto and other towns, and even controlled retail outlets. A huge enterprise, the guild had sixty-four members resident in Kyoto by the late fourteenth century. Although largely oriented to the Kyoto market, it was not a Kyoto-based operation.[34] Nor was another remarkable organization—the sedge hat guild of Fukae in Settsu province, which oversaw the production of hats by farmers in that area, transported and then sold them in Kyoto, Nara, and other towns. A single man reputedly formed the guild in the Warring States Period by uniting groups once under the control of different patrons and subsequently buying off the patrons with new business taxes.[35]

Such examples of the multistage organization of commerce are rare in wartime. Among them, Kyoto leadership was surprisingly absent. In the face of outside challenges, Kyoto's importers did not conspicuously seize the initiative to break new ground. They responded to crisis by invoking repeatedly the privileges conveyed by their patrons. Before we reflect again on this response, let us consider Kyoto's other economic sectors—the spheres of production and distribution—and the problems there.

Workers in the capital doubtless pursued many of the more humble trades—hulling rice, pickling vegetables, carding cotton, preparing hemp fiber. These employments tend to be hidden from the documents, however, and hidden, too, from the occasionally closer portraits we have of communities. A rare census report of 1593 from the neighborhood of Reizen (also read Reizei) and Muromachi lists fifty-nine workplaces and shops: workers produced or sold oil, charcoal, silver, copper, tin, needles, pongee, woven cloth, Buddhist vestments, *obi* (two shops), embroidered cloth (two), gold-flecked lacquerware, sword sheaths (two), armor (three), leather goods (three), blades, bamboo blinds, brushes (three), fans (eleven), umbrellas, tea scoops, paintings (three), medicines, *sake*, and rope (two); also living in this neighborhood were a metal forger, a thread spinner, five carpenters, three exchangers of coins, an otherwise unidentified "merchant," and a person of unclear employment.[36]

The neighborhood of Reizen-Muromachi was located in northern Kyoto's commercial center and may have been untypically dominated by trade in luxury goods. Nevertheless, the portrait we have of Reizen resembles the portrait we have of wartime production in Kyoto more generally. Commercial documents of the time, often generated by the more prosperous craftspeople in the fine trades, depict a city disproportionately producing rich textiles (superior dyed cloth, figured and glossed silk, embroidery), metal wares, military gear (long and short swords, bows and arrows, armor, saddles), and a range of other precious manufactures: fans, ink stones, paper, cypress bowls, and so forth.

Like Kyoto's importers, producers had patrons to whom they paid business taxes in exchange for protection from competition. Some craftspeople, such as the master of the lathe whom we encountered in

Chapter 3, produced (and probably sold) goods as individual purveyors licensed by (usually noble) patrons. Most carpenters and certain metalsmiths tended to work as individual purveyors, though it is likely that they managed sizable workshops and even satellite groups of manufacturers.[37] Other craftspeople were organized into guilds protected by either nobles or religious establishments. Shogunal patronage was unusual but weighty.[38] Although the scope of activity in particular guilds is often vague, some clearly engaged in several stages of production whereas others covered a single stage.[39] For example, the Konoe house protected the gold and silver foil guild and the Kuga house protected the guild of leather workers. Folders of fans were patronized by the court Bureau of Carpentry (and by the shogunate itself), paper makers by the court Bureau of Books and Drawings. The Gion shrine protected the producers of arrows, also the producers of brushes. The shogunate protected the weavers of figured and glossed silk as well as the forgers of iron and bronze pots, kettles, and bells. Some of these enterprises remained small, but some became extensive: the guild of fan folders, who also sold fans, included "original," "middle," and "new" members who operated shops across the city.[40]

No enterprise, however, could rival the *sake*-brewing industry in size. Reduced from its pre-Ōnin peak, the industry nonetheless included in wartime about 150 firms. Most of them both produced and sold *sake*, although pure retail operations began to increase in the sixteenth century. All owed business taxes to the shogunate, patron of the industry from the end of the fourteenth century, and provided the regime with its largest regular income. Usually levied against the volume of *sake* produced in two annual brewings, business taxes were collected by the *nō-sengata* in monthly installments that ranged, by firm, from 16 to 200 *mon*. This range suggests the diversity of a far-from-monolithic industry, with substantial organizations (possibly involved in an export trade) as well as minor businesses with sidelines in retail sales of rice or lumber or other goods. Many brewers also fermented bean paste and most served as pawnbrokers—activities separately taxed by the shogunate through, again, the *nōsengata*.[41]

As they appear in the documentary record, the troubles of Kyoto's wartime producers arose from familiar competition within traditional enterprises. Malt makers protected by the Kitano shrine continued venomous attacks against the *sake* brewers who preferred to make their own malt. The weavers of figured silk (protected by the Madenokōji house) struggled with the weavers of glossed silk (protected by the shogunate)

until, in 1547, the two guilds merged under shogunal patronage. The
shogun's silversmith, like the shogun's master of the lathe, railed against
imposters. A maker of sweet rice cakes appealed to the shogunate for a
monopoly on five varieties of sweets also produced by members of a rice
cake guild.[42]

The documents do not reveal significant war-related alterations in
production. Kyoto did not, for example, become a center of musket
manufacture when the industry began to expand elsewhere in the latter
part of the sixteenth century. If the manufacture of traditional arms increased substantially, if textile production expanded and changed course
to outfit armies, if leather goods or medicines or cured foods came to
play a bigger role in the economy—the record is silent. Nor do we find
traces of a large-scale immigration from the countryside by refugees
who brought rural crafts to the city or changed the organization of the
workforce.[43] In short, rather than dislocation and redirection in the pro-
ductive sector of Kyoto's economy (developments that may well have
occurred, in fact), we find at least superficial continuity from the medieval period.

Except in the realm of management. Just as wholesale *ton'ya* attempted to control the import trade, so too they took over certain urban manufactures. Producers had generally sold their own goods in the
prewar capital and continued to do so in many major and minor industries. Nonetheless, a division among manufacture, wholesale, and retail
enterprises became conspicuous. Late in the fifteenth century, the shogunate licensed the *obi* guild to wholesale silk textiles, forbidding manufacturers to engage in sales. Wholesale *ton'ya* also distributed long
swords, braziers, and Buddhist prayer beads. This development most
obviously concerned marketing but it also impinged on production: it
enforced greater control and a vertical organization upon manufacturers, narrowing their profits as well as their freedom. Benefits redounded
partly to patrons of the new wholesalers, who received additional business taxes, and mainly to the wholesalers themselves, who constituted a
new body of middlemen. Manufacturers fought this change, if we can
judge from repeated injunctions that they cease the now-illegal sale of
their products.[44] Yet the problem of new middlemen was not simply
one of constrained profits and freedom. It indicated profounder challenges in the realm of circulation, which must engage us now.

Much of what we know about the distribution of goods
in Kyoto and beyond has already been mentioned. The record is surpris-

ingly thin. Certain goods reached the market directly through either licensed purveyors or illicit peddlers. The more notable goods that the documents describe—rice, salt, oil, cotton, lumber, textiles, and blades, for example—were meant to reach the market through wholesalers. Some wholesalers were affiliated with subordinate retailers—in, say, the oil and *sake* businesses—but most retail operations are poorly documented. Urban producers probably conducted a fair portion of them. Although sellers of *sake* sold other goods as well (rice and bean paste appear to have been the main subsidiary items), mixed retailing was probably not common. In any case, retail sales, like wholesales, tended to be taxed by noble and religious proprietors who had acquired jurisdiction either over particular goods or a particular geographical market in the medieval period. Several nobles (the Oshikōji, the Nagahara) taxed retail sales of rice; the Nakamikado house taxed retail sales of noodles; the Bureau of the Palace Kitchen taxed sales of birds south of Sanjō avenue; another imperial bureau taxed retail sales of salt; the Takatsukasa taxed retail sales of fish.[45]

I have noted several problems concerning distribution—primarily illicit peddling and direct sales by producers of goods meant to be controlled by wholesalers—but the shrillness of complaints about these violations deserves attention. The shogunate, for example, responded in this fashion to imports of *sake:*

Although we have previously issued orders forbidding the transport of country *sake* into Kyoto, it is being selfishly brought into the capital under the pretext that it is intended for the use of courtiers and then being sold licentiously throughout the neighborhoods. This is utterly unprecedented. Sellers thus avoid taxes and violate the licensed brewers. With wicked scheming they operate in a libertine fashion.[46]

Brewers and shogunate alike tried repeatedly but unsuccessfully to halt *sake* imports from Nara, Sakamoto, Ōtsu, Kawachi, and Settsu. And as the document suggests, they were foiled in part by nobles who transformed the importers into "purveyors" and collected their own business taxes from them.[47] Again, to return to the shrillness of the complaints, consider this shogunal decree:

Because, of late, violators have licentiously broken the rules of the salt guild, devised strategies, brought these goods into Kyoto, and selfishly sold them, the business taxes have decreased. This is reprehensible.[48]

Or this shogunal decree to members of the *obi* guild, wholesalers of silk textiles:

We understand that the weavers are retailing directly and forcing sales on monasteries and temples. We also understand that, calling themselves retainers of the nobility, they are claiming exemptions from business taxes. These are utterly unspeakable offenses. The selling of silks recently without proper appointment is entirely corrupt. You are immediately to conduct your affairs in accord with precedent.[49]

Let me cite one further instance of what seems to be a disproportionate, and therefore arresting, response to trouble. This case is a thirty-year quarrel that we have briefly remarked before, between the noble houses of Takatsukasa and Yamashina over the conduct of the Awazu guild, whose members were licensed to wholesale fresh fish imported from Lake Biwa. The quarrel turned on the expansion of the guild into salted fish and tidal produce (items handled by rival organizations) and into direct retail trade, over which the Takatsukasa had tax jurisdiction. The latter inveighed against these transgressions to the shogunate, complaining particularly about the guild's recruitment of other fish dealers as affiliates and its refusal to pay retail taxes (because of the protection of the Yamashina house). The case is both mundane and exemplary in its duration, the acrimony between rival patrons, the inefficacy of repeated shogunal intervention (on behalf of the Takatsukasa), and the seeming insignificance of the money at stake.[50]

Shrill language and disproportionate responses have many sources—models in customary legal battles (though the wartime documents stand apart from their predecessors in intensity) or the momentum of the fight, for example. But much of Kyoto's conduct of trade in wartime appears to me symptomatic of the economic change that threatened the city. On the one hand, supply was increasing—a phenomenon that cannot be quantified for this period yet is clear from the growth of toll revenues, the larger numbers of licensed and maverick purveyors, and anecdotal evidence about swelling imports of *sake* or salted goods or the like. The increase in rural production for the market resulted in deflationary pressures and in organizational pressures as well: competition weakened the control of guilds and monopsonies as new traders engaged in smuggling or found eager patrons. On the other hand, demand presented real problems. Both regional and national demand were almost certainly increasing along with (if not fully in line with) supply. The challenge before Kyoto's merchants was to respond to this demand. And here the threats of the changing economy were felt most keenly, for they centered on consumption patterns within Kyoto and the organization of the export market. My analysis of these problems is inferential; there is little direct and even less quantitative evidence about the circulation of Kyoto's goods in wartime. There are significant signs of trouble in the process of distribution, however, which will lead us back to a discussion of the commercial suits and their meanings.

Until wartime, Kyoto's economy thrived on internal consumption. Manorial taxes from the provinces sustained a high level of consumption by the courtly nobility and the vast religious establishment; a variety of military taxes from the provinces sustained a high level of consumption by the shogunal bureaucracy as well as the large entourages of *shugo* from central and western Japan who resided in the capital. But war occasioned, in the first instance, a probably severe depletion (although we have no figures) through the full-scale departure of *shugo*, the collapse of major portions of the shogunal administration (the shogunal guard and the Board of Retainers), and the flight of some portion of the noble and religious population. Any replacements among the military ranks, moreover, were rotating and lower-ranking retainers without substantial incomes.[51] The income of the capital's surviving elite, more than its numbers, figured in the health of Kyoto's economy.

Here again evidence is largely anecdotal, but it all points to distress. Almost 90 percent of imperial landholdings ceased generating revenue for the court in wartime.[52] Provincial rebellion also cut off most estate income due to nobles and religious institutions. Aristocrats raised money as they could—pawning mosquito nets, selling manuscripts, lecturing on the classics in the provinces, practicing medicine; Buddhist temples sold off buildings.[53] Shogunal resources were more ample, but here too the situation was worrisome. The shogunate relied on forced loans for important ceremonies, imposed emergency rice levies around the capital when peasants on its own diminished holdings withheld taxes, and ordered the postponement of imperial enthronement rituals on one occasion because "preparations of the shogun's summer robes have not been carried out."[54] A significant (perhaps major) portion of shogunal income had always come, in any case, from Kyoto's business taxes rather than from the provinces; thus, whatever consumption the shogunate was able to sustain need not have resulted from the infusion of outside revenue into the city. Given the loss of revenues from Yamashiro through persistent tax delinquency and the far graver loss of revenues that *shugo* had once brought to Kyoto from their own provincial holdings, the wartime shogunate may have constituted a net drain on the capital's economy. And the civil elite put new pressures on the economy as well. As their manorial incomes declined, proprietors turned to (almost certainly heavier) commercial taxation for support—by adding wholesale taxes, licensing new purveyors, and expanding the size of guilds.[55]

Where, then, did the infusion of money come from? In a city dependent on imports, urban traders and craftspeople could not sustain the market simply by exchange among themselves. Extra-urban loans by Kyoto's brokers may have been enormously important, although, again, there is no quantitative evidence to support the contention. Nor is there any record of ties between Kyoto's brokers and provincial daimyo. And what records do exist suggest a pattern of defaulted loans to nobles, forced loans to the shogunate, and debt moratoria that strained brokers' resources. Yet even if provincial lending brought significant capital into Kyoto, exports too had to increase to redress the loss of elite expenditures within the city. In effect, an economy that had once thrived on internal consumption, supported by provincial taxation, had to find new outlets to prosper. Either through the transshipment of imports or the circulation of urban products, Kyoto's traders had to reach outsiders— a particular challenge if these products were damasks and lacquer boxes and ink stones and tortoise shell combs and such.

We have an incomplete picture of the import and production spheres in Kyoto, but the picture of the export sphere is almost blank. Information about foreign commerce focuses on the direct trade between China and Japan, which faced increasing restriction by the Chinese from the late fifteenth century and, more important for Kyoto, violent contests within Japan itself. As the Ōuchi daimyo of western Japan were seizing ever-greater control of this trade from the shogunate, western merchants were outfitting more ships and copper ore from the Ōuchi domain was dominating Japanese exports. The export of fans (presumably produced in Kyoto) dropped sharply after 1468, and although the export of swords (presumably produced in Kyoto) climbed steadily, the price per blade fell by 90 percent between 1483 and 1511. The loss of export revenue was exacerbated by the diversion from the shogunate to the Ōuchi of "gifts" sent by the Chinese throne through the tributary missions and mounting Chinese reluctance to meet shogunal requests for shipments of copper coins.[56]

What, then, of exports from Kyoto to other parts of Japan? We may assume that the various shippers who carried goods into the city left with return loads. It is probable, moreover, that provincial lords purchased goods in the capital through representatives there. And it is likely that long-distance itinerant traders, prototypes of the Ōmi merchants of the late sixteenth century, carried numerous items from Kyoto to provincial markets.[57] Such traders make oblique appearances in the laws of provincial daimyo, who encouraged them with exemptions from barrier and market fees, guarantees of safe passage, or cancellations of debts.[58] They also make an appearance in the planting songs of provincial farmers:

> What a sight! Merchants from the capital
> carrying chests of merchandise on their
> backs, traveling three together.
> In their chests are many, many treasures.
> With treasures on his back he came from the capital today,
> down from the capital with more presents than I expected.[59]

The difficulty is how to measure this domestic export trade.

One factor that seems to me significant, although I am not sure of what, is the apparent absence of export organizations in wartime Kyoto. Merchants there did not respond to restricted urban consumption by directing themselves aggressively toward provincial consumers. Kyoto was not, visibly at least, at the center of a new transshipment trade in basic commodities—as, for example, the Yodo fish market dominated the distribution of salt, salted fish, and sea products in the home provinces; or as the Ōyamazaki oil guild dominated both the production and the circulation of sesame seed oil in the same region. Indeed, Kyoto's wholesale rice market was organized against a substantial transshipment enterprise. We find none of the incentives to trade increasingly characteristic of daimyo domains—toll and other tax exemptions, creation of a futures market, and competitive bidding. Instead, pack-horse drivers compelled to pay tolls and to sell at fixed prices made intermittent war on the city by attacking the barriers. They supplied a market seemingly preoccupied with internal circulation. There were no conspicuous initiatives to export Kyoto's own products either. It is surely possible that existing outlets—itinerant traders, the purchase agents of daimyo—were sufficient to sustain the city. Hence, the absence of export organizations may signify tolerable levels of economic exchange in the capital. It is also possible that their absence signifies a failure to adjust to economic change and consequent stagnation or reversal.

The latter possibility seems stronger. Quite apart from Kyoto's internal troubles (and the constriction of the China trade), provincial commerce was developing sufficiently to challenge the city, which was no longer the unrivaled entrepot of western Japan. Emigrants from the capital during and after the Ōnin war, for example, had helped make nearby towns like Sakai, Ōtsu, and Sakamoto into production centers. Sakai's textile industry expanded and a foundation was laid among metal workers for a major arms industry that, unlike Kyoto's, included the manufacture of muskets.[60] These and other towns may also have become the target of goods once destined for Kyoto, reducing opportunities there for profit through transshipment. Particularly important in this respect was the growth, after the Ōnin war, of periodic country markets, which opened six (rather than a previously typical three) times a month and coordinated schedules to facilitate virtually constant mercantile activity along a circuit within a given region. Ōmi province, along the eastern and southern shore of Lake Biwa, was thus integrated as a commercial region early in the Period of Warring States. Merchants from four coordinated markets there organized a long-distance buying and selling trade that extended to northern Ise. The first recorded "free market" law—a policy that spread through much of Japan in the sixteenth century—was declared in Ōmi, in the town of Ishidera, in 1549. The law opened up trade at Ishidera by withdrawing local recognition of guild privileges.[61] But even short of such innovations, markets in Kyoto's hinterland could lure sellers and buyers by less costly restrictions than those prevailing in the capital.

Regional markets concentrated on the trade in foodstuffs and simple manufactures. Yet as the case of Sakai suggests, finer goods produced in the provinces also came to challenge the capital's trade. Metal work, paper, dyed silks, and pottery became common manufactures. Textile production was particularly notable as some regions (Kaga, Mino, Owari, and Kōzuke) put out high-quality silks and others (in the Tōkai and Tōsan circuits) achieved self-sufficiency in woven goods. Even the most refined items may not have closely approached Kyoto's standards, for Kaga's best figured silk commanded only two-thirds of the price of comparable stuffs from the capital.[62] What is at issue, however, is not Kyoto's preeminent workmanship but the availability of substitute manufactures in an expanding provincial market.

Hence, there are worrisome shadows on the still-blank picture of Kyoto's export sphere. Kyoto's traders evince no conspicuous evidence of an orientation toward the provinces—through export organizations, a transshipment operation, or wartime production. But provincial traders evince an increasing capacity to serve their regions—through expanding supply, locally integrated markets, and cottage or more sophisticated manufactures.

In sum, then, Kyoto's commercial sectors faced two immense challenges in wartime—reduced internal consumption as provincial tax revenue declined and the *shugo* dispersed to their domains, and increased competition from outsiders as the supply of provincial goods expanded and the number of provincial markets grew. These challenges affected all spheres of the economy. Control over imports was eroded by country merchants and daimyo organizations. The strength of the production and distribution sectors was drained by the elite's lost income, rival markets, and substitute manufactures. Kyoto certainly remained the commercial center of Japan. This position was guaranteed by the city's size, the unparalleled excellence and variety of its goods, its extensive transportation arteries, and its continuing ties to provincial warlords. But economic vitality depended on compensation somewhere—most likely in the domestic import sphere—for the wartime depletion of income from rural estates and the China trade. The record is quiet about such compensation.

Partial and deceptive, the record may conceal considerable movement toward innovation. And the lists of precious imports—gold and mercury, lacquer juice, and expensive dye stuffs—should warn us against any dire characterization of Kyoto's trade. Who, after all, could pay for such things in a depressed urban market? Yet there is a difference between depression and constriction. There are also differences between the experiences of divergent groups, and between reality and the perception of it. In a period with so few hard data, in which the growth rates of supply and demand or the size of traded volumes and profits cannot be reliably plotted, analysis must remain conjectural. Certain groups in Kyoto must have prospered during wartime while others retained their equilibrium: the luxury suppliers with connections to provincial daimyo, for example, the producers of bows and armor, the distributors of smuggled and unlicensed goods who undercut the guilds, the "new traders" who found a niche in the market. But many other groups must have suffered real losses or perceived grave threats in an economy they no longer understood. Among these groups were the largest and once most stable of the city's elite tradespeople: the *sake* brewers, who competed with rural producers and never recovered their pre-Ōnin strength in wartime; the weavers, who fought among themselves for a dwindling Kyoto trade, faced challenges from Kaga and Mino provinces, and finally reorganized by merging their guilds and creating a wholesale *ton'ya;* the dealers in madder, hemp, and copper, who were replaced by privileged merchants from provincial daimyo houses; and even the producers of long swords, who probably thrived in wartime but nonetheless organized a wholesale *ton'ya* after blade prices in the China trade collapsed.

This movement toward wholesale *ton'ya* to centralize the distribution of both imported goods and urban manufactures best indicates real and perceived trouble in Kyoto. By channeling (or attempting to channel) goods through wholesale operations and by controlling (or attempting to control) purchase and sale prices, merchants could still squeeze a profit from even a diminished trade. In the face of competition, important Kyoto enterprises responded conservatively to protect what they had rather than to seek new outlets in the expanding economy. For them, change appeared to signal dislocation, not opportunity. This perception is hardly surprising in an established community shaped by the habits of prosperity and stability, which was ill-accustomed to risk and disposed, perhaps, to regard any restructuring as a surrender to the ephemeral at the cost of everything durable in the past.

Thus, the shrillness and the juxtapositions in the commercial suits: at one pole they placed the old, the inside, the unchanged, the conformity to degree, the right, the orderly; at the other they placed the new, the outside, the devious, the illicit, the wrongful, the injuring. In the suits, actual losses combined with anticipation and fear to suggest the importance of security—a security, real or imagined, that litigants continued to associate with regulated trade. Barriers, licenses, added layers of wholesalers—these were the supposed bulwarks against competition. Internecine quarrels, mutual recrimination, rivalries among patrons—these were the symptoms of weakening bulwarks.

Patronage and the Calculus of Attachment

Change in the market may have been sufficient by itself to bind workers in Kyoto to their patrons. But the attachments that survive crises—especially when they provide dubious relief and engender tensions of their own—tend to bind in multiple strands. The exchange of licenses for fees was simply one aspect of relationships that bound workers in varied ways.

Implicit in the preceding discussion but separable from it is the additional role of patrons in regulating the licensed trade they helped create. In practice, regulation meant opening judicial channels to resolve commercial quarrels, a function ultimately lodged in the shogunate. The shogunate also established the basic rules of the marketplace by setting coinage exchange and interest rates.[63] These functions were clearly limited; neither proprietors nor military officials concentrated on such presumably indispensable tasks as policing trade and punishing offenders. Nonetheless, the limits of regulation seem less significant than the obvious importance of the functions that were undertaken and the elite's continuing responsibility for them. The shogunate extended vital services to Kyoto's traders that they failed to provide for themselves. Commoners produced no variant of a "guild regime" to amplify or supplant the shogunal role in regulating commerce. Under official commission, they guarded the barriers during the years of Hokke ascendancy. But we find no larger history, either within or across enterprises, of commercial tribunals, police networks, and trade councils among townspeople.

This retreat from action was pragmatic (though "retreat" may impute too high a degree of consciousness to conduct normally left unexamined). Particularly in confrontations with provincial rivals, Kyoto's traders needed the prestige and authority (however undermined) of the proprietary elite. The elite also became a buffer between city people and provincials in sensitive matters of policy. The shogunate, not an urban trade council, authorized the tolls on rural imports, established the coinage exchange rates that could be more easily manipulated by city merchants than country producers, stipulated the high rates of interest, and decreed the "partial debt cancellations" under terms that favored pawnbrokers over debtors.

Divisions between urban borrowers and lenders, and between many groups of urban competitors, were acute as well. Hence, the shogunate served, too, as a valuable buffer between city people. The development of some version of a guild regime in Kyoto required not only a remarkable shift in mentality but a perception of a common cause transcending divisions. And here were clear problems. Conflicts of interest separated small purveyors and guildsmen and monopsonists, producers and wholesalers, buyers and sellers. So, for example, we find differences between the weavers and the wholesalers of silk, among rival dealers in fish, between the licensed brewers and the importers of *sake,* and between the same brewers and the makers of malt. More to the point, since versions of self-rule among traders usually emerge from the mercantile elite, we also discover differences among Kyoto's leading tradesmen. Brewers dependent on rice imports had clashing interests with the organization of rice buyers who centralized distribution and raised prices. Brewers who sold their own *sake* directly had clashing interests with the silk wholesalers who gained the upper hand over producers.

The advantages of patronage systems, perhaps especially of weakened ones, are flexibility, particularity, and a kind of innocence for clients—who give to and take from their patrons outside larger systems of accountability and corporate order. When traders with profound internal differences resist such a system or temper it with guild councils and the like, we must look for either a severe provocation or a striking imbalance between its advantages and disadvantages. Provocation certainly occurred in Kyoto: pawnbrokers suffered from debt cancellations; licensed tradespeople suffered when patrons took on additional clients, authorized wholesale organizations, supported rival groups, and accepted the equivalent of bribes to allow the provincial representatives of daimyo to supplant their own enterprises. Yet conduct injurious to some traders was beneficial to others, thus diffusing the incentives for change. The mutual competition and economic needs of patrons also made them vulnerable to manipulation by their clients. Tradespeople found themselves able to change patrons, to find new patrons, to organize monopsonies, to break into the ranks of purveyors, and to write codes within individual enterprises that eroded the patron's jurisdiction over membership. Flexibility and particularity were everywhere apparent. And once possessed of a patron and a license, tradespeople found themselves able to sue adversaries through a shogunal office more committed to endorsing privilege than to rationalizing an extremely diverse economic order. The blame for the resolution of a suit, moreover, attached to the elite patrons and judges who had to take sides and set terms, not to a council of guildsmen.

Even without grave provocation, the patronage system might have been broken by disadvantages great enough to overcome its advantages. Two related problems threatened Kyoto: the challenges from outsiders who were sufficiently powerful or numerous to defy the controls on trade; the disaffection of insiders whose privileges were becoming sufficiently meaningless to provoke rebellion. The patronage system continued to absorb outsiders at a cost to insiders. We return, then, to a recurrent question: why didn't Kyoto's tradespeople seek better enforcement of their privileges, either on the part of their patrons or through a police force of commoners? A number of answers might serve well enough—a continuing belief (or hope) that consent to authority would prevail over force; a lack of experience in police control; a sense of problem so great that successful resistance seemed hopeless. Yet I am inclined to another sort of response, which takes account of the opportunism and cynicism among licensed traders in the changing economy.

Many of the commercial documents issued by the shogunate and individual patrons concerned not outside violators of trade privileges but licensed traders themselves.

No. 1.   We hear, of late, that in violation of previous policy the rice carried by pack-horses through the various Kyoto barriers is being sold directly to small dealers. . . . You are to cease these new practices.

[From shogunal magistrates to members of the rice market guild.]⁶⁴

No. 2.   Of late, the merchants of the blue ash *ton'ya*, in violation of past law, have been engaging lawlessly in trade.

[From shogunal magistrates to one of the blue ash wholesalers.]⁶⁵

No. 3.   The offense of smuggling salt and salted goods around the barriers into Kyoto and its environs has been strictly forbidden from of old. As soon as such offenses are discovered, the patron and [salt] guild members will be punished. Because, of late, you have lawlessly broken guild rules, devised strategies, brought these goods into Kyoto, and selfishly sold them, the business taxes have decreased. This is reprehensible. It is ordered that members of this guild understand that all persons who hereafter violate precedent and carry out deviant activity shall be in offense.

[From shogunal magistrates to members of the salt guild.]⁶⁶

No. 4.   Laws [concerning the exchange value of various issues of copper coins] are strictly established. Male violators will have their heads cut off and female violators will have their fingers cut off. If anyone selfishly selects coins [that is, specifies outside the law which coins will be accepted in payment], the violation is to be reported by the people of the neighborhoods. Anyone concealing such a crime shall bear the same guilt as the perpetrator. If there is private justice meted out, people of the neighborhoods are likewise to report it to us.

[Statutes issued by the shogunal administration.]⁶⁷

No. 5.   In the matter of the fermented bean tax: We have previously decreed that since there are many firms that combine the bean tax with the *sake* and brokerage taxes—paying only whichever is lowest—the shogun's tax revenue is lowered.

In the matter of [sales of] clear *sake* in various places in the neigh-borhoods, including all firms from those exempted from certain taxes to small retailers: Those selfishly selling *sake* are numerous beyond limit. Thus, the taxes of original firms are decreasing [as the volume of their trade is reduced through competition]. This occurs through wicked scheming and is outrageous. Even if the original firms are rendering their taxes, the names and addresses and resources [of all firms] throughout the neighborhoods and in all places—even to the smallest retailers—are to be closely investigated and reported imme-diately. All are to render taxes.

[Statutes issued by the shogunal administration.][68]

No. 6.   Taxes from the leather workers of Kyoto and its environs are part of your house vestiture. However, we hear that there are per-sons who are acting willfully and not paying taxes. This is entirely without reason.

[From shogunal magistrates to the household office of former Minis-ter of the Right Kuga.][69]

These and similar documents trace a history, though how deep I can-not tell, of commercial violations by Kyoto's privileged traders. Most complaints inveigh against the withholding of business taxes from pa-trons, typically through simple delinquency (No. 6) or chicanery (No. 5, first item). The third document describes a more complex scheme of collusion between smugglers and city firms dealing in salt and salted products. The scheme defrauds the court of barrier taxes and may, in addition, reduce wholesale and retail taxes as goods are concealed from the record. Although the content of the first two documents is less clear, here too smuggling may be at stake, as well as complicity to evade sales taxes. If rice wholesalers themselves were assisting direct sales from ship-pers to retailers (a suspicion raised by the dispatch of the first document to *ton'ya* members), the issue of bribery or payoffs arises. The second item of document No. 5 introduces a similar issue: the burgeoning of unregistered *sake* retailers, who are reducing the trade volume of older firms and hence the tax revenue of the shogunate. Yet retailers had to acquire their *sake* somewhere—either from importers or from Kyoto brewers. The latter source seems likely here, given the references to "wicked scheming" and "clear *sake*," a superior product first devel-oped in the capital. Thus, we encounter the suggestion that brewers (the "original firms") were conniving with unregistered retailers to transfer *sake* casks to them, to underreport production, and to defraud the shogunate of revenue.[70]

Document No. 4 in this sequence strikes an ominous note in its promise of horrible punishment for violations of coinage exchange laws. Such laws, reissued and recast over time, attempted to deal with a copper currency supply that was both inadequate and diversely stocked (with old and newer Chinese issues, different native issues, broken and damaged coins—all of varied purity). They stipulated what comparative values coins were to be assigned and what mix of coins (what percentage of "good," "bad," and "broken" coins) a seller was to accept from buyers. They invariably forbade sellers to set their own terms of payment. Yet in their draconian penalties, these laws suggest widespread violation by merchants (rice sellers are particularly condemned in one document) of basic market rules.[71]

In short, I suspect that licensed traders failed to pursue the stern enforcement of market controls—either by their patrons or by their peers—because they had accustomed themselves to laxity and its opportunities. Many tradespeople responded to a changing economy by lodging suits or forming *ton'ya;* others exploited what chances they could. Although corruption is inherent in commercial (and other) institutions, the documents of wartime indicate both a growing divisiveness among merchants and a faltering confidence in the very organizations they rhetorically invoked as indispensable in their suits. Tradespeople had divided minds. But even divided minds do not reject systems that provide irreplaceable services.

Patronage remained more than a system for licensing and regulating trade, however. The personal calculus of attachment and the mentality of dependency must also figure in our inquiry into work, for the services that patrons rendered belonged not just to the market economy but to the moral economy as well. As the petition of the lathe master cited in Chapter 3 suggests, issues of identity and prestige shot through the patron-client relationship, taking a mercenary as well as a psychological form.

Let us return to the twenty men who presented a "jointly signed petition" in 1539 to receive shogunal appointments as *nōsengata* (the collectors of business taxes from *sake* brewers and pawnbrokers). One of their immediate incentives was gain, or the hope of it, from tax farming, since these officials retained as a kind of salary some portion of the business taxes they collected for the shogunate from their fellow brewers and brokers. Not surprisingly, within three months of the appointment of the twenty, the chief of the *nōsengata* implored the shogunate to increase the tax burden on the brewers and brokers by 1,000 *hiki*— a startling request unless we assume that a fair part of the sum was destined for the collectors themselves.[72] If the new men expanded the total number of *nōsengata* (we do not know the full size or composition of the group), the increase might have been sought to cover their cut of the spoils. If, as is equally plausible, the new men replaced others (dissidents who split with the regime after the Hokke uprising?), the increase might have been sought to enrich loyalists, or opportunists, who hewed to the shogunate. Either way, cleavages in the brewer-broker community divided not only larger and smaller firms, but also officials and nonofficials, profiters from and payers of taxes, and, possibly, closer and more ambivalent adherents of the regime.

The gains of alliance extended beyond tax farming. As shogunal appointees, the *nōsengata* entered a larger population of privileged townspeople known generically as *kunin* (public people) or *hikan* (deputies), who were in the service of the civil and military authorities. Through customary practice or decree, these public people came to enjoy a variety of tax exemptions. Some were exempt from basic land rents, some from irregular levies on houses or land, some from proprietary exactions of labor and other services, some from business fees.[73] For example, a certain Mizutani, one of the city's major brewers, was excused from business taxes as a special retainer of the shogunate. He probably acquired other exemptions as well, for he enjoyed further appointments as a deputy of the noble Sanjōnishi house (with the responsibility to collect sales taxes on salted sea products) and as head of a guild protected by the court.[74] Tateri Sōkei, another brewer and broker, served (as his father and brother had before him) as "keeper of the imperial storehouses," a position that exempted him from land rents. Kawabata Dōki was a dealer in rice cakes who became an "imperial deputy" excused from both land rents and proprietary levies.[75]

Such biographical information is very rare in wartime Kyoto, yet it is fascinating in its illustration not only of the varied economic advantages open to certain commoners but also of the multiple alignments with the elite some of them were able to pursue. Mizutani was triply a "public person" and eventually expanded his influence as an "elder" in his neighborhood association.[76] More often than individuals, the record mentions special bodies of privileged townspeople, such as the otherwise unidentified *kodoneri* and *zōshiki* (different categories of shogunal retainers) who used their official connections to withhold land rents in properties held by the Hino house in southern Kyoto.[77]

The number of public people in Kyoto is impossible to fix. One wartime record identifies seventy-four in the southern sector of the capital, although this figure may be misleadingly small, inclusive only of shogunal deputies among the townspeople and perhaps solely those accorded regular exemptions from a specific tax. The very compilation of the list suggests an effort to control information about commoner privileges and, perhaps, consternation over promiscuous claims to the perquisites of public people.[78]

This implication of townspeople in official structures of authority was presumably one goal of the elite, which used selective rewards to fold commoners into a community of prestige. The selectivity was surely important. Even though the protection and regulation of trade involved group formation, the appointment of public people involved individuation and stratification. It entailed a movement from the commercial to the more broadly social plane, and the creation of a commoner hierarchy. Insofar as economic advantage partly defined the hierarchy, mercenary interests must have conspired in its formation. But the community of prestige was also defined by more symbolic expressions of honor.

The language and the symbols of honor in wartime Kyoto are often hard to detect and interpret. Some terms, which seem basically descriptive, may have conveyed great dignity: *danna*, for example, which designated the lay leadership of Hokke congregations; *utokunin*, or "men of virtue," which had evolved from a varied medieval usage to designate men of wealth; *shi*, or master, which designated superior artisans; *shukurō* and its variants for "elders," which designated the officials of emerging neighborhood associations.[79] Such terms belonged to worlds of their own, apart from the domains of patronage or elite control, but there were surprisingly few of them. The striking, if predictable, feature of the language and symbols of honor is their overwhelming association with the elite and traditional structures of prestige. For example:

In the matter of the rights to headship of the Kyoto *obi* guild [*obiza zatō-shiki*] and the rights of shogunal deputy [*kuyō daikan-shiki*]: We issue a decree entrusting these rights, as his vestiture [*tōchigyō*], to Kameya Goin'yō.[80]

The official of the Inner Palace Guards, Left Division [*sakon efu satanin*], Yoshimura Naoyoshi, and the official of the Inner Palace Guards, Right Division, Fujita Moriyoshi, bring suit: The rights of officials [*satanin-shiki*] of the palace palanquin bearers have been theirs for several generations. As an imperial favor, they have been granted tax revenues from the clothing guild of Kyoto and its environs.[81]

These documents concerning commoners insistently enumerate honorary courtly and military titles. They also evince an interest among townspeople in surnames and, though we cannot see it here, the use of polite closing forms, for privileged commoners increasingly came to be addressed as *dono*, a term of respect.[82] Especially important, they use the language of property, and even proprietorship, to define the special prerogatives of these townspeople. Rights in land were called *shiki;* so too were the guild headship and income rights of traders. The land vestitures of proprietors were called *chigyō;* so too were the offices of guildsmen. Privileged townspeople were not consigned to separate or alternate categories of honor; they were (just barely) lifted into a prevailing status system that measured distinction in terms of court title and estate rights.

Whereupon some commoners also took on the trappings of courtly honor. Naming themselves as their patrons named them, they signed their correspondence with *kaō,* the elaborate monograms used first by noble and later by military officials.[83] They, or their scribes, sometimes wrote in Chinese. They began to adopt the ritual calendar of the elite by carrying out initiation ceremonies (*genpuku*) for their sons, signifying the passage to adulthood by formally abandoning the name, clothing, and coiffure of the child.[84] On such occasions, and sometimes at the New Year, they received aristocratic guests. They gained entry, moreover, to the residences of the elite where they brought gifts (in the manner of the newly appointed *nōsengata*) or sought counsel (over guild and tax matters) or offered greetings (at New Year's and after momentous events like the wounding of the shogun) or gathered for musical entertainment.[85]

The meanings of such conduct are not transparent. These actions may belong to a world of genuine deference; they may convey either subversive or aggrandizing mimicry; they may signal the appropriation and translation of a culture that was no longer specifically elite. But the consequences of such conduct are less obscure. In conforming to the etiquette of honor, at least some commoners formed habits of behavior, if not of mind, that connected them to their masters and entangled their identities with conventional forms of prestige. And if only rhetorically, they relied on the conventions to locate themselves. Like the lathe master, like the lumber workers from Onoyama, commoners repeatedly centered identity in honorable attachment:

The silversmith Sea Ūemon Saburō Tsuneharu brings suit: Since the time of Lord Rokuon'in [Ashikaga Yoshimitsu, 1358–1408], our house has been awarded the name of Ichijō Sea and has for generations produced the honorable objects [of silver for the shogun].[86]

Time, blood, name, work, service, and patronage fuse here to make a person.

I associate such declarations with what I earlier called a mentality of dependency but might better be described as a reliance on customary frameworks of social definition. Despite massive upheaval, the structures of patronage continued to order work and workers for a variety of good reasons: these structures seemed to offer the best available defense in a changing economy; they provided necessary regulatory functions for traders with little incentive to govern themselves; and they differentiated a mercantile elite that found both economic advantage and social prestige within their compass. In short, the structures stood because they were useful. Yet I have also seen the structures as a complex of ideas, beyond utility, that confirmed familiar identities and, in the manner of the word wars, provided a rampart against confusion. By pursuing noble titles and assuming noble habits, commoners may well have been reconstructing old frameworks and thus exposing the mutability of the status order. Nonetheless, their terms of reference and the prestige they conveyed depended on an elite, hierarchical culture. Although cultural mimicry implies a delight in one kind of confusion (between the genuine and the imposter), it also precludes the ultimate confusion of anarchy; for mimicry can exist only as long as the categories of honor retain meaning. The deep reliance on these categories—whether through deference or through a more radical appropriation—invites speculation about the mentality, rather than the practical and perceived advantages, that bound workers to their patrons.

I know of only one substantial document produced by Kyoto's traders that leads us into the question of vision, or mentality, from an internal rather than an external perspective. The document is not directed to the authorities and not intended for litigation. It is a group of statutes composed by members of the blue ash guild, monopsonist purchasers and wholesalers of a fixing agent for dyestuffs, to guide the organization. Because these statutes were written early in our period (in 1517), and because we cannot compare them to similar records, they can only suggest the mental universe of the capital's tradespeople. They nonetheless resonate with the sentiments of public suits and petitions to indicate certain commonalities of thought.

1. Conforming to the dictates of the previous patron [*honjo*] in 1504, the number of firms dealing in blue ash has been fixed at four. . . . But since the patron interceded when both Sano Matasaburō and the wife of Urai Shin'emon pressed suits to control the business of the Kagame firm, and made a permanent ruling establishing Sano as the principal and the wife of Urai as the second head, there have been five individuals doing business although the number of firms remains four. . . . It is strictly forbidden to conduct business through any other than these [four] firms.

2. Insofar as the number of firms has been fixed in conformity with the wish of the previous patron, permission [to expand this number] is not to be given lightly, even if someone submits old writs of guarantee [*shōmon*] and seeks appointment. All members of the guild must accede in the same mind [to any such request before it can be granted].

3. If there are any merchants who fail to distribute their goods through our firms and lawlessly conduct [direct] business in other places, they will be punished as if they were handling stolen goods.

4. If there is a person in the guild who wishes to pawn or to sell his business rights [*ton'ya shiki*], he must first receive the permission of the patron and then consult the guild membership; only after receiving the consent of all the above may he proceed. . . .

5. Even if you are transferring business rights to a child or grandchild, you must describe the situation to the patron, procure an appointment of succession, and clarify the details of the succession to prevent quarrels in the future. . . .

6. If there is trouble over disagreements in business matters, you must first go through the offices of the patron and only thereafter address the shogunate. Should there be a decree in the matter from the shogunate, it should be issued in the name of the patron. If hereafter there is any person who brings direct suit to the shogunate, it is to be stopped as a violation of precedent.

7. Meetings of the patron and the guild members are held to prevent future quarrels. There is nothing better than meetings of all to secure permanent, peaceful good relations. Each one of us must make paramount the concerns of the patron and know full loyalty.

   These articles are established in conformity with the Way [or principle; *dōri*] of this guild and in protection of precedent. If there is any violation by a guild member, he shall forfeit the writs of guarantee transmitted to him and immediately cease his business activities. . . . We shall make six copies of this document and its specifications, conveying one to each of the guild members and one to the patron. The above is established to instruct succeeding generations.[87]

These regulations tell more than one story. In the very formulation of the code, in its insistence that guildsmen themselves accede to changes in membership or the disposition of business rights, in its leanings toward corporate rule by a body possessing its own Way—we discover a consciousness and a confidence that deny servility. The patron so lavishly invoked here may be a figurehead. He may even be something of a peer, since the code begins to imply parity between guild members and patron in its emphasis on unanimous agreement to decisions.

The alternative story appears both on its surface and in its assumptions. On its surface, the document speaks of the dictates and rulings and permissions of the patron, of the writs of guarantee and appointments of succession that issue from the patron. It speaks, too, of the paramount concerns of the patron, of loyalty to him. It speaks of conformity, sameness of mind, and preventing quarrels. It speaks, quite crucially, of disagreements that must be handled through the patron and, if further recourse is required, through the shogunate. Certainly this rhetorical structure does not preclude manipulation of the patron or struggles with him. Nor does it preclude the sort of cynical abuse of the patron I have noted earlier. To identify an authority, even one whose powers are shared with, or mitigated by, his clients, is not to eliminate conflict. And indeed, every article in this code is implicitly about trouble—internal antagonism, quarrels, violations, and rule breaking. Yet these are troubles of a particular kind—crimes of discord and disobedience—that are premised on a recognition of rightful power.

Thus, this code contains assumptions beneath its surface that are antithetical to revolutionary action: the patron must legitimate decisions since he is the source of just appointments that make it possible to identify and protest commercial disorder; the patron will prevent fragmentation within the guild since he is the guarantor of a harmony that derives from obedience. These premises have little to do with obsequiousness to a noble proprietor. Rather, they implicate the lord in (they make the lord necessary to) all rightful procedure and orderly relations. They implicate him, too, in something more, which emerges from the unstated contrasts in the final article and conclusion of the code. There the guild members invoke the values of the permanent against the specter of the ephemeral, the peaceful against the specter of the war-torn. They invoke the Way against the specter of lost direction; the precedent against the specter of the arbitrary; the continuity of succeeding generations against the specter of rupture. There are echoes of other contrasts already familiar to us: between the old and the new, the inside and the outside, the right and the wrongful, the orderly and the injuring. The lathe master and the silversmith extend the contrasts: between the real and the imposter; the named and the unnamed; the honorable and the dishonorable. In effect, the structures of patronage came to delimit the world of coherent meaning.

And so we return to the beginning. Is it really possible that the Hokke uprising died in 1536? And if so, how did the most sensational development in Kyoto's wartime history come to such an end? Certainly, the great displays of commoner militancy disappeared after 1536. This seems to me a result of the new costs of action after Hiei's raid on the Hokke temples. The decisive attack on Kyoto's sectarians came not from agrarian leagues or Ikkō armies but from a coalition of proprietary and shogunal forces. Between 1532 and 1536, the roles and demands of the commoners expanded within the confines of an alliance with the elite. Once Hiei broke the alliance so inalterably, continued uprising would have meant full and bloody rebellion against proprietors and shogunate alike. Rebellion might have been sustained, at least for a time. Guerrilla war might have been sustained indefinitely. Yet either course would have required commoners to dismantle the structures of work and patronage—to envision their patrons as their enemies and anticipate the loss of the practical as well as the symbolic benefits of protection. Even if this were possible for an undifferentiated mass of sectarians whose martial service remained unrewarded and whose political ambitions had provoked merciless reprisal, it would have posed an ultimately impossible challenge to silk weavers and rice dealers and pawnbrokers and swordsmiths.

But the structures that simultaneously protected and trapped Kyoto's workers were themselves fracturing into new shapes. On one level, workers were reorganizing their own relations: through the creation of *ton'ya* and a greater emphasis on specialization and vertical control; through the manipulation of elite alliances to define a hierarchy of prestige; through the intensification of competition, which exposed conflict as the norm. On another level, workers were reorganizing relations with their patrons: through the defiance and abuse of authorities; through movements toward greater parity and corporatism in making decisions; through the exploitation of patronage for private advantage. These realignments, which tended in contrary directions, would continue to cross Japan's economic history. While stratification divided workers from one another, shared conflict with patrons united them along the lines of class.

Class divisions appeared most dramatically in wartime Kyoto not in the commercial domain but in the political organization of neighborhoods. Yet what happened there derived from tensions that could not be released within the finally unbreakable structures of patronage. Even more, what happened in the neighborhoods derived from the Hokke uprising, for the conflicts of class that were mediated in the realm of work (by attachment and the habits of dependency, by crisis and the antagonisms among workers) were everywhere apparent in Hiei's invasion of 1536. Kyoto's Lotus sectarians could not have formed the undifferentiated mass that appears in the records of the elite. We may imagine, although we cannot uncover, many configurations of radical and conservative elements, of leaders and reluctant followers and dissidents, among the commoners who fought as the "Hokke army." But no such distinctions mattered in 1536. "Public people" suffered as grievously as peddlers. Hiei's troops made no compromises as they ravaged the capital and killed its townspeople. And thus commoners who imagined themselves divided and discretely grouped were forged from the outside and, no doubt, from the inside as well into a unit, a class. This consciousness found increasing expression in the new politics of post-Hokke Kyoto. The armed rebellion that workers could not undertake against their patrons metamorphosed into local organization.

6

Neighborhood:
The Reconfiguration
of Attachment

Around the middle of the seventeenth century, during a cartographic boom in Japan, surveyors began producing large, immensely detailed maps of Kyoto for both official and commercial audiences. The only earlier efforts to map the city had occurred, so far as we know, in the ninth century. Once resumed in the early modern period, the mapping of Kyoto became a formidable enterprise, as rival publishing houses issued annual editions of woodblock prints that combined ever-updated information about the cityscape with ever-splashier treatments of it—including color coding, pictorial details, dense indexes. One feature of these remarkable maps was the entry of a name for each of the hundreds of individual blocks (*chō*) that made up the city.[1] A distinctive construct described as a "two-sided block" (*ryōgawa chō*), the city block of this time included the properties fronting both sides of any street between significant intersections.[2] (See Map 5.) Eventually common to most of the early modern cities of Japan, such blocks emerged as the defining units of urban life. They were the first locus of administrative organization and of festive and ritual assembly. In popular literature as in official edicts, the block lay at the center of an intimate geography not only of place but of social and political connection. And the name of the block, far more than the name (if any) of the street or larger district, was the code of urban space. (As it is today.)

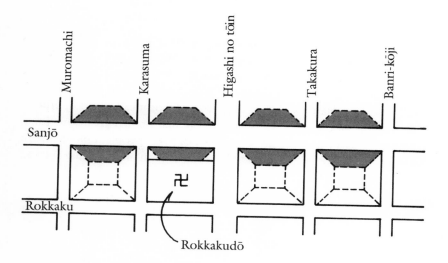

Map 5. The configuration of the block. The shading indicates the areas of four of the "two-sided blocks" (*ryōgawa chō*), which faced—in this case—Sanjō avenue. Based on Hayashiya Tatsusaburō, *Machishū* (Tokyo: Chūō Kōron-sha, 1964), 89. Courtesy of the publisher.

When the avid mapping of Kyoto began, however, the block was still a rather new element of the cityscape. As a unit of organization, it dates from the 1530s and its broader history is intertwined with the wartime experiences of Kyoto's commoners. Much more than a unit of residence, the block became a critical site of urban politics where a transformation in the relations between rulers and ruled was accomplished. This chapter traces early notions about place and neighborhood in Kyoto and then explores the politics of class that found expression in block associations from the time of the Hokke uprising. Like the uprising itself, these associations pose vexing problems of meaning and purpose. My reading of the evidence is, once more, hard rather than soft. I find in the blocks a new political community of townspeople, united against military overlords, who translated demonstration and uprising into an adversarial institution.

The Emergence and Early Organization of the Block

The more distant origins of the block lie sometime before the fifteenth century, when the street was reconceived as a binding agent rather than a boundary. In the classical and early medieval capital, land was allocated and administered in units framed, or set off, by the surrounding roadways. The increasing shift in orientation toward the street and its facing properties, apparent by the early fifteenth century, doubtless reflected a prior shift from a manorial to a more commercial attitude toward space: urban property that had once served as (walled and isolated) residential lots for landed proprietors and their satellites had become, over time, rental sites for craftspeople and merchants making the transition from household service for the elite to professional status in the marketplace. As the arteries of their trade, streets came to link the tradespeople who lined them and pushed into them with open frontages and portable displays.[3]

The notion of blocks as units dividing streets into limited stretches of facing properties within the compass of intersections is conveyed by the naming of these units as separate locales. The first name appeared around 1455, but not until the first three decades of the sixteenth century did block names become common. Thereafter, they were the norm.[4] Some names derived from local landmarks, typically shrines and temples or natural features; others derived from notable local employments, and still others from popular deities or saintly figures. A number of block names were variants of street names. For example, we find the blocks of the Myōden Temple, the Palace Hachiman Shrine, the Northern Boat Bridge, the Tenjin Hill, the Fan Guild, the Leather Workers, the Baths, the (god) Ebisu, the (goddess) Benzaiten, and the (priest) En no Gyōja. We also find the blocks of Ichijō Avenue at the Western Entry, Nishiki Street at Kamakiri Hill, and Shijō Avenue at Abura Street, Stone Well.[5]

We do not know who named these blocks. Historians have associated the impulse with the people who inhabited them, particularly the commoners who dominated not only the population at large but almost all settled areas as well—for zoning by class in Kyoto, rarely strict in the medieval capital, was essentially unknown in wartime.[6] If commoners did name their blocks, we might discover in that act a changing concept of place. The naming suggests a perception of the block as a reliable, long-term address of its occupants rather than a simple extension of the landlord/proprietor who suffered his tenants/servants to linger there. In effect, the naming suggests some confidence in the contractual relationship between landlord and renter, and in the ensuing conversion of rented property into a stable enclave of tradespeople. Overwhelmingly, the block names moved place from direct proprietary connections into a more public sphere. A few blocks, but only a few, bore the names of proprietary houses—the block of Lord Ichijō, for example, or the block of Lord Asukai.[7]

Not incidentally, this naming occurred among other signs of a more autonomous tenure among commoners. Although the trend was far from universal, increases in land rents were coming to substitute for the diverse lordly exactions of labor and tribute that had characterized the manorial system.[8] Economic relations were partially replacing complex social attachments to make land a market commodity accessible to those who could pay to occupy it. As commoners increasingly bought and sold the buildings they inhabited, their claims to space must have intensified. Townspeople also became land owners. There is clear evidence that commoners were buying and selling real estate, both with and without the required shogunal confirmation, and acquiring it through foreclosures on loans. Between 1474 and 1484, for example, as many as one-third of the land purchases documented by the shogunate may have been made by commoners. Although such figures are arresting (however scant in an incomplete record), debate continues to surround the issue of nonelite land ownership. Partial census data from the end of the sixteenth century seems to refute notions that land ownership was at all extensive among townspeople.[9] Nonetheless, the very existence of land sales to commoners loosened the elite's grip on property as it opened the possibility, even the expectation, of a tighter hold on urban space by the "people of the blocks."

Coincident with a greater security of land tenure among commoners, the naming of blocks also coincided with the accelerating street actions that I have chronicled before. As if creating a public space that could be occupied and altered by persons without title or office, townspeople took to the streets after 1480 to resist invasions of rural debtors and to avenge the injuries of officials and criminals. Finally and most dramatically, the years after 1527 saw fortification of the blocks, commoner battles against agents of the "Sakai shogun," mass tax delinquency, and the events of the Hokke uprising. The conduct of townspeople throughout these decades of war indicates a widening appropriation of physical places and a presumption that commoners had a role to play in urban politics. That role—a mixture of self-defense, self-redress, and alternating defiance of and alliance with the authorities—took changing and sometimes contradictory directions. Yet one constant in the activism of townspeople was its association with physical space. Let me review several familiar documents to draw out their attention to the blocks and particular locales of Kyoto.

Go-Hōkōin-ki. 1495, 10th month, 22d day.

I hear that several score participants in the debtors' uprising were killed at *Taka-tsuji and Muromachi.* They say the *people of the blocks* (*chōnin*) and the brokers fought together against them.[10]

Sanetaka kō-ki. 1506, 7th month, 16th day.

In *Tachibana alley,* children were parading with lanterns for the Ceremony of Myriad Lamps when retainers of a military official [*kaikō*] in the capital stopped them, declaring that prohibitions against such activity had been issued. Thereupon an argument broke out.[11]

Tōji hyakugō monjo. 1516, 9th month, 21st day.

In the matter of the recent dispute over water use in *the area of Shichijō and Suzaku*: Administrators of Tōjiin assert that, since the time of the original quarrel at the water source, Tōji has again gathered forces and sent them there. When we raised questions with administrators of Tōji, they asserted: "Matters did come to violence during the dispute over water. But when we attacked *the residents of Suzaku, people from the surrounding areas* [*kinpen no shosho*] joined forces with both sides, faced off against each other, and joined the battle."[12]

Tokitsugu kyō-ki. 1529, 1st month, 10th and 11th days.

Asserting that they were to collect a commissariat tax, two [military deputies] burst into the property of Lord Ichijō and, we heard, took his wife and children hostage.... Again the Kōdō bell sounded. *[People of] the blocks* rose up (*chōchō okite*) and surrounded [Lord Ichijō's residence].[13]

Tokitsugu kyō-ki. 1527, 11th month, 29th day, and 12th month, 1st day.

This morning about ten men from the gang of Awa invaded the house of the *tatami* maker of this neighborhood. *The people of northern Kyoto, all the way from Nijō avenue,* rose up and surrounded them with two or three thousand persons.... Again, in late afternoon, they invaded [a courtier's] *house on Musha-kōji.* And again, *the people of the various blocks* rose up and surrounded them, shouting and crying.... People here are building *fortified gates for the block* and hence asked me for bamboo. I gave them ten stalks.... I also sent over *sake* to the [people of the] block.[14]

The actions described in these documents were communal rather than solitary; they were conducted openly and violently, rather than privately and litigiously; and they drew together actors linked primarily by geography—by their blocks, residences, neighboring places, water sources, and sectors of the city—rather than by their employments, religion, proprietary attachments, or status. Litigation remained the battleground of internally divisive fights over commerce and the attendant matters of patronage and privilege. The streets became the battleground of elemental fights for physical security against invaders. On occasion, they also became the arena for battles against tax collectors and police. Although tax problems typically inspired petitions or the withholding of dues by the aggrieved groups, belligerent intervention by officials could galvanize substantial bodies united only by proximity. What we might begin to think of as "neighborhoods" closed ranks against assault.

The Lotus uprising was closely related to these earlier patterns of agitation, but it moved significantly beyond them. Street actions before 1532 had tended to be crowd responses to emergencies. However rooted in attachments to place, the actions appear undisciplined by a politics of place that transcended immediate concerns. Yet with the Hokke movement we find organization as well as agenda, which emerged from, and gave shape to, the events of four tumultuous years. Issues of place did not disappear during the Hokke uprising; for the movement always retained prominent aspects of self-defense of the city, and its participants were almost interchangeably described as "Hokke sectarians" and "people of the blocks." No symbols of spatial appropriation could be clearer, moreover, than the great circular processions around Kyoto or the outdoor assembly of a Hokke council to try and to execute three arsonists. The street arrests of enemies, the guarding of toll stations, the erection of fortifications—all affirmed the hold of townspeople on Kyoto. And even the religious dimension of the movement found a powerful physical expression in the twenty-one Hokke temples commanding extensive downtown locations, where commoners rallied before marches. Yet place during the Lotus uprising was not, primarily at least, a matter of blocks and particular attachments. The uprising was citywide, apparently organized through a transcendent institution and sustained by varied purposes that reached beyond neighborhood to military alliance and the pursuit of governing privileges.

In the aftermath of the uprising, Kyoto's townspeople reworked the legacies both of Hokke and of an earlier activism to form associations different in scope from those of the Lotus but animated by the hostilities the uprising had exposed. As we know them from a record created entirely by elite outsiders (by shogunal officials and noble diarists), the new associations may seem a tame enterprise, subject to manipulation by urban authorities, whose history only confirms a post-Hokke quiescence among commoners and an abandonment of once-extraordinary possibilities for change. Yet that quiescence itself is suggestive of an altered political outlook. And if we submit the record of the associations to a hard reading, we may find not a tame enterprise at all but a new challenge to current notions about power—a reproach that was subtle and insidious where the Hokke movement had been fatally blunt, and one finally instrumental in shaping postwar society in the capital.

One of the first indications that commoners were forming new associations, defined by blocks, appears in documents of 1533 and 1534, during the period of Hokke ascendancy.

Gion shugyō nikki. 1533, 6th month, 7th day.
In connection with the floats [the *yamaboko* used in the annual Gion festival], the monthly magistrates of the sixty-six blocks of southern Kyoto, as well as the commoner attendants to the shrine, came [for discussions] to the place of Yamamoto Daizō this morning. Even though the religious rituals of the [Gion] festival will not be carried out [this year], they wish to conduct the procession of floats.[15]

Here we discover that residents of individual blocks, as many as sixty-six of them in the southern sector of Kyoto where the Gion shrine was located and its festival centered, had organized in two ways: they were selecting representatives to speak to their interests; and these representatives were assembling as a group for negotiations with shrine officials. Neither in this document nor in subsequent records of the sixteenth century do we find reference to the process for selecting representatives. Only infrequently do we find the names of representatives or their individual blocks. Repeated mention of monthly magistrates (*gachi gyōji*), however, suggests frequent rotation of spokesmen and perhaps a disposition toward a semi-egalitarian management of the block.[16]

The negotiations at stake arose from an official decision to suspend the Gion festival, a rare though not unknown decision in years of particular crisis, and an apparent desire among the townspeople to schedule at least the parade of floats that brought entertainment to the participating blocks.[17] The Gion festival had long been a subject of tension, even rancor, between townspeople and shogunal authorities. Viewing the festival as a symbol of social cohesion and continuity, deputies of the shrine and the shogunate frequently inveighed against recalcitrant townspeople to muster both the floats and the funds required for the event. Although the festival became associated in the early modern period with popular culture and neighborhood pride, the evidence of the war years portrays it as an official rite that provoked commoner resistance as well as rowdyism against (even the murder of) official participants.[18] Thus, the negotiations of 1533 may have reflected not a genuine interest in the parade among townspeople but anger or obstinacy—a likely possibility in the light of succeeding events. The shogunate declined the request to hold the parade but then reversed the decision two months later, ordering the commoners to supply funds and floats. The commoners rejected the order, protesting against its "inconvenience."[19] In the end, the struggle seems less about the festival than about authority and compliance—particularly about the commoners' unwillingness to suspend and resume their affairs at the decree of the shogunate. (The outcome of this tug-of-war is unclear. The record mentions neither the convening nor the ultimate postponement of the Gion festival in 1533.)

Block associations appear again in a series of documents written between the second and fourth months of 1534. Two of these documents may serve to outline a complicated exchange between the court, the shogunate, and the people of the "six blocks."

No. 1.   1534, 2d month, 29th day.

> Since it is the imperial desire, you are to render service to the throne [by repairing] the eastern and southern moats of the palace. As overseer, Lord Yamashina will strictly order that this construction by the people of the six blocks be completed as an admirable act of service.
>
> [From (two imperial officials) to the monthly magistrates of the six blocks.][20]

No. 2.   1534, 4th month, 29th day.

> In accord with the imperial desire, it has been ordered that the imperial moat be repaired by [the people of] the two blocks of Ichijō, the two blocks of Ōgimachi, the block of Karasuma, and the block of Tachibana street. We understand that [this order] has caused hardship. This is entirely not as it should be. Hence, although work on the general [city] moats will consequently be delayed, you are first to attend exclusively to the imperial orders.
>
> [From (the shogunal deputy) Ibaragi Nagataka to the people of the several blocks.][21]

Immediately at issue were conflicting impositions on the residents of six blocks in close proximity to the palace. Ordered by the shogunate to join a citywide effort to rebuild the "general moats," they were also ordered by the court to repair the moats of the palace—a conflict eventually resolved, after elaborate negotiations between courtiers and military officials, by the shogunal concession that the double burden was an inappropriate "hardship" and that construction should proceed first (and perhaps only) on the emperor's ditches.[22]

More deeply at issue was the conduct of power. Yamashina Tokitsugu indicates in his diary that the original order for repair of the palace moats went out to the six blocks as early as the first month of 1534. This order was conveyed informally, however. The court decree of the second month (No. 1) appeared only after a request by block representatives for a document and subsequent consultations among courtiers. Negotiations then reopened when (on the seventh day of the third month) block representatives complained to the court about the conflicting demands for labor; whereupon Tokitsugu and other nobles pursued discussions of the matter with shogunal deputies for nearly six weeks. The eventual concession from the shogunate appeared in a formal document (a *bugyō-nin hōsho*) bearing the seal of the *kanrei*'s ranking deputy, Ibaragi Nagataka (No. 2). Possessing their two documents, the people of the six blocks began work on the imperial moats in the fifth month of 1534.[23]

We find in this case, as in the Gion case, the emergence of blocks as organized units and the appearance of monthly magistrates to represent them. We also find the formation of a block federation (*machi-gumi*), a coalition of individual units engaged in corporate action. Other federations like the "six blocks" (embracing Tachibana, Karasuma, the two blocks of Ichijō, and the two blocks of Ōgimachi) gradually spread through the city as intermediate levels of association between the single block and the more inclusive bodies (like the "sixty-six blocks of southern Kyoto") that covered the two major sectors of the capital.[24]

Most significant in this case is a distinct change in political relations. The magistrates of the six blocks succeeded in submitting to negotiation the demands of Kyoto's highest authorities and in winning from these authorities an obvious concession. Notable in themselves, these achievements were surpassed by the magistrates' success in procuring the two documents. The importance of the documents lay partly in their formality and deferential language and even more in their terms of address; for both went directly to the magistrates and their constituents, rather than through titled intermediaries, to make the block organizations immediate parties to official transactions. The blocks effectively acquired an official identity. Of equal importance, the documents transformed a lordly summons to labor into a specific order of record. Corvée levies belonged to the world of proprietary privilege: the right to service was presumed and it was exercised peremptorily. Without departing from that world, the two documents marked a shift in outlook. The demand for labor became a matter of decree; it was also circumscribed. And it just might become a basis for compensation or future bargaining, should the magistrates, who were accorded an official identity, represent the demand for labor as part of an implicitly reciprocal agreement.[25]

References to the block associations fade from the record during the last years of the Hokke movement (when attention was riveted on the larger drama being played out by the sectarians), and during the years immediately following the movement's collapse (when Kyoto's elite resumed complaints about mass tax delinquency among the commoners). Despite sanguine observations that normalcy had returned by 1537 (when "the various proprietors had their vestitures restored as they were originally"), the strident petitions from elite landlords who were denied their rents belies any image of "restoration."[26] By 1541 the shogunate was issuing threats to "all the people of northern and southern Kyoto":

In the matter of the domestic lot and field taxes of Kyoto and its environs: These are to be rendered, as of old, to the vested proprietors. This demand will be enforced by the troops of Ōmi should anyone raise difficulty. There is to be no further negligence [in submitting taxes].[27]

By 1544 a head priest from the temple of Shōkokuji was reflecting a general despair among proprietors by settling for whatever (if anything) he could get.

12th month.
16th day.   Residents have been withholding the land rents from Aya no kōji from the first month of 1540 until today, simply ignoring our various orders. I understand that a [new] demand will be pressed by troops from Ōsumi.

19th day.   The residents have offered apologies about the [delinquent] land rents from Aya no kōji. They propose to pay one-third of the rents for the past five years now, to pay one-third in the future, and to be excused of the remaining third. I am asked for an opinion. I consent.[28]

The Shōkokuji account contains a suggestive description of the relations prevailing broadly between commoners and the authorities after 1536. Retreating from armed conflict or open hostility, eschewing any violent break with their proprietors, commoners quietly ignored demands for taxes and then, under threat, offered perfunctory apologies and implausible schemes for restitution. On those rather rare occasions when threats actually led to "enforcement," the townspeople responded in kind.[29] Yet violent encounters became unusual in a now-wary capital where officials seemed to avoid confrontation and, like the Shōkokuji priest, to settle for however strained a calm.

More Snarls in the Shogunate, 1536–1553

In the background of this standoff and the emerging story of the block associations was continuing turmoil within the shogunal institution. Many of its features were old, some new. The turmoil might have invited a popular response similar to the Hokke uprising but instead gave way to a direct, adversarial politics. To establish the context of this change, let me return to the often punishingly familiar landscape of coups.

When the *kanrei* Hosokawa Harumoto returned to Kyoto in 1536, he could make a guarded claim to victory in a ten-year struggle for ascendancy: he had successfully usurped Hosokawa Takakuni; he had survived the internecine rebellions of Yanagimoto Kataharu and Miyoshi Motonaga; he had forced the Ikkō sectarians into a truce and suppressed agrarian uprisings in the home provinces; he had repelled the efforts of the Lotus army to redefine the power relations of the capital. Nonetheless, his victory proved ephemeral and his peace short-lived. Although Hosokawa Harumoto retained his office and nominal claims to control over Kyoto between 1536 and 1549, another series of contests opened swiftly before him. The campaigns of those years contain occasionally surprising details within a text of hypnotic sameness. I break the spell of nightmare here by giving the campaigns speed, chronology, and a plot of seven acts.

No. 1.   In 1539 Kyoto was invaded by the troops of Miyoshi Chōkei, the young son of Hosokawa Harumoto's one-time ally and subsequent enemy, Miyoshi Motonaga. (Motonaga had been defeated and killed in 1532 by the Ikkō sectarians and several of Harumoto's generals, preeminently Kizawa Nagamasa.) Chōkei was seeking both vengeance for his father and a major role in the Kyoto area for himself.

After a fruitless effort at conciliation by the shogun and an ensuing campaign by Chōkei in Settsu, a truce between Harumoto and Chōkei was achieved by the head of the Rokkaku house. Harumoto ceded a number of land rights in Kawachi to Chōkei and probably gave him an official appointment. Chōkei's power base, like that of his father, was in the Shikoku province of Awa.[30]

No. 2.   Probably as a result of the concessions to Miyoshi Chōkei, Kizawa Nagamasa, a major shogunal deputy and a castellan in Settsu, raised a rebellion against Harumoto in 1541. The shogun fled Kyoto for Sakamoto. After months of fighting, Miyoshi Chōkei and Hosokawa Harumoto defeated and killed Kizawa Nagamasa in the third month of 1542.[31]

No. 3.   Almost constantly from 1543, Harumoto faced challenges from Hosokawa Ujitsuna, the adopted son of Hosokawa Takakuni and now the principal avenger of his usurped father. Ujitsuna attacked Harumoto's troops at Uji, in Yamashiro, Tanba, and Sakai. Miyoshi Chōkei appears to have been at the heart of Harumoto's defense, which involved as many as 10,000 troops from the home and western provinces. To sustain this defense, Chōkei imposed war taxes around the capital, which he extorted under threat of fire.[32]

No. 4.   In 1546 the incumbent shogun, Ashikaga Yoshiharu, split with his *kanrei,* Hosokawa Harumoto, built and occupied a castle in Yamashiro to wage war against Harumoto, and imposed war taxes (for labor, rice, and building supplies) on the farmers of Yamashiro and Yamashina.

Yoshiharu formally allied with Hosokawa Ujitsuna in this campaign against Harumoto, which suggests that the grievances of twenty years may have provoked the rupture. (Harumoto had originally united with Ashikaga Yoshitsuna to oppose Hosokawa Takakuni and Ashikaga Yoshiharu in 1527. Harumoto and Yoshiharu had made peace, only after five years of battle, in 1532.) Yet a more recent history of antagonism also figured in the break, for Yoshiharu had several times halted efforts by Harumoto and his men to impose tax levies and debt cancellation orders around the capital. During his campaign against Harumoto, in the twelfth month of 1546, Yoshiharu resigned as shogun in favor of his ten-year-old son, Yoshiteru. This act seemingly ensured a succession favorable to Yoshiharu's interests and precluded intervention in the decision by Harumoto.

After intermittent fighting with Harumoto (who deployed troops from headquarters at Kyoto's Shōkokuji) and with Miyoshi Chōkei, Hosokawa Ujitsuna was forced to flee the capital area in 1547. The retired and the incumbent shogun, Yoshiharu and Yoshiteru, subsequently made a fragile peace with Harumoto and returned to Kyoto.[33]

No. 5.   And we return to the beginning. Provoked by the undesirable resolution of a succession dispute in Settsu, Miyoshi Chōkei went to war against Hosokawa Harumoto in 1548. Chōkei took up the cause of Hosokawa Ujitsuna (whom he had opposed for the preceding five years), began a campaign against Harumoto and his remaining allies, and, in the sixth month of 1549, gained a decisive victory against them in Settsu. Eight hundred of Harumoto's forces, we are told, died in the battle.

Hosokawa Harumoto fled to Sakamoto with Ashikaga Yoshiteru and Yoshiharu. Miyoshi Chōkei entered the capital, confiscated Ashikaga and Hosokawa properties, and sent his men throughout the districts of Yamashina to collect commissariat taxes. And thus the start of the fifth violent transition in power within Kyoto.[34]

No. 6.   The transition was anything but final. Between 1549 and 1553, war continued in and around Kyoto between Hosokawa Harumoto and Miyoshi Chōkei (whose campaigns were regularly complicated by Ashikaga Yoshiteru—who sometimes allied with one or the other of these opponents, and sometimes fought independently against them both). Each contestant tried to project authority over the capital by erecting and invading a new generation of local castles—Koizumi castle in Saiin, Nakao castle in Higashiyama, Reizan castle in Higashiyama—but each was forced into flight from the city under attack by the other. Residents of Kyoto endured the most intense and destructive battles in the city since the early 1530s.[35]

No. 7.   Kyoto's fifth violent transition in power came to an end in the eighth month of 1553 when Miyoshi Chōkei, having destroyed Hosokawa Harumoto earlier in the year, seized Ashikaga Yoshiteru's headquarters in Kyoto and forced the shogun into an exile that lasted five years. And then the purge. Chōkei paraded 25,000 soldiers into the capital, arrested the officials of the Board of Administration, appropriated the properties of his enemies, and oversaw the appointment of his puppet, Hosokawa Ujitsuna, as *kanrei*.[36]

There are several old themes in these unfolding acts. We encounter again disarray at all levels of shogunal power: the Hosokawa *kanrei* house was divided by vendetta and the ambitions of deputies; these deputies were divided against each other (in this case the main players were Miyoshi Chōkei and Kizawa Nagamasa); and the Ashikaga house itself was variously aligned with different parties to these contests. We also discover again full or partial vacuums of power in the capital: *kanrei* and shogun alike were periodically out of Kyoto after 1546; no overlord at all was able to hold the city between 1549 and 1553; and the ascendancy after 1553 of Miyoshi Chōkei kept the shogun in a five-year exile. Finally, we discover familiar patterns of suffering in Kyoto: the levying of heavy war taxes, the construction of castles, repeated battle in the streets, constant threats of invasion.

Yet three themes in these unfolding acts were new. The campaigns of Ashikaga Yoshiharu and Yoshiteru cast the shogun themselves as warlords. Not since 1490 had a shogun gone to battle, and then only briefly and in alliance with provincial governors to protect manorial rights in

Ōmi. But the purposes of the Ashikaga after 1546 were obscure from the start and only further confused by their shifting alliances (they fought for and against Hosokawa Harumoto and Miyoshi Chōkei, sometimes opposing both of them simultaneously). Whatever their purposes, they were acquiring immediate debts to vassals as well as a specifically martial and partisan role that could finally reduce the shogunate into a regional lordship up for grabs. And indeed, the eclipse of the shogun seemed to be the consequence of a second change in this period of conflict. Once in power in Kyoto after 1553, Miyoshi Chōkei dispensed with the Ashikaga presence altogether (he elevated no figurehead, allied with no mascot) and dispensed too with the Board of Administration (whose members he arrested and then dispersed into exile). He governed directly through edicts bearing his own signature, and he began aggressively to confiscate urban taxes. The search for control over Kyoto and the home province, unhampered by the shogunal and proprietary systems, may have been anticipated by Miyoshi Chōkei's father, Miyoshi Motonaga, in his struggles with the Sakai shogunate around 1530. But it was the son, two decades later, who began (though only began) to make a radical break in rule.[37] Throughout the years of conflict that led to Chōkei's takeover of Kyoto, however, Kyoto's residents were quiet. This quiescence, after the militancy of Hokke, is another new and problematic theme.

I have already discounted the likelihood of popular rebellion against proprietors and military officials in the capital after 1536. But absent completely was an independent defense of Kyoto by townspeople or their alliance with any of the contenders. Commoners who had mustered armies of up to 20,000 men in the 1530s stood apart from the new campaigns that ravaged their city and threatened to undo the proprietors and administrative officials who organized their normal universe. This disengagement may have resulted from terror or a sense of futility. Sorting sides and motives in these conflicts was all but hopeless, in a manner that conflict with the Ikkō sectarians never had been, and alliance promised only the betrayal met in 1536. Alternatively, the military disengagement of commoners may have resulted from new political calculations. Rejecting alliance with all overlords, townspeople entered instead into organizations that permitted direct, adversarial relations with military powers on the one hand, and a degree of separation and self-reliance on the other. Their organizations advanced a premise implicit in the autocratic rule of Miyoshi Chōkei: that the medieval corporate order was dying.

Rulers and Ruled, Power and Class

Back to the block associations. Their record, like the record of the Hokke uprising, is thin but provocative. The following documents trace their history from 1539 to the ascendancy of Miyoshi Chōkei in 1553.

No. 1.   1539, 12th month, 24th day.

In the matter of upper Ogawa, in front of Seiganji, about which the temple administration has brought suit: We understand that discussions have occurred with the Kajūji house [concerning public solicitations for rebuilding temples]. You are to understand that maintaining a solicitation place (*kanjinsho*) by the Senbon Enmadō and others, as well as constructing huts [around the solicitation site], is strictly forbidden.

[From (two shogunal magistrates) to the residents of Ogawa block.]³⁸

No. 2.   1541, 4th month, 12th day.

In the matter of Seiganji and, additionally, the other sacred places: We hear of late that there are persons constantly raising havoc in the temple with music and flutes, disturbing order. This is outrageous. You are immediately to understand that we have posted signs ordering this to cease. If there are violators, the blocks are to inform us of their names and they will be judged in offense.

[From (the shogunal deputy) Ibaragi Nagataka to the residents of the seven blocks of Ogawa.]³⁹

No. 3.   1542, 11th month, 14th day.

In the matter of the priests and monks scattered in the four directions: It is the imperial wish that you return now to Kyoto, resume full control over your original lands, and promptly rebuild.

[From (the imperial official) Uchūben Haruhide to the officials (*gobō*) of the twenty-one Hokke temples.]⁴⁰

No. 4.   1545, 8th month, 18th day.

In the matter of the four square blocks between Rokkaku and Shijōbōmon, Abura no kōji and Nishi no tōin in southern Kyoto: Although this land was the private holding of Sawamura Senmatsu, it is clear from the several documents of proof appended here that it has passed by sale to this temple. . . . Inasmuch as the documents are in order, it is ordered that there be no violation of this holding.

[From (two shogunal magistrates) to the administrative office of Honnōji.][41]

No. 5a.   1546, 11th month, 18th day.
In the northern Kyoto block of Muromachi-Tōichi, the following is forbidden:

> Barracking soldiers
> Levying extraordinary taxes

The aforementioned is absolutely to cease. If there is any violator, he will be immediately seized and strictly punished.

[Signed by two shogunal magistrates.][42]

No. 5b.   1546.
A similar document went to the block of Shiragumo-Kinuya.

No. 5c.   1549.
A document went to the block of Shijō-Abura no kōji forbidding the violence of warriors, the felling of trees or bamboo, the levying of war or commissariat taxes.

No. 5d.   1549.
A document went to the block of Shijō-Kawadana forbidding the barracking of soldiers and the levying of extraordinary taxes.[43]

No. 6.   1549, 4th month, 8th day.
The residents of the block of Shijō-Aya no kōji bring suit [to the shogunal administration]: "A person called Masakiyo resided on the southern corner of the eastern side of this block. When he died, his effects went to his daughter. She sold the house to a person called Takeyama Jirō Saburō of Karasuma block. This was an unspeakable offense. She sold, as well, the land on which the house stands and the additional land in the rear. . . . From of old officials have ordered [sales to outsiders] to cease. Accordingly, she was accused of an offense for selling the land despite previous regulations. But she replied that there had never been such regulations. Such conduct is outrageous. We would therefore be most grateful if [the shogunate] would issue an order to the effect that land in one block is not to be sold to persons from other blocks."[44]

No. 7. 1550, intercalary 5th month, 24th day.

Because this area is close to a battle encampment, troops must be present in Kyoto. Should there be violent havoc raised by them—such as lawless disturbance or the like—you are to respond immediately to terminate the havoc and need not inform us prior to your actions.

[From Tabuse Yōichi Iehisa to the body of monthly magistrates.][45]

No. 8. 1550, 7th month, 10th day.

Item: Taxes due on the lands taken by my men and on the various vestitures shall be collected promptly by the blocks and delivered to me.

Addendum: A senior person shall deliver them.

[From Miyoshi Chōkei to the residents of northern Kyoto, Kyoto, and its environs.][46]

No. 9.   *Tokitsugu kyō-ki.* 1549, 9th month, 7th day.

In order to enforce judgment and apprehend the two foot soldiers who had pillaged the fields of Shōgōin in eastern Kawara, 5,000 people of northern Kyoto set out for an attack. They apprehended both men, I hear, and put them to death.[47]

No. 10.   *Tokitsugu kyō-ki.* 1549, 11th month.

17th day.   After the moon came up, there was a quarrel at the corner of Ōgimachi-Tachibana-tsuji, I understand. One of Yotsusuji's men—Tanaka Heisuke—was attacked and killed.

18th day.   Yotsusuji came over. We discussed the events of last night. It is said that [the assailant] was Niwada's man, the green samurai Kada Yasaburō. Others think that is not the case. But they are saying there should be a thorough investigation of him. Ise also came over. We drank *sake.* Ise said that because [the assailant] is somebody known to the people of the block, the palace should order them to inform us of his identity. And so Yotsusuji went to Nagahashi to request this.

19th day.   I hear that Yotsusuji is going to invade Ōgimachi-Muromachi at dawn the day after tomorrow. They say the assailant is now clearly identified as a carpenter of the block. Since this may provoke a great confrontation, it is ordered [by the palace?] that [Yotsu-suji] delay [any action].

20th day.   Because there were rumors that Yotsusuji was going to invade Muromachi, I went over there. Justice should be rendered by this block. But since [the assailant] has fled, nothing will come of it. Nonetheless, they say that there should be some judgment as a form of private restitution. Therefore the group of elders of these six blocks joined with Yotsusuji's representatives, went out to destroy the house of the assailant, and burned it down, I hear. About 500 men were on hand as a precaution. This combined force stood guard. There was no disturbance. I had some *sake* at Yotsusuji's house.[48]

No. 11.   *Tokitsugu kyō-ki.* 1550, 5th month, 2d day.
There was a quarrel at Nijō-Muromachi near Oshi-kōji and Sanjō-bōmon. From about noon until late afternoon, the opponents confronted each other. I sent Ōzawa Kamon Kanimori to deliver word to Lord Nijō and to Sanuki no kami Tadamune. I hear that one hundred persons, on both sides of the quarrel, were wounded. The commoner elders of northern and southern Kyoto intervened. Lord Nijō also went out to the scene, I understand. The matter was settled without further incident.[49]

No. 12.   *Tokitsugu kyō-ki.* 1550, 7th month.
15th day.   For several hours there was a quarrel between occupants of the block before Lord Ichijō's residence and the block before Sei-ganji. One person was killed and many, on both sides, were wounded, I hear.

16th day.   The altercation resumed today, I understand, but it was mediated by the 120 blocks of northern Kyoto.[50]

No. 13.   *Tokitsugu kyō-ki.* 1551, 1st month, 24th day.
There was a quarrel between Muromachi and our neighborhood. One person from here as well as the priest Obata, who had acted as a mediator, were struck and killed. Hence, people of our neighborhood said they were going to attack Muromachi and this promised to eventuate in large-scale mayhem. So I went to consult Anzenji and then Hirohashi. I also went to consult Karasumaru and Nakamikado and shared a cup of *sake* with them. Then I went to Lord Ichijō and drank *sake* again. I heard that the elders of northern Kyoto had mediated the quarrel.[51]

These documents associate block residents or their representatives with four separate roles, none of them revealed extensively. People of the blocks emerge as correspondents of military officials who charge (or deputize?) them with various police and tax-collecting functions; as recipients of exemptions from war taxes; as regulators of certain internal affairs such as land sales; and as mediators and judges in a number of violent altercations. Like the Hokke record, this one invites both soft and hard readings, with quite different emphases; the brevity of the record, its elite authorship, and its failure to disclose much of a background make interpretation a hazardous challenge.

A soft reading of the record might find the roles of block residents not only compatible with military rule but supportive of it. It seems telling that successive officials simply took the blocks and their organizations for granted as convenient instruments of governance. Rather than oppose or purge these commoner associations, military men appear to have coopted them as placable extensions of themselves: the blocks were meant to understand (and enforce) a shogunal policy against putting up structures for religious solicitations (and possibly for neighborhood self-defense) (No. 1);[52] to report persons disturbing the peace "with music and flutes" in a temple precinct (No. 2); to intervene against rowdy soldiers preparing for battle (No. 7); to serve as an efficient mechanism for collecting and delivering land taxes (No. 8). As small and discrete units, moreover, the blocks appear especially vulnerable to higher control. Unlike the great Hokke congregations who were charged to patrol the city barriers, the block residents belonged to little pieces of place and received commensurately modest commissions. These commissions smell of corporate surveillance. Reporting troublemakers and gathering collective taxes—this work of intrusive mutual inspection recalls previous orders that townspeople inform on neighbors still practicing Hokke rites or traders violating laws on coinage exchange. The suit over the land sale (No. 6) may strengthen the impression that block residents were instruments of military officials, for we discover in it not just an appeal to shogunal authority but the very self-scrutiny that regulated entry into the block, helped control the conduct of occupants, and thus legitimated the principal of corporate responsibility.

The implication in the suit that block residents had compiled their own (written or unwritten) regulations raises the possibility that block associations were also presiding over a range of internal affairs—a possibility likely enough in any case and all the likelier given the subsequent history of Kyoto's blocks. Block codes and other records from the seventeenth century portray mature organizations that attended, for example, to local fire patrols; the upkeep of streets, bridges, and other public facilities; the supervision of neighborhood festivities; and the assignment to residents of dues for these and other purposes (such as "gifts" to officials).[53] Again, a soft reading of such developments might stress their obvious utility to military officials, their "civic" mindedness, and their conversion of place into neighborhood. Accordingly, the acts of mediation might appear as responsible efforts by block leaders to contain "the force of the self" when it erupted in local violence (Nos. 10, 11, 12, 13). The record does not, after all, describe a system of formal tribunals that supplanted shogunal justice but a sequence of emergency interventions by elders who might best be seen as surrogates. Episodes of commoner justice appear concentrated in the years between 1549 and 1553, when no overlord controlled or even routinely occupied the capital, and peacekeeping devolved of necessity onto available substitutes.[54]

The issuance of tax exemptions to the blocks (Nos. 5a, b, c, d) might be viewed as rewards for quiescence and good behavior, alternatively as incentives to good behavior. Because the exemptions went to individual blocks and were almost certainly temporary, they also appear to be selective concessions that could fragment the commoner population. Like the appointment of "public people," the dispensation of privilege to a block might create divisions and hierarchy useful to military rulers. In sum, the record of the block associations suggests an accommodation between ultimately compliant townspeople and a series of overlords who accrued distinct advantages from the associations—advantages seemingly superior to those enjoyed by block residents themselves.

A hard reading of the record, the one I embrace, would also acknowledge an accommodation between commoners and their overlords, even while insisting on the contention underlying it and the fundamentally new political relations resulting from it. My reading begins with the fact of organization itself. Indeed, to understand the perspective of the townspeople, the fact of organization provides the most critical information we have about popular politics. Although we know that officials issued orders to the blocks and that noblemen "heard about" the mediation of block leaders, we know really nothing about how townspeople took these orders or conducted these mediations. What, then, of organization? We know that the block had emerged as a unit of association by 1533 and was taken for granted by the 1540s. Such units expanded swiftly to cover most of the settled areas in Kyoto's urban islands by

1550. The Gion document cited early in this chapter indicates that 66 blocks from southern Kyoto participated in the negotiations of 1533; Yamashina Tokitsugu's account of the Ichijō-Seiganji quarrel (No. 12) indicates that 120 blocks from northern Kyoto participated in the mediation of 1550/7/16. These numbers increased somewhat by 1571 (when the fullest account of the block structure in wartime appeared in documents prepared for Oda Nobunaga), but the fortification of the city precluded significant growth until the late sixteenth century (when the numbers of blocks started to increase dramatically).[55]

We know, further, that organization began with the block itself, which was named and addressed, for example, in the decrees of tax exemption; and that these blocks were (sometimes) assembled into small federations (or *kumi*), such as the "six blocks" in proximity to the palace or the "seven blocks of Ogawa" (No. 2). (By 1573 there were apparently five federations in northern Kyoto and five in southern Kyoto.)[56] Finally, these blocks and federations were (on occasion) combined into inclusive organizations embracing the northern and southern sectors of the capital, either separately (Nos. 12, 13) or together (No. 11). We also know that "monthly magistrates" represented the individual blocks and that elders (*shukurō*) represented the federations (No. 10) and the sectors (Nos. 11, 13). *Elders* may simply be a different term for *magistrates* or may indicate a separate body of leaders—perhaps with longer tenures and higher standing—who engaged in activities transcending the individual block.[57]

Now what are we to make of the fact of organization? The organization of the blocks was apparently voluntary, neither mandated by power holders in the city nor forged under obvious duress. Further, the organization was both elaborate and unusual. Not only did the block organization spread across the capital, it could operate on various levels, from neighborhood to sector, and produce appropriate leadership bodies to represent all units. Here it reveals a striking departure from the trade guilds, which remained particular and insular, and perhaps from the Lotus organization as well. Although the Hokke movement may have provided a model for the blocks, what little we know of it suggests a more centralized structure of authority that radiated downward and probably lacked small, potentially autonomous, units at its base. Unusual in form, the block associations were unusual, too, in their lack of antecedents in the pre-Hokke capital and in their appearance in a city where popular, voluntary organization of any kind was all but unknown outside religious congregations.

All of these features indicate that block associations were formed deliberately. Deliberation implies motive. And motive implies a problem. Organization also posits the existence of a group—a "we," an "inside"—that shares a perspective on the problem. And the "we" requires a "they," a body of outsiders, or adversaries, who define the inside.[58]

The creation of such an unusual organization challenges, from the outset, a soft reading of the record. Any new organization introduces change; for it draws lines, confers identities, alters the consciousness of members, and heightens the attention of nonmembers. To tease out the possible meanings of the block associations, let me now speculate on the interlocking issues of motive, membership, and adversaries. First, the issue of membership.

The most obvious aspect of membership in the block associations was its unprecedented heterogeneity. All surviving evidence suggests that residents of the same block did different work (even though workers in related employments occasionally clustered in certain areas, diverse occupations in the block remained the rule); occupied different stations (landowners were mixed in with renters, "public people" with unprivileged craftspeople); and often owed taxes to different proprietors (the long history of land sales within the elite had broken down cohesive holdings).[59] Religion *might* have united a majority of block residents, but sectarianism appears nowhere as a principle of their organization. The block associations were secular bodies. We are left, then, with the sole unifying factor of place.

Certainly much of the record focuses on concerns of place, in the form of threats to physical security and local concord—invaders, felons, strangers, bad neighbors. Thus we might think of the block insiders as good neighbors, bound by a shared interest in defense, whose associations were products of a lengthening experience of street actions. But concerns over place are always and inherently political concerns; they involve power and authority. Some such concerns may be largely internal or hold only a low political charge. Many others, and most of those apparent in the record, engage external matters and display a high political charge: control over the Gion festival, demands for corvée labor, the levying of war taxes, or the sale of land. In effect, a politics of place is just that—a politics that arises from divided interest and contention. The divisions indicated here separated taxers from taxpayers, for example, and laborers from summoners of labor.

Hence the question arises of whether members of the elite could have belonged to the block associations. Did class define membership? This question tends to be finessed by scholars, who note that men of rank constituted significant portions of the population in at least two block federations and clearly shared some interests with their commoner neighbors. On four occasions, moreover, men at the margins of the nobility served as monthly magistrates in the six blocks (one of the heavily elite block federations).[60]

The ambiguity over the class composition of the block associations reflects deeper ambiguities in the political status of the nonmilitary elite. As we have seen, the courtly nobility and the religious establishment faced ongoing contests with the shogunate over judicial authority, tax exemptions, and other manorial privileges. The severe decline in manorial revenue and the accompanying decline of a ceremonial eminence only exacerbated the political problem. Although courtiers and priests prevailed in some contests with the military, their situation was precarious; the issue finally at stake—whether the vestiges of a proprietary power structure would vanish before a strictly vertical realignment headed by military men—remained undecided. There may be some room, then, for including courtiers and priests in the memberships of block associations. Inclusion might result from their sympathetic identification with commoner residents and from a joint antipathy to the shogunate. It might result from obvious collective interests (in physical security and fire prevention, for example) and occasional common grievances (nobles, too, were impressed by the shogunate for war taxes and laborers, for example).

The inclusion of members of the elite in the membership of the block associations is nonetheless extremely problematic. The record itself discourages such an identification. We might wonder whether orders to collect taxes or report troublemakers would have been addressed, without honorific language, to men of rank. We might observe that the decree about public solicitations went both to "the residents of Ogawa block" and to "the administrative office of Seiganji temple"—as if to distinguish unequivocally between two communities that shared a single location but not a collective identity.[61] And we might note in the diary entries of Yamashina Tokitsugu, who provides our fullest view of the blocks, a precise reference to "the *commoner* [*jige*] elders of northern and southern Kyoto" (No. 11). Tokitsugu also intimates repeatedly that neighborhood quarrels provoked quite separate deliberations among his fellow (*sake*-drinking) nobles and among the block elders who invariably conducted the decisive negotiations (Nos. 10–13). These groups may have acted in parallel, and they may have been cordial to each other. But they were not one.

We can approach the issue of class somewhat differently, if indirectly, by turning to the problem that motivated the organization of blocks in the first place. I do not think that problem was any immediate concern about place or, indeed, any other matter. Concerns over place were endemic to wartime society, as some concerns are endemic to the human condition. Rather, the problem was a need to find voice and presence sufficient to resolve, or at least to press the resolution of, those concerns most vital at the time to a constituency. The need to find voice and presence implies the prior absence of voice, or the inadequacy and abandonment of whatever voice had existed. Effective or not, the proprietary elite retained its voice and presence through titles and administrative offices, documents and decrees, direct connections to the throne. (Let me defer thoughts about the elite's possible abandonment of this presence.) But outside their trade associations, the only voice available to commoners before the Hokke uprising was an extension of the proprietary voice—in the case, for example, of the lumber workers from Onoyama who resisted a levy from the shogunate by invoking the imperatives of imperial service. Even the suits of privileged traders borrowed the authority of their patrons.

Absolutely fundamental to the experience of the block associations was the dropping of the proprietary voice and the separation from proprietary attachment. Block representatives, when we are able remotely to hear them, spoke for the blocks—in the negotiations over Gion, for example, and in the suit over the land sale (No. 6.). Residents of the six blocks detached themselves from the court in 1534 to elicit formal decrees concerning the moats, addressed directly to themselves, from both the throne and the shogunate. And block residents must also have negotiated on their own behalf to secure the decrees of tax exemption that the shogunate began issuing in 1546.

This new voice is startling in itself. Equally startling is its recognition by military officials. A shogunate that had made the six blocks a party to official transactions in 1534 made additional blocks a party to rule after 1539. Never before the Hokke uprising had townspeople been made privy to a suit that did not immediately engage them (No. 1), been involved in police actions (Nos. 2, 7), or been impressed as groups to gather taxes (No. 8). In these cases, as in the moat affair, intermediaries in the proprietary community were effaced to permit direct correspondence between the military and the townspeople. Contrast document No. 7, for example, with the pre-Hokke order that went from the shogunate not to townspeople but to the temple of Nanzenji:

[A] gang of bad men is conspiring to raise an uprising. . . . Hence, without wasting a day or an hour, you are to apprehend the ringleaders. . . . We order you to send directives to all your affiliates that, should anyone resist compliance, his lands will be confiscated.[62]

Or compare the imperial and shogunal orders concerning the moats with a pre-Hokke account of another demand for labor:

Kōzai Mataroku set out for the Kamo shrine and demanded men to assist him in the forthcoming campaign. Shrine officials refused on the basis of their formal exemption from surveillance and taxation by the shogunate.[63]

Setting aside the problem of manipulation (did military officials simply coopt the block associations?), as well as the problem of compliance (did block residents obey the officials?), these comparisons point to a changing structure of authority.[64] The structure incorporated organized townspeople into urban governance, bypassing the religious establishments and the manorial elite that had once served as exclusive channels of command and enforcement.

In another departure from past conduct, military officials began issuing decrees of tax exemption to certain blocks (Nos. 5a, b, c, d), a practice that continued through the remaining decades of war.[65] Until 1546, only temples, shrines, and proprietary houses had received such exemptions. Most decrees, and all those granted to the blocks, stipulated exemptions from various war taxes: barracking duty, claims on building materials, or cash levies for battle. They were typically written on public signboards and displayed around the precincts affected.[66]

But why did military officials recognize the block associations and accord such concessions to them? To a large extent, surely, they chose to conspire in the eclipse or marginalization of the proprietary establishment, which these developments accelerated. The emergence and acceptance of the block organization pointed to a radical division of society into rulers and ruled without mediating ties of attachment. The society of multiple corporations, of autonomous jurisdictions and complex privileges, was being undercut from within. Yet the shogunate was also driven by compulsion in its relations with the blocks. The decrees of tax exemption were hardly necessary to marginalize proprietors. And because they cost the military a good price, they are hardly credible as voluntary favors. What was the compulsion? The exemptions may have represented compensation for specific services. That is, they may belong to the domain of reciprocal agreement that I earlier associated with the pursuit by the six blocks of proper orders to repair those moats: the exemptions may have been a form of payment for conduct no longer coerced through lordly fiat. (There is evidence that the six blocks, for example, received a routine exemption from war taxes in exchange for services to the throne that gradually extended beyond repair of the moats to guard duty and maintenance of some palace buildings.)[67]

Still, relations between the townspeople and the shogunate remained sufficiently tortured to discourage us from any notion of harmony in a contractual exchange. The exemptions occurred in a context of trouble: not only did new battles assail the shogunate; tax defiance among commoners was endemic. The ineradicable specter of the Lotus also continued to dominate the chronology of men who dated their experiences "before" and "after" the Hokke uprising. And on the occasion of that uprising, the shogunate had declined to pay the price of agrarian taxes in exchange for military service and barrier policing by the sectarians.

Yet instead of deterring the shogunate from accommodation with the blocks, the troubles after 1536 may have provided the essential condition of accommodation. This possibility implies that the block associations were able to operate from a position of strength—that they were able to convert turmoil to advantage in a fashion ultimately denied the Hokke movement. Part of their strength derived from the substantially lower price they were exacting from the shogunate: the recognition of, and concessions to, the block associations involved a different order of accommodation than the surrender to commoners of tax privileges reserved for the proprietary elite. Just as important, their strength derived from the combined power of memory and what I have called quiescence. Fortified by the continued withholding of land rents, the memory of the Hokke uprising must also have been fortified by the terror of victors who lived daily, and interdependently, with townspeople capable of brute reprisal. And quiescence may heighten rather than relieve alarm: it is an instrument of bloodless war. Ominously still and unaligned, townspeople refrained from actions that invited easy counterattack and easy interpretation. Thus, the concessions of the shogunate seem to me more than the price of real or expected services. They were the price of a truce, extorted under the compulsion of fear.

Nor was the price of the truce an entirely discrete matter between individual blocks and the shogunate. In 1542, by "imperial wish," the

Lotus sect was revived in the capital, granted "full control over [its] original lands," and urged to rebuild (No. 3). Two years later, the shogunate confirmed the purchase of an immense property by the Hokke temple of Honnōji (No. 4). No soft reading of this development appears tenable. Probably the result of hard negotiations and certainly influenced by awful tension, the development looks like an act of appeasement.[68]

Back to the issues of membership, motive, and adversaries that forged the block associations. A muddled definition of membership also hopelessly muddles the politics of organization. Insofar as organization gave voice to the voiceless, sharpened the edges between rulers and ruled, and worked through the compulsions of fear, divisions by class appear inseparable from that organization. If nobles or priests joined the block associations as more than peripheral sympathizers, the move indicates a decision to surrender the voice of privilege and unite with commoners before a shared adversary. Such a move blurs the lines of class a bit, but it clarifies the lines of power by requiring men of rank to assume a new identity among the ruled. In my view, the block associations emerged as commoners united by class and by place (the "we," the ruled) resolved to acquire a presence and a voice (the motive) before an authority ultimately made up of military overlords (the "they," the rulers).

We-they structures can assume many forms. The record suggests that military officials tried to neutralize the new organization through recognition and concessions and thus to infer an underlying consent to authority from the block associations. From their perspective, the organization was premised on a clear vertical relationship and an implicit acceptance of their own legitimacy. And so we see the absorption of the blocks into urban governance as presumptively compliant units of rule. (And thus the possibility of the soft reading.)

But the expectation of the commoners is another matter. They may have wanted what they got—the recognition and the concessions, the radical clarification of rulers and ruled with its opportunities for direct access and confrontation, a measure of self-rule, a changed political climate that discouraged heedless impositions, a certain security in position after the trauma of the Hokke uprising. These results alone contradict a soft reading of the record. Yet it is always possible that the commoners wanted more—either greater concessions, say, or a rather different we-they structure, premised not on orderly vertical relations but on something else. The most suggestive evidence of a different structure lies in the acts of mediation and justice by commoner "elders" between 1549 and 1553 (Nos. 9–13).

The references to mediation are embedded in descriptions of extraordinary mayhem—murder, mass wounding, threats of retaliatory invasion. Here is the society of self-redress, of concern to us in Chapter 2, in which the "power of the I" explodes into violent marches and five-hour melees. Yet in the face of mayhem on a great scale, commoner elders exerted sufficient authority to end the hostilities, at least for a time, in a fashion unremarkable to the diarist who tells us of them. They worked fast and they worked together in large numbers—as the elders of the six blocks, the elders of northern Kyoto, the elders of northern and southern Kyoto. Such action exceeds civic responsibility or resourcefulness in an emergency and indicates a capacity for alternate governance. Although the blocks had no formal tribunals and justice became a function of mass witness and demonstration (the vengeance of 5,000 commoners, the house burning before 500 guards, the assembly of 120 elders), we nonetheless find a singular ability to organize and to impose resolutions in the stead of a debased shogunal institution. The administration of justice in the blocks necessarily discredited the governance of military officials.

The creation of an alternate government, however limited and however short-lived, pushes we-they relations out of a vertical structure into a parallel one. At least in part and on occasion, the block organization involved the separation and sealing off of commoners from their overlords. Some version of self-rule in the blocks, focused on the administration of justice, may have been far more routine than the record suggests, for that record is exceedingly incomplete. Shogunal documents take no regular account of "outside" justice; noble diarists rarely make note of block affairs; and the exceptional Yamashina Tokitsugu concentrates on his own locale (the six blocks) and, almost certainly, on particularly grievous quarrels there. Yet even the record we have exposes one period of separate rule and the potential for more of the same. In its silences, moreover, the record of military action after the Hokke uprising exposes a different, though related, separation of we and they. The disengagement of commoners from battle that I described earlier as an instrument of bloodless war might also be seen as an instrument to set boundaries. It appears the result of some unspoken agreement about divided interest and separate domains: the overlords were left to fight their own campaigns; the townspeople employed the compulsion of fear to escape, on occasion, even the levying of war taxes. Common cause was no longer possible.

The setting of boundaries—between rulers and ruled, between parties to hegemonic battle and the unaligned—took neighborhood organizations in a direction opposite to that of the Hokke movement. The organizations turned away from one sort of radical political structuring to another. They insisted on the existence of conflicts of interest generated by class and the necessity of expressing these conflicts institutionally. They also opened possibilities for ameliorating injuries—through the confrontations that resulted in tax concessions, a contractual sense of public obligation, and the revival of Hokke devotion; through the entry of commoners into a regular political process and the self-consciousness that implied; through the development of some self-rule and a separate (even separatist) politics. These are positive things, though I cannot measure them against the hypothetical advantages of a successful Hokke uprising or direct revolutionary action.

Yet we should not ignore the singular transformation that the neighborhood associations achieved: the exclusion of the proprietary voice and the breaking of mediating ties of attachment, as the political community was reorganized into two simple parts—military authorities and townspeople. This change had been anticipated by the word wars of concern to us earlier. However insistent on the privileges deriving from proprietorship, those suits acknowledged the final weakness of the old elite and the ultimate role of military officials in all areas of conventional governance. Still, there is an enormous leap between acknowledging weakness and bypassing proprietors altogether, particularly through the creation of new organs of representation. The leap was occasioned, I think, by the absolute political splits exposed by the Hokke uprising. A further transformation was the acceptance of the neighborhood associations by Kyoto's military rulers as part of a normal political life.

We can account for such acceptance in two ways: by the military's perception of neighborhood associations as useful instruments of control; or by the military's growing commitment, most apparent in the tenure of Miyoshi Chōkei, to dismantle the medieval corporate order. But to suggest that officials could view the associations differently from commoners and that a popular movement might even resonate with the objectives of warlords is not to find the organizations a retrograde development made captive to military power holders. It is, rather, to identify the peculiar genius of a development that is capable both of multiple readings and of integration into an emerging polity, and thus of persistence when other forms of agitation failed. Although neighborhood organizations could fail their members through official cooptation, they nonetheless created opportunities for a popular politics that commercial associations and the Hokke uprising itself had not.

I close, however, by returning to paradox. My descriptions of work and neighborhood have been contradictory. In the world of work I have found continuity, dependency, fragmented and insular organization focused on patrons, structures of privilege and honor binding townspeople to the elite. There the language of particularism and attachment prevailed (and continued to prevail, for commercial suits framed in conventional terms in no way abated after the Hokke uprising). In the world of neighborhood I have found rupture, the raising of an independent voice, encompassing organization focused on place, structures of conflict and fear separating commoners from their rulers. There the language of class and division prevailed. At times, the two descriptions have intersected. Cynicism and change eroded the relations of work. Manipulation by the elite compromised the identity of the block organizations. Yet we are still left with colliding visions of power.

And we are left with a stepping back from collision. After the Hokke uprising, men and women on opposite sides of the social and political divides chose to tolerate a fair degree of ambiguity in their relations with each other. Proprietors in financial trouble relied only on strident verbal threats to recover their land rents. Overlords unable to control the capital excused certain blocks from war taxes and avoided public conscription. Armed and presumably vengeful commoners created a voice through nonviolent neighborhood associations. Like the equally profound contradictions in many other societies, those in Kyoto may have been reconciled, or suspended, by divergent interests and needs. Thus, the trader who sought protection from a commercial patron within the organization of a guild might also have sought protection against proprietary or military taxes within the organization of a block. And the patron still capable of collecting guild fees might have safeguarded this income by enduring the withholding of land rents. Kyoto's many constituencies were both intertwined and divided. Even though neighborhood associations moved away from proprietary attachments, they continued to welcome whatever leverage the old elite, and particularly the throne, could afford them.

But in Kyoto the compulsions of interest were always complicated by the extremities of war. With its brute revelations about disorder in the economy, polity, and society, war exposed differences and built contradictions. These tensions might have forced resolutions, for we often suppose that war has a rationalizing influence. This influence was exercised very gradually in Kyoto, however, and when it did come to bear (in the emergence of block associations), the change was insidious rather than dramatic. The toleration of ambiguous relations surely reflected the awful vulnerability of the capital to outside threats. It reflected even more clearly the risk of internal disintegration revealed in the Hokke uprising. The residents of Kyoto chose to live with paradox.

7

Play: The Freedom of Invention

In 1591 the man who had finally unified Japan's warring states condemned his tea master to death. Sensational both to contemporaries and to generations of historical detectives, the act has provoked a host of interpretations that turn on the politics and the temperaments of the two principals: Toyotomi Hideyoshi, the great general and peacemaker, and Sen no Rikyū, the most eminent leader in the culture of tea. All we really know is that Rikyū was permitted to take his own life, at the age of sixty-nine, in a residence surrounded by more than three thousand of Hideyoshi's troops.[1] But I am convinced that the event developed from a crisis described by one chronicler of the time:

In [tea] objects he liked, [Rikyū] declared good points bad and bought them for mean prices. In vessels he disdained, [Rikyū] declared bad points good and bought them at high prices. He called new old and old new. No he made yes, false he made genuine.[2]

Here is an exceptionally vivid indictment of arbitrary standards and slippery meanings. In the domain of play, or of art, Rikyū stood accused of wreaking havoc, exposing the volatility of aesthetic and economic value, of judgment and cultural authority. Good and bad, even old and new or true and false, dissolved in his hands as constants to become ephemeral verdicts of ephemeral leaders and the men and markets they could influence. It is, of course, the power of art and play to test constants and endanger certitudes. And it is an odd conceit to imagine that such power may be confined to a ludic sphere without encroaching on politics and society. For Hideyoshi, a man resolved to fix the moorings of a world at drift, the havoc of play registered and helped propel havoc everywhere. Rikyū was sacrificed to the goal of clear meanings and certain authority.

This is a chapter about wartime play—about the havoc Rikyū came to represent and men like Hideyoshi tried to tame—and the ways in which it registered havoc elsewhere. It is a chapter about the union of play and politics. On one level, the union derived simply from the political content of play; for in the realms of dance and tea, issues of political power were everywhere. Dancers and tea men discarded the authority of tradition, form, and masters; they broke open notions of value and taste; they challenged all presumptions about the custodianship of art. Wrenching play out of familiar contexts and scrambling the elements and the rules of procedure, these practitioners used improvisation to re-create their arts day after day. Wartime play thus moved simultaneously into transgression and invention; it rejected stability to explore the boundaries of imagination. This exploration gradually revealed new definitions of communal and personal identity, new conceptions of style and artistic authorship. The transformation occurred, moreover, through dramatic acts of performance that, in the case of dancing, occupied the streets in wild nighttime spectacles defiant of urban regulations.

As these observations suggest, the union of play and politics involved something more than the political content of dance or tea (or other practices—linked verse, for example). On the deepest level, the play and politics of wartime were manifestations of a single culture in which distinctions between the playful and the political, between art and power, had collapsed. Although I have called this culture the culture of lawlessness, it might better be called the culture of performance.

Culture is a chameleon term. I use it here to describe dominant forms of public conduct that both project and create attitudes about selves, attachments, and values. Although word wars and commercial practices continued to evoke the presumptively normative attitudes of the past, lawlessness describes the prevailing direction of the age. The term refers, in part, to the unleashing of the "force of the self" in the pursuit of interest; it also refers to experimentation with new modes of confrontation and melioration in a society that had lost confidence in precedent and institution. Essential to these developments, but particularly to the demonstrations that became a central mode of urban conflict, were mass performances of coercion and appeal in the streets. As the medium of expression for lawlessness, performance conveyed new attitudes about selves, attachments, and values that rejected norms. In politics as in play, spectacle began by slipping out of the constraints (of statute, custom, legal structure, corporate hierarchy) that I have signified with the word *law*. Protest was often overt (in the debtors' marches, for example), sometimes oblique (in the dancing, for example). Yet spectacle moved beyond transgression into improvised encounters that tested the desire of participants and the responses of audiences. Many transformed desire into alternative visions of social order: uprisings opened the possibility of horizontal self-rule; the Hokke movement posited a reconfiguration of the elite and ultimately provoked a class-based organization of neighborhoods; purges separated legitimacy from institutions; tea (as we shall see) redrew the lines of prestige in new communities of wealth. But whether visions took clear and durable form, they emerged from dynamic group actions and reactions that insisted on process over closure. Performance created a culture of motion in which men and women chose fluidity over fixed definitions of identity and authority.

Motion had a special importance in play. By using the word *vision* and linking political demonstration to alternative forms of governance, I have implied that performance was instrumental to the discovery of goals. Yet performance in play, and often in the political theater as well, was an act of liberation in itself, dependent for satisfaction not on any future effect but on the very movement of the rebellious body.[3]

Dancing

Toward the end of the seventh month of 1520, the *Nisui* diarist made the following entry in his journal:

At nightfall five or six of us went out together to see the dancers and musicians. Tonight the sponsor was Kanrōji. I understand he was reciprocating last night's [sponsorship of the dancing] by some of his retainers. Such things occur every night this year, in a fashion unseen and unheard of in recent times. Is it because the realm appears peaceful? Or is it the beginning of a new commotion? On my way home, [I saw that] dancing had even taken over the bamboo grove [at the imperial palace]. It overpowers every eye and ear.[4]

On the same day Sanjōnishi Sanetaka noted Kanrōji's sponsorship of the dancing in his diary, concluding: "It is beyond explanation. Beyond explanation." Three days later he added, "There is music and dancing all over southern Kyoto."[5]

Unlike the *Nisui* diarist, Sanetaka refrained from suggestions that the frenzy was novel—something "unseen and unheard of in recent times"; for years, this stern old aristocrat had been observing, always with disapproval, the eruption of music and dance in the capital. In the seventh month of 1505, for example, he had made this entry in his diary:

Ever more throughout Kyoto, the sounds of dancing, of bells and drums, exhausts the ears. Today there are orders that there be no such vulgarity off the battleground. This is just as it should be.[6]

In the next year he welcomed new laws by the shogunate that forbade "violations of coinage exchange laws, theft, arson, armed assault, quarrels, sumō wrestling, and dancing."[7] These laws too appeared in the seventh month.

Similar laws and similar observations occurred across the decades of war in connection with an activity sometimes called, simply, dancing, sometimes called *hayashi*—which referred to the accompaniment of flutes and drums, and probably to singing. Most often the activity was identified as *fūryū odori*—literally, "the dance of the wind flowing." Just what this was, however, remains a mystery. Like the tantalizing expression *uchimawari*, which named the circular processions of the Hokke sectarians, *fūryū odori* evoked without defining an apparently sensational scene. The emphasis of the phrase itself was on spectacle. When it first came into use in the early classical period, *fūryū* referred to a showy elegance, particularly in dress, although it could also indicate splendor in music or poetry. By the early medieval period, the word designated elaborate constructions as well—such as floats or festooned umbrellas or other ornaments that appeared in festival gatherings. Yet it retained strong associations with flamboyant costume, especially in the periodic sumptuary laws where "*fūryū* attire" was lined up with the flaunting of "figured silk and embroidered brocade and silver blades" as symptoms of "lunacy" (*monogurui*) and "wild excess" (*basara*).[8] Indeed, *fūryū* was interchangeable with *basara*—a word that went beyond visual images of gaudiness and tactile images of opulence to evoke dizzying noise, pungent tastes, and rich aromas.

The clearest representation of *fūryū* dancing occurs quite late, during the period of political unification, in screens depicting the events that marked the seventh anniversary of Toyotomi Hideyoshi's death. The screens capture highlights of a commemoration stretching over seven days in the eighth month of 1604, which included processions, theatrical performances, gift exchanges, and prayers around the precincts of

Fūryū dancing.
Details from *Hōkoku sairei-zu byōbu* (a pair of screens representing events that commemorated the seventh anniversary, in 1604, of the death of Toyotomi Hideyoshi). Both scenes appear on the left member of the pair of screens; the scene on the left appears in the second and third panels, and the scene on the right in the fourth and fifth panels. Painted by Kanō Naisen (1570–1616). 167 cm. × 352.5 cm. (each screen); gold leaf and color on paper. Registered as an Important Cultural Property. Courtesy of Hōkoku shrine, Kyoto.

two Toyotomi monuments: Hōkoku shrine, where Hideyoshi's divine spirit was worshiped; and Hōkōji temple, where Hideyoshi had built a massive statue of Vairocana Buddha. Together with a narrative account of the proceedings prepared by Hideyoshi's biographer, the screens offer a compelling interpretation of one experience of *fūryū* dance—the central event of the fourth day of commemorative ceremonies.[9]

Both the painter and the biographer assail us with size and color. What appears in the screens as a sea of bodies in motion is described in the account as an assembly of five hundred dancers divided into five groups, three from northern and two from southern Kyoto. They came from block federations, identified in the screens both by the handsome

placards carried by attendants and by the distinctive costumes and ornaments arraying the dancers. The biographer focuses attention on brilliant umbrellas, hats embossed with flower patterns, fans and hand
props, while the painter gives us robes of bold designs and sharp colors.
The biographer listens to the music of drums and flutes and voices,
while the painter watches the limbs of dancers who stomp and fly in
concentric circles around crazed ensembles at the hub. The painter also
watches the watchers—crowds of nobles, priests, and military households observing the dancers from viewing stands along the parade
route.

Is this the sort of activity that so disturbed military officials and diarists in wartime? It is likely that several features of the dancing represented in the screens also characterized the dance of war. Striking trappings of some sort, for example, appear inextricable from *furyū,* although these must have been far simpler in wartime than the robes and ornaments of the screens. In a rare description of the clothing worn to dance in 1571, Yamashina Tokitsugu tells us of the "gold and silver," the "Chinese fabric," and the "red plum dye" in the "splendid attire" of participants from northern Kyoto.[10] Yet I suspect that such opulence came to popular dancing late in the sixteenth century, and that the *furyū* dimension of earlier gatherings derived from lesser, still-dramatic elements—the similar costumes of dancers, perhaps, or repeated patterns in their fans and headgear, the use of props like umbrellas or decorative lances.[11]

Heightening the impact of display was the force of numbers; for the size of the commemorative dancing honoring Hideyoshi was probably roughly consonant with wartime experiences. By the 1560s, Yamashina Tokitsugu commented on an assembly of more than 250 dancers.[12] Few single gatherings may have been that large, but the emphasis in the sources on the frequency and the many locations of the dancing conveys the impression of great expanse. And heightening the impression of size was the frenzy of movement and sound; for the conduct of the commemorative dancing probably preserved older traditions. Here speculation is fraught with trouble. Dance, particularly amateur dance, is not static, and neither written nor pictorial evidence makes possible a close comparison of its sixteenth-century forms. Diarists tell us of flute and percussion accompaniment and the "havoc" they associate with the dancing. They sometimes link it to *nenbutsu odori*—ecstatic dancing invoking the Buddha Amida which, as we encounter it in medieval painting, involved moving circles of devotees stomping their feet and swinging their arms in apparent delirium.[13] In very general terms and without imputing to dance a stability it rarely has, I think of the *furyū* dancing of wartime as a group activity in which performers moved in concert through circular formations with some speed and abandon.

But if, to some extent, the *furyū* dancing of wartime shared trappings, size, and conduct with the dancing of 1604, it shared nothing else. Irreducible differences marked the distance between something forbidden in wartime even to children and something celebrated in peacetime as fitting homage to a newly proclaimed god. In effect, the dancing at Hideyoshi's shrine had a context, and the dancing of war did not. Although the screens may intimate an appealing bedlam, the dancing portrayed there fitted into intelligible frames: its participants had clear identities; they gathered at the behest of the powerful military sponsors of the event, who observed them from elevated viewing stands; they performed in an arena reserved for them at religious (and political) monuments; they took their place at an appointed time during the day, in a sequence of carefully scheduled activities. As the closing remarks of the narrative account indicate, the dancers also had, in the eyes of their official patrons, an obvious and admirable purpose: their performance signified the peace and cohesion of the realm. Lest the proceedings slip into anything unseemly, we are further told that five hundred guards, five hundred attendants with portable stools, and a body of block elders equipped with (gold!) sticks were patrolling the perimeter of the action. (*Fūryū* was not, then, entirely tame.)

What is striking in wartime accounts of *fūryū* is the seeming absence of frames and controls. Let me amplify the observations of *Nisui* and Sanjōnishi with later comments from Yamashina Tokitsugu, the most consistent reporter on the dancing.

No. 1.   1532, 8th month, 20th day.
Until late tonight, there was extraordinary *fūryū*, everyone gripped by lunacy.[14]

No. 2.   1544, 7th month, 14th day.
Today, all *fūryū* throughout Kyoto has been forbidden. Also forbidden are all excursions with lanterns.[15]

No. 3.   1553, 7th month.
19th day.   Hamuro is journeying out of Kyoto. Is he going to see the *fūryū* dancers? I understand the Yoshida group is planning [dancing] today. . . . Tonight Yoshida Kanemigi called and we went out together. There was *fūryū* dancing in front of the Daiban. Many people gathered to watch, including [five nobles] and seven or eight children. There were four dances.

20th day.   Because there were rumors that the people of Muromachi, from this area, would be doing *fūryū,* the head carpenter of the Seiryōden came to call to say that I should go over to the palace [to watch]. However, they say it has been postponed. There are rumors everywhere that [dancing] throughout Kyoto is being postponed these days. What are the details?

21st day.   Because *furyū* dancers from southern Kyoto came up [to northern Kyoto], I went out to my gate to watch them. I also gathered [with the crowds] to watch when the *furyū* dancers went over [to perform] at the palace.[16]

No. 4.   1565, 7th month, 18th day.

Five or six people from the blocks came over today to practice. We settled on the rhythm and other matters. They say they will [use the music] tonight.[17]

No. 5.   1567, 7th month, 24th day.

Because there were rumors that the *furyū* from Awata-guchi would be performed at Yoshida, I went out to Yoshida at nightfall. There were twenty large lanterns, and the [dancing area] spread over two square *ken*. It was an amazing sight, unknown to previous ages. There were groups from all over the vicinity of Kyoto. Four dances took place. Then there was *nenbutsu* dancing from Ichijōji. There were 100 women and 140 or 150 men. The *nenbutsu* was admirable, exceeding the [descriptive power] of brush or tongue.[18]

With few exceptions, the references by noble diarists to *furyū* were made toward the end of the seventh month, the period of *obon,* when the living greeted the spirits of the dead who returned briefly to commune with their descendants. The seasonal recurrence of the dance, as well as occasional allusions to the lanterns that illuminated it, establish seemingly obvious connections with *obon* rituals, which originated in the courtly ceremony of lighting lamps donated by aristocrats to Buddhist temples.[19] Yet the diarists themselves never made this connection. Perhaps they took it for granted. Perhaps, however, it went unspoken because it was both there and not there. It was there insofar as the ritual calendar provided a broadly legitimating motive and occasion for the gatherings; and there, too, insofar as, seeking an occasion to meet, the dancers selected a festival of ghosts. Inhabiting a universe outside time and place, beyond the custodianship of institutions or authorities, these ghosts belonged (if they had to be fitted into categories of belonging) only to memory and family. And in greeting them in the preternatural space of reunion, the dancers too might break for a moment all mundane ties other than those of blood.

Such connections between *furyū* and *obon* may have been sufficiently unsettling, of themselves, to discourage acknowledgment by our noble diarists. They may also have been so fragile or coincidental as to recede entirely for men left baffled by what they saw. The *Nisui* diarist was moved to wonder whether the dancing signified a joyful response to peace or a round of new disturbances. Sanjōnishi Sanetaka compared it not to religious rites but to the misbehavior of troops readying for battle. Yamashina Tokitsugu found it lunatic, with no reference to ritual excitement. Ancestors, priests, temple precincts do not figure in their records.

Night does figure—as the only constant other than the unremarked concentration of the dancing in the seventh month. Observers set off in darkness to watch the proceedings; they stayed (when they tell us at all) for four rounds of dancing; they returned home much later to notice the outbreak of dancing in new locales; and they prepared themselves for the possibility of more *furyū* when dusk fell again. They presumably carried torches, and they presumably viewed the dancers through pools of lamp light and smoke. Along with the performers, they defied the taboos against nighttime excursions and fire.

Where did they go? Usually they "went out" to unnamed locations, some beyond the city boundaries. Other times they were summoned to the palace for a viewing or watched the dancing from their own gates. Toward the end of the period, they saw *furyū* in a rather formal setting in the district of Yoshida. The earlier accounts place the dancing "all over" or "throughout Kyoto." In every case, however, the accounts suggest that observers went out suddenly, in response to "rumors" or unexpected "summons," to watch an activity without a fixed location (or a fixed schedule). The dancing moved from place to place, may have occurred simultaneously in several places, and at least sometimes became a carnival in motion as dancers progressed from station to station, stopping to perform before this or that residence. They seemingly appropriated the streets and other open areas to transform the fortress city into a free arena of play.

The apparent absence of any schedule for the dancing suggests that it was provoked by impulse or opportunity. Clearly, toward the end of wartime *furyū* involved considerable planning: performers were practicing the musical accompaniment (No. 4) and many troupes were assembling in a well-prepared setting (No. 5). Throughout the period, someone had to coordinate the dancers, gather suitable trappings, and circulate word about likely assemblies. And allusions both to sponsorship of the dancing and to dancing at the palace (which implies prior invitation?) build an impression of organization. Still, *furyū* seems to have emerged from private arrangements and a popular will, and planning seems to have remained secret. Spectators (at least noble ones) had little notice of dancing that could be postponed (through fear of official intervention?) as surprisingly as it could be initiated.

But secrecy in planning did not extend to secrecy in execution. *Fūryū* was not the hidden play of shuttered rooms and small, quiet parties. Conspicuous enough in its noise, color, size, and location to draw an audience, *fūryū* also sought out an audience. To launch an activity that required display and encounter, not simply the gratification of participants, rumors were floated, sponsors attracted, and spectators brought to their gates. Yet the identities of observers and performers, and the relations between them, are as obscure and variable as the setting and timing of the dancing. The observers specifically mentioned by the noble diarists also belonged to the nobility. Several times an apparently supportive Yamashina Tokitsugu even provided songs and instruction for *fūryū* performers. But was the nobility a critical part of the *fūryū* audience? In what role, or roles, was it cast? Were courtiers patrons of the dancers, interested neighbors, voyeurs, fellow conspirators and law breakers, instruments of a crowd that manipulated them into participation? Did courtiers actually join in the dancing?

The main body of dancers was made up of commoners. By the latter part of the sixteenth century, Yamashina Tokitsugu was identifying performers with certain geographical areas on the periphery of the city (Yoshida and Awata-guchi, for example) and with individual blocks in the city (Muromachi, Karasuma, Tachiuri, and Nishijin, for example).[20] The identification of dancers with place moved *fūryū* closer to the realm of intelligibility after 1550. But even then, identity attached to a crowd without clear leaders or structures in an environment—of darkness, costume, repetitive movement in unison, possibly of intoxication—that blurred everything particular about the participants. It may also have blurred distinctions of sex. Yamashina Tokitsugu notes that one hundred women joined the dancing at Yoshida in 1567, though without indicating whether they danced separately or in company with men. It is tempting to imagine that women regularly joined the dancing, together with male performers, in headgear and robes bound by low-slung sashes, effacing gender.

The censure of officials and the disquiet of observers might have been provoked by any of the discordant elements of *fūryū*—its tenuous links to the ritual calendar, its unpredictability in timing and location, its invasion of the streets and open spaces, its associations with darkness and fire, its insistent but obscure relationship with an audience, its identification with crowds merged and stimulated through spectacle.[21] Quite simply, *fūryū* disturbed the peace. Potentially alarming in any situation, it posed a particular challenge to a fearful city where encounters of all kinds—debates over the Buddhist law, the redemption of pawned articles, the collection of taxes, the drawing of water from a well—were correctly perceived as occasions for violence. But the conjunction of so many discordant elements in *fūryū*, as well as the persistence of the activity despite the threats of reprisal, invites a broader meditation: what did observers make of *fūryū*, and what did participants find in it?

Fūryū deeply resembled the politics of demonstration and witness. Observers would have characterized the resemblance differently, if compelled to characterize it at all, but I suspect they found, if unconsciously, a parallel between the dancing and the political theater that had come to substitute for the rule of law. They saw that theater everywhere in the conduct of military rule: in the massing of armies that engaged in sporadic battle seldom attended by large casualties; in the parades of severed heads, humiliated shogun, and recent victors; in the rites of purge that included the burning of the enemy's residences and the humiliation of the old guard.

The residents of Kyoto also saw political theater in the conduct of popular mobilizations: in the debtors' uprisings that began at night when supporters gathered with torches at the city entrances, and continued at sunrise when phalanxes descended with shouts on the city's pawnbrokers; in the street actions of commoners who assembled in crowds to resist tax collectors or military police; in the acts of private justice; and, most flamboyantly, in the circular processions of Hokke sectarians.

The politics of demonstration occurred in spaces open to view, generally in the streets of the capital, and demanded attention with noise or fire or grotesquerie or the trappings of parade. And we know of it now, as great numbers of people were surely meant to know of it at the time, through the testimony of the riveted spectators who spread word of what they saw. Almost invariably, those spectators too had "gone out" to the political theater in response to "rumors" or a "summons," to engage in something they called *kenbutsu*, "sightseeing" in modern parlance but closer to "watching spectacles."[22] Indeed, watching became a consuming activity of wartime, as spectacle became the currency of almost all transactions. Religious establishments, for example, used mass witness not only in public debates and martial displays but also in important rituals:

Gensuke onen-ki. 1525, 2d month, 2d day.
The abbot of Yamashina Honganji died. The funeral will occur on the seventeenth day of this month. I understand tens of thousands of people will be gathered.[23]

Tokitsugu kyō-ki. 1553, 3d month, 25th day.
I understand that three thousand priests will be reading the sutras in succession (at the Saga Shakadō). Temporary quarters have been put up for them to the east and west of the Shakadō. I do not know how many listeners there are throughout Saga. They come and go in astonishing numbers. There are limitless numbers of beggars and people soliciting contributions.[24]

Fūryū conformed quite remarkably to the patterns of political theater and the broader patterns in wartime society of display and appeal to audience. But to what end? Purposes were not at all apparent to the diarists, who repeatedly convey the mysterious quality of the dancing and hence, its exceptional challenge to observers. Perhaps *fūryū* looked to them like a display of power aimed at the defiance of military authorities, the reclaiming of the streets, and the intimidation of an often-inadequate police force. A type of guerrilla insurgency, it could have appeared as an extension of uprising that combined terror and carnival. Yet the dancers willfully broke the contexts that made uprisings and other forms of demonstration at least superficially intelligible. Purges and debtors' marches, for example, were not mysterious. Thus lacking an overt purpose, *fūryū* might have seemed a form of parody. Holding up a fun-house mirror to political spectacle, the dancing contorted the features of demonstration to reflect a face of transitory ascendance, impulsive organization, mob sway, and a lunatic ethos. As parody, *fūryū* mocked all efforts at political structure.

From a different perspective, *fūryū* surely looked less like a parody than the logical unfolding of political spectacle. On one hand, the politics of demonstration worked according to rules of encounter and retreat that forestalled brute force. On the other hand, demonstration rejected institutional authority in coercive acts that always threatened greater violence. Demonstration was an uneasy compromise between control and riot. *Fūryū* confirmed the fragility of control and the nearness of riot. The dancers easily took over the garrison town of walls, fortified gates, and moats. They shed identities under the cover of darkness and in the anonymity of costume and crowd. They slipped the ties of place and neighborhood during a progress of movable feasts that might halt anywhere. They snapped the attachments of work and sect and patronage in groups united only by agitated motion. They muddled surviving hierarchies of power and prestige through encounters with spectators that defied any simple hierarchical interpretation. Had control prevailed during the day, the madness of night might have appeared as a fitting release from mundane confinements, say, or as an escape into an alternate world whose passing freedoms sated, rather than stimulated, the appetite for transgression. But *furyū* was not a reversal of daytime certainties. It was an extreme version of the routine denial of constants. The authors of word wars may have constructed a stable idyll. Even military men may have met the influx of green and naked soldiers of fortune with new ranking systems and a heightened attention to symbols of honor.[25] The battle between control and riot remained, nonetheless, an unequal contest.

Furyū's play with notions of hierarchy doubtless left elite observers most uneasy. The allusions in the sources to noble spectators and sponsors, and to commoner dancers from the blocks, hint at encounters of class. But what sort of encounters were they? Yamashina Tokitsugu chose to give them a benign quality, depicting courtiers as patrons of an activity compatible with orderly class relations. Alternatively, since Tokitsugu mentions nobles joining the dancing by 1568 and identifying with the performers of the six blocks, the courtiers appear as participants in a common frenzy.[26] These developments seem to belong to a late stage of *furyū*, when it was tamed by context.[27] But even if noble patronage and participation were common to *furyū* throughout wartime, they were hardly benign acts. The leveling of hierarchy through the union of courtly audience and commoner dance troupe must have raised again the specter of the Lotus uprising. And although this union may have implied the binding together of a new community, it may also have implied the escape of all participants from community into a bedlam where solitary release was possible. Crowds wear equally well the face of solidarity and the face of atomization. Yamashina Tokitsugu's image of benevolent nobles and deferential dancers acting within their strata raises its own vexing questions about what these groups wanted from each other, wanted enough to break shogunal law together and join in the disturbing play of night. The partial rebinding of ties that were breaking in the spheres of trade and governance? The translation of a once-pervasive relationship into a more purely symbolic form? The joint manipulation of the other?

The two versions of class encounter that Yamashina Tokitsugu provides do not exhaust the possibilities. We might remember that commoners were periodically obstinate about cooperating with officials to mount the Gion festival, even as they were persistent in mounting their own *furyū*. What, then, of Tokitsugu's image of harmony? If we suppose that commoners sought control over their own festival life and thus moved *furyū* out of generally intelligible contexts into a world totally of their own making, the encounter between performers and audience must have assumed aspects of confrontation reminiscent of the street actions of commoners. Confrontation could have been soft or hard—soft insofar as it sublimated contention in play; hard insofar as it extended contention into play. But some element of confrontation was inherent in *furyū*, for it was unmistakably an act of aggression. Night, fire, mobs, noise—all its parts battered the audience. Even if the battering was delicious for some, even if Tokitsugu chose to sympathize with *furyū* and other nobles to appropriate it, the essential violation of the dancing remains.

So what, in sum, did the violation signify to observers? Alarming enough in its surface disturbance of the peace, *furyū* was still more powerful, surely, in the multiple associations and potential meanings it opened up. In the first instance, the dancing looked sufficiently like the political theater to suggest either that the participants had their own political agenda or that they were mocking the conduct of power. The dancing also looked like a manifesto of confusion, a statement that the riot of night conveyed the real—but suppressed—riot of day; for although it took place in the domain of play, where dancers might be seen as escaping or reversing the certainties of "normal" life, *furyū* exposed rather than denied the final absence of normalcy. And the dancing looked, too, like a form of class encounter: a leveling of hierarchy or a defiance of power relations by subordinates, who were prepared to resist with belligerent spectacles solely under their own control.

These associations and meanings sometimes collide, sometimes overlap. I suspect the problem of *furyū*, for spectators no less than historians, was the abundance of connections that the dancing intimated. But there was its potency—its ability to use the world of strange play to engage the images and fears and contests at the center of the mundane world.

What observers made of the dance and what participants found in dancing may often have been the same, although basic differences are likely as well. Let me suggest the differences by outlining the obvious: the participants in *fūryū* made choices about what they did— they chose to dance and to dance in a certain way; they also chose to dance often and over the course of decades despite official disfavor. I conclude that the dancers liked what they did and the way they did it. It is this pleasure that interests me most.

Pleasure surely came from the dramatization of conflict: from the battering of the audience, the mockery of power, the confusion of hierarchy, and the exposure of slipperiness. Yet apart from whatever black pleasures *fūryū* offered, it was also driven by an excitement that drew in spectators who surmounted their fears in the presence of something thrilling. The association in the diaries between dancing and lunacy suggests a taste, in at least some parts of wartime society, for stronger and stronger stimulation.[28]

The issue of lunacy, which has long engaged historians, invites several comparisons. Writing of violence in the "gratification of passion" during the Renaissance, Jacob Burckhardt observed:

The restraints of which men were conscious were but few. Each individual, even among the lowest of the people, felt himself inwardly emancipated from the State and its police, whose title to respect was illegitimate, and itself founded on violence; and no man believed any longer in the justice of the law.[29]

Writing of the effects of the great plague upon Athenian society, Thucydides observed:

Seeing how quick and abrupt were the changes of fortune which came to the rich who suddenly died and to those who had previously been penniless but now inherited their wealth, people now began openly to venture on acts of self-indulgence which before then they had used to keep dark. . . . Money and life seemed equally ephemeral. And as for what is called honor, no one showed himself willing to abide by its laws. . . . It was generally agreed that what was both honorable and valuable was the pleasure of the moment. . . . [30]

The connections made here between political or physical trauma and reverberating license guide much of my discussion. They are especially revealing in the domain of *homo ludens,* where Burckhardt in particular went on to trace the moral and psychological upheaval produced by political dislocation.[31] Thus, we might interpret the lunacy of *fūryū* as a collapse of restraints once fortified by lawful rule—as the unleashing, through misrule, of an always-latent disorder, which emerged as libertine dancing. Viewed in this way, *fūryū* becomes more than functional play (an antidote to, or an outlet for, mundane expectations), and more, too, than symbolic play (a dramatization of the obsessions of an age).

Fūryū had a good deal to do with "the pleasure of the moment." And it was more than a functional or symbolic response to trouble. We lose something essential to *fūryū* if we ignore its hectic thrill. Still, the dancers took to the streets in a particularly fraught political context; they used the forms of contemporary political theater; and they appeared in public again and again, over the course of decades, in actions that were ephemeral but ever renewed. It is difficult to dismiss *fūryū*, then, as a random explosion of passion set off simply by the moment. It appears, rather, a distinctive and continuing source of strength for commoners in a distinctive situation. I find its power (and pleasure) less in the statements about conflict that *fūryū* conveyed to its audience than in the experiences of freedom it provided to the dancers themselves.

The freedom of the dancing was, first of all, a practical matter of autonomy. Separating themselves from intelligible structures and authority, the dancers assembled by themselves all the elements of their play, without external compulsion or expectation. They also denied stasis by re-creating the event day after day, if only by varying its setting and other elements. The variety gave the performers control over each episode of the dancing to set it apart from a past and a tradition, a pattern of fixed ritual reenactment. And control delivered a message about the authorship of art—about its continual transfer away from formulators or custodians to current performers, its accessibility to anyone who asserts presence and voice by seizing the arena of performance. Finally, the freedom of the dancing was a matter of style. What little we know of *fūryū* suggests a taste for the weird. Darkness and clamorous music, splashy trappings and gyrations—such features rejected harmony and elegance to embrace shock and incongruity.[32]

In effect, *fūryū* defined a series of oppositions: between freedom and subordination, shifting authorship and stable authority, invention and stasis, iconoclasm and reverence, license and discipline, present and past. The choices made by the dancers, in every case for freedom and its correlates, implied political statements—except that the term *statement* obscures the performance aspect of *fūryū*. The actual dancing of the dance (the massing of bodies, the invasion of the cityscape) was an immediate (and renewable) act of freedom felt in the flesh. Unlike other forms of political demonstration—the processions of the Lotus sectarians, for example—the dancing was a complete experience. It waited for no future consummation of goals. It asked for nothing.[33] It was no instrument, no symbol or protocol, but the very realization of an autonomous power. Thus, the dancing could not be fought or defeated in the manner of an uprising. Official decisions about debts or taxes could not touch it; the most vigilant policing could only disperse it; brute repression would only suspend it for a time while confirming its potency.

Tea

1533
3d month, 20th day
To [the residence of the priest] Shishōbō [the host]
Hisamasa, one person [the guest]
In the alcove: [the painting] *Kawachisa*
    [by] Mokkei [Mu-ch'i; of the Southern Sung dynasty]
On a board: a *hiragumo* [-style kettle]
    next to it, a *hoya* censer [used as a lid rest]
On the shelves: a *tsurukubi* [tea caddy] on a tray
    a *daikoshi* fresh-water container
    an *usu* tea bowl
    a metal *hiraki* waste-water receptacle
Following the tea, there were noodles (*sōmen*)[34]

This is the first entry in a tea diary kept by Matsuya Hisamasa, a privileged purveyor of lacquerware in the service of Tōdaiji temple in Nara. Hisamasa kept up the diary for sixty-three years, from 1533 until 1596, as a record of the noteworthy tea parties he attended as a guest. His son and his grandson kept similar journals, which extend the collective tea record of the Matsuya house to 1650. Three other tea diaries, all from prominent merchant families, also survive from the sixteenth and early seventeenth centuries. The Tsuda diary (1548–90), begun by Tsuda Sōtatsu of Sakai and continued by his son and grandson, consists of a series of journals that separately describe parties attended by, and parties hosted by, the several authors. The diary of Imai Sōkyū, another Sakai merchant, chronicles the tea parties given and attended by Sōkyū between 1554 and 1587. The diary of Kamiya Sōtan of Hakata chronicles tea parties given and attended by Sōtan between 1586 and 1613.[35]

The form of Matsuya Hisamasa's first entry came to govern both his own subsequent entries and the accounts of later tea diarists, shaping what we might now regard as a genre but what, at the time, was probably an unusual enterprise. We have earlier descriptions of certain notable gatherings for tea.[36] (We also have accounts of sessions to compose sequences of linked verse, which may have influenced the tea records.[37]) Yet the Matsuya diary is the first extant work that tracked, on a regular basis, the seemingly vital information about individual tea meetings: time and setting, the names of host and guests, details concerning objects on display and in use in the tea room (with notes about their presentation), and menus of the food served during any ensuing meal. Occasional entries may omit some of these remarks or introduce others—about the character of the tea itself, for example. Sometimes we encounter sketches of a pot or a flower arrangement in the increasingly encyclopedic records of later years. But these are variations on a form, an almost-telegraphic form often dependent for sense on an insider's knowledge of the code, in which the identities of the participants and the material things they savored loom largest.

The tea diaries of the sixteenth century trace both a social and an aesthetic transformation in the culture of tea. The tea parties preceding the transformation, those of the later fifteenth century, were gatherings of the elite to appreciate precious, frequently Chinese, objects. Some were held in Zen monasteries, some in aristocratic mansions, but those best known to us took place in the circles of ranking military men, preeminently the shogun. They were set in distinguished reception rooms ornamented (even loaded) with prized continental objects—celadon vases, for example, Sung landscape paintings, bronze censers for incense, and iron-glazed bowls on carved stands. There eminent guests gathered, on occasion in substantial numbers, to receive tea from a group of attendants who had typically prepared the beverage in adjacent rooms concealed from view. Guests were served the tea simultaneously, in individual bowls, perhaps as part of a long day of entertainment that included poetry composition, walks through the gardens, and banquets. In the early years of wartime, a certain disciplining of the tea meeting occurred: parties were sometimes held in more intimate rooms, some as small as four-and-one-half mats, where fewer objects and fewer guests could be assembled; attendants sometimes prepared the tea in front of the guests, making the service central to the gathering and heightening attention to the physical acts of preparation and drinking.[38] The parties nonetheless remained vehicles of elite encounter and the display of Chinese treasures. But in these and other matters, the parties recounted by the diarists were very different.

The social transformation revealed in the diaries of the sixteenth century began with the appropriation of the tea party by commoners. Both as hosts and as guests, they came to dominate a wartime tea culture that eclipsed the tea of elite salons. The separation of tea from the salon affected the geography as well as the class composition of tea society; for gatherings moved into the homes of commoners and into the urban centers where certain merchant houses flourished—most notably into Sakai, Nara, and Hakata, as well as Kyoto.

This movement occurred outside the bounds of elite patronage and control. A number of attendants to the shogunal house, men of humble origin but artistic proficiency who were called *dōbōshū,* had acquired some cultural authority in military circles. They cared for and catalogued the objects owned by their masters, specified the manner of their display in reception rooms, prepared and served tea, and probably influenced the transition to more intimate settings where tea was actually whisked before the guests.[39] Yet despite the importance of these attendants to salon society, they remained attendants—fixed in webs of service. Commoners in the tea culture of the sixteenth century were autonomous practitioners, men of means with mercantile livelihoods, who had neither patrons nor artistic masters. They may have had mentors, for tea historians of the late sixteenth century looked back on decades of change to identify leaders who drew in bodies of "disciples" and thus generated "lineages" with distinctive styles.[40] But even in their retrospective ordering of the tea experience, we discover no formal teaching establishment. The diarists themselves suggest patterns of affinity and influence among practitioners, yet without imputing clear notions of hierarchy to tea society. And those tea men vested with prestige by the diarists were fellow commoners.[41]

Another aspect of social change apparent in the diaries is the shift from tea as an event to tea as a practice. Tea became a practice when the host himself prepared the beverage before his guests, dispensing with the services of attendants.[42] More important, it became a practice when interested men made it a regular, sometimes daily, part of their lives—when they exchanged hospitality with sufficient frequency and scrutiny to make tea a sort of avocation. Tea men were amateurs, but amateurs of a certain kind: they nourished their interest over years and decades, traveled in pursuit of knowledge, developed a language and an etiquette that shaped their culture, and accumulated the trappings that defined their tastes. The individual tea meeting, as event, certainly remained at the center of tea society. Yet as the word *society* suggests, it was also part of an ongoing experience of cultivation that forged a group (and inspired the record keeping of the diarists).

The aesthetic transformation revealed in the diaries turned primarily on the choice and assembly of the objects in the tea space—both those simply on display and those actually used in the tea service. Outside observers, later historians, and the physical remains of the period draw attention to dramatic changes in the tea space itself: to the reduction in its area, as a four-and-one-half mat room became common; to the erection of separate tea huts, surrounded by gardens, for the gatherings; and to a preference for "rustic simplicity" in the methods and materials of construction.[43] The diarists' attention, however, remains on the objects personally arrayed by the host, not by attendants conforming to a rubric of style, and to the implicit statement these things conveyed about taste, or tastes.

For both the early and the continuing historians of tea, who tend to construct a narrative emphasizing the consistent development of the tea culture, the diaries are particularly interesting in their disclosures about an emerging, finally ascendant(?), appreciation for *wabi*—the quality of modesty, often of roughness or crudeness, that characterizes mundane things and is reflected, for example, in a muddy or accidental glaze, an asymmetrical shape, a cracked surface.[44] Among the earliest entries in the tea diaries, we find notations about the use of native Japanese wares, one critical departure from the tea of the salon, and notations about the use of vessels with a *wabi* flavor: found objects, for example, rude pots fired at the Shigaraki or Bizen kilns for daily service in the kitchen, and utensils formed of simple materials like bamboo or grainy clay.[45] Yet stunning as this departure in taste surely was, it appears less a consistent aesthetic than an unending search for the variety and surprise that made wartime tea an art of invention and reinvention. The *wabi* element moves in and out of the diaries as hosts combined noble and vulgar objects, relished the elegant in native wares and the flawed in continental wares, turned for novelty to Korean pots, and routinely foiled expectation. In the end, the aesthetic transformation of wartime tea had less to do with the definition of a new taste than with freedom from all orthodoxies.

The social and the aesthetic transformations apparent in wartime tea were deeply intertwined and mutually reenforcing. Before I return to the actual play, or art, of tea, and its various meanings, let me look somewhat more closely at the social configuration of the tea culture. The things that bound, and did not bind, its members may suggest the multiple sources of artistic change, as well as the multiple satisfactions of a change that was never purely artistic. My remarks about tea society are not intended to reproach a history that has often focused on presumptive leaders and the philosophies imputed to them, but to locate tea in the environment of communal encounter that formed it.[46]

The society described in the diaries was male. The point might hardly bear mention, except that we do find some weakening of sexual barriers in sixteenth-century cities. Women were guild members, sometimes guild heads; they danced in public, though perhaps typically in female troupes that also appeared in popular theatricals (*sarugaku*); they joined public, as well as private, audiences for various entertainments (such as noh drama); they were present in political street actions. Their exclusion from the tea world is a reminder, though, of the still-formidable boundaries of sex in an age otherwise characterized by breached boundaries. The exclusion also hints at an additional feature of tea society itself: a presumption of some equality among members.

On the other hand, age barriers were not of apparent consequence in the tea world. Matsuya Hisamasa began his tea journal at the age of twenty-two, perhaps some years after his first entry into tea society. He initiated his own son into that world at the age of eighteen and began to accompany Hachiya Matagorō of Nara to tea parties when Matagorō was nineteen. Sen no Rikyū made an appearance by the age of twenty-two, possibly by the age of sixteen. And young men were hosts as well as guests at tea gatherings; they frequently entertained, and were entertained by, men of a venerable age who remained in tea society until they died. Matsuya Hisamasa continued his journal until the age of eighty-seven. Thus, the wartime tea community appears to have been an adult male community—free of age stratification, of prolonged (or even clearly defined) apprenticeships, and even of a preference for gatherings of age peers.[47]

It is possible that induction into tea society, in the company of a parent or sponsor, was a rite of manhood in certain commoner circles. Fathers and young sons entertained and were entertained together in the Matsuya, Tsuda, and Sen families, for example.[48] Once inducted, however, the newcomer could assume an independent place in the tea world. Matsuya Hisamasa's son was entertained often and privately following his debut with his father. Such evidence tends to confirm the current wisdom about the life cycle in late medieval Japan: a single, and critical, division seems to have been made between youth and adulthood, probably in the mid- rather than the late teens.[49] Such evidence also points to the complex transmission, in at least some merchant families, of a

Water container (*mizusashi*), made in Shigaraki.
Late Muromachi period. Height 17 cm., mouth 14 cm. Courtesy of the
Tokyo National Museum.

patrimony that went beyond house and business to include culture. This
culture was only partly a matter of artistic interest or proficiency, for tea
also became a vehicle of wealth, identity, prestige, and connection.

Certainly the most striking aspect of the tea society revealed in the
diaries is its class composition. The diarists themselves were traders and
artisans; the hosts and the guests they mention were, overwhelmingly,
commoners as well. On occasion, biographical information from other

Tea caddy (*chaire*), made in Seto.
Late Muromachi period. Height 7.6 cm., mouth 4.2 cm.; brownish-black iron glaze. Courtesy of the Tokyo National Museum.

sources helps us identify some of the more prominent merchants and tea celebrities.[50] But the members of the tea world appear more vividly in the parade of surnames in the diaries. Some of them disclose particular trades: we find dealers in salt, lumber, oil, copper, lacquer, silk, textiles, needles and blades, dyestuffs, and pots. Other surnames with geographical associations suggest linkages between urban merchants and distant suppliers—from Satsuma, Wakasa, Takase, Hibiya, Chikugo, or Kawasaki. From time to time in the diaries, we encounter simple personal names, unprefaced by surnames, with a strong downtown flavor—Magobei, Shinbei, Genbei, and Jirō.[51]

The men identified in the wartime diaries were not all commoners. Matsuya Hisamasa, as his first entry suggests, was entertained by high-placed clerics, most notably by Shishōbō Shūjo, the supervisor of instruction at Tōdaiji for monks from the imperial house. Hisamasa traveled to out-of-town parties in the company of other priests. He and his fellow diarists also describe gatherings attended, or hosted, by regional military lords (like Miyoshi Masanaga).[52] But not until the late 1560s do the diaries indicate the entry into tea society of substantial numbers of powerful military men (and some aristocrats). This movement led, for a time, to a heady and seemingly democratic transcendence of class in the tea room, and then to the ascendancy of daimyo practitioners—who converted merchant adepts into household retainers, on stipends, and thus gradually (though never completely) redrew the lines of patronage and authority.[53] The early tea diaries provide something less than an exhaustive record of wartime tea society, particularly since none issued from Kyoto. There and elsewhere, significant class mingling may have occurred before the closing years of wartime. Still, the Kyoto people we encounter in the diaries—those visited by the diarists and those who left the capital to visit other tea men—were commoners. And the records of Kyoto residents offer little evidence either of a mixed tea society there or of parallel societies—one of commoners, one of elite participants in a surviving salon culture.[54] Whatever variety the tea world of wartime preserved or encouraged, the portion of it we know was largely a commoner world, entered on occasion by priests and warriors.

Which is hardly to say that it lacked complexity. The tea world reached across trades, and across what we can reconstruct of personal backgrounds. It also reached across space: tea men from Nara, Sakai, Kyoto, and Hakata (and elsewhere) visited each other in years of constant danger. The entries of Matsuya Hisamasa's diary, for example, describe journeys to Kyoto, Sakai, and other towns, where Hisamasa stayed for as many as fourteen days at a time, visiting different hosts each day in a hectic round of inspection.[55]

The association of disparate commoners occurred in an environment constructed to conceal disparity. Although we find surnames indicative of a variety of livelihoods, numerous participants mentioned in the diaries after the mid-1540s bear a single name unrevealing of background: not a personal name but a tea name or an art name of monastic origin, elected by, or bestowed on, certain practitioners to signal an identification with their art.[56] The use of tea names does not clearly separate central from marginal participants; nor is it consistent, for the same man might variously appear in the diaries with a surname, a personal name, and a tea name. The development is nonetheless one of the strongest indications of tea's transformation into a practice (a "Way") pursued by highly conscious followers and marked by a defining language—not only to designate participants but to designate objects and grades of tea as well. The use of the tea name also indicates an interesting play with identity by effacing the mundane self and creating a new person measured by the standards of a (partially) separate world. Unlike costume or darkness, tea names did not obliterate or level the particular. They bestowed and demanded identities of their own. Yet they permitted a certain escape from conventional distinctions among men, an escape that is also revealed in the rankings assigned to guests in the tea room.

The diarists list guests in the order that tea was served to them, which indicated precedence and, in time, seating arrangements and various duties.[57] The order did not conform predictably to distinctions of age or class (when classes mixed in tea gatherings). Nor did it conform predictably to historical judgments on the reputations of conspicuous practitioners.[58] When hosts entertained the same, or very similar, groups of guests, moreover, a seemingly well-established order of precedence might be unexpectedly mixed or reversed.[59] Sometimes the rankings seem dictated by courtesy: the principal guest appears, on occasion, to be a first visitor to the host's home, or a man from another city, a host of a recent gathering whose hospitality is being returned. Yet these "rules," too, were regularly thwarted. In effect, we find in the tea room a freedom from convention that invited, if not an arbitrary or egalitarian assignment of prestige, then a constant reappraisal and redistribution of it.

Among the commoners who actually entered the tea room, two groups emerge from the record. One included apparently infrequent visitors. Tsuda Sōtatsu, for example, refers to the presence at certain parties of unnamed "neighbors," or "two men from Bingo," or "eight of the block elders" of Sakai. Many men appear once or twice in the diaries and then disappear.[60] Hence, to some extent, I imagine, the tea room was used for business or political entertainment in a society of townsmen with negligible alternative spaces for meeting and, as far as I know, no earlier tradition of professional entertainment.[61] This function suggests a growing self-awareness and connection within a mercantile community. The second, and dominant, group revealed in the diaries included the committed practitioners—the "tea men," many with tea names, who regularly entertained and visited each other for the practice of their art. It is likely that some practitioners found and nurtured friendships within their tea circles. A certain Yasa appears again and again in the diary of Tsuda Sōtatsu as host, guest, and companion. Ejun,

Matagorō, and Shōsei traveled again and again with Matsuya Hisa-masa.[62] Such habits of association hint at an intimacy stronger than art, though art may have been its foundation, and a place reserved in the tea world for male affection. Yet affection was not the essential bond within tea society. To discover what was, we must look more closely at the attributes of the tea men, the pattern of their entertainment, and the size of their society.

Two of the more conspicuous attributes of the diarists were literacy and leisure. They wrote in an educated Japanese, correctly recording the names of Chinese and Japanese painters and calligraphers; the courtly or monastic titles of elite participants in the gatherings; the colophons of scrolls; the names of continental objects; and the names of places and people useful in describing the tea vessels. Leisure is implicit in the time required for such an education and for the very keeping of the diaries. It is apparent, too, in the time the diarists were able to commit to their art. They could afford visits of a week or more to other cities for intensive rounds of tea; when at home, they could attend gatherings day after day. In some years, Tsuda Sōgyū made notes about 120 or more parties he hosted and attended—which was probably not a complete record, but an indication of notable meetings.[63] Most of these parties, moreover, were crowded into the months of winter and early spring—when jars of "new tea" were opened and the New Year and cherry blossoms were celebrated. Summer gatherings remained rare. Yet in the last and first months of the year, an avid tea man might attend a meeting almost daily, sometimes twice a day.[64]

The extent of literacy in wider tea circles is difficult to chart, although we might presume that a basic education was common among tea men in a society whose privileged tradesmen brought suit and wrote guild laws. We might also suspect that various pressures—the high standard of competence set by men like the diarists and the training of some practitioners in the poetic tradition—elevated the level of aspiration and performance among tea men beyond that of other commoners.[65] Similar pressures may have moved many of them to invest a considerable amount of time in the practice of tea, an investment often demonstrable in the diaries. Yet however important these and other elements, the universal attribute of serious practitioners was wealth sufficient to assemble a suitable collection of objects; for the tea service was inseparable from its vessels, and these, in turn, required an uncommon, even an extraordinary, expenditure.

It is not surprising that vessels attracted attention in merchant tea circles. Membership in tea society, as opposed to occasional access to it, derived from reciprocity in entertainment. Because serious practitioners exchanged hospitality, serving alternately as hosts and guests, all of them needed the basic items for the tea service. And such items invited notice and conveyed affluence. Iron kettles, lacquer or ceramic tea caddies, appropriate tea bowls, water containers, braziers, whisks, scoops, ladles, stands—these assemblages, large enough to permit some rotation of objects from party to party, were clear marks of prosperity in a world where the possession of quilts and sliding doors identified the well-to-do tradesman.[66] But the tea men made these objects central to their gatherings; they were obsessed with the collection and connoisseurship of eminent things. This preoccupation is well attested in the early histories of tea and in schemes for classifying tea adepts that turned on the merit of the items they owned. It appears most blatantly in the stories of legendary, often ruthless, collecting that attended the rise of daimyo practitioners in the late years of wartime.[67] Yet this preoccupation was an old one. It is clear from the inception of the tea diaries and, indeed, probably drove the diarists to keep their journals.

With negligible exceptions in an immense record, the accounts of tea gatherings focus on the items displayed in the tea room and used in the tea service: what they were, where and how they were placed, what sequence they appeared in. Diary entries note the names of painters, the provenance and pedigrees of objects, and the characteristics of these objects—the shade and texture of a glaze, for example, the material and shape of a bowl or stand or tray, the design in gold or silver on lacquerware, the content and treatment of a painting. Some accounts include exceedingly close measurements of scrolls and vessels (did guests carry around measuring tools?) or a count of the characters in a colophon (in lieu of a quotation or paraphrase when the diarist reached the limit of his knowledge?). Observations about the tea itself, the setting, food, conversation, and etiquette—all were dispensable. Observations about the objects were not.[68]

The objects commanding such attention were not simply serviceable utensils, although many tea men doubtless used a number of unremarkable items that went appropriately unremarked in the diaries. Attention centered on pieces of peculiar attraction around which a collection was built. And built for display. Both by fitting tea rooms with alcoves and shelves to exhibit varied possessions (such as scrolls, vases, and censers) and by preparing tea before guests with vessels necessarily inspected as they were handled, practitioners brought objects conspicuously into view.

Precious Chinese objects continued to have immense cachet for merchant tea men, some of whom managed to obtain (from pawnbrokers?) items from the shogunal collection. Among the continental "items of fame" in merchant hands were Sung and Yuan paintings and calligraphy, iron-glazed (*tenmoku*) bowls and caddies, bronze vases and censers, celadon pots, and heavily glazed storage jars. Murata Jukō, regarded as one of the great formulators of the tea service, reputedly owned as many as thirty, and Takeno Jōō as many as sixty, "objects of fame."[69] Fragmentary but consistent evidence indicates that fame went together with breathtaking prices in Chinese wares. (Rikyū appraised a Sung storage jar at 1,000 *kanmon*.) More arresting, though, is the turn toward native objects, particularly "withered" objects expressing a *wabi* taste, that acquired similar (but never, in wartime, equal) renown and value. Simplicity was not synonymous with a meager presence or price in a bamboo tea scoop valued, in 1538, at 500 *hiki*. (This, at a time when a fourteenth-century manuscript in 123 fascicles sold for 800 *hiki*.) A bowl, probably a wooden bowl, associated with the Asakura house sold in the same year for 350 *kanmon*.[70] Some of the most agitated reports on price came from Portuguese missionaries who commented, for example, on an earthenware caddy appraised at 30,000 ducats. The Jesuit Alessandro Valignano wrote of another caddy "for which, in all truth, we would have no other use than to put it in a bird's cage as a drinking trough; nevertheless, [the daimyo of Bungo] had paid 900 silver *taels* (or about 14,000 ducats) for it, although I certainly would not have given two farthings for it."[71]

The importance of objects to the diarists and their fellows is reflected only partly in the fastidious entries about fastidiously collected and dearly valued things. It is also reflected in the pattern of entertainment indicated in the diaries. In 1550, Tsuda Sōtatsu made notes about twenty-three tea parties that he himself hosted.[72] He entertained a total of fifty-five people at these parties, typically in groups of three or four, although he had a single guest on five occasions, eight guests on one occasion, and ten on another. Of the fifty-five guests mentioned in the entries for 1550, forty-six appear a single time. Three others appear twice, making their second visit for the largest of Sōtatsu's gatherings, which was held in a large reception room overlooking flowering cherry trees. Three men took part in three gatherings, two others took part in four, one man (Yasa) took part in five. When Tsuda Sōtatsu entertained a repeated visitor, he changed the objects in the tea space.

During the same year, 1550, Sōtatsu also made notes about thirty-three tea parties that he attended.[73] He visited twenty-six hosts: twenty-two of them once, three of them twice, one of them (Yasa) five times. Most of these hosts were entertained by Sōtatsu in 1550. Only eight of them were not. When Sōtatsu repeated a visit to the same host, the objects in the tea space were changed.

A similar pattern is apparent in the diary of Matsuya Hisamasa. Although the diary is extremely sparse for the first twenty years, Hisamasa kept close account of his trips from Nara to Sakai. In 1542 he spent seven days in Sakai, visiting seven different hosts for seven parties. In 1544 he spent ten days in Sakai, visiting nine different hosts for nine parties.[74] None of the hosts mentioned in 1544 appear in his accounts of 1542. Never did he see the same object twice. We have no record of the tea parties Hisamasa himself certainly gave.

The evidence in other diaries and for other years repeats the patterns sketched here, although I have not attempted a full tally.[75] Tentatively, let me suggest that we find in the diaries an interest in wide encounters with changing hosts and changing guests and a consequently wide exposure to objects, as the tea man examined the vessels of many collectors and displayed his own possessions to a broad circle of visitors. We find infrequent mention of repeat encounters over the course of a year. Over longer periods repetition appears common—not only to refresh acquaintances but also to exhibit or view new pieces and different combinations of vessels, perhaps to inspect again a marvelous item. Matsuya Hisamasa's whirlwind excursions to Sakai vividly illustrate a commitment to wide encounters, which was shared by the hosts who welcomed him with his traveling companions and brought out their most esteemed goods for viewing. Indeed, Takeno Jōō sent Hisamasa a note the night before a party, asking which of two particular "items of fame" in his collection Hisamasa would prefer to see on display. Since Hisamasa was undecided, Jōō showed them both: a painting by Gyokkan (Yü-chien) and the tea storage jar named "Matsushima."[76]

The tea diaries are surely incomplete chronicles of a year's teas: the entries fluctuate greatly in number from year to year and are sometimes oddly thin even in the high season.[77] All diarists are selective but the tea men concentrated their attention, I suspect, on parties requiring a place in memory because of the people and the objects they brought together. They were probably less likely to describe parties when the objects were unremarkable, or the hosts somehow undeserving of mention—perhaps because they were marginal practitioners, perhaps because they (and their possessions) were too well known to the diarist to need regular note. And they were probably less likely to describe parties given by themselves when, again, the objects were all too predictable, or the guests either too distant or too intimate to bear remark.

If such principles of selection were at work in the diaries, the entries may particularly distort the dimensions of the wider tea world. Although many occasional participants appear as a result of the special distinction of themselves or their hosts and fellow guests or the objects in use, a great many other men on the edges of tea society may have disappeared from the record—hence concealing a possibly extensive practice of tea for pure diversion or for business and political contact. Similarly, selective entry may conceal frequent encounters of intimates who discovered in tea a forum for friendship. Perhaps Tsuda Sōtatsu shared tea with Yasa far more often than the eighteen times he chose to record in 1550. In this and other cases, the diaries probably include only highlights of repeated teas in particular circles, which—though probably small (Sōtatsu mentions only six men whom he saw three times or more in 1550)—may have been neither quite as small nor as infrequently renewed through meeting as the entries indicate.[78]

However broad the tea world was at its periphery, and however narrow at its core, the diarists principally explored that (middle?) ground where like-minded men entertained each other widely and thus saw and showed objects widely as well. Collecting and connoisseurship were not simply private pleasures, enjoyed personally or in closed groups, but instruments of display and encounter in a substantial society. How substantial? Any good calculation requires a painstaking collation of all the diaries, although even that will (if attempted) probably underestimate the size of the periphery. My guess is that the tea world was neither large nor small—that it included several hundred regular practitioners in Sakai, Nara, and Kyoto.[79] A catalog of "items of fame" compiled late in the sixteenth century lists 430 objects divided among 190 holders in these and several other cities.[80] Because such items were found only in excellent collections, the catalog implies the existence of (considerably?) more than 200 serious tea men. If we consider the periphery, as well as sub-strata in the tea world never touched by the diarists, the number of tea participants grows accordingly.

But not inexhaustibly. The configuration of tea society that I have traced through the early diaries was, in many respects, open: it embraced males of diverse ages who, though overwhelmingly professional traders and thus members of the commoner class, were able to mix occasionally with priests and warriors and regularly with one another—despite differences in employment, background, and geographical location; it also displayed a tendency toward horizontal association as tea men escaped the hierarchies of patronage and master-disciple relations, and as they concealed distinctions by adopting tea names and unpredictable rankings of guests. Some closing of this society may have occurred if the high standards of cultural literacy set by men like the diarists came to prevail more broadly and if access to the tea community came to depend on acquaintance or connection with the more active practitioners identified in the diaries. The level of activity itself surely helped set the dimensions of tea society; while the routine "practice" of tea separated an inner from an outer circle of participants, even that outer circle, to retain any shape at all, must have included occasionally visible and committed members. Commitment required a degree of leisure and hence some freedom from consuming toil; it also required a lift of spirit that is one of the most absorbing yet elusive features of wartime tea, since it was very rarely a subject of the early masters and never a subject of the diarists. Their primary subject, and the interest that served essentially to form a bounded rather than a boundless tea society, was the collection and connoisseurship of valuable objects. Tea society was a community of wealth organized around the display of things.

What sort of an art form, what sorts of choices, did this community make? And what correspondence existed between the structure of tea society and the structure of the tea practice it fashioned?

The early merchant tea men began with an elite pastime, associated with court and monastery and shogunate, that was consequently indicative of prestige. Yet tea was a particular sort of pastime. Unlike many other elite pursuits (such as poetic composition, painting, and musical performance, which commoners took up on occasion but in apparently small numbers[81]), tea lacked rules and the codification of form and practice. More to the point, it lacked texts and an esoteric tradition.[82] With only rudimentary formal requirements, tea was thus peculiarly accessible to the uninitiated, even to the uneducated. The tea of the elite salon nonetheless had two appealing principles of organization: it turned on decorous social gatherings involving performance of the tea service; it entailed the display of wealth in the form of eminent objects.

   The initial attraction of commoners to tea is congruent with the attributes of the tea society described by the diarists. The early tea men were
traders and artisans, united mainly by wealth, cultural ambition (if not
achievement), and a desire for connections. Tea provided them an honorable occasion for meeting, for wider or more intimate connections in
groups that were potentially open to disparity but not infinitely elastic,
insofar as affluence and objects continued to matter. That they mattered
was neither necessary nor inevitable. We can easily imagine tea without
precious objects, as we can imagine noh without splendid robes and war
without stunning armor. In borrowing from the high culture, prosperous tradesmen selected a malleable form that, however bent in time to
their own dispositions, retained by design the features of collecting and
connoisseurship. Yet in crucial respects, the new men broke with salon
tea: their practice put the host, not just his objects, on display; this development led, in turn, not just to ruptures in taste but also to the subordination of objects to style. Here again, artistic choice responded to
the social construction of the tea community.
   The prominence of the host derived partly from his responsibility to
prepare the tea personally before his guests, without attendants. Because the diaries mention the full range of tea utensils, we may imagine
the wartime host, like his successors in a later tea world described to us
more fully, performing a sequence of careful acts: ladling hot water to
the bowl from the kettle (suspended over a hearth or standing on a
brazier); warming, cleaning, and emptying the tea bowl; measuring out
the powdered tea from a caddy; whisking fresh water and tea; offering
the bowl to the principal guest.[83] The basic performance was elaborated
by wartime tea men, in further departures from salon tea indicated in
the diaries. The host might open a gathering by "breaking the seal"—
cutting the paper cover on a storage vessel for tea leaves, selecting a
particular type of tea from the bags kept within, and having the leaves
ground in earshot of the guests. He might prepare thin tea in addition
to the heavy tea that was passed from guest to guest in a communal
bowl. For thin tea, the tea service was performed repeatedly: after the
principal guest consumed a serving, the host recovered the bowl,
cleaned it, and prepared a serving for the second guest, and so forth.[84]
Although we know very little of wartime tea etiquette, the emphasis and
elaboration on physical action implies a keen attention to deportment.
It is likely that tea was a medium of physical discipline and an expression
of the host's grace and civility.[85]
   The control of the host extended to the entire tea environment.

Many men contributed to this environment: carpenters and gardeners; painters and potters; workers in metal, wood, lacquer, and the like. Yet all of these creative talents gave way in the tea room to the maestro who understood what was estimable in their work and assembled it personally in a distinctive fashion. Except for painters, artists often remained anonymous in a craft tradition that assigned importance to workmanship, occasionally to workshop or kiln, rather than to individuals—a feature of connoisseurship apparent in the diaries' concentration on the execution of objects, with fleeting remarks on their makers.[86] For the diarists, however, the objects were not lifeless products of nameless artisans that required, for appreciation, only a full description. They took meaning from the multiple decisions of the host.

We are told where the host put things: objects for display might be in an alcove, on shelves or boards or trays of various shapes; utensils might be on shelves within portable frames (*daisu*) or on trays, sometimes directly on the *tatami*. We are told the sequence of presentation: one object might replace another in the alcove during the service; an interesting vessel might be brought out on a stand after the tea was served. We are told in detail which items appeared together: an artless Korean tea bowl might be juxtaposed against a lacquer caddy on a square tray, an eggplant-shaped caddy against a poem fragment containing the word *eggplant,* a rough water container from Shigaraki against an array of Chinese "items of fame," a brazier against a censer.[87] We are told of displays of wit: of a host who hung a scroll depicting seven kinds of sweets during a meal lacking sweets, of another who displayed an ink stone in front of mounted calligraphy. We find a host placing a ladle rest in his alcove.[88]

The authority, akin to authorship, exercised by the host also inspired a certain identification between him and the vessels he brought to life. Thus, some objects bore the names of the men who owned them; others were described as "to the taste" of the men who used them; still others were described in terms of their pedigrees, as connoisseurs noted the successive generations of owners who had given them a history.[89] And owners sometimes conspired in this identification by placing their ciphers directly on their treasures.[90]

In effect, the tea environment became an extension of the host who created and re-created it, independent of advisers or institutions. He neither massed objects in static, museumlike displays nor presented them in formulaic arrangements dictated by cognoscenti. And in pursuing tea as a regular practice, he constantly revitalized his art. The host reconstructed the environment for successive parties; he observed the assemblies of the many other hosts whom he visited; he responded to these encounters with new parties and new decisions of his own—always under the eye of interested guests. This interplay among practitioners gave tea both its dynamic and its split focus on individual and group. To an exceptional degree, tea was a solo performing art. Both as preparer of the tea and as inventor of a particular experience, a single man put a stamp on each gathering. In a society of ensemble performance (in linked verse, drama, dance, and music), tea stood out in its celebration of the solitary host/actor. But performance requires witnesses—a mindful audience capable of seeing, reacting, and remembering. The principal tea audience was composed of singularly alert fellow collectors and fellow performers and, thus, of judges and rivals as well. This layering of roles in the tea room was surely one of tea's most stimulating features. The host was the giver of hospitality to his guests, the independent performer and author of experience, the analyst of previous performances (his own and those of others) on which his current decisions provided a commentary, a future guest and witness, a future host, a continuing collector. The guest was the recipient of hospitality, the witness and critic and rememberer, the future host, the future guest, the continuing collector. A pleasing tension consequently emerged between the communal and the competitive dimensions of the tea practice.

The roles of objects in such a practice were also complex. In small part, objects were the simple props of hospitality. In large part, they were symbols of wealth among men who collected items of established value and then, when they turned to native and even vulgar pieces, drove up their prestige and prices as well. This aesthetic shift indicates that objects were more than safe depositories of predictably high value. The selection of a piece became a declaration of personal taste, the assembly of pieces an act of artistic interpretation. Objects made wealth expressive. They linked affluence to invention—not just to a standard connoisseurship of treasures but to a risky exploration of new visions. Knowing was not enough. Seeing—seeing with fresh eyes—was necessary, too. In the end, objects were the medium of a lively art.

Hence, choices about objects took many directions. We may detect, in the diaries, certain patterns of choice. Some tea practitioners appear to have concentrated on Chinese objects and other pieces of established value (old Ashiya tea kettles, for example, or Seto bowls). Some nurtured "courtly" interests by displaying the gilded lacquerware and refined native paintings and calligraphy associated with clients of the nobility.[91] But most often, the diaries reveal eclecticism. Combining objects surprisingly, tea men also collected surprising objects—notably, flawed or strange or vulgar items suggestive of *wabi*.

The concept of *wabi* has loomed large in Japanese cultural history because it both identified a remarkable taste in things and provoked a substantial discourse on the philosophy and aesthetics guiding that taste. A term of classical origin with numerous medieval associations as well, *wabi* came to the center of tea discourse from the end of the sixteenth century. It was linked to various traditions—classical and medieval poetry, noh drama, Zen Buddhism, eremetic practices. It was glossed by a rich, not specifically artistic, vocabulary—by words like *chill, withered, rustic, lonely, pure, austere, lowly,* and *imperfect.* Descriptive of peculiar objects (crudely lacquered caddies, celadons with yellow-brown glazes, storage or water jars of rough workmanship), it also evoked a mentality.[92]

Although wartime allusions to *wabi* are either fragmentary or extant in documents of unclear authenticity, it is very likely that the discourse originated in early tea circles, as practitioners entered into inquiry (and debate) concerning artistic meanings. The following remarks, said to be addressed to the young Sen no Rikyū, are attributed to the Sakai tea master Takeno Jōō (1502–55):

The word *wabi* has been used in a variety of ways by men of the past in their verse, but in recent times it has come to indicate an open and straightforward attitude, deeply modest and considerate, and free of arrogance. In the year, it is the tenth month that embodies the spirit of *wabi*. . . . The source of the spirit of *wabi* in the land is the goddess Amaterasu. The great master of Japan, if she desired to construct a shrine hall by inlaying gold, silver, and precious gems, what person could say it should not be so? But, with a thatched roof, offerings of unhulled rice, and in everything else down to the least detail profoundly modest and never negligent, the deity is the finest of tea practitioners.[93]

Takeno Jōō may well have written this (or some similar) letter and may well deserve his reputation as a formulator of tea aesthetics.[94] Yet more critical than the attribution of such records is their suggestion that experimentation was accompanied by a high degree of artistic self-consciousness and even by articulate efforts to link practice and theory.

And this consciousness was connected not merely to the *wabi* taste but to the notion of taste itself. Important as the *wabi* revolution surely was, it represented one direction in a tea world resistant, in its eclecticism, to any single direction. The appreciation of variety is conveyed by the word *suki,* a term virtually synonymous with the practice of tea. ("They refer now," the poet Sōchō tells us, "to the practice of tea in southern Kyoto as *suki.*"[95]) *Suki* meant discrimination among things— the act not just of connoisseurship but of choice, the establishment in practice of a style. Tea, then, was the art of discrimination and of the discriminator, the man who declared taste through his art. In usage, the term remained neutral, unmodified. We do find note of *wabi-suki,* or the *wabi* taste, apparently as a category of discrimination.[96] But taste was not "good" or "bad," "old" or "new," "conventional" or "deviant." *Suki* implied a suspension of all commitment to an orthodoxy. It acknowledged a multiplicity of styles (what I have inadequately called eclecticism), even as it indicated the inseparability of each tea from the expression of some style.

Thus, the aesthetic break between medieval and wartime tea was only partly a matter of aesthetic change. As merchant tea men put the host uniquely on display (as, indeed, they invented the host), so they reconceived objects as vehicles of expression for that host, rather than items of inherent, perhaps absolute, value and meaning. Variety and flux in artistic choice followed. Inquiry and debate concerning aesthetic philosophy probably followed, too. Yet at the center of the tea culture was the insistence on individual taste. Style became the very definition of tea practice, not simply a consequence of it. And style remained free from canons, as tea men both escaped the rule of the past and refused to formulate a substitute.

Wartime tea produced very few (if any) critical treatises, guides to procedure, or tracts on connoisseurship.[97] We find nothing like the texts of shogunal advisers, which ranked objects and specified the manner of display. Instead, we find diaries. In part, surely, diarists wrote to prod memory—to record obligations and track the particular gatherings of objects and guests that would influence future gatherings. The very need to remember a distinct event implies the absence of rule-driven patterns. In greater part, however, I imagine diarists wrote to hold knowledge that was precious in itself, independent of its application. Tea offered them, and perhaps many of their peers, the pleasure not just of performance and witness but also of specialized learning. The diarists were savants; they knew what was what, who owned what and did what. Yet knowledge was forever incomplete, amplified as it was in daily practice and observation. It derived from experience. Thus, the diary alone could contain, or begin to contain, such knowing. Diaries may become the stuff of tradition. They may exalt the savant's learning over the performance he observes and the eccentric vision performance requires; they may convert experience into history, revealing the patterns that become hallowed directions and the practices that become nascent rules. Indeed, diaries may well be symptoms of a tradition-seeking, rule-seeking consciousness. They originate, however, from those longings for knowledge that can be felt only when knowledge is still remote and obscure.

In many ways, the differences between the tea practice of wartime and *fūryū* dancing are pronounced. The dancing was an affair of crowds, clamorously arrayed at night, in which impulse appeared stronger than organization. We know of it through the random accounts of outsiders, whom it baffled and alarmed. Tea was an affair of intimate groups, drawn from an affluent minority of commoners, who pursued their art privately and decorously in tea rooms. Organization rather than impulse governed their practice, which is revealed in the extensive accounts of insiders. Unlike dancing, tea was not an object of official regulation or proscription in the war years. Yet, in time, it proved more disturbing than the dancing: Hideyoshi's condemnation of Sen no Rikyū was only the most sensational of a series of acts that imposed order (and intelligibility) on the practice of tea.[98]

Wartime tea eventually provoked a reaction because it posed social challenges similar to, and in some ways deeper than, the challenges of *fūryū*. Tea also provided its participants with similar pleasures. Let me consider the challenges as well as the pleasures of tea before returning to the connections between its social and aesthetic transformations and thus, the connections between society and play in wartime.

Like the *fūryū* dancers, tea men snapped the relationship between play and context: they moved tea from the salon to the tradesman's reception room, and they showed there the prizes once monopolized by the elite. The move immediately challenged assumptions about the access not only to wealth but also to precious objects, the custodianship of civility, and the ties linking class to particular entertainments. Although the invasion of the streets by *fūryū* dancers was a more public act of aggression, the flaunting of Chinese celadons by townsmen may have been more bruising to noble bones. And to what purpose did they acquire these celadons? Was the appropriation by commoners of salon play just a troubling version of cultural mimicry (surely not parody?)? Or did it suggest a struggle over the control of culture? In either case, tea men were playing with class boundaries—breaching them or dissolving them—and hence, to return to another earlier theme, exposing a certain slipperiness in society. Elite identities that were enhanced, if not established, through wealth and ceremony and etiquette were secure against neither assault nor trespass. Because tea involved conspicuous material accumulation, as well as a ceremony that had conveyed both cultural and political power in the salon, its practice by commoners could hardly have been dismissed as a simple diversion in the alternate universe of play, without implications for the "real" world.

The challenge of wartime tea did not stop, however, with cultural appropriation and its attendant challenges. In their new concern with performance and taste, tea men emancipated tea from authority. Gone were patrons, professional connoisseurs, and established values. Ascendant were many individual, essentially autonomous hosts (or authors), iconoclasm, and style. Having already confused the connections between symbols and status, the tea men went on to confuse the meanings of symbols and the sources of prestige. Choice and act mediated the always-changing view of objects, as they did the position of tea practitioners. Neither value nor prestige was fixed or, indeed, fixable; to define these notions at all—in effect, to judge—was to reimpose a version of the canonical standards that had been rejected when tea men invented the host and subordinated objects to style.

Like the pleasures of *fūryū,* the pleasures of tea for its practitioners probably derived, in part, from the inherent challenges tea posed to its society—from the dark thrill of boundary play, unseemly consumption, and flirtations with *lèse majesté.* But again like *fūryū,* tea also offered brighter pleasures. Or rather, tea practice was constructed to provide a number of positive satisfactions that came to entail social dislocation and its peculiar excitement, although this dislocation was not a (primary) motive of tea's wartime formulators. I presume the first of these satisfactions turned on mimicry: engaging in an honorable pastime, commoners acquired a sort of honor. Yet the pleasure of mimicry seems to have been quickly superseded by the pleasures deriving, as in dancing, from the freedom of invention. My view of this phenomenon is now familiar: disparate authorship replaced authority; the creation and recreation of performance replaced static forms; individual styles replaced fixed notions of value; seeing and acting replaced knowing. Invention also led to bracing (and abrasive) explorations of taste—sometimes to declarations of antitaste, as harmony yielded to dissonance; sometimes to enchantment with the strange (if not the weird). Leaving objects aside, we find arresting experiments with the food served at the feasts that often followed the tea service. Tea men might offer grilled birds on gold and silver skewers, badger broth, or thin slices of Ise crustacean.[99]

The freedom of invention was linked in tea, as it was not in dancing, to the celebration of the solo performer and the conversion of wealth into an instrument of expression. In both respects, tea offered pleasures that were as deeply social as they were artistic. The same is true of several additional developments. Tea emerged as a practice, and consequently provided a regimen and even a culture for its participants, a distinct object of knowledge for its savants. It produced a community—larger and smaller circles of regular and less frequent associates—that sustained the practice and surrounded performing hosts with suitable witnesses. The organization of this community, more horizontal than vertical, concealed significant differences among its members. All of these features were elaborated to meet particular needs. I am back, then, at the intersection of art and society.

Wartime tea was shaped, in a new and unusual fashion, as a source of individual identity and communal relationship for prosperous commoners. It emerged in a particularly conducive environment: the age of merchant tea was also the age of organization among politically mobilized commoners and the age of profoundly altered relations between townspeople and their various patrons, proprietors, and rulers. Yet unlike other commoner associations and movements, tea transcended the linkages of trade, sect, and neighborhood as well as the agendas they implied. However often (if obliquely) the tea room became a site for politics and business, it remained a place of hospitality and fraternity, deliberately porous of access, without a specific utility that defined a specific constituency. Tea meetings worked on the premise that commoners might offer each other support and esteem, perhaps solace, too.

Because wealth was a criterion for entry, tea society was certainly both elite and exclusive. It departed, however, from the sort of social climbing I have noted before—the pursuit by commoners of privilege and title, the exchange of gifts and visits with noble associates, the adoption of aristocratic signatures and rites of passage—to forge internal and horizontal bonds among townsmen in the stead of external and vertical bonds with men of rank. The appropriation of a salon art led not to a replication of salon tea but to its dynamic refashioning by commoners responsive to one another. And in their response, they made tea a medium of culture as well as a medium of community. Tea men wanted not only connection and its pleasures; they also wanted a form of cultivation.

Thus, to the issue of identity. As we have encountered the concept earlier, identity derived for commoners from lineage, family, and name; from work, duration of service, and patronage; from whatever titles and honors were occasionally available to them. Guilds, congregations, and neighborhood associations bestowed identity on groups as well. But identity in the tea world was fundamentally different: it derived from the self and an elective community rather than traditional attachment; from interest rather than occupation or place. Entry required the will to be there and the wealth to sustain a presence. Membership required the expression of will in distinctive performance, the expression of wealth in distinctive style. Tea's emphasis on cultural invention by the individual, within the context of regimen and community, broke open the notion of identity.

But why the emphasis on the individual and wealth? Wealth may well have been a source of anxiety for prosperous commoners. Disjunctions in the distribution of resources and status must always be problematic in hierarchical societies, although I am not sure whether the extreme ruptures of war exacerbate or diminish the concern. War's gravest trials can overshadow such disjunctions, for example, or the confusion un- leashed by war can license them. Certainly, the tortured discourses on wealth—its appropriate distribution, practical and symbolic use, ratio- nalization, and significance—awaited the Tokugawa period and the pro- nounced transfer of capital from the samurai to the mercantile popula- tion. Nonetheless, the affluence of certain wartime commoners must have been a complicated issue, which tea men necessarily addressed on some level. Thus, sensational acquisitions and expenditures might have been efforts to resolve the problem of wealth by giving it civility and dignity, for example; or they might have been unabashed acts of trans- gression that simply rejected hierarchy.

But even if wealth represented a problem in need of resolution, it more clearly represented an opportunity in search of realization. On the most obvious level, it offered a principle for selective entry into an otherwise-unbounded tea society. Further, it purchased the objects that made merchant tea immediately conspicuous. Wealth gave notoriety to tea as crowds and darkness gave notoriety to *furyū*, in both cases by design. Yet its role in forming a vigorous creative practice distinguished wealth as something more than a principle of selection and a source of notoriety. Wealth acquired a broadly cultural and not specifically eco- nomic value, insofar as it provided access to artistic achievement (thus opening new avenues to prestige) and a foundation for social attachment (thus offering new modes of union and division among men). Wealth emerged, in short, as a category of identity separable from class and status.

And it identified groups of individuals, of solo performers. We might, in part, associate this celebration of the self with an entrepreneurial ethic, for at least some tea men (outside Kyoto) represented the new money and the adventurous trading practices that marked both mercantile and tea circles toward the end of the sixteenth century.[100] But because the sources do not allow a close correlation of the mercantile and the tea elites, we might better associate the celebration of the self with the general growth of commoner leadership. Although we rarely know their names, we know (in Kyoto and elsewhere) of guild and monopsony heads, of licensed purveyors to the daimyo, of major brokers and brewers. We know of commoner patrons and councillors (and suspect the existence of commoner military leaders) in religious congregations; we know of magistrates and elders in neighborhood associations. Even as movement and aggression in the realms of commerce, religion, and politics focused on groups, they produced leaders whose individuality cannot be obliterated by the titles that substitute for personal names in the documents. The individuality of the tea room was clearly different from leadership in a neighborhood, say. Tea freed its participants from the constraints of representation and the burdens of service, giving play to imagination in a community of peers driven not by grievance but the pleasure of self-expression. Arising from a new experience of personal power, the attention to the host in tea practice offered a model of gentility and a basis for respect outside the bounds of practical roles.

Capturing the meaning though departing from the spirit of the quotation that opened this chapter, an admiring contemporary of Sen no Rikyū observed that the tea master had "changed mountains into valleys and east into west."[101] The remark is an apt commentary on the broader achievement of wartime tea men—the appropriation and transformation of a salon art, the replacement of authority with the freedom of invention, the unleashing of the power of money and the power of the self, and the provision for themselves of new forms of identity, communal attachment, and esteem. Yet so crisp a summary of something summarily called an "achievement" misses the craziness conveyed in images of flattened peaks and reversed directions (the image, again, of the fun-house mirror). The practice of tea came to offer structures of community and discipline and, thus, visions of social change that remained elusive in *fūryū* dancing. It nonetheless shared with the dancing a basic impulse toward iconoclasm, porous boundaries and horizontal association, constant reinvention and reencounter. It was not quiet and not stable.

Afterword: Scenes In
and Around the Capital

I am ending this book without an ending—or, what is much the same thing, without a fresh beginning, for one subject is rarely complete without movement into another. Ending and beginning, of an untidy sort, would be possible if we followed Kyoto's story into the seventeenth century. Then the lines of a peacetime political system, and the outlines of new social and economic systems, come (often obscurely) into view. But such a conclusion would not really belong to this book. The events of the "unification" era, which we normally date from 1568 to 1615, did not unfold inevitably from earlier events—nor did they develop in a single direction. Although *unification* implies an integral narrative of change, the word conceals an upheaval as complex and surprising as that of the warring states before 1560. I resist conclusion, however, not only because it would take me through tough new territory without clear linear connections to the past. I resist because the long century of war of concern to me here was about the absence of closure and the murkiness of genesis.

The most notable feature of the Era of Warring States was rupture, as the force of the self moved dynamically across every boundary to create a systemic crisis in all relations of power. We have seen cleavages open throughout the shogunal institution: between the Kyoto regime and its provincial governors; between the Ashikaga shogun and the Ho-sokawa *kanrei,* as well as between rivals for these offices; between the *kanrei* and their deputies, as well as between the deputies and men of the land. Military government in the capital belonged to strongmen whose titles were contingent on force, whose legitimacy derived from the purge. Fracture also occurred throughout proprietary institutions. Cut off from provincial estates and debilitated in Kyoto by jurisdictional battles with the shogunate, the civil elite was most deeply riven by the radical politics of commoners. Townspeople who periodically withheld land and business taxes moved on to a lengthy uprising under the ban-ner of the Lotus and then organized themselves—independent of pro-prietary attachments—into neighborhood associations that directly confronted martial rulers.

The medieval polity—which I described in the Introduction as a complex corporatist state—had neared collapse. The shogunate was barely credible as a superior authority that could still legitimate power through appointment, judicial decisions, statutory edicts, official dis-pensations, and public favors. The diverse corporate units within which power was actually distributed (the units, for example, of estate and guild and military lordship) were dissolving into new configurations. Thus, both the discrete vertical attachments that had organized medi-eval society and the shogunal institution that had mediated those vola-tile relations seemed to have little more than a vestigial character.

Still, both shogunal and proprietary institutions retained a half-life. The perquisites and nominal legitimacy of office continued to focus the ambitions of warlords in the capital (and to some extent in the prov-inces). The judicial organs of the shogunate continued to serve the ur-ban population. A source of remonstration against misrule, the throne and the civil elite remained significant of the inchoate values of stability and continuity; patrons remained crucial to the organization of com-merce in Kyoto.

But it was not just the tenacity of the past that figured in the irresolu-tion of the age. The most ambitious departures from the medieval order had assumed momentum only to be stalled or deflected. Variations in the *ikki* model of rule—the Yamashiro version of self-governance in hor-izontal communities, and the Hokke version of a reconfigured elite in-clusive of townsmen proprietors and administrators—were suppressed by otherwise-divided civil and martial powers who closed rank against insurrection. The sectarian uprising of Ikkō was repelled as well (at least in the capital region), by warlords and townspeople alike. And efforts by military leaders to replace the shogunate with a form of daimyo rule in the home provinces were equally frustrated. Neither Miyoshi Motonaga around 1530, nor Miyoshi Chōkei between 1553 and 1558, succeeded in detaching warrior control of Kyoto from the shogunal framework.

This suspension in a world of possibilities—where halting initiatives and retreats left open many choices—gave the age its peculiar tension. But why did it last so long? The simplest answer turns on the logic of violently divided interest. Because the cleavages exposed by war broke apart the units of medieval power, movement into a new settlement required new coalitions. These coalitions regularly arose, in coups or uprisings, for example, only to provoke the sort of mass reprisal from (ephemeral) countercoalitions that I have just noted. We find cycles of insurgency from nascent allies, repression by temporarily aligned opponents, and renewed agitation and resistance from disparate quarters. Nor were wartime coalitions assailed only by external enemies. The warlord regimes of Kyoto splintered into factions; the Yamashiro men of the land faced competition among themselves and recruitment into rival armies; the Hokke sectarians were deflected from rebellion by the crises of work. Indeed, all constituencies in the capital were variously divided and entangled. No group maintained a durable preponderance of force that could withstand both retaliation from outsiders and contests within.

For all these violently divided interests, the capital did not devolve into chaos or even into a sequence of martial tyrannies. The more interesting question about the age, then, concerns not the long duration of inconclusive battles but the structures of order that regulated conflict: why did prolonged warfare stop short of apocalypse?

To a fair extent, I have found a stabilizing influence in the medieval polity itself—which remained something more than a vestigial survival in the absence of compelling alternatives. This influence was essentially conservative. The old polity bound patrons and workers in still-cogent trade alliances; it bound proprietors and shogunal officials in exchanges of privilege that, however faltering, still organized formal governance in Kyoto. Less conservatively, the verbal politics of litigation served as an instrument of protest against warlord rule, of indirect participation in urban administration, and of bloodless confrontation over quarrels of all sorts. But protest was always leashed. Throughout their suits and petitions, litigants constructed identities for themselves that diminished rebellion. As they reaffirmed the ties of ancestry, name and title, patronage and proprietorship, time and honor, so these men and women of all stations linked their present to the past. This past was largely a fabrication—an idyll representing "things as they should be." It could become a vantage for trenchant social criticism. It could also become a place of retreat.

Stronger than the impulse toward restoration, however, was the impulse toward invention. Loosed in the force of the self, this impulse provoked the rupture of the age. Transformed into the politics of demonstration, this impulse conveyed the mentality of the age. We have seen demonstration in many forms—in the conduct of battles and purges; in the marches of debtors and the processions of Lotus sectarians; in the street actions of grievants, the justice of ad hoc tribunals, and the dancing of Kyoto's townspeople. This conduct represents not a random series of events but a culture of performance that used mass public witness, often accompanied by exemplary violence, to test notions of identity, attachment, and value. Demonstration was a coercive statement of power. But it carried distinctive premises about power: that neither battle nor appeal to law was sufficient to resolve the profoundly divided interests of wartime; and that interest itself—whether of allies or opponents—was an often-obscure and variable matter requiring exploration.

Demonstration took rupture as a given, denied the possibility (or desirability) of familiar melioration, and then accorded contenders a theater of negotiation in which to examine their emerging purposes. Its genius was the combination of realization and deferral. Even as performance allowed immediate gratification to the debtors who destroyed brokerages or the men of the land who occupied an aristocratic temple, it also allowed the constant recalculation of advantage and conviction. This process of encounter left open the ultimate definition of attachments and identities. Indeed, the culture of performance signifies a societal agreement to leave relations fluid rather than freeze them, to tolerate a high degree of ambiguity in the polity rather than confront apocalypse.

Yet everything was not ambiguous. The demonstrations that resisted closure also precluded any real return to an older polity. In themselves, they were sources of continuing upheaval—not only because they employed selective violence and sometimes provoked grisly retaliation but also because they set changes in motion that were irreversible. Demonstration was a powerful, dangerous activity that provoked reprisal precisely because it rejected the past and thus required the remaking of the world. In an age of considerable irresolution, the world of Kyoto went through two major changes.

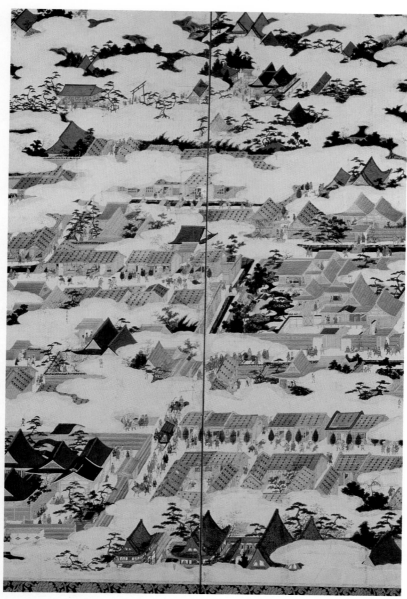

"Scenes In and Around the Capital."
Detail from the *(Uesugi-bon) Rakuchū rakugai-zu byōbu*. These scenes appear in the third and fourth panels of the left member of the pair of screens. Notice the shogunal mansion (lower left), the Hosokawa mansion (middle right), Shōkokuji (red roofs at bottom), the two noble residences of the Konoe (cypress-barked roofs just above the shogunal mansion), and the Asukai (below the Hosokawa toward the left). Courtesy of Yonezawa City.

"Scenes In and Around the Capital."
The left member of the pair of screens *(Uesugi-bon) Rakuchū rakugai-zu byōbu*. This screen, probably representing Kyoto in the late 1540s, features the western and northern areas of the city and its outreaches. Attributed to Kanō Eitoku (1543–90). 159.4 cm. × 363.3 cm. (each screen); gold leaf and color on paper. Registered as an Important Cultural Property. Courtesy of Yonezawa City.

"Scenes In and Around the Capital."
Detail from the *(Uesugi-bon) Rakuchū rakugai-zu byōbu*. These scenes appear in the lower part of the third panel on the right member of the pair of screens. The commoner residences depicted here front Nishi no tōin and Muromachi avenues. Honnōji appears at the bottom left. Courtesy of Yonezawa City.

First, class replaced corporation as the primary locus of political organization and social identification. After the failed Lotus uprising,
townspeople moved outside vertical alliances with their patrons and
proprietors to construct horizontal associations within their neighborhoods. No longer mediated through discrete units of attachment, conflict and power were negotiated between military rulers and commoner
bodies. In their associations, townspeople remade the institutions of urban politics. In the circles of tea and dance, they remade the premises
of urban culture. Here, new alignments founded on class were also centered on ambition, wealth, and invention, as practitioners reconceived
the nature of prestige and redrew the lines of community. Their performances entailed dazzling acts of improvisation that freed art from authority. Their porous ensembles demanded choices of style that located
art in encounters between artist and audience. The union of politics and
culture, which was always implicit in demonstration, became overt in
play: commoners used assembly, motion, and iconoclastic display not
only to alter relations of power but also to open the social imagination.
Fixed notions of value and meaning, no less than fixed notions of corporate hierarchy, were broken.

The second major change in wartime Kyoto involved a shattering of
the deepest assumptions about legitimacy. What now validated authority—in art, in the household, in the polity? Demonstration conspired
with "private war" and the "force of the self" to loose authority from
all the old frameworks of ancestry, office, custom, and religious belief.
Despite the attraction of old titles and the tenacity of old pieties, political power floated free of traditional rationales. In practice, power depended on either superior violence or successful negotiation in the
streets, sometimes both. Force on the one hand, and demonstration on
the other, replaced the dense constraints of medieval "law." Although
the two approaches resembled each other on occasion, they advanced
very different conceptions of social order: force presumed the ascendancy of the conqueror's will; demonstration presumed a process of encounter and conversion. In both cases, medieval propositions about
authority were denied.

These changes in wartime culture—in political structure, social
imagination, and theories of authority—were momentous but not pre-
scriptive. They provided no formula for the distribution and integration
of power. They posed excruciating questions about the ultimate conduct and rationalization of authority. Produced by convulsion unknown
since the founding of the classical state, the changes belong less to the

stories of states—their endings and beginnings—than to the struggles that resist statist solutions.

My own ending occurs where most urban histories begin—with a long look at physical place, at least as painters have captured it for us. Perhaps the best known of all the documents from wartime Kyoto (but documents I have barely alluded to so far) are pairs of gold-emblazoned screens that represent the city and its environs in a sweeping and celebratory panorama. Although the first such screens may have appeared around 1500, the earliest extant pair depicts Kyoto in the 1520s. Also surviving are two pairs that probably depict Kyoto before 1550. In time, as similar versions of the cityscape mounted in number, the screens came to form a genre described as *Rakuchū rakugai-zu,* or "Scenes In and Around the Capital." These paintings were not without forerunners of a sort: classical and medieval mandalas representing individual temples and shrines, for example; hand scrolls and screens illustrating seasonal passage and the annual ritual calendar; portrayals in various formats of workers, or "the people of skill." Never before, however, had the city of Kyoto—the whole city, the city as a city—been a subject for painters. The panoramic screens are singular in their leap from the part to the whole—in their projection of a synoptic vision of a world always apprehended earlier in pieces.[1]

I began this book with some of those pieces: the discrete and tortured entries from Nakamikado Nobutane's diary that drew us into the universe of wartime in Kyoto. As I draw now away from that universe, the screens provide a vantage (the only encompassing one known to me among the texts of the period) for the longer views that invite integration. The contrast between the screens and the diaries is greater than the distance between a holistic and a fragmentary, even fractured, perspective, for the screens also excise the pain inescapable in the words of contemporary writers. The paintings offer no hint of a world "dark, dark for all infinity," where streets had become a "lair of foxes and wolves" surrounding a palace transformed into "a tangle of summer grasses." Hence, in taking a last look at Kyoto through this wide and brilliant lens, I may seem to abandon the terrain I have surveyed thus far.

Surely, we can discover no "real" Kyoto where disconsonant images might be reconciled or dismissed. Cities are mental landscapes no less than physical places. The diarist's vision, mixed of memory and daily suffering, is as much an invention as the golden screens that portray an irreproachable palace and shogunal mansion in a period when both were regularly uninhabitable. The challenge, in the end, is to enter the mental landscape as best we can and try to recover the imagination that made it possible.

The imagination of the painters, like the imagination of the diarists, emerges as a divided one. For all their attention to a benign cityscape, the artists also offer us a tentative interpretation finally suggestive not of the serene control we might easily impute to them but of agile compromises. At its most challenging, their work frames questions. The experience of warfare, which is nowhere their explicit subject, is everywhere their animating concern. And as the screens address that concern, they also chart—though from an exceptional perspective—the terrain we know: one of possibilities rather than obvious contours.

On one level, the earliest screens of Kyoto offer an immensely assured statement responsive to an urgently felt need. There can be little mystery about their inspiration. A capital that men and women had once taken for granted was being consciously shaped, just as the very notion of capital seemed to lose coherence, into a symbol of consolation and hope. The screens project an image of a center in a centerless world, of stability in the face of explosion. As the poet Sōchō felt the "breezes of the Capital of Flowers," discovering that "in an instant, this word— Capital—captures peace," so too, the screens play on the desire for orientation. They do so, moreover, with a sweetness of tone rare in the emotionally raw narratives of war.

The consolation of the screens derives from the integration of several subjects. The first is place itself, a subject treated with both scope and detail, for the screens are, or at least seem to be, inclusive. With an apparent maplike integrity that permits the geographical adept to use them as a fair guide to real space, the paintings move in their central portions across many identifiable streets and their many, many markings.[2] The screens are not about a few emblematic buildings in a highly reified cityscape. Rather, they take us from major sites (like the imperial palace and the shogunal mansion), to the residences of noble and military households and the greater and lesser compounds of numerous temples and shrines. They take us, too, with particular attention, into the homes and shops and backyards of Kyoto's commoners. We move across bridges, around neighborhood wells, past bath houses and privies. Ordered by the grid of avenues and alleys, as well as by the framing device of gold leaf clouds, these scenes converge into a whole that pleases with its vivid colors and excellent repair. Gardens and the compounds of the elite are immaculate; commercial quarters are prosperous and inviting. The very plenitude of such images speaks to the seemingly universal good fortune of a capital where concord runs deep.

Surrounding the city proper, we find the outreaches of the Kyoto valley and the hills girdling it to the east, north, and west. This sweep allowed painters to illustrate the scenic beauties and the countrylike religious sanctuaries that enhanced Kyoto's metropolitan attractions. I believe it also evoked an image of the capital as the fixed and central place in the national landscape extending from it, much as the earliest maps of Japan represented the home province of Yamashiro rather like a flower calyx from which all other provinces unfolded. Lacking clear boundaries, the screens encourage the viewer to imagine a vast, spreading hinterland presumably oriented toward the capital.

But place is not the only subject of the Kyoto screens. They are concerned, too, with time—partly historical time, but primarily the cyclical time of the seasons and the ritual calendar. The foliage and colors of succeeding months link sites to the natural order, insisting again that place is not a matter simply of location but also of intersection: between the rural and the urban, say, the center and the periphery, space and time, and man and nature. The ceremonial of the festive and religious calendar unites the city in patterns of renewal, insisting that the deepest rhythms govern what seems a volatile universe.

Implicit in my reference to ritual is one more subject of acute importance to the screen painters: the connection between place and society. Their paintings are not bloodless studies removed from human commotion. The time that is marked by winter snow or autumn maples is also marked by the summer processions of Gion, the shuttlecock games of the New Year, and the blossom-viewing parties of spring. The space that is organized by the great physical works of man and nature is also punctuated by the daily activities of labor and play. We discover nursing babies and trysting lovers, peddlers hawking their wares, fishermen returning home with their catch. People are all over these screens. Indeed, one pair depicting Kyoto in the 1540s includes about 2,500 individual figures in a cityscape where buildings and other sites become more a backdrop for human hurly-burly than independent foci. Full of purpose, comfortable with the tasks before them, these figures bring vitality—and a future—to a city of gracious landmarks and steady rhythms.

Thus, in many ways the Kyoto screens may be read as another, singularly masterful statement of "normalcy"—a declaration, like the word wars or the guild laws, that instilled belief in some cohesion between past and present and future. The declaration is the more emphatic (perhaps the more defiant) insofar as the painters systematically excluded trouble. They eliminated from their vistas damaged buildings, charred lots, conspicuously deserted neighborhoods, and hastily constructed shantytowns. They suggest something of the contraction and fortification of the city—by depicting cultivated fields just south of the palace where elite mansions once stood and by tracing, rather modestly, the gates at certain intersections. But the retreat into urban islands is not apparent, nor is the prominence of the watchtowers and rudimentary castles, and the heavily barricaded temple compounds, that defined the garrison town.[3] Filtering out injury and ignoring the martial presence, the painters give us a civilian capital impervious to armies and armed camps.

Just as war is excluded, so too are other sources of disquiet. Entirely wiped from view are the firms of the brewers and pawnbrokers (as many as 150 of them) as well as the toll barriers ringing the city. The lunatic dancing of *fūryū* is transformed into one harmless and decorous vignette while the Gion festival becomes a celebration of civic pride. Despite a seemingly fastidious attention to religious landmarks, the painters ignore the temple of Enryakuji on Mount Hiei and reduce the Hokke presence to the single, meagerly depicted sanctuary of Honnōji (when, in the case of the screens from the 1520s, twenty-one Hokke complexes, all large and formidably defended, commanded prime locations). Thus withdrawing from provocative or fraught images, the painters also discourage the eye from lingering over anything discordant. We find, for example, no large residences for commoners, and very few two-story buildings.

By purging Kyoto of fractious scenes, the artists return us to the world where diarists labeled turmoil as ephemeral and some version of an old order as durable. Except that, unlike the parties to word wars, the painters lacked a model and a syntax for "things as they should be." Although they borrowed images from temple mandalas and other sources, they nonetheless had to invent contexts and connections in the previously uncharted landscape. The decisions they made—the integration of place and time and society in panoramas that console in multiple ways—may appear so ingenious and successful (indeed, so obvious to the many observers who have learned to see Kyoto in the terms established by the screens) that their surprising, essentially radical, aspects are obscured. I want to look more closely now at three aspects of these decisions and thus suggest some of the unresolved problems residing below the assured surfaces of the screens.

The greatest surprise in the screens, one that is almost unrecoverable to the modern eye, is their total invasion and appropriation of place. Even more aggressively than maps (which plot space without picturing and hence entering every site), the paintings take hold of the city from a low, unfixed aerial perspective to make the closed into the open and the private into the public (at least in imagination). The barriers of walls—which signify the barriers of privilege and station—dissolve. One result is the transformation of once-mysterious compounds into accessible landmarks or monuments, into objects (rather than subjects) of observation—an effect much intensified by the introduction of identifying labels near certain buildings and other locations.[4] A corresponding result is the transformation of viewers into spectators or voyeurs.

Here is a break with earlier paintings featuring some aspect of Kyoto life. The mandalas of temples and shrines preserved buildings as holy sites tied explicitly to the deities worshiped there, in iconographic studies that presumed attitudes of reverence in the viewer. The narrative scrolls (concerning, for instance, the historical founding of sanctuaries or even the fictional interpretations of life at court, such as the *Tale of Genji*) merged places with a story and a moment, a text, that captured the viewer in its world, if not as a participant, at least as an engaged visitor controlled both by the narrative and the physical action of unrolling the scroll. The screens, however, invite the gaze of strangers to move freely through a secular representation of immense size and complexity, lacking a clear master plot. There is great control and selection in the screens, as well as the temptation to narrative involvement in individual vignettes. Still, as the eye copes with constant choices and distractions, the sheer act of looking takes over. Interpretation is deferred or suspended altogether.

The invasion and appropriation of the cityscape, the creation of monuments and voyeurs, reveal new ways of seeing; for the objectification of place required its separation from the tangled personal histories that had defined Kyoto's medieval society. The geography of the Ōnin war was governed by the geography of personal power: fire did injury to buildings perceived as physical extensions of the men (enemies) who occupied them. And this pattern of reprisal was born of the more general association of place (even temple compounds and shogunal mansions) with individual groups and loyalties, lineages and affiliations, political and social alliance. Nowhere in the medieval world of household and corporation were there symbols of integration or civic (public) identity. The medieval city contained no common gardens or meeting halls or central markets; no sanctuaries without walls; no offices with open access. Place was organized as society was—by units of attachment to individual patrons and proprietors. Nowhere in this society was there even a word for Kyoto-ite. The very conception of the screens, then, demanded a reimagining of the city—a reimagining that accorded with the broader reconfiguration of attachment among townspeople, who were finding in class, neighborhood, and communities of wealth the identities that once centered on corporate hierarchies.

Making parts into a whole, removing powerfully charged sites into a public field, the painters invited viewers to identify with place itself. The Kyoto that dancers claimed for their nighttime spectacles and demonstrators circled or invaded for their street actions was emerging as a collective property. A general "idea of the capital" began to take hold during the period of civil war. Thus, provincial warlords built replicas of Kyoto's buildings in their castle towns and encouraged associations between local rivers or hills and the topography of the capital, transforming their headquarters into "small Kyoto."[5] And in a wartime collection of provincial folk songs we discover a verbal analogue to the depictions of the screens:

> The fascinating Capital of Flowers
> The brush not supple enough to write of it!
> In the east—Gion, Kiyomizu,
> And, in the spray of Otowa's crashing falls,
> The cherry blossoms of Jishū scattering.
> In the west—Hōrin, the temple of Saga,
> And the river waves at the dam of Risemu
> Where waterwheels circle and circle.[6]

Here again Kyoto becomes the imaginary possession of a diffuse audience. The city is both a whole—the "fascinating Capital of Flowers"—and an array of spatial images that listeners must inflect.

But among the images of Kyoto, even in screens that excised most signs of trouble, were the symbols of the problematic old order: the palace, the shogunal mansion, the residences of the courtly and military elite, and the great temples of religious proprietors. Inextricable from most perceptions of the capital and indispensable to any statement on continuity and perduring order, these sites were also emblematic of upheaval. In their treatment of these images, the painters made a second significant choice: they neutralized and made innocuous, indeed banal, the centers of medieval power.

This effect is achieved primarily by balance and dispersal. Part of a panorama where nothing protrudes and most images compete for attention, the sites of authority are scattered over a landscape that juxtaposes them equitably against one another (as we pick out here a temple, there a shrine or noble residence, elsewhere another temple or perhaps a military mansion) and against the extensive street scenes and the countryside that tend to swallow them up. Because three compounds do receive more prominent treatment—the palace, the shogunal mansion, and the enclave of the Hosokawa *kanrei*—they are sometimes described as dominant motifs. Yet *dominance* is a poor characterization of an only marginally pronounced presence that fails to organize the entire composition and fades into a blur once the viewer stands a few feet away from the screens. The painters do not orient the city toward these sites; they accord none of them a size or location of outstanding visual privilege; they intimate no hierarchy of power among them. (This was not always the case either in later depictions of Kyoto or the still later panoramic studies of Edo. Edo castle occupies the greater part of three panels in a pair of seventeenth-century screens covering twelve panels, whereas the shogunal mansion in the Kyoto screens of the 1540s occupies about one-quarter of one panel and a small portion of a second in, again, a total of twelve. Not incidentally, the mansion is located at the *bottom* of the left member of the pair of screens.[7])

The painters further neutralize the elite presence through attenuation and the projection of innocuous tableaux. The great Hokke temple of Honnōji receives particularly abbreviated attention, but such constriction is a feature of all elite sites in the screens. Just as the painters conceal from us the wartime damage done to these complexes, they conceal the often-extensive grounds of religious institutions, the networks of submonasteries and halls and offices that made many temples into small towns, and the array of household structures that spread over even the most badly injured noble compounds. We normally find, instead, a cluster of grand roofs or a single striking building with perhaps a few satellites, in depictions that function as synecdoches both for an individual site and the larger community it might represent. Thus, a finely gabled roof of cypress bark and a garden stream overhung with pine can represent the particular residence of Lord Nijō, even as they evoke the many aristocratic homes that do not appear in the paintings. This translation of complex, distinctive places into formulaic images is completed by the human tableaux within them. Aristocrats in classical robes admire their stylized gardens (which seem to be inspired by classical paintings); they play the refined games of the past, such as the exqui-

site version of kickball known as *kemari;* they observe the festive calendar in the third month by staging a contest between bush warblers to
determine which has the sweetest voice. Courtiers at the imperial palace
greet the New Year with the ancient, almost motionless dancing of *bugaku.* And at the shogunal and *kanrei* mansions the emphasis shifts to
domesticity: servants and attendants hold quiet postures of waiting
while women distract and play with children.

In sum, the painters create a denatured elite. It has no particular face
(and certainly no identifiable representatives such as a shogun or an
emperor) and no clear structure of power or immediate relevance. Its
buildings are gracious, but they are also impersonal monuments requiring labels in a hectic cityscape. Its life is bound both to the ritual clock
and to the historical time of an enduring past, but these are effectively
realms of timelessness. Spectators themselves, again, must sort meanings. The elite presence can be merged with something called tradition,
perceived as a still-vital source of unity, broken into parts variously mag-
nified or ignored by the onlooker, transposed into a history or a future.

But not the commoner presence. This presence scatters and con-
stricts the elite, emphasizing through contrast the stasis and antiquarian
charm of the old centers of power. In their treatment of townspeople,
the painters made a third significant choice: they described urbanity in
terms of the commoner class. Streets and neighborhoods fill the screens
not as fields for other subjects but as the primary content of citiness.
The city is a place for commerce—variously for the transport, manufacture, selling and buying of fans, paper, cloth, blades, arrows, combs,
dishes, pots, tea, lacquer, love, and all manner of foodstuffs. The screens
portray a richly diverse market where the pleasures of shoppers mingle
with the apparent satisfactions of workers. The city is also a place for
entertainment—for high festivals and low street carnival, for mixed
bathing in saunas (with female attendants) or visiting a theatrical performance, for hiding anonymously in a crowd or parading conspicuously
in a new costume, for watching and walking. And not least important,
the city is a place of mundane life where roofs are repaired, pieces of
laundry set out to dry, children fondled, and beggars given an occasional coin.

The treatment of the commoner world in these screens is carefully
modulated. Not only have vexing images been deleted, the uniform rendering of neighborhood architecture combines with the uniform good
cheer of human caricatures to suggest a cartoon. Yet the commoner
world also displays the final insistence of the cartoon: it cannot be dis-

missed as some separable element in the cityscape that a noble might overlook or a pilgrim avoid. The life of the street pervades the screens as no monument, not even the total of all monuments, is permitted to pervade them.

The wartime screens of Kyoto were almost certainly painted by professional artists of the capital, most likely for military patrons in the provinces.[8] It is probable, in effect, that they were produced by insiders for outsiders. The painters' sense of audience surely helps account for their long, synoptic view of Kyoto as they looked at it with the distant eye of a daimyo to capture an intelligible general portrait. Yet even if the dynamic of patronage explains, in part, the perspective of the artists (which was fundamentally different from the vantage of diarists and litigants), it could hardly provide a formula for the many complex decisions required by the act of representation. Those decisions were artistic ones, but they were also grounded in the mentality of the time. The painters rejected many of the images and moods of their age. Nowhere do we find in their screens the pathos of *The Chronicle of Ōnin*, the severed heads of Nakamikado Nobutane's diary, the apprehension that transformed the "Flower Capital" into a garrison and boating into crime. Everywhere, though, we find the exploration of identity that defined wartime culture. In the screens, as in demonstration, the old frameworks of corporation, of a fixed polity and a stable hierarchy, were bent beyond recognition. And whatever frames replaced them belonged to a popular politics of class and neighborhood. The painters elided the most radical aspects of change—uprising, the riotous spectacle of dancing, the reimagining of authority and community among affluent practitioners of tea. Still, they broke with every tradition known to them by inventing a cityscape dominated by commoners in motion. Consigning the elite to a reified domain of monuments, those painters located Kyoto in the performances of the street.

Notes

Introduction

1. The most extensive project on warring states (*sengoku*) history yet undertaken is the eighteen-volume *Sengoku daimyō ronshū*, under the general editorship of Nagahara Keiji. Each volume is a collection of essays that focus upon one or more of the daimyo houses in different geographical regions. (Honganji and the *ikkō* movement are covered in volume 13 as well.) Even in the various thematic works—concerning wartime law, for example—domains provide the organizing framework. Other topics have not been neglected, however; an increasing attention to social history has provoked substantial studies of villages (Fujiki, *Sengoku no sahō*, for instance), popular life (see Nagahara, *Nairan to minshū no seiki*), uprisings, and a host of subjects from trade to archeology. Yet much of this research broadly concerns the medieval period, with variable attention to wartime. Monographs on such subjects as warring states commerce, foreign relations, and religion, for example, have yet to appear. For an introduction to the Japanese bibliography, see the May issues of *Shigaku zasshi;* also see Tōhō Gakkai, under the auspices of the Japan Foundation, comp., *An Introductory Bibliography for Japanese Studies,* vol. 6, pt. 2, *Humanities 1983–86,* and vol. 7, pt. 2, *Humanities 1987–88.*

2. The history of wartime Kyoto has received extended treatment in three exceptionally fine works that have very much influenced my analysis: Imatani, *Sengoku-ki no Muromachi bakufu* and *Tokitsugu kyō-ki;* and Takahashi, *Kyōto chūsei toshi-shi kenkyū.* Wakita Haruko has written widely on medieval cities (carrying their stories into the warring states period); see *Nihon chūsei toshi-ron,* especially the excellent "Chūsei Kyōto no tochi shoyū." The multivolume

Kyōto-shi, ed., *Kyōto no rekishi*, which provides broad, diverse treatment of wartime in volume 3, covers the entire Ashikaga period from the early fourteenth century to the entry of Oda Nobunaga. A substantial number of articles consider aspects of late medieval urban history, but still few extended studies treat the particular experiences of the warring states period.

3. The events before unification are consigned, for example, to volume 3, *Medieval Japan* (ed. Kozo Yamamura) in *Cambridge History of Japan*. The linkage of wartime at least to the Ashikaga experience, if not to the Kamakura experience as well, is normal in series publications; see, for example, Rekishi-gaku Kenkyū-kai and Nihon-shi Kenkyū-kai, eds., *Kōza Nihon rekishi*. Throughout the historical literature, the break between *chūsei* and *kinsei* has concealed other temporal divisions. Thus, outside the huge bibliography committed to wartime domains, the *sengoku* experience tends to be either adamantly medieval (ending around 1560) or early modern (beginning around 1560).

4. The directions and the turbulence in medieval studies are apparent in Yamamura, ed., *Cambridge History of Japan: Volume 3, Medieval Japan*. For reviews equally suggestive of turbulence, see Steenstrup, "Middle Ages Survey'd"; Farris, Review; and Berry, Review. One of the earlier and more trenchant discussions of ferment in medieval historiography is Ishii, "Chūsei shakai-ron." Also see Nagahara, ed., *Nihon rekishi taikei 2: Chūsei*; Kuroda, *Rekishi-gaku no saisei*; and Wakita, "Shinpojiumu chūsei mibun-sei no kenkyū jōtai to kadai."

5. For a particularly clear and accessible history of classical Japan, see the relevant sections of Hall, *Government and Local Power in Japan*. Also consult the essays, particularly those by Cornelius Kiley and Elizabeth Sato and G. Cameron Hurst, in Hall and Mass, eds., *Medieval Japan*.

6. Two histories of warrior development in the classical period have just appeared—Friday, *Hired Swords;* and Farris, *Heavenly Warriors*.

7. Jeffrey P. Mass has laid authoritative claim to the history of the Kamakura regime in English. See, in particular, *Warrior Government in Early Medieval Japan, Development of Kamakura Rule*, and his contribution to *Cambridge History of Japan: Volume 3, Medieval Japan* (ed. Kozo Yamamura). I follow Mass in associating Yoritomo with this radical vision of power.

8. Mass discusses the problem of nomenclature in "What Can We Not Know About the Kamakura Bakufu?"

9. Mass discusses *jitō* and *shugo* experiences in *Warrior Government in Early Medieval Japan*. Also see his *Lordship and Inheritance in Early Medieval Japan* for illustrations of *jitō* fortunes in the Kamakura period.

10. See Imatani, "Muromachi Local Government." Also, for the history of the Ōuchi *shugo* house, see Arnesen, *Medieval Japanese Daimyo*.

11. See Imatani, with Yamamura, "Not For Lack of Will or Wile." Hall is emphatic about the statist and monarchical dimensions of Ashikaga rule in his contributions both to *Japan in the Muromachi Age* and to Yamamura, ed., *Cambridge History of Japan: Volume 3, Medieval Japan*. Grossberg follows a similar direction in *Japan's Renaissance*. The issue of kingship in Japan has received intense treatment recently in Japanese scholarship; see, for example, Sakurai, *Chūsei Nihon no ōken, shūkyō, geinō*.

12. See Harrington, "Regional Outposts of Muromachi Bakufu Rule."

13. For excellent essays in English on Ashikaga period villages, see Naga-hara, with Yamamura, "Village Communities and Daimyo Power," and Naga-hara, "Decline of the *Shōen* System" and "Medieval Peasant."

14. In addition to *Cambridge History of Japan*, readers interested in a taste of the debates might consult Hall and Toyoda, eds., *Japan in the Muromachi Age;* Mass and Hauser, eds., *Bakufu in Japanese History;* and Arnesen, *Medieval Japanese Daimyo.*

15. I first discussed this formulation in Berry, Review. It has much in com-mon with views of classical Japan advanced in Kiley, "Estate and Property in the Late Heian Period." A much more ambitious and cogent analysis of the medi-eval polity during the Kamakura period appears in Satō, *Nihon no chūsei kokka;* also see Kasamatsu, *Hō to kotoba no chūsei-shi.*

Prelude

1. *Nobutane kyō-ki*, Eishō 1 (1504)/9/4–21, 45:75–77.

2. Guicciardini's *Storia d'Italia* was begun in 1538, first published in 1562. For the text in English translation, *The History of Italy*, trans. Sidney Alexander. For discussion, see Gilbert, *Machiavelli and Guicciardini.*

3. Ōmura Yukō, secretary and scribe to Toyotomi Hideyoshi, probably completed *Tenshō-ki* (a biographical portrait of his lord covering the years 1577–90) in the last decade of the sixteenth century. Subsequent biographies of Hi-deyoshi include Ōta, *Taikō gunki*, written soon after Hideyoshi's death in 1598; and Oze, *Taikō-ki*, probably completed around 1626. The earliest biography of Oda Nobunaga is Ōta, *Shinchō kō-ki*, completed around 1610. See Kuwata, ed., *Taikō shiryō-shū;* Oze, *Taikō-ki;* Ōta, *Shinchō kō-ki.* Also see Kuwata, *Taikō-ki no kenkyū.*

4. See, for example, Matsunaga, *Taion-ki.* Donald Keene discusses the frag-ile sense of peace that the poet Matsunaga Teitoku (1571–1653) conveys in his account of the early Tokugawa years and, implicitly, the deep uncertainty surrounding what we now think of as the transition into a stable political order; Keene, "Nikki ni miru Nihon." I am grateful to Fujiki Hisashi for these refer-ences.

5. See, for example, *Go-Hōkōin-ki*, Eishō 1 (1504)/9/20, 8:227.

6. Katsumata, "Mimi o kiri" and "Shigai tekitai"; *CHSS/MBH*, 123–24, nos. 385–89.

Chapter 1. The Culture of Lawlessness, The Politics of Demonstration

1. Translated in Varley, *Ōnin War*, 139–40. This book is an extremely useful analysis of the Ōnin war and its origins. For the text of *Ōnin-ki*, see Hanawa, ed., *Shinkō gunsho ruijū* 16:252–97; also Wada, ed., *Ōnin-ki.*

2. For detailed treatments of the succession quarrels, the general background, and the progress of the Ōnin war, see Nagashima, *Ōnin no ran;* Suzuki, *Ōnin no ran;* Momose, "Ōnin, Bunmei no ran"; Imatani, ed., *Ōnin no ran.*

3. For studies of the great provincial *shugo* and their houses, see Imatani, *Shugo ryōgoku shihai kikō no kenkyū;* Tanuma, "Muromachi bakufu to shugo ryōgoku" and "Muromachi bakufu, shugo, kokujin"; Ike, "Daimyō ryōgoku-sei no tenkai to shōgun, tennō"; Nagahara, *Nihon chūsei no shakai to kokka,* 119–48. For studies in English, see Arnesen, *Medieval Japanese Daimyo;* and Kawai with Grossberg, "Shogun and Shugo."

4. The issues of family headship (succession) and inheritance are intimately linked and complex. By the time Ashikaga rule was consolidated, practices of partible inheritance had yielded to unitary vestiture and the consequent concentration in one heir of both the family headship rights and the household wealth and holdings. Competition over headship was thus severely aggravated. See *KR* 3:307–8; and Kawai, *Chūsei buke shakai no kenkyū,* 157–74. For the Kamakura period situation, see Haga, *Sōryō-sei,* and Mass, *Lordship and Inheritance in Early Medieval Japan.*

5. See, for example, Kitazume, "Kokujin ryōshu to dogō"; Kawai, *Chūsei buke shakai no kenkyū,* 203–61; Fujiki, "Zai-ichi ryōshu no kōri-gashi kinō ni tsuite"; Imatani, "Muromachi Local Government."

6. *KR* 3:316–17.

7. Imatani Akira insists on the centrality to the Ōnin quarrel of competition over the position of Yamashiro *shugo; Ōnin no ran,* 203–4.

8. *KR* 3:316–17.

9. *KR* 3:318–19; Nagashima, *Ōnin no ran,* 229–40.

10. *KR* 3:300–306; Kawai with Grossberg, "Shogun and Shugo," 72.

11. The standard biography is Kawai, *Ashikaga Yoshimasa.* Also see Varley, *Ōnin War,* 101–19; and *KR* 3:309–14.

12. *KR* 3:314–15; Imatani, *Ōnin no ran,* 202; Nagashima, *Ōnin no ran,* 75–80.

13. *KR* 3:315–16.

14. Imatani, *Ōnin no ran,* 204, 206.

15. Ibid., 204.

16. Nagashima, *Ōnin no ran,* 55–112; Varley, *Ōnin War,* 86–96, 123–35.

17. *CHSS/MBH,* 124 (no. 390); see also ibid., 16 (no. 15), 21 (no. 26), and 30 (no. 58), for the important legislation of the fourteenth century. I have followed Kobayashi Seiji ("Sengoku sōran no tenkai," 16) in interpreting *kōsen* not just as an aggressive (in contrast to defensive) battle, but as a "private" battle that emerges from personal intentions, causes, and circumstances.

18. *CHSS/MBH,* 16 (no. 15), 21 (no. 26), 30 (no. 58), 126 (no. 396); also see Berry, "Public Peace and Private Attachment," 243–51.

19. *KR* 3:317; Nagashima, *Ōnin no ran,* 81–91, 94–103.

20. For overviews of the problem of jurisdiction and the administration of justice, see Ishii, *Nihon hōsei-shi teiyō,* 73–95; Fujiki, *Sengoku shakai-shi ron,* esp. 1–117. The sources cited in notes 3 and 5 are also useful.

21. Jeffrey P. Mass has extensively explored this subject, in relation to the

Kamakura bakufu, in such works as *Kamakura Bakufu* and *Development of Kamakura Rule*. For the Muromachi bakufu, see Gay, "Muromachi Bakufu Rule in Kyoto"; Ishii, *Nihon hōsei-shi teiyō*, 68–119; the *tsuika-hō* of the bakufu itself, in *CHSS/MBH* (translated by Kenneth A. Grossberg and Kanamoto Nobuhisa in Grossberg, ed., *Laws of the Muromachi Bakufu*); and the administrative documents in *MBMS/BHH* 1:13–206.

22. Imatani, *Ōnin no ran*, 204–6. Throughout this period, dates and sources can be quickly confirmed by consulting *KR*, vol. 10, which contains a detailed chronology and source guide.

23. *KR* 3:319–20, 335–36.

24. Konoe Masaie, quoted in Akiyama, *Kinsei Kyōto machigumi hattatsu-shi*, 10.

25. *KR* 3:333–44.

26. Imatani , *Ōnin no ran*, 206–7; *KR* 3:319–23.

27. Varley, *Ōnin War*, 172–73. Also see the map in Imatani, *Ōnin no ran*, 204–5, indicating the provinces involved in Ōnin, the sides their leaders took, the pattern of engagement.

28. *KR* 3:320–32.

29. Akeda, *Ransei Kyōto* 1:179–236; *KR* 3:319–32.

30. *KR* 3:323–24; Nagashima, *Ōnin no ran*, 128–36.

31. Wada, *Ōnin-ki*, 85; *KR* 3:338.

32. *Ōnin ryakki*, quoted in Akiyama, *Kinsei Kyōto machigumi hattatsu-shi*, 14.

33. Akeda, *Ransei Kyōto* 1:224.

34. *KR* 3:339–40; Akiyama, *Kinsei Kyōto machigumi hattatsu-shi*, 10–11.

35. *KR* 3:35–37; also see the map of Ōnin damage, ibid. 3:348.

36. Katsumata, "Ie o yaku."

37. I find no record of, or reference to, food embargoes, nor is there mention of severe food shortages in the city. The documents of shogunal administrators (*bugyō-nin*) display a concern with maintaining both the tax barriers around the capital and the taxes on imports due to various proprietors. This attention to collecting tax revenue from imports, rather than to canceling taxes and opening the barriers in order to stimulate the movement of supplies into Kyoto, indicates a stable and adequate supply system. See *MBMS/BHH* 1:236 (no. 837), 237 (no. 841).

38. The word *protocol* is very close in resonance to *sahō*, the term employed by Fujiki Hisashi in *Sengoku no sahō*. Though concerned essentially with rural protocols, the book—and Fujiki's counsel—have been important in the conception of this manuscript.

39. Fujiki, *Sengoku no sahō*, 129–64; also see Berry, *Hideyoshi*, 89–90, 95.

40. Amino et al., *Chūsei no tsumi to batsu*, esp. 15–26, 44–58, 133–52.

41. Owada, *Ōmi Asai-shi*, 247–50; Kuwata, *Yodogimi*, 19–24.

42. I know of no good, inclusive tally of temple and shrine destruction. See, however, Akeda, *Ransei Kyōto* 1:225–26; and *KR*, vol. 10, for the Ōnin years.

43. Takahashi, *Kyōto chūsei toshi-shi kenkyū*, 291–93; Akiyama, *Kinsei Kyōto*, 12–13.

44. Nagashima, *Ōnin no ran,* 113–36, 140–46, 149–53, 158–62.

45. *Daijōin jisha zōjiki,* Bunmei 9 (1477)/11/10; see the rebuttal to these assertions in Imatani, *Sengoku-ki no Muromachi bakufu,* 151–52.

46. Imatani, *Sengoku-ki no Muromachi bakufu,* 155–58; *KR* 3:353–54.

47. *KR* 3:358–60, 365–67.

48. Ibid. 3:360–62; Takahashi, *Kyōto chūsei toshi-shi kenkyū,* 293–96.

49. *CHSS/MBH,* 96–98 (nos. 276–92); *MBMS/BHH* 1:306–80 (for example, 308 [no. 1098], 311 [no. 1107], 325 [no. 1157], 326 [no. 1161], 332 [no. 1184], 336 [no. 1197], 339 [no. 1209]). See Kawasaki, "Muromachi bakufu no hōkai katei," 62–67, for a discussion of the 20 percent tax levy.

50. *KR* 3:362–65.

51. *Nobutane kyō-ki,* Eishō 4 (1507)/8/24, 45:201–2.

52. *Nisui-ki,* Eishō 17 (1520)/8/4, in *SKR* 5:254–55.

53. *KR* 3:376–78; Kobayashi, "Sengoku sōran no tenkai," 16.

54. See Nihon-shi Kenkyū-kai and Rekishi-gaku Kenkyū-kai, eds., *Yamashiro kuni ikki,* for an excellent chronology and bibliography of this uprising. This book also contains citations of the most relevant contemporary documents (pages 230–37); see, in this case, documents 13–16. Also see *KR* 3:369; Imatani, *Ōnin no ran,* 214. Particularly interesting and bearing further consideration are the documentary references to the use of sacred water and fire.

55. Nihon-shi Kenkyū-kai and Rekishi-gaku Kenkyū-kai, eds., *Yamashiro kuni ikki,* documents 19, 20; *KR* 3:370; Imatani, *Ōnin no ran,* 214.

56. See Kawasaki, "Muromachi bakufu no hōkai katei," 49–82. Kawasaki links the uprising closely to impositions of the half-tax in Yamashiro (in 1478, for example, when 20 percent rather than 50 percent of proprietary revenues was demanded by the shogunate) and the steady depletion of local resources by the Hatakeyama and the bakufu alike. A half-tax was also ordered by the shogunate in 1483.

57. *KR* 3:368–69; Nihon-shi Kenkyū-kai and Rekishi-gaku Kenkyū-kai, eds., *Yamashiro kuni ikki,* documents 21, 23.

58. Nihon-shi Kenkyū-kai and Rekishi-gaku Kenkyū-kai, eds., *Yamashiro kuni ikki,* documents 22, 25; *KR* 3:370.

59. For an extensive discussion and analysis of *ikki,* see Katsumata, *Ikki;* Nakamura, *Do ikki kenkyū;* Murata, "Sō to do ikki"; Kurokawa, "Chūsei kōki no nōmin tōsō."

60. Other *kuni ikki* had taken place in 1429, against the Akamatsu house in Harima, and in 1468–71, against the *shugo-dai* in Bitchū; *KR* 3:368.

61. Standard descriptions of this uprising (for example, *KR* 3:370–73) associate it with the *jizamurai* and their putatively conservative and pragmatic concern for expanding their own particular land interests.

62. *KR* 3:372–73; also see Imatani, *Ōnin no ran,* 212–15.

63. *KR* 3:68–71. Not only did the office of Yamashiro *shugo* rotate regularly among shogunal favorites and heads of the *samurai-dokoro,* the opportunities of the incumbent to build a land base in the home province were much constrained by the extensive development of *shōen* there and the consequent paucity of *kokugaryō.* The authority of civil proprietors in Yamashiro also limited *shugo* opportunities to use judicial decisions to enrich themselves or their vassals.

64. Yamashiro was anomalous among the provinces for its intense development of *shōen* (eighty at their numerical height), the relatively close surveillance of the proprietary community (which resided close by, in the city of Kyoto, and regarded the home province as the most reliable source of revenue), and the connections between proprietors and their managers that helped defend the managers against the encroachments of their peers. These factors made possible the survival of managers of medium-size holdings who, though highly competitive, remained roughly equal. See *KR* 3:270–304, particularly the *shōen* map on page 274; also see Tanaka, "Sengoku-ki ni okeru shōen sonraku to kenryoku," concerning the history of Kami-kuze no shō.

65. *KR* 3:375–76; also see, for the larger and ensuing structure of vassalage, Morita, "Sengoku-ki Kinai ni okeru shugo-dai, kokujin-zō no dōkō."

66. *KR* 3:373–75; Imatani, *Ōnin no ran*, 212–15.

67. Murata, "Sō to do ikki," 135–76.

68. *SKR* 3:310–11 (no. 6).

69. *KR* 3:378. The retired shogun Yoshimasa also died in 1490, thus depriving Masamoto of a valuable ally.

70. Katsumoto was *kanrei* in 1445–49, 1452–59, and 1467–73; Masanaga was *kanrei* in 1473 and, after a period when the office went vacant, in 1477–86. Masamoto held the office briefly in 1486, Matsunaga recovered it for another year, and Masamoto reclaimed it in 1487.

71. *SKR* 3:309 (no. 2).

72. *KR* 3:482–83; Imatani, *Sengoku Miyoshi ichizoku*, 35–37.

73. *KR* 3:483; Imatani, *Sengoku Miyoshi ichizoku*, 37–39.

74. *KR* 3:483. Sumiyuki's *genpuku* occurred in 1504, when he was presumably fifteen years old or so.

75. *KR* 3:483–84; Imatani, *Sengoku Miyoshi ichizoku*, 40–43; *Sanetaka kō-ki*, Eishō 4 (1507)/6/23, 4:742. Sanetaka describes Masamoto's murder as a "judgment of heaven" and adds that "high and low are amazed and in an uproar."

76. *Sanetaka kō-ki*, Eishō 4 (1507)/8/1–2, 4:751; *KR* 3:484; Imatani, *Sengoku Miyoshi ichizoku*, 43–44.

77. *Sanetaka kō-ki*, Eishō 5 (1508)/4/16, 5:36; *KR* 3:484; Imatani, *Sengoku Miyoshi ichizoku*, 45–46; Morita, "Hosokawa Takakuni to Kinai kokujin-zō." Sanetaka describes the departure of the shogun's wife into hiding in Kyoto.

78. *Nisui-ki*, Eishō 18 (1521)/3/8, in *SKR* 3:318; also see the chronology in *KR*, vol. 10, for the clearest summary of these events. Sanetaka describes the amazement among the *kuge* over Yoshitane's departure and his problems with Takakuni.

79. Kobayashi, "Sengoku sōran no tenkai," 14–18; Imatani, *Sengoku Miyoshi ichizoku*, 40. The Isshiki rebelled, and the Asakura refused service.

Chapter 2. Dancing Is Forbidden: The Structures of Urban Conflict

1. *Sanetaka kō-ki,* Eishō 3 (1506)/7/11, 4:574.
2. *Chikatoshi nikki,* Tenbun 11 (1542)/2/10, 14:13.
3. *Tokitsugu kyō-ki,* Tenbun 13 (1544)/7/14, 1:484.
4. *MBMS/BHH* 2:171 (no. 2775); 2:189–90 (no. 2841); *KR* 3:341; *Gen'i Hōin gejijō,* no. 36. A good reproduction of such a placard appears in Imatani, *Ōnin no ran,* p. 207.
5. *Mandokoro-gata hikitsuke,* Meiō 3 (1494)/11/14, in *SKR* 3:343 (no. 1).
6. The *tokusei-rei* of Kyōroku 3 (1530)/12/19 in *CHSS/MBH* 2:139–40 (nos. 480–82).
7. *Chikanaga kyō-ki,* Bunmei 16 (1484)/6/2, 40:218.
8. *Go-Hōkōin-ki,* Meiō 5 (1496)/6/24, 27, 7:260–61.
9. *Motonaga kyō-ki,* Eishō 4 (1507)/4/23, 23:136; also see *Sanetaka kō-ki,* Eishō 4/4/23, 4:720–21.
10. *Nisui-ki,* Daiei 7 (1527)/11/29, in *SKR* 4:281–82 (no. 6).
11. *Sanetaka kō-ki,* Daiei 7 (1527)/11/28–29, 7:144.
12. Quoted in Akiyama, *Kinsei Kyōto machigumi hattatsu-shi,* 12.
13. *Gensuke onen-ki,* Tenbun 5 (1536)/7/27, in *SKR* 4:269 (no. 23).
14. *Go-Hōkōin-ki,* Ōnin 1 (1467)/6/22, 5:107.
15. *Kin'yori kō-ki,* Daiei 7 (1527)/7/2, in *SKR* 4:269 (no. 22). The sense of loss also lives vividly in the writings of European Christian missionaries, who first came to Japan in the 1540s; it clearly derived from comments of Japanese acquaintances, who must have inherited it from their parents and grandparents. See, for example, remarks by Gaspar Vilela in *SKR* 4:277 (no. 48).
16. *Sōchō shūki,* Daiei 6 (1526)/3/28, 88.
17. *Ōnin-ki,* quoted in Akeda, *Ransei Kyōto* 1:224 (for the reference to foxes and wolves); Ichijō Kanera, quoted in Akiyama, *Kōdo enkaku-shi* 1:21.
18. See Takahashi, *Kyōto chūsei toshi-shi kenkyū,* 293–97.
19. The various troubles at the imperial palace are noted in the successive entries of the chronology in *KR,* vol. 10. See *Sanetaka kō-ki,* Eishō 4 (1507)/7/26, 4:750, for one description of the huts for refugees built on the palace grounds. In 1521 the head of the Takeda house of Wakasa received a promotion to the third rank for a donation to repair the north gate of the palace; *KR* 3:669.
20. A thorough discussion of the palace moats, in the context of the development of block associations, appears in Takahashi, *Kyōto chūsei toshi-shi kenkyū,* 453–61. For the quotations, from the *Nisui-ki,* Daiei 7 (1527)/12/17, see *SKR* 5:264 (no. 17).
21. *Morimitsu kō-ki,* Eishō 12 (1515)/6/4–5, in *SKR* 3:368 (no. 32). The phrase I have translated here as beggars is *kanjin hijiri,* which describes persons seeking contributions for temples.

22. João Rodrigues, *História da Igreja do Japão,* translated in Cooper, *This Island of Japon,* 115.

23. *Rojin zatsuwa,* in *SKR* 4:272 (no. 33).

24. Takahashi, *Kyōto chūsei toshi-shi kenkyū,* 294–97.

25. Ibid., 393–94, 411–12.

26. Teishitsu Rin'ya Kyoku, *Go-ryōchi shikō,* 239–41; Okuno Takahiro, *Kōshitsu go-keizai-shi no kenkyū,* 227–41.

27. For the reference to the mosquito net and the sword, *Tokitsugu kyō-ki,* Tenbun 1 (1532)/6/7, 18, 1:189, 191; for the copying and selling of manuscripts, *Sanetaka kō-ki,* Eishō 17 (1520)/3/7–10, 5:706, and Kyōroku 2 (1529)/8/24, 8: 23–24, also Bunki 3 (1503)/4/29, 4:125; for a series of documents concerning postponed rituals, *SKR* 5:252–56 (nos. 21–24, 28–32, 38–40).

28. *Daijōin jisha zōjiki,* Bunki 2 (1502)/6/16, 36:466.

29. *Nobutane kyō-ki,* Eishō 14 (1517)/1/1, 45:251.

30. Takahashi, *Kyōto chūsei toshi-shi kenkyū,* 296 (for the failure to redevelop the *hōkōshū* quarter); *SKR* 3:309 (no. 2) and Imatani, *Sengoku Miyoshi ichizoku,* 36 (for the events of 1493).

31. See the Afterword for a discussion of the *Rakuchū rakugai-zu* screens and the pictorial treatment of military mansions. Typical of documentary references to the Hosokawa presence is *Sanetaka kō-ki,* Eishō 4 (1507)/6/23–24, 4: 742–43, which describes the attack on Masamoto's residence and the destruction of the palace by fire.

32. There is not yet, nor is there likely to be, any precise description of shogunal residences and shogunal movements during wartime. The Hana no gosho (between Kamidachiuri and Imadegawa on the north and south, Karasuma and Muromachi on the east and west) was restored around 1479 but subsequently damaged again by fire. The ninth shogun may rarely have used it, turning, instead, to the mansion of the Ise house and the Ogawa gosho (a temporary residence or retreat, with apparently modest facilities, which was built by Hosokawa Katsumoto above Ichijō). The tenth and eleventh shoguns may have moved back and forth between the Hana no gosho, the Ogawa residence, and (in the case of the tenth) the residence of Hosokawa Masamoto.

The inadequacy of these arrangements was acknowledged in 1515 when construction of a new residence was undertaken near Sanjō-bōmon. What very little we know of this effort comes from a thin and questionable account in a text called *Towazu-gatari* (*SKR* 4:267 [no. 13]). *Nisui-ki* refers to a temporary shogunal residence north of Yanagihara-Muromachi in 1521 and then to construction of yet another new residence in 1524, which, according to *Kugyō bunin,* the shogun Yoshiharu entered on the thirteenth day of the twelfth month in 1525. No document specifies the exact location of this residence, although it is now referred to as the Willow Mansion (Yanagi gosho), since *Nisui-ki* refers to its location north of Yanagihara.

By 1527 Yoshiharu was taking shelter in Shōkokuji. From 1528 until 1534 he lived outside Kyoto. From 1534 until 1542 he apparently lived in a series of temples and private mansions (Kenninji, Nanzenji, the Ise mansion). In 1542 the shogun moved into the restored Hana no gosho, although he and his son (the thirteenth shogun, Yoshiteru) had moved back into fortified temples by 1547 and then into outlying castles. Yoshiteru did not resume regular residence in Kyoto until 1558, when he lodged at Shōkokuji and Honkakuji.

A new shogunal mansion, known as the Konoe gosho, was completed by 1560 at Muromachi–Made no kōji. But again the Hana no gosho was rebuilt, and the shogun moved there in 1564. This building burned in 1565 when a coup was mounted against the shogun.

See Takahashi, *Kyōto chūsei toshi-shi kenkyū*, 293–97; the chronology in *KR*, vol. 10; *KR* 3:400–401; the notes on shogunal buildings in Ishida et al., eds., *Rakuchū rakugai-zu taikan;* also Imatani, *Tokitsugu kyō-ki*, 110–50, concerning the castles. The most vivid description of a shogunal mansion comes from the missionary Luis Frois, who described (glowingly) a visit to Ashikaga Yoshiteru's residence in 1565; quoted in Cooper, comp., *They Came to Japan*, 110.

33. See note 32 above, esp. Imatani, *Tokitsugu kyō-ki*, 110–50.

34. Imatani, *Tokitsugu kyō-ki*, 110–50.

35. My understanding of the physical transformation of wartime Kyōto derives almost entirely from the work of Takahashi Yasuo. See, for example, his *Kyōto chūsei toshi-shi kenkyū*, 291–372, esp. 343–72; his *Rakuchū rakugai-zu*, esp. 22–31; and his visualization of the Kyoto landscape in Imatani, *Ōnin no ran*, 208–9. João Rodrigues confirms a number of details in Cooper, ed. and trans., *This Island of Japon*, 110–15.

My measurements of the urban islands derive from maps drawn to scale that accompany (as inserts) *KR*, vols. 3 and 4. The prewar distribution of the population concentrated between Tera no uchi and Rokujō (north to south), Tomi no kōji to Ōmiya (east to west), an area of roughly 7.5 square kilometers; see the map in *KR*, vol. 3.

36. Takahashi, *Kyōto chūsei toshi-shi kenkyū*, 348–53.

37. See the maps in Takahashi, *Rakuchū rakugai-zu*, 22–23. The principal baths that we know of appeared at Ichijō, Ōgimachi-Muromachi, and Sanjō-Muromachi; *SKR* 5:251 (nos. 13–15).

38. For tax concessions on the vacant site, see *Gen'i Hōin gejijō*, no. 1; for the census data (concerning Reizen-chō) see Yoshida, "Kōgi to chōnin mibun," 102–5, and Takahashi, *Kyōto chūsei toshi-shi kenkyū*, 433–35.

39. A comparison of the maps showing the Ōnin destruction and later reconstruction of Kyoto during wartime indicates both a lasting retreat from some destroyed parts of the city (primarily the immense stretch of land between Tsuchimikado and Nijō, the western sector of southern Kyoto, and the area east and north of the palace) and the resettlement of other such parts. It also indicates that residents withdrew from certain sectors that remained undamaged in the Ōnin war (primarily the area east from Takakura to the Kamo River, and south from Gojō to Rokujō). The capacity for regular and purposeful rebuilding is suggested, for example, by the rapid recovery of the weaving district after Ōnin (see Takahashi, *Kyōto chūsei toshi-shi kenkyū*, 324–33), and the reconstruction of the Hokke temples (see *KR* 4:148–65). For missionaries' comments on the state of the city, see, for example, Cooper, comp., *They Came to Japan*, 276–82.

40. Takahashi, *Kyōto chūsei toshi-shi kenkyū*, 291–99, 366–72; *Tokitsugu kyō-ki*, Tenbun 2 (1534)/4/29, 1:183–84.

41. Takahashi, *Kyōto chūsei toshi-shi kenkyū*, 366–72, 400–404; *SKR* 4:281–82 (nos. 3–7), also 4:278 (no. 51) concerning Luis Frois's remarks on gates, and 2:278–79 (no. 52) concerning references in an undated *kyōgen* play to the walls and fences protecting the homes of affluent commoners.

42. Yoshida, "Kōgi to chōnin mibun," 98–99, 101–5; Takahashi, *Kyōto chūsei toshi-shi kenkyū*, 327–33; *Nisui-ki*, Bunki 4 (1504)/11/29, in *SKR* 4:266 (no. 11), concerning a fire that destroyed half the homes on a block, calculated at twenty buildings. Takahashi, in a conversation of June 29, 1987, estimated that most wartime homes were 2 *ken* wide and 2 *ken* deep (1 *ken* = 6 *shaku*, 5 *sun*, or roughly 2 meters). Anything larger was the exception. Narrow but deep homes (in the "eel" style) appear to have been later peacetime phenomena. In wartime, shallow buildings on back alleys were constructed behind shallow buildings facing the street. Although wartime homes were probably no narrower than prewar homes, the crowding I have associated with stockade conditions derived both from the development of back lots and from the lining up of buildings alongside one another, eliminating the spaces that had once provided comfortable margins between structures.

43. For the mention of *zushi*, or new alleys, in wartime blocks, see, for example, the tax registers from Daitokuji in *SKR* 4:270 (nos. 26 and 27). Takahashi Yasuo believes the *zushi* were no more than 2 meters wide. The old avenues, such as Muromachi, were probably about 8 meters wide.

44. A discussion of population appears in *KR* 3:33–41. Takahashi Yasuo prefers a figure of 100,000 (conversation of June 29, 1987). Although all such population estimates remain large, very large, I know of no scholar who proposes smaller figures.

If we assume that there were 224 settled blocks in Kyoto around 1572 (68 in southern Kyoto, 150 in northern, and 6 in the Rokuchō-gumi; Takahashi, *Kyōto chūsei toshi-shi kenkyū*, 348–53) and that each included 40 homes occupied by 8 people (the number suggested by figures available just before and after 1700; *KR* 10:99–100), we arrive at a population estimate of roughly 72,000. Takahashi believes that many homes harbored more than 8 people, and that many tiny dwellings outside the block structure were crowded into back gardens.

To arrive at a population density of 1 person to 20 square meters, I calculated the area of settled Kyoto at 2 square kilometers and the population at 100,000.

45. *Nisui-ki*, Daiei 6 (1526)/10/27, in *SKR* 5:263 (no. 13).

46. *SKR* 4:283 (no. 14; Tenbun 19 [1550]/intercalary 5/24).

47. *SKR* 3:323 (no. 44; Eiroku 5 [1562]/3/23).

48. *Kamikyō monjo*, Tenbun 19 (1550)/7/10, in *SKR* 3:321 (no. 37).

49. *KR* 3:341–43; *Tokitsugu kyō-ki*, Tenbun 18 (1549)/11/17, 2:279.

50. Imatani, *Ōnin no ran*, 206–7.

51. *KR* 3:333–35, 338, 341.

52. *Shinnyodō engi emaki*, in Imatani, *Ōnin no ran*, 203, 207.

53. *KR* 3:337; *SKR* 3:323 (no. 44; see article 4); also see note 71 below.

54. *Daijōin jisha zōjiki*, Bunmei 3/1/24, 30:61.

55. *KR* 3:351.

56. *Tokitsugu kyō-ki*, Tenbun 18 (1549)/11/17, 2:279.

57. Imatani, *Tokitsugu kyō-ki*, 131–33.

58. *Go-Hōkōin-ki*, Meiō 7 (1498)/12/4, 8, 10, 11, 7:380–81.

59. *Rokuen nichiroku*, Meiō 8 (1499)/10/1, in *SKR* 5:262 (no. 9). For a somewhat different version of the same events, see *Go-Hōkōin-ki*, Meiō 8 (1499)/10/5, 7:418.

60. *Nisui-ki*, Tenbun 1 (1532)/8/23, 24, in *SKR* 5:265–66 (no. 250).

61. Fujiki, *Sengoku no sahō*, 131–39, discusses the taking of such hostages in agrarian villages.

62. *SKR* 3:310–12 (nos. 3–10).

63. *SKR* 3:309 (no. 2); *KR* 3:482–83; Imatani, *Sengoku Miyoshi ichizoku*, 35–37.

64. *Sanetaka kō-ki*, Eishō 4 (1507)/6/23–24, 4:742; Eishō 4/8/1–2, 4:751; Eishō 5/4/16, 5:36. See also *Tamon'in nikki*, Eishō 4/8/1, 1:197; *KR* 3:483–84.

65. See notes 7 and 8 of Chapter 4. This transition, which is discussed at length in Chapter 4, was never concluded successfully. The coup created two rival administrations and resulted in protracted warfare.

66. *KR* 3:66–68; Imatani, *Sengoku-ki no Muromachi bakufu*, 18–27.

67. See the "Biographical Sketches of the Wartime Shogun," Chapter 3.

68. *Nisui-ki*, Eishō 18 (1521)/7/6, in *SKR* 5:318 (no. 29).

69. *Nisui-ki*, Eishō 18 (1521)/3/8 and 5/28, in *SKR* 3:318.

70. The most startling act of compliance involved the promotion in 1527 of Ashikaga Yoshitsuna to a rank and title that anticipated his appointment as shogun, despite the fact that the incumbent shogun (Ashikaga Yoshiharu) was actively resisting the rebel Yoshitsuna and apparently retained the throne's support; see Chapter 4.

71. See *Tokitsugu kyō-ki*, Eiroku 8 (1565)/5/19, 3:502–3. This extraordinary description of the shogunal assassination of 1565 condemns the event but goes on to describe the presumptive Ashikaga successor in honorific and respectful language.

72. *Sanetaka kō-ki*, Eishō 6 (1509)/10/26–27, 5:275–77.

73. Imatani, *Tokitsugu kyō-ki*, 257–58.

74. See, for example, *KR* 3:499–502.

75. *SKR* 3:323 (no. 44).

76. *Kamikyō monjo*, Tenbun 19 (1550)/7/10, in *SKR* 3:321 (no. 37).

77. These events are considered again in Chapter 4.

78. Imatani, *Tokitsugu kyō-ki*, 67–72.

79. *Tokitsugu kyō-ki*, Daiei 7 (1527)/11/29 and 7/12/1, 1:88; Takahashi, *Kyōto chūsei toshi-shi kenkyū*, 400–403.

80. *Sanetaka kō-ki*, Daiei 7 (1527)/11/28, 7:144. Invaders are called "villains" here and "thieves" in *Sanetaka kō-ki*, Daiei 7/11/29, 7:144.

81. *Tokitsugu kyō-ki*, Daiei 7 (1527)/12/1, 1:88.

82. *Tokitsugu kyō-ki*, Daiei 7 (1527)/12/13, 14, 1:90–91; *Nisui-ki*, Daiei 7/12/17, in *SKR* 5:264 (no. 17).

83. *CHSS/MBH,* 123–24.
84. *Honnōji monjo,* Tenbun 5 (1536)/intercalary 10/17, in *SKR* 3:363.
85. *SKR* 4:290 (no. 38; Tenbun 18 [1549]/4/8).
86. Laws of the Blue Ash Guild, *Sano monjo,* Eishō 14 (1517)/9/21, in *SKR* 4:315–17 (no. 15).
87. *Tōji hyakugō monjo,* Eishō 11 (1514)/5, in *SKR* 4:280–81 (no. 2; articles, 5, 3).
88. Imatani, *Sengoku-ki no Muromachi bakufu,* 18–27.
89. Takahashi, *Kyōto chūsei toshi-shi kenkyū,* 352–63, 461–66.
90. Ibid., 291–93, 297–99; *Tokitsugu kyō-ki,* Tenbun 3 (1534)/4/29, 1:334; Tenbun 3/3/1, 1:313; also *KR* 3:337.
91. Imatani, *Tokitsugu kyō-ki,* 110–50.
92. For an excellent overview of forest depletion, see Totman, *Green Archipelago,* esp. 34–80.
93. For this calculation, I am assuming a commoner population of about 75,000 and assigning 5 persons to each household (to yield 15,000 houses). If we assume a commoner population of 100,000 and assign 8 people to each household, the yield is 12,500 houses. Obviously such figures are only suggestive. See note 44 above.
94. *Sanetaka kō-ki,* Meiō 6 (1497)/10/11, 12, 18, 21, 3:451–56; Meiō 6/11/2, 3:460.
95. *Go-Hōkōin-ki,* Eishō 1 (1504)/9/22–23, 8:227; *Nobutane kyō-ki,* Eishō 1/10/10, 45:78–79.
96. *Sanetaka kō-ki,* Eishō 4 (1507)/9/3, 4:759.
97. *Nisui-ki,* Eishō 2 (1505)/9/10, 11, 21, in *SKR* 3:314–15 (no. 16).
98. Imatani, *Sengoku Miyoshi ichizoku,* 44–46.
99. *Tokitsugu kyō-ki,* Kyōroku 2 (1529)/1/10–11, 1:128–29. See ibid., Tenbun 16 (1547)/1/10–11, 2:178, for a description of an almost-identical raid in 1547. Imatani, *Tokitsugu kyō-ki,* 232–33, describes the earlier raid in conjunction with a military tax, *hyōrōmai.*
100. See note 89 of this chapter.
101. See note 1 of the Prelude for recruitment in 1504. See Imatani, *Tokitsugu kyō-ki,* 233–34, for recruitment in *shimo-gyō* by the Sakai shogun.
102. *Nanzenji monjo,* Meiō 4 (1495)/10/21, 2:19.
103. *Honmanji monjo,* Tenbun 2 (1533)/7/23, in *SKR* 3:362 (no. 5).
104. Accounts of the uprisings focus on the vulnerability of the capital, its defense by the townspeople, and the disposition of the weak shogunate to placate debtors with debt cancellations. See the discussion later in this chapter, and notes 109, 115, 116, and 117 below.
105. Imatani, *Sengoku-ki no Muromachi bakufu,* 161–66.
106. Ibid., 164.
107. See note 63 concerning the purge and retirement of the *hōkōshū* in 1493; also see Kobayashi, "Sengoku sōran no tenkai," 16.
108. Imatani, *Sengoku-ki no Muromachi bakufu,* 151–66, concerning Hosokawa military power and reliance on provincial *kokujin.*
109. *Chikanaga kyō-ki,* Bunmei 16 (1484)/6/2, 40:218.

110. For a discussion of *ikki*, see Katsumata, *Ikki;* Nakamura, *Do ikki ken-kyū;* Murata, "Sō to do ikki"; Kasamatsu and Katsumata, eds., *Tokusei-rei.* Also see Hayashiya, *Machishū,* 95–103.

111. *Nisui-ki,* Eishō 17 (1520)/1/12, 28, in *SKR* 5:263 (no. 12); also see notes 58 and 62 above.

112. Imatani, *Sengoku Miyoshi ichizoku,* 34–5; *KR* 3:334–35; note 125, below, concerning the aristocratic benefits from *tokusei.*

113. See, for example, Murata, "Sō to do ikki," 135–76; Imatani, *Ōnin no ran,* 196–200.

114. The best chronology of *ikki* appears in the annual entries of *KR* 10:216–28.

115. *SKR* 5:263 (no. 14; Daiei 6 [1526]/12/1). Also see, concerning 1504, *SKR* 5:250 (no. 6; Eishō 1 [1504]/9/11).

116. *Sanetaka kō-ki,* Meiō 6 (1497)/9/28, 30, 3:446–47; also *Go-Hōkōin-ki,* Meiō 6/9/28, 7:326; Meiō 8 (1499)/9/27, 7:417.

117. *Go-Hōkōin-ki,* Meiō 4 (1495)/10/20, 7:220.

118. Ibid.; also *Go-Hōkōin-ki* for 10/22, 7:220; *Daijōin jisha zōjiki,* Meiō 4/10/24, 35:740. Word of this uprising came as early as 10/4; see *SKR* 5:261–62 (nos. 3, 4).

119. *KR* 3:244–46.

120. Ibid. 3:245–46.

121. *CHSS/MBH,* 78–81 (no. 212–31); also *KR* 3:244–50, 298–304, 309–12, 486–88.

122. *CHSS/MBH,* 84 (no. 238), 87 (no. 249), 89 (no. 258), 97 (no. 283).

123. *KR* 3:246–47.

124. *CHSS/MBH,* 109 (no. 333), 129 (no. 409), 138 (no. 478); also *KR* 3:486–88, 246–47.

125. *KR* 3:247.

126. See Kamiki, "Chūsei kōki ni okeru bukka hendō," for a discussion of rice prices. I am grateful to Mark Metzler for this information. See Yamamura, ed., *Cambridge History of Japan: Volume 3, Medieval Japan,* 37–38, for a chronology of famine.

127. *Tōji hyakugō monjo,* Eishō 13 (1516)/6/26, in *SKR* 4:289 (no. 34), for the first quotation concerning the water dispute; and ibid., Eishō 13 (1516)/9/21, in *SKR* 4:289 (no. 35), for the second quotation.

128. My thinking concerning *jiriki kyūsai* has been deeply influenced by the works of Fujiki Hisashi, particularly *Toyotomi heiwa-rei to sengoku shakai* and *Sengoku no sahō.*

129. *Sanetaka kō-ki,* Eishō 3 (1506)/7/16, 4:576; Takahashi, *Kyōto chūsei toshi-shi kenkyū,* 395–96.

130. *Chikatoshi nikki,* Tenbun 8 (1539)/8/3, 13:261–62.

131. *Sanetaka kō-ki,* Tenbun 2 (1533)/2/14–15 8:394–95.

132. *Tokitsugu kyō-ki,* Tenbun 2 (1533)/2/18, 1:225.

133. *Tokitsugu kyō-ki,* Tenbun 18 (1549)/9/7, 2:258; *KR* 3:587.

134. *Tokitsugu kyō-ki,* Tenbun 19 (1550)/ intercalary 5/2, 2:338.

135. *Tokitsugu kyō-ki,* Tenbun 20 (1551)/1/24, 2:414.

136. *Tokitsugu kyō-ki,* Tenbun 23 (1554)/5/21, 3:137; also see *Ninagawa-*

ke-ki, Tenbun 23/5/29, in *SKR* 3:340 (no. 23); and, for a discussion, Imatani, *Tokitsugu kyō-ki*, 151–66.

137. Imatani, *Tokitsugu kyō-ki*, 123.

138. *KR* 3:587.

139. For another case, see Imatani, *Sengoku Miyoshi ichizoku*, 34–35, concerning Miyoshi Narinaga's protection from punishment after leading the 1485 *ikki*.

140. There is a certain disposition among scholars, which I do not fully share, to regard the ascendancy of self-redress and local justice as an enlightened alternative to a state Leviathan. See, for example, Sakai, Review.

141. *Tokitsugu kyō-ki*, Tenbun 18 (1549)/11/17–20, 2:279–80; also see note 55 above.

142. For a discussion of justice in the village and the search there for supra-judicial methods to halt reprisals (particularly through the use of scapegoats and hostages), see Fujiki, *Sengoku no sahō*, 129–64.

143. *Go-Hōkōin-ki*, Meiō 3 (1494)/8/4, 9, 17, 19, 7:161–64.

144. Ibid., Meiō 3 (1494)/7/6, 3:157; *Tokikuni kyō-ki*, Meiō 3/7/6, in *SKR* 4:265 (no. 3). Sixty-eight *chō*, rather than fifty-four, may have burned.

145. *KR* 10:220.

146. *Nobutane kyō-ki*, Bunki 2 (1502)/4/6, 45:21.

147. *Go-Hōkōin-ki*, Bunki 3 (1503)/9/9, 8:178; *Tokitsugu kyō-ki*, Tenbun 3 (1534)/1/28, 1:304.

148. *Nisui-ki*, Daiei 7(1527)/5/6, in *SKR* 5:270 (no. 41).

149. *Tokitsugu kyō-ki*, Daiei 7 (1527)/5/29, 1:41–42.

150. *Nobutane kyō-ki*, Bunki 2 (1502)/4/6, 45:21.

151. *Tokitsugu kyō-ki*, Daiei 7 (1527)/12/13, 1:90; *Go-Hōkōin-ki*, Meiō 4 (1495)/10/30, 7:221; Takahashi, *Kyōto chūsei toshi-shi kenkyū*, 453–60.

152. *SKR* 5:269 (no. 37) also concerns private settlement.

153. *Go-Hōkōin-ki*, Bunki 3 (1503)/10/18, 20, 8:182.

Chapter 3. Word Wars: The Refuge of the Past

1. *Nobutane kyō-ki*, Bunki 2 (1502)/4/6, 45:21.

2. *Sanetaka kō-ki*, Eishō 4 (1507)/4/23, 4:720–21; *Kazunaga kyō-ki*, Eishō 6 (1509)/10/26, in *SKR* 5:270 (no. 40); *Chikanaga kyō-ki*, Bunmei 16 (1484)/6/2, 40:218–19.

3. *Sōchō shūki*, Daiei 6 (1526)/3/28, p. 88.

4. *Tokitsugu kyō-ki*, Daiei 7 (1527)/8/15, 28, 1:61, 63. The entries describe the exchange between several nobles of a text called *Kingen wakashū*, a collection of poems by an anonymous but educated poet, presumably a noble himself. See Hanawa, ed. *Zoku gunsho ruijū*, ser. 33, pt. 2, vol. 983, pp. 40–59.

5. *Morimitsu kō-ki*, Eishō 12 (1515)/5/11, in *SKR* 3:317 (no. 26).

6. *Watarase Nobushige nikki*, Eishō 6 (1509)/10, in *SKR* 3:326 (no. 51).

7. See, for example, *Oyudono no ue no nikki*, Tenbun 7 (1538)/3/3, in *SKR* 3:340 (no. 21).

8. *Kyōkō hōin nikki*, Tenbun 1 (1532)/11/24, in *SKR* 3:328–29 (no. 57). The quotation is part of a document sent by Ibaragi Nagataka to a district official in the five southern districts of Yamashiro. The order responded to nobles' complaints about the withholding of land taxes.

9. *MBMS/BHH* 2:366–67 (no. 3418).

10. *SKR* 4:287 (no. 29).

11. *Chikatoshi nikki*, Tenbun 11 (1542)/7/14, 14:73.

12. *MBMS/BHH* 2:99 (no. 2529).

13. *Ukagai-goto kiroku*, Tenbun 9 (1540)/12/6, in *SKR* 3:358 (no. 44).

14. *Morimitsu kō-ki*, Eishō 14 (1517)/8/30, in *SKR* 3:349–50 (no. 17).

15. *Tokitsugu kyō-ki*, Tenbun 14 (1544)/3/2, 2:41–43.

16. *SKR* 4:321 (no. 8).

17. The language of invective included the terms *sendai mimon no gi, midari ni, jiyū ni, hoshii mama ni*. The past was invoked with phrases such as *senki no gotoku, arikitaru no gotoku, kono izen no gotoku, sakizaki yori ima motte*.

18. Written on the back of a page of *Watarase Nobushige nikki* for Meiō 2 (1493)/11/29; see *SKR* 3:324 (no. 46).

19. Imatani, *Sengoku-ki no Muromachi bakufu*, 155–59.

20. *Nisui-ki*, Eishō 18 (1521)/3/8, in *SKR* 3:318 (no. 28).

21. Imatani, *Sengoku-ki no Muromachi bakufu*, 152–53; *MBMS/BHH* 1:3–6. The continuing activities of the *magistrates* are best understood through a survey of the documents of the *bugyō* in *MBMS/BHH*, primarily in volume 2, which covers the record from 1502 through 1568; also see the *ikenjō* of the board in *CHSS/MBH*, 275–86. For a discussion, see Kuwayama, with Hall, "Bugyōnin System."

22. For a particularly good illustration of the fastidious deliberations of the magistrates, see *CHSS/MBH*, 281 (no. 323).

23. Imatani, *Sengoku-ki no Muromachi bakufu*, 159–66.

24. References to *hibun kayaku* are most plentiful in decrees of specific exemption from them. See Takahashi, *Kyōto chūsei toshi-shi kenkyū*, 354–56, for a list of tax exemptions granted to various neighborhoods. Also see *MBMS/BHH* 2:180–81 (nos. 3131–33), 377 (no. 3454), 420 (no. 3594), 433 (no. 3636). In these decrees of tax exemption (to both proprietary and commoner addressees), *hibun kayaku* emerges as a kind of shorthand for all manner of emergency tax levies.

25. *Nanzenji monjo*, Tenbun 4 (1535)/10/26, 2:73–74.

26. *Tokitsugu kyō-ki*, Tenbun 3 (1534)/4/29, 1:334–35.

27. *Naginata boko-chō monjo*, Tenbun 18 (1549), in Takahashi, *Kyōto chūsei toshi-shi kenkyū*, 354.

28. *Kanrei narabi ni mandokoro kabegaki*, Meiō 9 (1500)/9, in *SKR* 3:352 (no. 25).

29. *Tanaka Mitsuharu-shi shozō monjo*, Tenbun 13 (1544)/12/18, in *SKR* 3:358 (no. 45).

30. *MBMS/BHH* 2:210 (no. 2907).

31. For an excellent analysis of Hosokawa relations with vassals and the con-

cessions granted to them, see Morita, "Hosokawa Takakuni to Kinai kokujin-zō" and "Sengoku-ki Kinai ni okeru shugo-dai."

32. See Imatani, *Sengoku-ki no Muromachi bakufu,* esp. 180–82, 191–92, concerning shogunal moderation (even conservatism) after 1536 and the "reverse course" steered by Ibaragi Nagataka away from martial absolutism and back toward a shogunal rule in concert with the proprietary system.

33. See, for example, Sasaki, "Rakuichi rakuza-rei to za no hoshō ando," for a discussion of the provincial regulation of commerce. While Sasaki finds the policies of provincial daimyo more conservative than radical, he nonetheless illuminates patterns of change and liberalization that would not affect Kyoto until the 1570s.

34. Morita Kyōji represents Masamoto as a basic defender of the medieval polity, who was supported both by *shugo* and civil proprietors; see "Hosokawa Takakuni to Kinai kokujin-zō," 272, and "Sengoku-ki Kinai ni okeru shugo-dai," 280–85.

35. For an extended analysis of one *shugo* house and its use of public authority to build a private domain, see Arneson, *Medieval Japanese Daimyo.*

36. Even though Imatani Akira declares that the middle ages died in Kyoto in 1549, when Miyoshi Chōkei defeated shogunal forces and brought to Kyoto a vision of daimyo power, a sort of shogunal restoration occurred after 1558 and basic transformations of the polity were suspended. See *Tokitsugu kyō-ki,* 158–66; also see Chapter 6.

37. See note 31 of this chapter.

38. Imatani, *Sengoku-ki no Muromachi bakufu,* 166–81, 191–207.

39. The outstanding example is Ibaragi Nagataka; see Imatani, *Sengoku-ki no Muromachi bakufu,* 182–93. Although a deputy of Hosokawa Harumoto, Ibaragi was also an official within the *shōen* order.

40. All population figures for this period are extremely speculative and, I suspect, much inflated. For widely cited figures, see the approximations of Harada Tomohiko in *Chūsei ni okeru toshi no kenkyū,* 142.

41. *Sanetaka kō-ki,* Eishō 4 (1507)/9/3, 4:759.

42. *Oyudono no ue no nikki,* Tenbun 7 (1538)/3/3, in *SKR* 3:340 (no. 21).

43. *Nisui-ki,* Eishō 16 (1519)/10/10, in *SKR* 5:254 (no. 30).

44. For one treatment of the cautious behavior of the unifiers, see Berry, "Restoring the Past."

45. *Haretomi Sukune-ki,* Meiō 5 (1496)/7/13, in *SKR* 5:249 (no. 1).

46. *Tokitsugu kyō-ki,* Tenbun 2 (1533)/9/10, 12, 13, 15, 1:251–53.

47. *Sōchō shūki,* Daiei 6 (1526)/8/15, p. 92.

48. *Tokitsugu kyō-ki,* Kyōroku 2 (1529)/3/3, 1:145.

49. *Tokitsugu kyō-ki,* Eiroku 3 (1560)/1/18, 3:284–85, for the New Year's worries; Takahashi, *Kyōto chūsei toshi-shi kenkyū,* 412, for the leaking roofs; Imatani, *Tokitsugu kyō-ki,* 96–101, for Tokitsugu's gifts during a visit to the shogun at Karashigawa.

50. *SKR* 5:252 (no. 20) for the ground-breaking; *SKR* 3:366 (nos. 22, 24) for the Gion festival.

51. *SKR* 4:318 (no. 21).

Chapter 4. Popular Insurrection

1. *Sōchō shuki,* Daiei 7 (1527), p. 117.

2. Imatani, *Sengoku Miyoshi ichizoku,* 61–62.

3. Ibid., 62–63; *KR* 3:486–93, 544; Imatani, *Tokitsugu kyō-ki,* 67–69; Kobayashi, "Sengoku sōran no tenkai," 22. Also see the chronology for 1527 in *KR* 10:232–33; and *SKR* 5:263 (nos. 13, 14) for the *tokusei* report and other descriptions of events in Kyoto.

4. *KR* 3:488; Imatani, *Sengoku Miyoshi ichizoku,* 65.

5. See Morita, "Hosokawa Takakuni to Kinai kokujin-zō," 240–75; *KR* 3:488–89.

6. *Tokitsugu kyō-ki,* Daiei 7 (1527)/2/13, 1:13. Also see Imatani, *Tokitsugu kyō-ki,* 69–70; and Takahashi, *Kyōto chūsei toshi-shi kenkyū,* 397.

7. *Tokitsugu kyō-ki,* Daiei 7 (1527)/2/14, 1:14. Also see Imatani, *Tokitsugu kyō-ki,* 70–71, and *Sengoku Miyoshi ichizoku,* 61.

8. Imatani, *Sengoku Miyoshi ichizoku,* 70–76, *Tokitsugu kyō-ki,* 71–79, and *Sengoku-ki no Muromachi bakufu,* 166–74. The Ōmi documents appear in *MBMS/BHH* 2:279–86 (nos. 3130–51). Imatani emphasizes throughout his analysis the ascendancy of the Sakai administration and the essentially symbolic role of the Ōmi administration. Takahashi Yasuo is more guarded about the relative strength of the two administrations and tends to emphasize the uncertain military situation; see, for example, *Kyōto chūsei toshi-shi kenkyū,* 399.

9. Imatani, *Tokitsugu kyō-ki,* 79–81, and *Sengoku Miyoshi ichizoku,* 76–77.

10. Imatani, *Sengoku Miyoshi ichizoku,* 77–81. Imatani discounts the military oscillations in power to insist on the ascendancy of the Sakai administration virtually from the time of its inception; see, for example, *Sengoku-ki no Muromachi bakufu,* 178–79. Also see his discussion of the dating of the Sakai and Ōmi documents and its revelations about the existence and structure of the Sakai administration as well as the throne's apparent recognition of the Ōmi administration as legitimate; *Tokitsugu kyō-ki,* 71–77.

11. *KR* 3:489–90; Imatani, *Tokitsugu kyō-ki,* 80–84; *Tokitsugu kyō-ki,* Tenbun 1 (1532)/6/22, 1:191–92.

12. Imatani, *Tokitsugu kyō-ki,* 79–80, *Sengoku-ki no Muromachi bakufu,* 179–82, and *Sengoku Miyoshi ichizoku,* 66–68 (for speculation on the selection of Sakai as headquarters). Imatani posits a split between Motonaga and Ibaragi Nagataka (as he later posits a split between Miyoshi Chōkei and Ibaragi Nagataka) that emerged because Motonaga seemed committed to daimyo power and a new order on the one hand, while Ibaragi remained committed to proprietary authority and the medieval order on the other hand.

13. Kobayashi, "Sengoku sōran no tenkai," 18–20. Also see Morita Kyōji's response to Kobayashi in "Hosokawa Takakuni to Kinai kokujin-zō," 240–43.

14. See, for example, Imatani, *Sengoku Miyoshi ichizoku,* 76–83. The principal Kyoto battles after the Katsura engagement occurred in Daiei 7 (1527)/11, when Asakura and Miyoshi troops met at Saiin; Daiei 8 (1528)/1, when Miyoshi and Yanagimoto troops met at Muromachi-Tachiuri; Kyōroku 2

(1530)/12, when Rokkaku and Yanagimoto troops met at Hōshōji; Kyōroku 4 (1531)/2, when the same forces met in the area of the palace; and Kyōroku 5 (1532)/1, when Miyoshi Motonaga attacked Yanagimoto Kataharu's son at Sanjō.

15. Imatani, *Sengoku Miyoshi ichizoku*, 70; *Oyudono no ue no nikki*, Daiei 7 (1527)/8/16, 3:255.

16. *Sanetaka kō-ki*, Daiei 7 (1527)/2/15, 7:20. Also see notes 148 and 149 of Chapter 2; and the chronology for 1527 to 1532 in *KR* 10:232–35.

17. *Tokitsugu kyō-ki*, Tenbun 1 (1532)/6/7, 1:199; *KR* 3:601.

18. *Tokitsugu kyō-ki*, Daiei 7 (1527)/8/2, 1:57–58; also see *KR* 3:586–87.

19. *Tokitsugu kyō-ki*, Daiei 7 (1527)/11/29, 1:88.

20. The sequence and the documentation of neighborhood purge is discussed in Takahashi, *Kyōto chūsei toshi-shi kenkyū*, 397–404. For many of the important documents, see *SKR* 4:281–82 (nos. 3–7); *SKR* 5:264 (nos. 16, 17).

21. *Tokitsugu kyō-ki*, Kyōroku 2 (1529)/1/10–11, 1:128–29; also see Takahashi Yasuo's discussion in *Kyōto chūsei toshi-shi kenkyū*, 451–52.

22. See, for example, *Sanetaka kō-ki*, Kyōroku 2 (1529)/7/11, 8:5–6 (for lumber taxes), Kyōroku 2/7/13–14, 8:6–7 (for a form of commissariat tax); *SKR* 3:339 (no. 19; for court orders to desist from levying roof taxes in Yamashina, quoted from *Oyudono no ue no nikki*, Kyōroku 2/8/8); *MBMS/BHH* 2:284 (no. 3142; for a shogunal exemption to Tōji from the half-tax). On Kyōroku 3 (1530)/4/11, one of Harumoto's generals tried to impose roof taxes throughout Yamashiro.

23. *Sanetaka kō-ki*, Kyōroku 3 (1530)/3/29, 8:122.

24. Ibid., Daiei 8 (1528)/2/17–20, 7:198.

25. *SKR* 3:319 (no. 31).

26. See the sources cited in note 8 of this chapter, especially Imatani, *Tokitsugu kyō-ki*, 72–75, and *MBMS/BHH* 2:279–86. The documents include, for example, land confirmations, tax exemptions, and decrees concerning commercial privileges that responded to conventional suits and petitions. Documents to Tōji were issued by both the Sakai and the Ōmi administrations, suggesting that some litigants sought to protect themselves by appealing to both shogunates for justice during the years of dual military administration.

27. Takahashi Yasuo (*Kyōto chūsei toshi-shi kenkyū*, 397–404) makes a cogent and often-passionate argument concerning the illegitimacy of the Sakai deputies in the eyes of many Kyoto residents.

28. See note 24 above; also see Chapter 1 for a discussion of the Yamashiro uprising.

29. *Gion shugyō nikki*, Kyōroku 5 (1532)/7/28, Tenbun 1 (1532)/8/7, and Tenbun 1 (1532)/8/10–12, in *SKR* 5:264–65 (nos. 18, 19, 21).

30. The term *muhon* appears, for example, in document no. 18, cited immediately above. For a further reference to *uchimawari*, see *Gion shugyō nikki*, Tenbun 1 (1532)/9/26, in *SKR* 4:282–83 (no. 10).

31. *Nisui-ki*, Tenbun 1 (1532)/8/7, in *SKR* 5:264–65 (no. 20).

32. *KR* 3:547–49; Imatani, *Tokitsugu kyō-ki*, 82–84. Tokitsugu reports 3,000 dead after the battle of Tenbun 1 (1532)/6/17, and he estimates the combined Ikkō strength at 210,000 for the battle of Tenbun 1/6/20 (in his

entry for 6/22); see *Tokitsugu kyō-ki* 1:190–92. For a detailed account of these battles, and the ensuing Hokke uprising, see Imatani, *Tenbun Hokke no ran.*

33. *Tokitsugu kyō-ki,* Tenbun 1 (1532)/6/22, 1:192.

34. For a discussion of Shinran and Jōdo Shinshū, see, for example, Asao, "'Shōgun kenryoku' no sōshutsu"; Dobbins, *Jōdo Shinshū;* and Weinstein, "Rennyo and the Shinshū Revival."

35. For an extensive treatment of the Ikkō organization, see Minegishi, ed., *Honganji, Ikkō ikki no kenkyū,* esp. 35–52, 53–64, and (for the Kaga events) 66–245.

36. Imatani, *Sengoku Miyoshi ichizoku,* 89.

37. Ibid., 90.

38. Imatani, *Tokitsugu kyō-ki,* 84–86.

39. Ibid., 86–89; *KR* 3:549–50.

40. *Nisui-ki,* Tenbun 1 (1532)/8/16, in *SKR* 5:265 (no. 22).

41. *Gion shugyō nikki,* Tenbun 1 (1532)/8/17, in *SKR* 5:265 (no. 23).

42. *Tokitsugu kyō-ki,* Tenbun 1 (1532)/8/19, 1:199.

43. *Kyōkō hōin nikki,* Tenbun 1 (1532)/8/23–24, in *SKR* 5:266 (no. 26).

44. *Nisui-ki,* Tenbun 1(1532)/8/25–26, in *SKR* 5:266 (no. 27).

45. Imatani, *Tokitsugu kyō-ki,* 87; *KR* 3:555.

46. *KR* 3:540–41; Akiyama and Nakamura, *Kyōto "chō" no kenkyū,* 284–85.

47. *Tokitsugu kyō-ki,* Tenbun 2 (1533)/3/7, 1:229–30. Also see *KR* 3:554–55; and Imatani, *Tokitsugu kyō-ki,* 90.

48. For survey discussions of Hokke faith, see, for example, Nakao, *Nichiren-shū no seiritsu to tenkai;* Tamura and Miyazaki, eds., *Nichiren shinkō no rekishi;* and *KR* 3:134–45, 545–47. Also see Rodd, trans., *Nichiren;* and Yampolsky, ed., *Selected Writings of Nichiren.*

49. *KR* 3:142, 545.

50. Ibid. 4:153. The Gotō code dates from 1560.

51. Ibid., 151–56. Information about particular commoners and their linkages to the Hokke faith tends to be limited and rather late in date.

52. *KR* 3:144–45.

53. *KR* 3:144, 543; *KR* 4:156–57.

54. *Sanetaka kō-ki,* Meiō 5 (1496)/8/6, 3:265.

55. *Daijōin jisha zōjiki,* Bunki 1 (1501)/4/26, 36:434.

56. *Sanetaka kō-ki,* Bunki 3 (1503)/3/5, 4:105.

57. *KR* 3:142–44; Aiba, "Junkyō no hitobito."

58. *KR* 3:142.

59. *KR* 3:543–45. See *KR* 4:148–50 for missionaries' accounts of the rebuilt Honkokuji.

60. See notes 31, 75, and 81 of this chapter.

61. The aspects of class conflict between peasants and urban merchants are emphasized by Imatani Akira in *Sengoku-ki no Muromachi bakufu,* 187–89, and *Tokitsugu kyō-ki,* 88.

62. *Tokitsugu kyō-ki,* Tenbun 2 (1533)/2/12, 1:223, concerning the assumption that Harumoto had died, and Tenbun 2/3/7, 1:229–30, concerning the size of the Hokke force.

63. For general narratives of the events after the fall of Yamashina Honganji, see *KR* 3:550–53, and Imatani, *Tokitsugu kyō-ki*, 88–90.

64. *Gion shugyō nikki*, quoted in *KR* 3:553.

65. *KR* 3:551–53.

66. Ibid. 3:551, for the battle against debtors; *Nisui-ki*, Tenbun 1 (1532)/ 12/10, in *SKR* 5:266–67 (no. 28), for an account of the debtors' uprising and the Hokke response; *SKR* 3:328–29 (no. 57), for three documents concerning claims to tax cancellations; *KR* 3:553–54, for league action in 1533. Also see Imatani, *Tokitsugu kyō-ki*, 87–88, concerning the claims to tax cancellations.

67. *Honmanji monjo*, Tenbun 2 (1533)/7/23, in *SKR* 3:362 (no. 5).

68. *MBMS/BHH* 2:316 (no. 3253).

69. *Tokitsugu kyō-ki*, Tenbun 2 (1533)/12/8, 1:277, concerning the disorder; *Oyudono no ue no nikki*, Tenbun 2/12/8, in *SKR* 5:267 (no. 30), concerning the quiet.

70. *Tokitsugu kyō-ki*, Tenbun 2 (1533)/12/25, 1:285. For another example of Hokke brutality, see Imatani, *Sengoku-ki no Muromachi bakufu*, 188.

71. *KR* 3:553–54. For a map of the campaigns of these years, see *KR* 3:557.

72. *Honmanji monjo*, Tenbun 2 (1533)/6/28, quoted in *KR* 3:553.

73. Imatani, *Tokitsugu kyō-ki*, 90–93. Imatani cites five critical documents that illustrate the military and police role of the Hokke forces—a role that, even if played under some general bakufu supervision, gave the sectarians primary police responsibility in the capital in practical terms.

74. *Sanetaka kō-ki*, Tenbun 2 (1533)/2/14, 8:394.

75. *Tokitsugu kyō-ki*, Tenbun 2 (1533)/2/18, 1:225.

76. *MBMS/BHH* 2:315 (no. 3249); see also Imatani, *Tokitsugu kyō-ki*, 91 (document D).

77. *MBMS/BHH* 2:329 (no. 3298).

78. *Tokitsugu kyō-ki*, Tenbun 3 (1534)/3/16, 1:320.

79. *SKR* 4:284 (no. 19).

80. *MBMS/BHH* 2:335 (no. 3318) and 2:334 (no. 3316).

81. *SKR* 4:284–85 (no. 20).

82. *SKR* 4:286 (no. 26).

83. Imatani, *Tokitsugu kyō-ki*, 92.

84. Ibid., 96–101.

85. See, for example, *SKR* 4:286 (no. 24) and 4:288 (no. 30).

86. *KR* 3:559–63, begins with an analysis of the religious issues motivating the Hokke uprising and then goes on to consider the importance of self-government to the townspeople and the implicit challenge to elite interests. Imatani Akira (*Sengoku-ki no Muromachi bakufu*, 187–89) emphasizes, rather, the antipeasant aspects of the uprising.

87. Imatani, *Tokitsugu kyō-ki*, 87–88.

88. *SKR* 3:328–29 (no. 57).

89. See note 73 of this chapter. Imatani does not make the analogy with the *samurai-dokoro* himself, but I find the inference unmistakable.

90. Imatani, *Tokitsugu kyō-ki*, 93–96.

91. Ibid.
92. *Rokuon'in nichiroku*, Tenbun 5 (1536)/5/29, in *SKR* 4:285 (no. 21).
93. *SKR* 5:267 (no. 32).
94. *SKR* 5:252 (no. 19).
95. *SKR* 5:267 (no. 32).
96. *SKR* 5:278 (no. 16).
97. *SKR* 5:267 (no. 32).
98. *SKR* 4:269 (no. 23).
99. *KR* 3:560–62.
100. *KR* 3:558.
101. *KR* 3:562–63. Imatani (*Tokitsugu kyō-ki*, 86–91) sees Ibaragi Naga-taka as the real power behind these reprisals.
102. *SKR* 4:269 (no. 24).
103. For additional references to the intensity of the attack, see *SKR* 4:269 (no. 25).
104. *Honnōji monjo*, Tenbun 5 (1536)/intercalary 10/7, in *SKR* 3:363.

Chapter 5. Work: The Structures of Daily Life

1. *Rokuon'in monjo*, in *SKR* 4:286 (no. 26).
2. *Honnōji monjo*, Tenbun 5 (1536)/intercalary 10/7, in *SKR* 3:363.
3. The most intriguing early texts on *shokunin* are *shokunin uta awase*, or imaginary poetic competitions between different people of skill. These scrolls depict selected workers in characteristic clothing and include poems (*waka*) fashioned for them by anonymous poets. There are four principal examples of the genre, each in several versions, all anonymous: *Tōhokuin shokunin uta awase* (early thirteenth century); *Tsurugaoka Hōjō-e shokunin uta awase* (late four-teenth century); *Sanjū ni-ban shokunin uta awase* (fifteenth century); *Nanajū ichi-ban shokunin uta awase* (late fifteenth century). Some versions of the last work, depicting 142 people of skill, are attributed to Tosa Mitsunobu, and some have calligraphy attributed to Kanrōji Chikanaga. See *KR* 3:524; Amino, *Nihon chūsei no minshō-zō*, 103–65; also see, for reproductions of the scrolls, Mori, ed., *Nihon emakimono zenshū*, vol. 28.
4. The earliest extant list of local manufactures and products is *Teikin ōrai* (probably produced sometime between 1394 and 1428), which notes 22 spe-cialties for Kyoto and its environs. *Kefukigusa* (preface written in 1638, work published in 1645; 1943 version edited by Takenaka Wakae) lists more than 1,800 products of the country, 39 percent of them issuing from the home prov-inces; *KR* 3:418–19.
5. These screens are discussed in the Afterword. For the illustrations, see Ishida et al., eds., *Rakuchū rakugai-zu taikan*, which includes complete repro-ductions of the Machida, Uesugi, and Funaki screens.
6. See note 3 above.

7. For these designations, see *SKR* 4:321 (no. 28), 3:353 (no. 27), and 4:325 (no. 38).

8. For a discussion of medieval and wartime commerce, see, for example, Wakita, *Nihon chūsei shōgyō hattatsu-shi no kenkyū*, "Towards a Wider Perspective on Medieval Commerce," and "Muromachi-ki no keizai hatten"; Sasaki, *Chūsei shōhin ryūtsū-shi no kenkyū; KR* 3:186–268, 503–39; Yamamura, "Growth of Commerce in Medieval Japan"; Miura, "Sengoku-ki no kōeki to kōtsū." The often-impressive scholarship on the medieval economy remains much constrained by limited and uneven information and therefore tends to combine a high level of generalization and speculation with close treatments of certain cases (where detailed evidence does exist) that are taken to be emblematic. We have no extended study of the wartime economy specifically, nor do we have a clear picture of Kyoto's commerce (Wakita's resourceful and thoughtful efforts notwithstanding). Economic historians have identified certain trends in commercial development, however, that seem unobjectionable when interpreted liberally: for example, the authority of noble and religious patrons was weakening; guild organization was giving way to transport and wholesale monopolies; the market economy was penetrating the countryside.

9. For references to various licenses, see, for example, *SKR* 3:358 (nos. 45, 46), 4:318 (nos. 19, 21). For the language of invective, see, for example, *SKR* 4:321 (no. 28), 4:323 (no. 35), 4:312–13 (no. 8), 4:321–22 (no. 29), and 4:322 (no. 30). References to the Way and peaceful good relations appear in *SKR* 4:315–17 (no. 15, closing paragraph).

10. Ibid. 4:321–22 (no. 29); also see 4:322 (no. 30).

11. Ibid. 4:325 (no. 38).

12. *Chikatoshi nikki*, Tenbun 8 (1539)/12/30, 13:335–36.

13. Kyoto's farmers have not, to my knowledge, been the subject of scholarly analysis, although the proprietors and wealthy peasants of the area have received fair attention; see, for example, Tabata, "Chūsei kōki Kinai dogō no sonzai keitai"; Imatani, *Sengoku-ki no Muromachi bakufu*, 102–9, concerning the Tōji and Tōfukuji properties. One subject of increasing interest and attention in medieval scholarship has been peoples marginal to the dominant social structures; see, for example, Wakita, "Chūsei hisabetsu-min no seikatsu to shakai"; and Koyama, "Chūsei senmin-ron."

14. This motley and idiosyncratic list is based on documents that identify import organizations, records from one of Kyoto's barriers, obvious deductions about the products required by Kyoto's leading craftspeople, and lists of medieval guilds. Other than *Kefukigusa*, I know of no efforts by wartime chroniclers or modern scholars to compile a list of goods imported into, and produced in, the capital. See *KR* 3:190–91 for the barrier information and 3:200–202, 221–24, 522–23 for information concerning provincial manufactures; Toyoda, *Nihon hōken toshi*, 51, and Takayanagi and Takeuchi, *Kadokawa Nihon-shi jiten*, 1034, for tallies of medieval guilds in Kyoto; *Gen'i Hōin gejijō* for indications of the guilds operative during Toyotomi Hideyoshi's tenure in the city; and the documents cited throughout this chapter for the identification of import organizations and craft guilds in Kyoto.

15. *KR* 3:208–10.

16. *KR* 3:205–8, 213–15, 220–21; Wakita, "Nihon chūsei toshi to ryōshu kenryoku," 353–59. My summary of commercial organization, here and elsewhere, is general and synoptic and tends to introduce too much clarity and simplicity where confusion and complexity would better reflect the record.

17. See, for example, *KR* 3:210–18; Wakita, *Nihon chūsei shōgyō hattatsu-shi no kenkyū*, 235–74; and Yamamura, "Development of *Za*." For the Awazu guild, see *KR* 3:205, 210; and the sources cited in note 50 of this chapter.

18. *SKR* 4:321 (no. 28).

19. *KR* 3:224–30, 511–14; Wakita, *Nihon chūsei shōgyō hattatsu-shi no kenkyū*, 275–356 and 395–404; also see Toyoda, *Chūsei Nihon shōgyō-shi no kenkyū*, 194–263. *KR* 5:105–44 discusses *ton'ya* growth in the Edo period.

20. *KR* 3:200, 201, 203–4, 205, 212–13, 226–28, 518–19. The wholesale rice sellers numbered 120 in 1438. The exact number in wartime is unclear.

21. For references to direct sales, see *SKR* 3:345 (no. 6) and 3:357 (no. 41). For the relations between suppliers and *ton'ya*, see Wakita, *Nihon chūsei shōgyō hattatsu-shi no kenkyū*, 395–404.

22. For illicit sales of rice, see *SKR* 3:345 (no. 6); of salt, *SKR* 3:352 (no. 24); of fruit, *SKR* 4:321 (no. 28); of blue ash, *SKR* 3:346 (no. 9); of bamboo, *SKR* 4:326 (no. 41).

23. See, for example, *KR* 3:204–5, 226–28, 508–9. The organization of 1543 is discussed on 3:514–15.

24. *SKR* 4:321 (no. 28).

25. *SKR* 3:345 (no. 6).

26. I know of no reference to scarcities of goods in Kyoto after the Ōnin war. The general story of wartime commerce seems to be one of steady provincial development and competition to reach, and profit from, both rural and urban markets. Such development and competition is not necessarily concomitant, of course, with significantly expanded urban demand. Embargoes on exports from the capital did not, apparently, occur in wartime. One document (*SKR* 3:344 [no. 3]) does forbid salt exports for a time, but this order was probably intended to control trade rather than to injure provincial consumers.

27. Wakita, *Nihon chūsei shōgyō hattatsu-shi no kenkyū*, 395–96; *KR* 3:507–8. The figures come from the Nagasaka-guchi and cover a period of 140 years.

28. *KR* 3:509–11; Wakita, *Nihon chūsei shōgyō hattatsu-shi no kenkyū*, 396–98. In 1477 the treasurer granted 539 toll exemptions to peasants, half of them for the transport of goods into Kyoto.

29. *KR* 3:218–20, 510–11; *SKR* 4:326 (no. 41).

30. *KR* 3:511 for the indigo trouble; *SKR* 4:319 (no. 24) for salt markets outside Kyoto; and the sources cited in note 61 of this chapter for the expansion of periodic markets.

31. *KR* 3:504–5; Wakita, *Nihon chūsei shōgyō hattatsu-shi no kenkyū*, 371–83.

32. *KR* 3:193–94, 508; Wakita, *Nihon chūsei shōgyō hattatsu-shi no kenkyū*, 380–83.

33. Sasaki with Hauser, "Sengoku Daimyo Rule and Commerce"; Kishida, "Chūsei kōki no chihō keizai to toshi," 83–124.

34. *KR* 3:224–25; Wakita, *Nihon chūsei shōgyō hattatsu-shi no kenkyū*, 371–72.

35. *KR* 3:519–20.

36. *KR* 3:414–16; Takahashi, *Kyōto chūsei toshi-shi kenkyū*, 433–35.

37. *KR* 3:529–30; *SKR* 4:323 (no. 34) and 4:318 (no. 21).

38. Wakita, *Nihon chūsei shōgyō hattatsu-shi no kenkyū*, 297–303. The bakufu protected the *sakaya-dosō*, the weavers of glossed silk, the madder importers, and, perhaps, the makers of long swords and fans.

39. Many *sake* producers combined the making of malt, the brewing of the *sake*, and sales of the product. The Iwashimizu oil makers combined all phases of production from purchase of the sesame seeds to retail sales of the oil. Cloth production, however, was divided into successive stages, from silkworm cultivation to sales, which were largely separated among different concerns. The making of blades was separated from the making of hilts and fittings. Fan making seems to have been divided into paper production, painting, the production and spreading of ribs, and the folding and sales of the finished products. Production patterns clearly varied by enterprise, and a universal movement toward separating the various stages of production does not appear obvious in wartime.

40. *SKR* 3:358 (no. 44) for the foil guild; *SKR* 3:356 (no. 38) for the leather workers; Wakita, *Nihon chūsei shōgyō hattatsu-shi no kenkyū*, 297–303, and *KR* 3:196 for the fan folders, paper makers, and shogunal interests; *KR* 3:194–96 for more on fans, 3:199 and 530–31 for the iron forgers. The record is often frustratingly unclear concerning the identity of patrons, the actual work of a guild (how many stages of production were really combined?), and the duration of patronage.

41. *SKR* 4:307–11 (no. 5); *KR* 3:231–44. The only other very large organization in Kyoto known to me is wholesale rice distribution (which seemingly involved more than 100 firms). Affiliates of the Iwashimizu oil guild may have constituted the next most numerous group. The textile industry was probably very large, although its workers were divided into many separate concerns. Takahashi Yasuo identifies 31 members of the *ōtoneri* guild living in the Nishijin area (*Kyōto chūsei toshi-shi kenkyū*, 324–33) but offers no more general figures for the size of the textile enterprise.

42. For instances of conflict and competition, see, for example, *SKR* 3:358–59 (no. 47), 4:311–13 (nos. 6, 8, 9), 4:318 (no. 21), 4:323 (nos. 34, 35).

43. One of the *very* few suggestive documents concerning immigration involves the demography of the eastern side of Reizen-chō in 1593. The document indicates the duration of residence of the commoners named there. See Yoshida, "Kōgi to chōnin mibun," 102–6. In general, the picture of wartime migration and its effects on Kyoto remains in shadows.

44. *KR* 3:198–99, 225–26, 515–19, 522–23, 529; *SKR* 4:317 (no. 17) concerning long swords; *SKR* 4:317–18 (no. 18) concerning beads; *SKR* 3:357 (no. 41) concerning injunctions against direct textile sales.

45. *KR* 3:210; *SKR* 3:354 (no. 31); *SKR* 4:318 (nos. 19–20). I do not know how retail taxes were calculated or collected, or how widespread they were.

46. *SKR* 3:346-47 (no. 10, item 3).

47. *KR* 3:243-44; *SKR* 4:306 (no. 3).

48. *SKR* 3:352 (no. 24).

49. *SKR* 3:357 (no. 41).

50. *SKR* 3:349 (no. 16), 3:358 (no. 46); *SKR* 4:320 (no. 26), 4:321 (no. 27), 4:324 (no. 36). Also see Imatani, *Tokitsugu kyō-ki*, 184-87.

51. After 1493 Hosokawa Masamoto apparently gathered in Kyoto the *shugo-dai* (or deputy military governors) of the seven provinces under the influence of the Hosokawa house, constructing something of an elite military enclave around his own mansion; see Morita, "Sengoku-ki Kinai ni okeru shugo-dai," 282. This practice, which was not repeated in successive *kanrei* tenures, was the closest equivalent to the pre-Ōnin assembly of the military elite in Kyoto.

52. Teishitsu Rin'ya Kyoku, comp., *Go-ryōchi shikō*, 171-235. Also see Wakita, *Nihon chūsei shōgyō hattatsu-shi no kenkyū*, 358-69, for a discussion of the income of the Yamashina house.

53. For distress among nobles, see, for example, *SKR* 5:252-58 (nos. 21-49). For the selling of temple buildings, see *Nanzenji monjo*, Tenbun 3 (1534)/12/15, 2:71.

54. See *SKR* 3:357 (no. 42) for the emergency rice levies; *SKR* 5:254-55 (no. 31) for the problem with summer robes.

55. See *KR* 3:447-52; Morisue, "Nō to hogosha," for a discussion of Noh troupes that turned to public performances to replace the support of elite patrons—another indication of the reverberating consequences of elite penury.

56. See Wang, *Official Relations Between China and Japan*, esp. 98-99, for the information on fans and blades.

57. Watanabe, *Ōmi shōnin*, identifies shops controlled by Ōmi merchants in Kyoto by 1555 (p. 119) but generally discusses the late sixteenth-century significance of their trade.

58. See, for example, Sasaki, "Rakuichi rakuza-rei to za no hoshō ando"; Sasaki with Hauser, "Sengoku Daimyo Rule and Commerce"; and the codes of the Imagawa and Takeda houses in *CHSS/BK*, 115-226.

59. Hoff, *Genial Seed*, 107.

60. See, for example, Toyoda, *Sakai*, 12-16, 87-88; *KR* 3:503; Asukai, ed., *Ōtsu-shi shi*.

61. Wakita, "Chūsei sangyō no hatten"; Sasaki, "Rakuichi rakuza-rei to za no hoshō ando," 170.

62. *KR* 3:190, 196-97; also see Nagahara and Yamamura, "Shaping the Process of Unification," esp. 98-99.

63. For statutes concerning lending and interest rates, see *CHSS/MBH*, 73 (no. 203), 74 (no. 205), 77 (nos. 210-11), 90 (nos. 260-61). For the *erizeni-rei*, see *CHSS/MBH*, 105 (no. 320), 109 (no. 334), 110 (no. 335), 111 (no. 344), 112-13 (nos. 345-48), 117 (nos. 360-62), 120 (nos. 372-74), 123 (nos. 385-89), 141 (nos. 486-88), 141-42 (nos. 489-90).

64. *MBMS/BHH* 2:112 (no. 3576).

65. Ibid., 2:137 (no. 2662).

66. Ibid., 2:438 (no. 3654).

67. *CHSS/MBH,* 123–24 (nos. 385–89).

68. Ibid., 121 (nos. 378–79).

69. *MBMS/BHH* 2:210 (no. 2907).

70. In this and similar cases (see, for example, *SKR* 3:352 [no. 25]), the interest of the shogunate was in registering retailers and taxing them—not in closing down or otherwise inflicting punishment on illicit operations.

71. For the condemnation of the rice sellers, see *MBMS/BHH* 2:67–68 (no. 2422). For a discussion of the bakufu's profit from currency exchange and its investment in the laws, see *KR* 3:265–68; also see Yamamura, "Growth of Commerce in Medieval Japan," 386–88.

72. *SKR* 3:351 (no. 21).

73. *KR* 3:216–17, 235; Takahashi, *Kyōto chūsei toshi-shi kenkyū,* 344–48; Yoshida, "Kōgi to chōnin mibun," 99–102; Wakita, *Nihon chūsei shōgyō hattatsu-shi no kenkyū,* 297–303. *Kunin* status had a high correlation with large household frontages.

74. Takahashi, *Kyōto chūsei toshi-shi kenkyū,* 346–47.

75. Ibid., 427–33.

76. Ibid., 347.

77. *SKR* 4:286 (no. 24); Takahashi, *Kyōto chūsei toshi-shi kenkyū,* 345–48.

78. Takahashi, *Kyōto chūsei toshi-shi kenkyū,* 345–46.

79. I know of no substantial study of the problem of honor among urban commoners, although the work of Yokoi Kiyoshi often moves in this direction; see, for example, *Chūsei minshū no seikatsu bunka* and *Gekokujō no bunka* (especially the essay "Machishū no seikatsu bunka").

80. *SKR* 3:357 (no. 41).

81. *MBMS/BHH* 2:443 (no. 3671); *SKR* 3:359–60 (no. 50).

82. See, for example, *SKR* 3:346 (no. 9), 3:353 (no. 27), 3:355 (no. 34).

83. See, for example, *SKR* 4:311 (no. 5), 4:326 (no. 41).

84. Takahashi, *Kyōto chūsei toshi-shi kenkyū,* 427, 429–30.

85. See, for example, *SKR* 4:289–90 (no. 36), 4:326 (no. 41); *Tokitsugu kyō-ki,* Eiroku 8 (1565)/7/17, 3:517; Takahashi, *Kyōto chūsei toshi-shi kenkyū,* 429–30.

86. *SKR* 4:323 (no. 34).

87. *SKR* 4:315–17 (no. 15).

Chapter 6. Neighborhood:
The Reconfiguration of Attachment

1. For illustrations of early Kyoto maps, see Nakamura, ed., *Nihon kochizu taisei;* Harada and Nishikawa, eds., *Kinki no shigai kozu.*

2. For a discussion of the *ryōgawa chō,* see Akiyama, *Kinsei Kyōto machigumi hattatsu-shi,* 1–43; Akiyama and Nakamura, *Kyōto "chō" no kenkyū,* 146–60; Hayashiya, *Machishū,* 88–90.

3. See the sources mentioned in note 2 for a general discussion of the street and its changing functions. Hayashiya Tatsusaburō (*Machishū*, 90) cites a document of 1401 to date the clear emergence of the *ryōgawa chō* and the perception of the street as a binding agent, but Akiyama Kunizō and Nakamura Ken (*Kyōto "chō" no kenkyū*, 157–58) prefer a dating sometime later in the century.

4. Takahashi, *Kyōto chūsei toshi-shi kenkyū*, 348–49; see ibid., 332–33, concerning the Daitokuji area of Nishijin and the presumption that the payment of land rents constituted a guarantee of occupancy rights (which subsequently led to the naming of the *chō*).

5. *KR* 4:106–7 lists the names of *chō* that appear in documents related to Oda Nobunaga's plan for general civic support of the imperial house in 1571.

6. Takahashi Yasuo illustrates the considerable class mixture even in areas normally associated with the courtly nobility (see, for example, *Kyōto chūsei toshi-shi kenkyū*, 391–97, 411–26, 433–37). He identifies the Higashi no tōin area as a rare example of a noble enclave, and the Reizen neighborhood as an anomalous example of a pure commoner neighborhood.

7. See note 5 above. The few blocks with proprietary names appear in the northern sector of Kyoto.

8. See, for example, Takahashi, *Kyōto chūsei toshi-shi kenkyū*, 345, for a discussion of the Hino property in Nakagumi, where high rents substituted for other exactions; and Wakita, "Chūsei Kyōto no tochi shoyū," 119–80.

9. Wakita Haruko ("Chūsei Kyōto no tochi shoyū," 164–66) provides a chart of land sales between 1474 and 1484 and duly notes the participation of commoners in these transactions. Her essay as a whole, however, argues against significant land ownership among commoners: Wakita associates the Hokke uprising with resistance to proprietors and their land rents and argues that the events of 1532–36 could not have occurred in a commoner population that included a fair proportion of land owners. Also see Takahashi, *Kyōto chūsei toshi-shi kenkyū*, 348, for a discussion of the Hino vestiture, where land sales to commoners, though forbidden, did occur; and Yoshida, "Kōgi to chōnin mibun," p. 99, chart 4, for a synopsis of some cadastral information about landed proprietors in certain neighborhoods.

10. *Go-Hōkōin-ki*, Meiō 4 (1495)/10/22, 7:220.

11. *Sanetaka kō-ki*, Eishō 3 (1506)/7/16, 4:576.

12. *Tōji hyakugō monjo*, Eishō 13 (1516)/9/21, in *SKR* 4:289 (no. 35).

13. *Tokitsugu kyō-ki*, Kyōroku 2 (1529)/1/10–11, 1:128.

14. Ibid., Daiei 7 (1527)/11/29 and 7/12/1, 1:88.

15. *Gion shugyō nikki*, Tenbun 2 (1533)/6/7, in *SKR* 4:283 (no. 13).

16. For the identification of several magistrates in the Rokuchō-gumi, see Takahashi, *Kyōto chūsei toshi-shi kenkyū*, 435–36. Such information remains, however, extremely limited. Yoshida Nobuyuki's analysis of Reizen-chō and the rotation of magistrates there indicates a certain egalitarian approach to office holding; "Kōgi to chōnin mibun," pp. 104–5, point 6.

17. *KR* 3:171–76, 600–610. The Gion festival was suspended between 1467 and 1500, postponed in 1504, canceled in 1525 and 1532.

18. See, for example, *SKR* 3:366–67 (nos. 21–24) for documents concern-

ing the difficulty of resuming even a very modest version of the Gion festival by 1500. See *Gion sha-ki*, Bunki 3/6/5, in *SKR* 4:314 (no. 11) for complaints in 1503 that the *ōtoneri* weavers' guild was withholding contributions for the festival (the guild was said to be 200,000 *kanmon* in arrears!); and Imatani, *Tokitsugu kyō-ki*, 241, for the violence surrounding the festival.

19. *KR* 3:608–10; *Gion sha-ki*, Tenbun 2 (1533)/8/9, in *SKR* 3:369 (no. 33).

20. *Tokitsugu kyō-ki*, Tenbun 3 (1534)/3/1, 1:313.

21. Ibid., Tenbun 3 (1534)/4/29, 1:334–35.

22. For the background and context of the quarrel, see Takahashi, *Kyōto chūsei toshi-shi kenkyū*, 452–68.

23. Ibid., 468–72.

24. Ibid., 377–491, esp. 446–81. Takahashi Yasuo argues that the six blocks constituted Kyoto's first block federation. While he traces the gradual emergence of a neighborhood consciousness and corporate activism before 1534, he insists on the novelty, importance, and relatively late development of formal organization. The Gion negotiations of the sixty-six blocks in 1533 were probably anterior to the creation of block federations. See Imatani, *Tokitsugu kyō-ki*, 244–45, for reflections on the possible importation of the notion of monthly magistrates from village society and the appointment of such officials before the organization of block federations. On page 236 Imatani rebuts the claims of Akiyama Kunizō (*Kinsei Kyōto machigumi no hattatsu-shi*, 36–38) that federation occurred before the 1530s. The work of Takahashi and Imatani does not deny that local solidarity in Kyoto had a long history, but it separates that history from the new and systematic process of organization.

25. See *SKR* 4:283–84 (no. 15) for a receipt from a palace official to a monthly magistrate for funds used in palace repairs during 1556. See Takahashi, *Kyōto chūsei toshi-shi kenkyū*, 465–68 and 472–74, for a discussion of concessions granted to the six blocks for service to the throne and protests from the six blocks over what they saw as excessive impositions. A pattern of negotiation and semicontractual exchange seems to be emerging here. Takahashi (pp. 460–61) points out that the throne was not the proprietor of the land constituting the six blocks and hence could not presume unconditional access to its resources.

26. For documents concerning tax problems after Hokke, see, for example, *SKR* 4:287–88 (nos. 27, 29, 30, 32); and the numerous decrees to Kyoto proprietors issued between 1537 and 1540 by shogunal officials in *MBMS/BHH* 2:351–90.

27. *MBMS/BHH* 2:390 (no. 3494).

28. *Rokuon'in nichiroku*, Tenbun 13 (1544)/12/16, 19, in *SKR* 4:288 (no. 33).

29. As, for example, in *Chikatoshi nikki*, Tenbun 8 (1539)/8/3, 13: 261–62.

30. For an extended treatment of this and the following six acts, see Imatani, *Tokitsugu kyō-ki*, 96–161, *Sengoku Miyoshi ichizoku*, 93–122, and *Sengoku-ki no Muromachi bakufu*, 191–207; Kobayashi, "Sengoku sōran no tenkai,"

18–33; *KR* 3:491–99. Hosokawa Harumoto's strength in these years centered on Settsu, Kawachi, and Izumi, and on two particularly important vassals— Ibaragi Nagataka and Kizawa Nagamasa.

31. *KR*, vol. 3, points out the inherent difficulty of maintaining Miyoshi Chōkei and Kizawa Nagamasa in the same administration because Kizawa had been instrumental in the death of Chōkei's father, Miyoshi Motonaga. Imatani Akira (for example, *Sengoku-ki no Muromachi bakufu*, 191–92) downplays the importance of Kizawa to represent the larger struggle after 1541 as a contest between Miyoshi Chōkei (representing a domainal and daimyo-centered vision of power) and Ibaragi Nagataka (representing a traditional order of proprietary and shogunal authority).

32. For Chōkei's ferocity, see, for example, Imatani, *Tokitsugu kyō-ki*, 106–9. Chōkei raised havoc in Uji, Fushimi, Daigo, and other areas, where he collected war taxes of up to 20,000 *hiki;* after 1549 he imposed commissariat taxes throughout the seven districts of Yamashiro.

33. Miyoshi Chōkei was still fighting on Hosokawa Harumoto's side, providing Harumoto with critical support from Shikoku, Tanba, Harima, Ōmi, and Settsu. At the same time, Chōkei was acting like a local daimyo of these areas— taking districts over as fiefs and confiscating estates.

34. Imatani Akira defines Chōkei's victory in 1549 as the end of Japan's middle ages; *Sengoku-ki no Muromachi bakufu*, 192.

35. For a close study of castle construction in Kyoto and its environs, see Imatani, *Tokitsugu kyō-ki*, 110–50. Firearms were in use in many of the battles between 1549 and 1553, thus changing significantly the experience of war.

36. By 1553 Miyoshi Chōkei's domain extended into seven provinces, as well as into port towns in Harima and Iyo. Imatani Akira represents Chōkei as a major Warring States daimyo who meets the four conditions established by Nagahara Keiji for that designation. See *Tokitsugu kyō-ki*, 156–58. Kobayashi Seiji resists the characterization of Chōkei as a daimyo warlord, and hence as a destroyer of Kyoto's medieval order, by emphasizing his continuing compromises with landed proprietors and his partial defense of the estate system; see "Sengoku sōran no tenkai," 28. For a description of Chōkei's entry into Kyoto in 1553, see *Tokitsugu kyō-ki*, Tenbun 22/8/1, 3:61–62.

37. Imatani, *Sengoku-ki no Muromachi bakufu*, 197–207; *SKR* 3:320–21 (nos. 36, 37). A partial restoration of the bakufu and the old order followed the return of the shogun to Kyoto in 1558; see Imatani, *Tokitsugu kyō-ki*, 158–66.

38. *MBMS/BHH* 2:373 (no. 3440); for a discussion, see Imatani, *Tokitsugu kyō-ki*, 237–39, and *Sengoku-ki no Muromachi bakufu*, 146–50.

39. *Seiganji monjo*, Tenbun 10 (1541)/4/12, in *SKR* 3:364 (no. 3).

40. *SKR* 3:364 (no. 14).

41. *Honnōji monjo*, Tenbun 14 (1545)/8/18, in *SKR* 3:320 (no. 34).

42. *MBMS/BHH* 2:433 (no. 3636).

43. See a list of such exemptions in Takahashi, *Kyōto chūsei toshi-shi kenkyū*, 354–55.

44. *SKR* 4:290 (no. 38).

45. *Muromachi tōchō monjo,* Tenbun 19 (1550)/intercalary 5/24, in *SKR* 4:283 (no. 14).

46. *Kamikyō monjo,* Tenbun 19 (1550)/7/10, in *SKR* 3:321 (no. 37, item 3).

47. *Tokitsugu kyō-ki,* Tenbun 18 (1549)/9/7, 2:258; also see *KR* 3:587.

48. *Tokitsugu kyō-ki,* Tenbun 18 (1549)/11/17–20, 2:279–80.

49. Ibid., Tenbun 19 (1550)/5/2, 2:338–39.

50. Ibid., Tenbun 19 (1550)/7/15–16, 2:359–60.

51. Ibid., Tenbun 20 (1551)/1/24, 2:414.

52. Imatani Akira insists that the block associations became a tool of Ibaragi Nagataka, who placed a stranglehold on them. Much of his analysis focuses on the Seiganji documents. He also finds illustrative the burning by military officers of a Sanjō neighborhood in retaliation for the killing of a bakufu affiliate during the Gion festival of 1545. See *Sengoku-ki no Muromachi bakufu,* 190–91, 146–50, and *Tokitsugu kyō-ki,* 241.

53. See, for example, Yoshida Nobuyuki's analysis of *chō* expenditures in Tachiuri and Reizen during the late sixteenth and early seventeenth centuries: "Kōgi to chōnin mibun," p. 106, charts 9 and 10. See Noda, "Shimogyō monjo, Sanjō-Karasuma Manjūya-chō monjo" for the character of chō organization and activities in the Edo period.

54. Imatani Akira argues that judicial authority in the *chō* disappeared after 1536, when the neighborhoods entered the grip of Ibaragi Nagataka, except for the period 1549–52, when *chō* officials filled, perforce, a political vacuum created by shogunal wars; *Tokitsugu kyō-ki,* 240–44.

55. Takahashi, *Kyōto chūsei toshi-shi kenkyū,* 348–57. Takahashi is satisfied that blocks in the southern sector of Kyoto did not number much more than 68 by 1571 (only 2 more than the count of 66 in 1533) but thinks the northern sector may have included more than 120 blocks in the 1570s (although the documents compiled for Nobunaga include only about half that number in the structure of block federations). For increases after wartime, see *KR* 4:105–21 and 5:74–76.

56. The Nobunaga documents identify five federations in northern Kyoto and three in southern Kyoto, but two additional federations in the south can be identified from other documents; see *KR* 4:108. The federation of the six blocks is not included in these numbers. Hence, the total of federations is eleven.

57. Imatani, *Tokitsugu kyō-ki,* 245–46. See Yoshida, "Kōgi to chōnin mibun," pp. 104–5, point 6, for a discussion of the title *toshiyori,* another term for "elder."

58. Takahashi Yasuo is particularly clear about the antagonisms between "we" and "they"—between the residents of the six blocks and the authorities demanding labor for the moats—that galvanized the *chōnin* into forming the first block federation in 1534; *Kyōto chūsei toshi-shi kenkyū,* 456–57.

59. See, for example, Takahashi, *Kyōto chūsei toshi-shi kenkyū,* 434, concerning the variety of occupations in Reizen; 332–33, concerning the variety of occupations in Nishijin, often considered a weavers' enclave; 345–46, concerning

the distribution of seventy-four "public people" throughout twenty-four blocks. See Yoshida, "Kōgi to chōnin mibun," 99, concerning the variety of proprietors in four different blocks; and 100, concerning the distribution of "public people" in Tachiuri; also see note 6 of this chapter.

60. Courtiers, military men, and priests were particularly conspicuous in the six blocks and in the Nakagumi federation. For the appointment of members of the elite as monthly magistrates, see Takahashi, *Kyōto chūsei toshi-shi kenkyū*, 435–36. The finessing of class identity can be seen in Hayashiya Tatsusaburō's well-known work *Machishū*, where the term "people of the blocks" tends primarily to designate commoners even though it can include members of the elite who participated in neighborhood life.

61. See *MBMS/BHH* 2:372–73 (no. 3439) for the document to the temple, 2:373 (no. 3440) for the document to the neighborhood. For the background of these documents and a discussion of the possibly divided interests between the temple and the neighborhood (and the military officials and the neighborhood), see Imatani, *Sengoku-ki no Muromachi bakufu*, 146–50.

62. *Nanzenji monjo*, Meiō 4 (1495)/10/21, 2:19.

63. *Motonaga kyō-ki*, Eishō 4 (1507)/4/23, 26:136.

64. Despite his representation of the block associations as fully subordinate to men like Ibaragi Nagataka, Imatani Akira does acknowledge a reformulation of neighborhood identity through organization and direct contact with military authorities; *Tokitsugu kyō-ki*, 237–39.

65. Takahashi, *Kyōto chūsei toshi-shi kenkyū*, 331, 354–55.

66. See, for example, *MBMS/BHH* 2:279–81 (nos. 3130–3133), 2:351–52 (no. 3371), 2:377 (no. 3454), 2:420 (no. 3594).

67. Takahashi, *Kyōto chūsei toshi-shi kenkyū*, 357, 461–68, 472–74; *SKR* 4:283–84 (no. 15).

68. *KR* 3:563–64.

Chapter 7. Play: The Freedom of Invention

1. The literature concerning Sen no Rikyū is vast. Two of the more important biographies are Haga, *Sen no Rikyū*, and Murai, *Sen no Rikyū*. Also see Sen et al., eds., *Rikyū daijiten*.

2. Quoted from *Chadō yōroku* in Murai, *Sen no Rikyū*, 235.

3. Comparative sources on the subject of play that have been of interest to me include Spencer, ed., *Society and the Dance;* Radcliffe-Brown, *Structure and Function in Primitive Society;* Turner, *Ritual Process;* Bakhtin, *Rabelais and His World*.

4. *Nisui-ki*, Eishō 17 (1520)/7/22, in *SKR* 5:251 (no. 11).

5. *Sanetaka kō-ki*, Eishō 17 (1520)/7/22 and 7/25, 5:736–37.

6. Ibid., Eishō 2 (1505)/7/18, 4:433.

7. Ibid., Eishō 3 (1506)/7/11, 4:574.

8. For the sumptuary law cited here, see *CHSS/MBH* 2:4 (the first item of

Kenmu shikimoku). *Fūryū* emerged in the literature as early as the eighth century (in *Shoku Nihon-gi*), and became a subject of sumptuary legislation as early as 1070 (when it clearly denoted spectacular dress). The term referred to elaborate props as early as the twelfth century (when the usage appears in *Konjaku monogatari*, *Imakagami* and other sources). The early history and continuing development of *fūryū* may be traced in the following sources: Gorai, "Fūryū no odori"; Atsuta, "Minshū bunka no genryū"; Misumi, "Fūryū-ko" and "Minzoku to geijutsu no aida"; Hayashiya, "Machishū no seikatsu to geijutsu," esp. 215–35; Geinō-shi Kenkyū-kai, ed., *Butō—kinsei no uta to odori;* Honda, "Fūryū"; Iwasaki, *Nihon geinō-shi*. Also see *KR* 3:600–23; and Imatani, *Tokitsugu kyō-ki*, 253–57.

The great difficulty with these works (and, of course, with my own study) is the paucity of sources concerning any particular manifestation of *fūryū* in a specific time and place. The scholarship consequently tends to finesse issues of genre, to link disparate snatches of evidence from disparate periods into a continuative analysis, and even to infer historical practice from present-day examples. The scholarship is nonetheless extremely interesting concerning *fūryū*'s various roles in building communal identity, in challenging social boundaries, in either containing or releasing conflict. Hayashiya is the most sympathetic to radical interpretations of the dancing and its potential for social subversion.

My own treatment of *fūryū* is limited not only to wartime Kyoto but also to the mysterious outbreaks of dancing described in the sources, which do not fit into the ritual calendar or other intelligible frames. I do not consider, for example, the dancing clearly associated with specific temples (like Shakadō or Katsura Jizō), with ritual events (like the *matsu-bayashi* of New Year's), or with individual festivals (like Gion).

9. Oze, "Toyotomi daimyōjin sairei-ki." The most famous of several pairs of screens depicting the anniversary festivities was painted by Kanō Naisen (1570–1616) and remains in the collection of the Hōkoku shrine in Kyoto; see Tanaka, "Hōkoku-sai no byōbu ni tsuite." For illustrations, see Kyōto Kokuritsu Hakubutsu-kan, *Rakuchū rakugai-zu*, and Takeda, *Fuzoku-ga: Sairei, Kabuki*.

10. *Tokitsugu kyō-ki*, Genki 2 (1571)/7/25, 4:515–16.

11. References to *fūryū* change during the 1560s, when we find increased mention of named dances, dancers from specific neighborhoods and locales, very rich costumes, and even instruction in music. See, for example, the sources cited in notes 12, 17, 18, and 20 of this chapter. For further discussion, see note 27.

12. *Tokitsugu kyō-ki*, Eiroku 10 (1567)/7/24, 4:159.

13. *Tokitsugu kyō-ki*, Eiroku 9 (1566)/7/15, 4:52–53, for the reference to *nenbutsu odori*.

14. *Tokitsugu kyō-ki*, Tenbun 1 (1532)/8/20, 1:199.

15. Ibid., Tenbun 13 (1544)/7/14, 1:484.

16. Ibid., Tenbun 22 (1553)/7/19–21, 3:58–59.

17. Ibid., Eiroku 8 (1565)/7/18, 3:517.

18. Ibid., Eiroku 10 (1567)/7/24, 4:159.

19. *KR* 3:620–23.

20. *Tokitsugu kyō-ki*, Tenbun 22 (1553)/7/19, 3:58; Eiroku 10 (1567)/

7/24, 4:159; Eiroku 11 (1568)/7/26, 4:257–58; Genki 2 (1571)/7/25, 4:515–16.

21. See Yokoi, *Gekokujō no bunka*, especially " 'Kyōki' no koto," for one of the boldest and most provocative analyses of madness and the strange in late medieval culture.

22. The word *kenbutsu* is ubiquitous in diary descriptions of public spectacles and seems to connote something quite different from passive acts of seeing. The term resonates with purposeful action and the adoption of a role that is indispensable to the total event of performance.

23. *Gensuke onen-ki*, Daiei 5 (1525)/2/2, in *SKR* 5:277–78 (no. 12).

24. *Tokitsugu kyō-ki*, Tenbun 22 (1553)/3/25, 3:31.

25. See, for example, Kawai, *Chūsei buke shakai no kenkyū*, 262–404.

26. *Tokitsugu kyō-ki*, Eiroku 11 (1568)/7/26–27, 4:258; Genki 2 (1571)/ 7/16–17, 4:513.

27. The changes in *fūryū* mentioned in note 11 become most conspicuous in Tokitsugu's entry for Genki 2 (1571)/7/25, 4:515–16. Here we find organized dancers from specific neighborhoods performing specifically named dances, and processing around the city to stops at the shogunal residence and different noble residences. The clothing of the dancers is also mentioned in detail. Tokitsugu claims that more than 100,000 people watched the dancing. I associate this development of *fūryū*, in part, with increased organization over time as dancers formed stable groups, elaborated distinctive styles, and gradually replaced guerrilla improvisation with form and order. But I also associate the development with the changed politics of the neighborhood associations— with the formal structuring of political identity, the channeling of conflict into organization and negotiation, and the withdrawal of commoners from violent encounter with the authorities.

28. Again, see Yokoi Kiyoshi and his analogy between *fūryū* and *kyō*, or madness, in a realm of the extraordinary (the realm of *hare* as opposed to the realm of *ke*) which provides him with an entry into a new sense of the period; " 'Kyōki' no koto," esp. 100–101.

29. Burckhardt, *Civilization of the Renaissance in Italy*, 283.

30. Thucydides, *Peloponnesian War*, 155.

31. *Homo ludens* is a phrase made famous by Johan Huizinga (in a book of the same title), but Jacob Burckhardt's analysis resonates more deeply with the themes of my work; see *Civilization of the Renaissance in Italy*, 271–351.

32. One particularly obscure aspect of *fūryū* is the lyrics of its songs. Some anonymous songs appear on the back of a page of Tokitsugu's diary (Daiei 7/ 1/14, 1:5.), and both Tokitsugu and Sanetaka mention composing *kouta*, perhaps to accompany the dancing. (*Tokitsugu kyō-ki*, Genki 2/7/11, 4:511–12, and Kōji 2/2/16, 3:225; *Sanetaka kō-ki*, Kyōroku 2/7/11, 8:5–6.) Also see Asano, *Chūsei kayō*, and Atsuta, "Minshū bunka no genryū." Discussion of *fūryū* lyrics remains conjectural, however, and only in Oze Hoan's account of the anniversary of Hideyoshi's death do we find songs that can be confidently associated with *fūryū* performance. See note 9 above.

33. See Katerina Clark and Michael Holquist, *Mikhail Bakhtin*, 426, con-

cerning the self-sufficiency of carnival and its refusal to make explicit demands to the authorities.

34. *CKZ* 9:1.

35. *Matsuya kaiki* includes the diaries of Hisamasa (1533–96), Hisayoshi (1586–1626), and Hisashige (1604–50). *Tennōjiya kaiki* includes the diaries of Tsuda Sōtatsu (1548–66, during which time he made records both of the parties he gave and the parties he attended); Tsuda Sōgyū (1565–85 for the parties he attended, 1566–87 for the parties he gave); and Tsuda Sōbon (covering the parties he attended in 1590). *Imai Sōkyū chanoyū nikki nukigaki* chronicles the parties Sōkyū gave and attended between 1554 and 1587. *Kamiya Sōtan nikki* chronicles the parties Sōtan gave and attended between 1586 and 1613. The diaries appear in *CKZ*, vols. 6–10.

36. Accounts survive, for example, of Go-Komatsu's visit to Ashikaga Yoshimitsu's residence in Kitayama during 1408 (which included a tea service); Go-Hanazono's visit to Ashikaga Yoshinori's residence in 1437 (which is described in *Muromachi-dono gyōkō okazari-ki*); and a party given in 1469 by the Furuichi (which purportedly included bathing and as many as 150 participants). *Kissa ōrai* (mid-fourteenth century, included in *CKZ* 2:163–213) also describes the environment and procedure of tea ceremonies of the elite at the time. For a discussion of the early tea service, see Kumakura, *Chanoyū no rekishi*, 55–96; Murai, *Sen no Rikyū*, 12–31; Haga and Nishiyama, eds., *Cha no bunka-shi*, 43–106. Murai Yasuhiko describes the Furuichi party in "Development of Chanoyū," 20. For an interesting comparison of the tea service described in *Kissa ōrai* and the service performed in Rikyū's time, see Kumakura, *Chanoyū no rekishi*, 68–69.

37. See, for example, Carter, *Three Poets at Yuyama*, for the account of a linked verse sequence composed in 1491. Also see Kumakura, *Chanoyū no rekishi*, 116–30 ("Takeno Jōō to renga"). A number of tea men—including, for example, Murata Shukō, Takeno Jōō, and Tsuda Sōtatsu—studied and practiced linked verse and knew some of its masters. The linkages between the two art forms are clearly complex and important, although a full-scale study has yet to be undertaken.

38. A number of sources in English offer good introductions to the early tea service; see Varley and Elison, "Culture of Tea"; Varley and Kumakura, eds., *Tea in Japan* (especially the contributions by Murai Yasuhiko, Kumakura Isao, H. Paul Varley, Theodore M. Ludwig, and Haga Kōshirō). Also see Sen, ed., *Chanoyū*, for a detailed description of the modern practice of tea.

39. The *dōbōshū* are discussed in Varley and Elison, "Culture of Tea," 202–11; also see Tani, "San'ami." The most important product of the *dōbōshū* circle, and the most significant guide to the aesthetic values of late Muromachi salon society, is *Kundaikan sōchō-ki*. This work lists and ranks Chinese paintings owned by the Ashikaga house, describes the organization and ornamentation of the reception rooms where precious objects were displayed, and discusses ceramics and other objects arrayed in the salon.

40. *Yamanoue Sōji-ki* is the earliest extant effort to provide a history and analysis of wartime tea. Composed around 1589 by a daimyo tea practitioner,

the work has been enormously influential in structuring all later understandings of tea "masters" and their lineages (one section is entitled "Chanoyū-sha no den," 95–98), even though the work includes apocrypha and dubious information.

41. I believe certain basic questions about wartime tea will never be adequately answered: were there patterns of instruction in the tea service that constituted a prototype for a formal teaching regimen? were there really any "professionals" among early tea men who made a living by offering such instruction or accepting the gifts of patrons? was tea society governed by some hierarchical order? My sense is that instruction remained an informal affair of watching and emulating one's seniors (particularly in the use of the *daisu*, a portable frame with shelves to hold the tea implements); that some practitioners depended on the support of admirers without quite moving into the realm of fees or stipends or formal employment; and that hierarchy was unstable and inchoate, reflected in the diaries only by the naming of objects after their presumably distinguished owners.

42. Kumakura, *Chanoyū*, 64–69. The host fully emerged in the tea service when he replaced attendants as the preparer of tea in front of his guests. Murata Shukō (d. 1502) was apparently one of the first practitioners to satisfy this definition.

43. The poet Sōchō remarks on the appearance of a tea hut in Kyoto by 1526 (*Sōchō shūki*, Daiei 6/8/15, p. 92). Tsuda Sōtatsu frequently mentions tea huts in accounts of tea parties he himself hosted from the 1550s (*CKZ*, vol. 8), although he does not describe their construction. See Horiguchi and Inagaki, eds., *Cha no kenchiku to niwa*, for an excellent survey of the subject with illustrations.

44. The modern literature on tea, excellent though it often is, seems overly concerned with a narrative of progress. It traces a history of deepening aesthetic consciousness as practitioners abandoned the tea competitions and the salon extravaganzas of the medieval period to commit themselves to a style of personal cultivation and artistic discrimination that "culminated" in the *wabi* tea of Sen no Rikyū. Men like Murata Shukō and Takeno Jōō emerge as precursors of Rikyū, and their possibly spurious documents emerge as harbingers of the *wabi* taste. Although the general lines of such analysis may be correct, I am concerned that this narrative makes too sharp the often-shadowy profiles of men we know little about, that it focuses attention on individuals rather than the larger tea society, and that it obscures the variety and complexity of the wartime tea culture.

45. For example, Matsuya Hisamasa mentions a Korean tea bowl in his entry for Tenbun 6 (1537)/9/12, a Shigaraki fresh-water container in his entry for Tenbun 11 (1542)/4/9, and a bamboo tea scoop in his entry for Tenbun 13 (1544)/4/20; *CKZ* 9:2, 7, 8. For an excellent discussion of the *wabi* taste, see Cort, *Shigaraki*, 104–82. Cort begins with an interesting economic argument concerning the appreciation of *wabi* vessels (pp. 109–10), although she does not make it primary. Also see Hirota, "Practice of Tea 1: Heart's Mastery," for a discussion of a document that addresses the issue of native and foreign wares and the necessity of dissolving the boundary between them.

46. See note 44 of this chapter. The "great man" concern in the modern tea literature reflects the historical analysis of *Yamanoue Sōji-ki* and the later treatments of Sen no Rikyū (in, for example, *Nanbō-roku;* see *CKZ* 4:1–333). Biographical information concerning early practitioners is scant, however, even in the case of the early Rikyū (see note 78 of this chapter). We know only that Murata Shukō may have been a monk (although some scholars doubt even his historicity), and that Takeno Jōō came to Kyoto from an obscure background to study poetry with Sanjōnishi Sanetaka.

47. For Matsuya Hisayoshi's debut, see *CKZ* 9:121 (Tenshō 14 [1586]/2/ 24); for Hachiya Matagorō's appearance, see 9:3 (Tenbun 8 [1539]/13/18). Matsuya Hisamasa attended a tea party in Sakai hosted by "Sen no Sōeki" in 1544 (*CKZ* 9:9, Tenbun 13/2/27), but also notes, as early as 1537, a party in Kyoto attended by a "Sōeki" (9:2, Tenbun 6/9/13). The only clear evidence known to me concerning the possibility of apprenticeship in the practice of tea is the compilation of *Chagu bitō-shū*, possibly around 1554, which Louise Cort describes as "a lexicon of terminology intended for the novice tea man"; *Shigaraki,* 114–15. A letter attributed to Murata Shukō (the authenticity of which is debated) speaks of tea practitioners as "adepts" (*kōsha*) and "beginners" (*shōshinsha*), terms that imply stages of induction and proficiency. See Hirota, "Practice of Tea 1: Heart's Mastery," 9–10.

48. Tea traditions were also passed down in the Murata, Hariya, Jūshiya, and Kobori households. I presume that one of the strongest inducements to such continuity was the importance of vessel collections.

49. See Yokoi, "Chūsei minshū-shi ni okeru 'jūgo-sai' no imi ni tsuite." In the Edo period, a clearer stage of adolescence emerged with the spread of schooling and commercial apprenticeships.

50. *Yamanoue Sōji-ki* provides most of what (often-uncertain) biographical information we have, although the author's concerns focus on the possessions and circles of tea people rather than on their employments and mundane activities.

51. See, for example, the names that appear in Tsuda Sōtatsu's accounts of 1550: Shioya, Akaneya, Aburaya, Nuriya, Hibiya, Tajimaya, Kawasakiya, Shinbei, Genbei, Jirō, Magobei; *CKZ* 7:16–26; 8:12–17.

52. From the late 1540s Miyoshi Masanaga and other members of the Miyoshi house begin appearing in the Matsuya and Tsuda diaries. Tsuda Sōtatsu also mentions, among others, Matsunaga Hisahide, members of the Ikeda and Hatakeyama houses, priests from the Honganji headquarters, and nobles such as Lord Kujō. The indexes of *CKZ,* which are detailed and extremely useful, provide the best access to this sort of information.

53. Oda Nobunaga placed at least three tea masters on stipends (Imai Sōkyū, Tsuda Sōgyū, and Sen no Rikyū). Toyotomi Hideyoshi appointed eight men as his tea masters. Nobunaga also retained the right to grant permission among his men to practice the tea service, *KR* 4:665–69; Kumakura, *Chanoyū no rekishi,* 164–76; Kuwata, *Sadō no rekishi,* 108–22. Perhaps the most significant act of control was Nobunaga's militant collection of vessels, especially "items of fame," which led to the concentration (for the first time since Ōnin) of objects of prestige in the hands of the dominant military authority. The codi-

fication of objects and the ranking of practitioners (undertaken first by Yamanoue Sōji, who served Hideyoshi as one of his tea masters) further advanced the ordering and rationalizing of the tea culture.

54. The aristocratic and military diaries of Kyoto do not focus on tea, although occasional references do appear. The tea practitioners of Kyoto, at least the leading ones, may be identified from the tea diaries, particularly *Matsuya kaiki*, in which Hisamasa notes the names of the Kyoto men who entertained him on his periodic visits to the capital. He identifies almost twenty Kyoto practitioners; *CKZ* 9:2–3, Tenbun 6 (1537); 9:19–23, Kōji 3 (1557); 9:88–90, Tenshō 10 (1582). Yamanoue Sōji also identifies certain Kyoto disciples of Murata Shukō, and Tsuda Sōtatsu and Tsuda Sōgyū further amplify the record. The tea society of Kyoto was probably substantial, given Matsuya Hisamasa's commitment to traveling there and the city's identification with the circles of Murata Shukō and Takeno Jōō. One list of tea utensils placed fifty-one "items of fame," held by twenty-nine owners, within Kyoto; Murai, "A Biography of Sen Rikyū," 7–8.

55. Matsuya Hisamasa spent seven days in Sakai in 1542; ten days in Sakai in 1544; fourteen days in Kyoto in 1557; and ten days in Kōriyama in 1586. For something of the variety of the tea culture, see note 60 below.

56. Overwhelmingly, tea names include the character *sō*. The first such name (Kinuya Sōrin) appears in *Matsuya kaiki* in 1539. The index for Tsuda Sōtatsu's and Tsuda Sōgyū's diaries (those chronicling parties they hosted themselves; *CKZ*, vol. 8) lists 132 different tea names with the *sō* character. The origin of the names and the process by which individuals adopted them are unclear.

57. Etiquette and procedure in the tea room receive attention in documents attributed to Murata Shukō and Takeno Jōō; see Hirota, "Practice of Tea 2: The *Wabi* Tea of Takeno Jō-ō." See Sen, *Chanoyū*, 120–41, for the modern conduct of the first and other guests.

58. Although rankings can often be interpreted without great difficulty, puzzles abound. The older Matsuya Hisamasa could take a second seat to Kinuya Sōrin or Sen no Sōeki; Sōeki could take a lower seat than various merchants now unknown to us; Takeno Jōō could rank below Tsuda Sōtatsu. See *CKZ* 9:10, Tenbun 21 (1552)/10/21; 9:13, Kōji 2 (1556)/10/13; 8:62, Kōji 4 (1558)/12/1; 7:38, Tenbun 23 (1554)/2/1.

59. See, for example, variations in Matsuya Hisamasa's traveling party of 1542 (*CKZ* 9:4–7) or in the ranking of Sōtatsu and Sōgo in the parties of 1550 (7:16–26).

60. In Tsuda Sōtatsu's account of parties he himself hosted, for example, see references to eight elders (Tenbun 19 [1550]/5/27); two people from Bingo (Tenbun 19/1/18); neighbors (Tenbun 19/2/3); travelers from Osaka (Eiroku 3 [1560]/1/17), Uji (Eiroku 3/1/27), and Hirado (Eiroku 3/5/17); twenty-seven prosperous people of northern and southern Sakai (Eiroku 4 [1561]/6/22); a group of elders (Eiroku 5 [1562]/1/7); twenty-seven townspeople (Eiroku 7 [1564]/2/21); more than thirty townspeople (Eiroku 7/7/27). Tsuda Sōgyū refers to travelers from Matsue (Eiroku 9 [1566]/10/27). *CKZ* 8:12–17, 75–81, 82, 87, 107, 108, 117. These examples are random.

61. Townspeople did not, for example, have guild halls; nor, other than their

own homes, did they control other spaces for entertainment. Although I have found no evidence concerning their patterns of social encounter, I presume that (like Kyoto's nobles) they visited each other, met at baths, and participated in versions of the *shiru-kai* (or "soup clubs") to which members alternately contributed food, drink, and a site for gathering. It seems likely, however, that tea parties brought to commoner society an unprecedented opportunity for regular, cultivated meetings.

62. Yasa and Sōtatsu participated together in at least eighteen teas in 1550; *CKZ* 7:16–26; 8:12–17. For Hisamasa's companions, see, for example, *CKZ* 9:4–10, 19–23.

63. Tsuda Sōgyū made notes of sixty-six parties he gave and fifty-six parties he attended in 1578; *CKZ* 7:272–92; 8:272–310. In general, entries increase significantly in the diaries from the Tenshō period (from 1573). Matsuya Hisamasa's early diary is sparse and seems largely devoted to chronicling his trips outside Nara.

64. Christy Bartlett has been making a close study of the seasonal occurrence of parties noted in Tsuda Sōtatsu's diaries. She finds parties frequent in the 1st, 2d, 10th, 11th, and 12th months; infrequent in the 6th, 7th, and 8th months.

65. Biographical sketches of tea men, noting their interests in poetry and painting and music, appear in Haga, "Chanoyū no kaiso," and Yonehara, "Sakai no machi no chajin."

66. For styles of life among Kyoto's townspeople, see Yokoi, *Gekokujō no bunka*, 65–77, 149–75, and *Chūsei minshū no seikatsu bunka*, 135–60.

67. Early efforts to list and classify vessels include *Chagu bitō-shū* (Tenbun 23 [1554]); the "Chaki meibutsu-shū" portion of *Yamanoue Sōji-ki* (Tenshō 17 [1589]); *Chanoyu dōgu nayose* (Tenshō 5 [1577]); *Enshū onkura moto chō;* and *Sencha-shū* (Bunroku 2 [1593]). For the collection of vessels by Oda Nobunaga, see Haga and Nishiyama, eds., *Cha no bunka-shi*, 127–31; Murai, *Sen no Rikyū*, 99–103; Kumakura, *Chanoyu no rekishi*, 164–76. The twin processes of classification and collection of vessels (by men like Oda Nobunaga) began to force an aesthetic code on tea that was new to the late sixteenth century and fundamentally important to its structuring as a fixed art form.

68. For measurements, see, for example, *Matsuya kaiki*, Tenbun 11 (1542)/4/3 (*CKZ* 9:4). For the counting of characters see the same diary, Eiroku 11 (1568)/1/5 (*CKZ* 9:65). Measurement and counting occur fairly frequently in the diaries. Tsuda Sōtatsu regularly mentions the grade of tea provided at parties, using five rankings. Most other diarists fail to mention the tea with any frequency.

69. See *Yamanoue Sōji-ki*, 54–90, for a catalog of vessels that traces the past and current ownership of important pieces. The best modern guide to the possessions of individual tea men is Iguchi and Nakashima, eds., *Genshoku chadō daijiten*, which notes collections under the biographical entries. For illustrations of notable vessels, see Noma and Oyama, *Cha no bijutsu to kōgei;* and Kyōto Kokuritsu Hakubutsu-kan, ed., *Tokubetsu tenrankai yonhyaku-nenki Sen no Rikyū ten.*

70. See Kyōto Kokuritsu Hakubutsu-kan, ed., *Tokubetsu tenrankai yonhya-*

ku-nenki Sen no Rikyū ten, 104, for the appraisal of the storage jar. For the tea scoop, see *SKR* 5:259 (no. 59); for the manuscript, *SKR* 5:253 (no. 25); for the bowl, *SKR* 5:259 (no. 58).

71. Quoted in Cooper, comp., *They Came to Japan,* 264 (Luis de Almeida, S.J., on 30,000 ducats), 261 (Alessandro Valignano, S.J., on the bird's cage).

72. *CKZ* 8:12–17 (Tenbun 19 [1550]).

73. Ibid. 7:16–26 (Tenbun 19 [1550]).

74. Ibid. 9:4–7 (Tenbun 11 [1542]); 9:7–10 (Tenbun 13 [1544]).

75. Although it is an enormous task, I urge the close collation of the diaries to permit exact studies of the size and composition of the tea world, patterns of entertainment and sociability, movement of vessels and changes in taste. Such a collation would encourage detailed studies in social history that few other (if any other) sources of the time permit.

76. *CKZ* 9:4 (Tenbun 11 [1542]/4/3).

77. Tsuda Sōtatsu, for example, notes thirty-three parties he attended in 1550 and five in 1555. He notes twenty-three parties he gave in 1550, five in 1553, thirty-three in 1562, fifty to sixty a year during the 1570s.

78. One puzzling aspect of the Tsuda diaries, for example, is the infrequency with which Sen no Rikyū appears as a guest or a host. Sōtatsu and Sōgyū entertained him only fifteen times between 1548 and 1585. (See the index to *CKZ,* vol. 8.) Does this fact suggest questions about Rikyū (was he reasonably obscure before the rise of Nobunaga and Hideyoshi? was he on distant terms with the Tsuda?) or does it suggest questions about the diaries (are they very incomplete? do they attend to parties only within particular circles?)? I am grateful to Christy Bartlett for pointing out the rare appearance of Rikyū in *Tennō-jiya kaiki.*

79. This vague figure is a yet-impressionistic response to data that can be assessed in greater detail: the lists of hosts and guests in the diaries; the late sixteenth-century lists of vessels and their owners. Short of the quantification of this information, the indexes to the individual diaries (which are extensive but not inclusive) can be collated and organized chronologically to give gross figures for the size of the tea community that is identified in the diaries.

80. Murai, "A Biography of Sen Rikyū," 7–8.

81. See, for example, *KR* 4:688–89; Hayashiya, *Chūsei bunka no kichō,* 258–69 and *Machishū,* 112–44; Keene, "Jōha, a Sixteenth-Century Poet of Linked Verse."

82. Medieval tea included no tradition of instruction or secret transmission, and its only texts were *Kundaikan sōchō-ki* and *Kissa ōrai.* Neither was a guide to tea practice itself.

83. No wartime text records the procedure of the tea service, although certain documents attributed to Murata Shukō and Takeno Jōō take for granted some shared sense of a basic etiquette and some notion of "formal" (presumably as opposed to informal) rites governing the preparation of thin tea; see Hirota, "Practice of Tea 2: The *Wabi* Tea of Takeno Jō-ō," 18–23.

84. *Kuchi-kiri* is noted, for example, by Matsuya Hisamasa (Tenshō 14 [1586]/10/6) and Tsuda Sōgyū (Genki 2 [1571]/10/21); *CKZ* 9:125;

8:164. Tsuda Sōtatsu frequently refers to *usu-cha,* which was typically served after a first round of thick tea.

85. For a modern discussion of this issue, see Sen, *Chanoyū,* 120–41.

86. Although paintings are almost invariably identified with their creators, vessels are described by shape, glaze, sometimes by kiln locale (Ise, Shino, Shigaraki), or style ("a Kinrinji-type lacquered caddy"). The principal exceptions before Rikyū's time (when craftsmen came to be named more often) were objects made by tea men themselves—we find tea scoops, for example, made by Jōō or Jūtoku; *Matsuya kaiki,* Tenbun 13 (1544)/2/20 (*CKZ* 9:8).

87. *Matsuya kaiki,* Tenbun 6 (1537)/9/12, for the Korean bowl and lacquer caddy; Tenbun 6/9/14, for the eggplants; Tenbun 11 (1542)/4/9, for the Shigaraki pot with items of fame; Tenbun 11/4/8, for the brazier and the censer. *CKZ* 9:2, 3, 7.

88. *Matsuya kaiki,* Tenbun 11 (1542)/4/7 (*CKZ* 9:6), for the sweets; *Tennōjiya kaiki,* Tenbun 19 (1550)/2/14 (*CKZ* 7:17), for the ink stone, displayed at a party Sōtatsu attended; *Tennōjiya kaiki,* Eiroku 3 (1560)/2/3 (*CKZ* 8:76–77), for the ladle rest, displayed at a party Sōtatsu hosted.

89. We find, for example, a "Jōō *nasu*" (a type of caddy), a "Shukō tea bowl," a "Zenkō censer," a "Matsuya *katatsuki*" (another type of caddy). See *Matsuya kaiki,* Shōhō 5 (1648)/2/8 (*CKZ* 9:436) for a reference to items conforming "to the taste" (*konomi*) of a tea practitioner. For several of the objects named after the owners, see illustrations in Kyōto Kokuritsu Hakubutsu-kan, ed., *Tokubetsu tenrankai yonhyaku-nenki Sen no Rikyū ten,* nos. 12–35. The pedigrees, though occasionally mentioned in the diaries, were kept most faithfully on the boxes holding vessels, which were inscribed with the names of owners; Cort, *Shigaraki,* 130–31.

90. See Jōō's cypher on a black *natsume*-type caddy in Kyōto Kokuritsu Hakubutsu-kan, eds., *Tokubetsu tenrankai yonhyaku-nenki Sen no Rikyū ten,* no. 33. Sen no Rikyū later adopted the practice.

91. See Noma and Oyama, ed., *Cha no bijutsu to kōgei,* 73–77, 103–22, 216–25, 210–13. Also see the modern commentary on *Matsuya kaiki, CKZ* 9:473.

92. Haga, "*Wabi* Aesthetic Through the Ages"; Kumakura, *Chanoyū.*

93. Hirota, "Practice of Tea 2: The *Wabi* Tea of Takeno Jō-ō," 9–10.

94. Ibid., 7–24, for a discussion of the letter and Jōō's place in tea. Hirota argues for the authenticity of the letter.

95. *Sōchō shūki,* Daiei 6 (1526)/8/15, p. 92.

96. See Kumakura, *Chanoyū no rekishi,* 131–44, for an excellent discussion of both *wabi* and *suki* and the linkages between the terms.

97. The exceptions include the Shukō and Jōō letters, if they are authentic (see Hirota, "Practice of Tea 1: Heart's Mastery" and "Practice of Tea 2: The *Wabi* Tea of Takeno Jō-ō"), and *Chagu bitō-shū,* if it does date from 1554.

98. See notes 53 and 67 of this chapter. Also see, for an excellent discussion of the contested structure of artistic authority in the early Edo period, Kumakura, "Kan'ei Culture and *Chanoyū.*"

99. See Nagashima, *Chūsei bunkajin no kiroku,* 169–82.

100. Tsuda Sōtatsu, for example, was one of the thirty-six councillors of Sakai, and Imai Sōkyū was a quartermaster who provided Toyotomi Hideyoshi with gunpowder and niter; Kuwata, *Taikō no tegami*, 14.

101. *Yamanoue Sōji-ki* (*CKZ* 6:102).

Afterword

1. In a diary entry for 1506, Sanjōnishi Sanetaka refers to a pair of screens representing Kyoto painted by Tosa Mitsunobu for the Asakura house of Echizen (*Sanetaka kō-ki*, Eishō 3/12/22). This is the earliest explicit reference to portrayals of the city, although the content of these Mitsunobu screens is unknown. (The reference may be to screens depicting scenes of the monthly ritual calendar.) Until recently, scholars have been familiar with only two extant pairs of screens depicting the capital and its environs that date from wartime: the "Machida" (or "Sanjō") pair, in the collection of the National Museum of History and Ethnography, which pictures Kyoto after 1525 and before the Hokke uprising; and the "Uesugi" pair, in the possession of Yonezawa City, which pictures Kyoto in the late 1540s. A copy of a third pair, no longer surviving in the original, is held by the Tokyo National Museum. (This is known as the Tōhaku copy.) An additional pair of screens depicting the capital and its environs was found in 1986. Known as the Takahashi pair, this set may predate the Uesugi screens (and certainly postdates the Machida screens), although considerable debate surrounds the issue. For reproductions and close analyses of the screens, with discussions of their dating and authorship and precursors, see Ishida, ed., *Rakuchū rakugai-zu taikan;* Kyōto Kokuritsu Hakubutsu-kan et al., eds., *Rakuchū rakugai-zu;* Okami and Satake, *Hyōchū rakuchū rakugai byōbu;* Takahashi, *Rakuchū rakugai-zu;* Imatani, *Kyōto 1547 nen;* and the special edition of the journal *Kokka*, no. 1105 (1987), "Rakuchū rakugai-zu." The *Kokka* number contains an extensive discussion of the Takahashi screens in Kobayashi, "Shinshutsu no shoki rakuchū rakugai-zu byōbu ni tsuite"; Takahashi, "Shoki rakuchū rakugai-zu byōbu no kaiga shiryō ronteki saikentō"; and Tsuji, "Uesugi iemoto rakuchū rakugai-zu saikō."

2. The screens are only apparently maplike. With a certain fidelity to the geography of the city and the location of its landmarks, they nonetheless mix and transpose sites, invent and eliminate buildings, in representations that contrive their subject. Takahashi Yasuo is particularly emphatic on the fictionality of the screens; "Shoki rakuchū rakugai-zu byōbu no kaiga shiryō ronteki saikentō."

3. For a discussion of the screens' reflection of fortification during wartime, see Takahashi, *Kyōto chūsei toshi-shi kenkyū*, 364–72.

4. Separate labels were actually affixed to the Machida screens, either at the time of their creation or later. Labels on the Uesugi screens were inscribed on the surface itself, probably at the time of creation. The Takahashi screens lack labels.

5. For a discussion of the "small Kyoto," see *KR* 3:663–75; Miyata, *Shō-Kyōto hyakusen.*

6. *Kangin-shū,* 62–63.

7. For reproductions and analysis of the Edo screens, see Suzuki, ed., *Edo-zu byōbu.* For Momoyama and Edo period representations of Kyoto, in which various monuments associated with the military loom prominently, see Kyōto Kokuritsu Hakubutsu-kan et al., eds., *Rakuchū rakugai-zu.*

8. None of the early screen painters nor any of their patrons has been identified with certainty, although the Kanō (sometimes the Tosa) school of artists is often associated with them. The widespread attribution of the Uesugi screens to Kanō Eitoku has been forcefully challenged by Imatani Akira but defended by Tsuji Nobuo ("Uesugi iemoto rakuchū rakugai-zu saikō"). The patronage issue is equally fraught with controversy, but I believe the content of the screens discourages their association with a local patron. The commoner world lacks the notable Hokke temples, the presumably gracious residences of the affluent townspeople, and the acknowledgment of an important brewer/broker community that I suspect we would find in paintings commissioned by a prosperous merchant. The military presence is at once so innocuous and so harmonious as to discourage association with a Hosokawa or Ashikaga patron. It is unlikely that courtiers could have financed the paintings and equally unlikely that the content corresponded with the aristocratic perception of the capital.

Bibliography

Abe Kin'ya, Amino Yoshihiko, Ishii Susumu, and Kabayama Kōichi. *Chūsei no fukei.* 2 vols. Tokyo: Chūō Kōron-sha, 1981.

Aiba Shin. "Junkyō no hitobito." In Tamura Yoshirō and Miyazaki Eishu, eds., *Nichiren shinkō no rekishi,* 99–114. Tokyo: Shunshū-sha, 1972.

Akeda Tetsuo. *Ransei Kyōto.* 2 vols. Kyoto: Shirakawa Shoin, 1969.

Akiyama Kunizō. *Kinsei Kyōto machigumi hattatsu-shi.* Tokyo: Hōsei Daigaku Shuppan-kyoku, 1980.

———, ed. *Kōdo enkaku-shi.* 2 vols. Kyoto: Gen Kyōto-shi Kōdo Rengō-kai Jimusho, 1933–34.

Akiyama Kunizō and Nakamura Ken. *Kyōto "chō" no kenkyū.* Tokyo: Hōsei Daigaku Shuppan-kyoku, 1975.

Amino Yoshihiko. *Chūsei tennō-sei to hi-nōgyōmin.* Tokyo: Iwanami Shoten, 1984.

———. "Chūsei toshi-ron." In *Iwanami kōza Nihon rekishi 7, chūsei 3:* 253–304. Tokyo: Iwanami Shoten, 1976.

———. *Nihon chūsei no minshū-zō.* Tokyo: Iwanami Shoten, 1980.

———. "Some Problems Concerning the History of Popular Life in Medieval Japan." *Acta Asiatica* 44 (1983; "Studies in Japanese Medieval Social and Economic History"): 77–97.

Amino Yoshihiko and Abe Kin'ya. *Chūsei no saihakken.* Tokyo: Heibon-sha, 1982.

Amino Yoshihiko, Ishii Susumu, Kasamatsu Hiroshi, and Katsumata Shizuo. *Chūsei no tsumi to batsu.* Tokyo: Tōkyō Daigaku Shuppan-kai, 1983.

Arnesen, Peter Judd. *The Medieval Japanese Daimyo: The Ōuchi Family's Rule of Suō and Nagato.* New Haven: Yale University Press, 1979.

———. "The Provincial Vassals of the Muromachi Shoguns." In Jeffrey P. Mass and William B. Hauser, eds., *The Bakufu in Japanese History,* 99–128. Stanford: Stanford University Press, 1985.

Asano Kenji. *Chūsei kayō.* Tokyo: Haniwa Shobō, 1964.

———, ed. *Shintei chūsei kayō-shū.* Tokyo: Asahi Shinbun-sha, 1973.

Asao Naohiro, ed. *Ken'i to shihai. Nihon no shakai-shi* 3. Tokyo: Iwanami Shoten, 1987.

———. " 'Shōgun kenryoku' no sōshutsu," part 1. *Rekishi hyōron,* August 1970.

Asukai Masamichi, ed. *Ōtsu-shi shi.* 10 vols. Otsu: Ōtsu Shiyakusho, 1978–87.

Atsuta Kō. "Minshū bunka no genryū: Machishū bunka, odori to matsuri." In Nihon-shi Kenkyū-kai, ed. *Ōnin-Genroku. Kōza Nihon bunka-shi* 4:111–81. Tokyo: San'ichi Shobō, 1962.

Bakhtin, Mikhail. *Rabelais and His World.* Trans. Helene Iswolsky. Bloomington: Indiana University Press, 1984.

Berry, Mary Elizabeth. *Hideyoshi.* Cambridge: Harvard University Press, 1982.

———. "Public Peace and Private Attachment: The Goals and Conduct of Power in Early Modern Japan." *Journal of Japanese Studies* 12, no. 2 (Summer 1986): 237–71.

———. "Restoring the Past: The Documents of Hideyoshi's Magistrate in Kyoto." *Harvard Journal of Asiatic Studies* 43, no. 1 (June 1983): 57–95.

———. Review of Kozo Yamamura, ed., *Cambridge History of Japan: Volume 3, Medieval Japan. Journal of Japanese Studies* 18, no. 2 (Summer 1992): 479–92.

Burckhardt, Jacob. *The Civilization of the Renaissance in Italy.* Trans. S. G. C. Middlemore. New York: Penguin Books, 1990.

Carter, Steven D. *The Road to Komatsubara: A Classical Reading of the Renga Hyakuin.* Cambridge: Harvard University Press, Council on East Asian Studies, 1987.

———. *Three Poets at Yuyama. Japan Research Monographs* 4. Berkeley: University of California, Institute of East Asian Studies, 1983.

Chagu bitō-shū. In Sen Sōshitsu, ed., *Chadō zenshū* 15:583–98. Tokyo: Sōgensha, 1946 [1936].

Chanoyū dōgu nayose, appendix to *Enshū onkura moto chō.* See *Enshū onkura moto chō.*

Chikanaga kyō-ki. See Kanrōji Chikanaga.

Chikatoshi nikki. See Ninagawa Chikatoshi.

CHSS/MBH. See Satō Shin'ichi and Ikeuchi Yoshisuke, eds. *Muromachi bakufu hō.*

CKZ. See Sen Sōshitsu, ed. *Chadō koten zenshū.*

Clark, Katerina, and Michael Holquist. *Mikhail Bakhtin.* Cambridge: Harvard University Press, 1984.

Cooper, Michael, comp. *They Came to Japan.* Berkeley and Los Angeles: University of California Press, 1965.

———, ed. and trans. *This Island of Japon: João Rodrigues' Account of Sixteenth-Century Japan.* Tokyo: Kodansha International, 1973.

Cort, Louise Allison. *Shigaraki, Potters' Valley.* Tokyo: Kodansha International, 1979.

Daijōin jisha zōjiki. Takeuchi Rizō, ed. *Zōho zoku shiryō taisei* 26–37. Tokyo: Rinsen Shoten, 1978.

Davis, David L. "*Ikki* in Late Medieval Japan." In John Whitney Hall and Jeffrey P. Mass, eds., *Medieval Japan: Essays in Institutional History,* 221–47. New Haven: Yale University Press, 1974.

Dobbins, James. *Jōdo Shinshū: Shin Buddhism in Medieval Japan.* Bloomington: Indiana University Press, 1989.

Elison, George, and Bardwell L. Smith, eds. *Warlords, Artists, and Commoners: Japan in the Sixteenth Century.* Honolulu: University Press of Hawaii, 1981.

Enshū onkura moto chō. In Sen Sōshitsu, ed., *Chadō koten zenshū* 12:113–329. Kyoto: Tankō-sha, 1962.

Farris, William Wayne. *Heavenly Warriors: The Evolution of Japan's Military, 500–1300.* Cambridge: Harvard University Press, Council on East Asian Studies, 1992.

———. Review of Kozo Yamamura, ed., *The Cambridge History of Japan: Volume 3, Medieval Japan. Harvard Journal of Asiatic Studies* 52, no. 1 (June 1992): 327–38.

Friday, Karl F. *Hired Swords: The Rise of Private Warrior Power in Early Japan.* Stanford: Stanford University Press, 1992.

Fujiki Hisashi. "Ikkō ikki ron." In Rekishi-gaku Kenkyū-kai and Nihon-shi Kenkyū-kai, eds., *Kōza Nihon rekishi 4, chūsei 2,* 199–232. Tokyo: Tōkyō Daigaku Shuppan-kai, 1985.

———. *Sengoku daimyō no kenryoku kōzō.* Tokyo: Yoshikawa Kōbun-kan, 1987.

———. "Sengoku no dōran." In Rekishi-gaku Kenkyū-kai and Nihon-shi Kenkyū-kai, eds., *Hōken shakai no tenkai. Kōza Nihon-shi* 3:265–96. Tokyo: Tōkyō Daigaku Shuppan-kai, 1970.

———. *Sengoku no sahō.* Tokyo: Heibon-sha, 1987.

———. *Sengoku shakai-shi ron.* Tokyo: Tōkyō Daigaku Shuppan-kai, 1974.

———. *Toyotomi heiwa-rei to sengoku shakai.* Tokyo: Tōkyō Daigaku Shuppan-kai, 1985.

———. "Zai-ichi ryōshu no kōri-gashi kinō ni tsuite." In Murata Shūzō, ed., *Kinki daimyō no kenkyū,* 205–37. Tokyo: Yoshikawa Kōbun-kan, 1986.

Gay, Suzanne. "Muromachi Bakufu Rule in Kyoto: Administrative and Judicial Aspects." In Jeffrey P. Mass and William B. Hauser, eds., *The Bakufu in Japanese History,* 49–65. Stanford: Stanford University Press, 1985.

Geinō-shi Kenkyū-kai, ed. *Butō—kinsei no uta to odori. Nihon no koten geinō.* Tokyo: Heibon-sha, 1970.

Gen'i Hōin gejijō. See Maeda Gen'i.

Gilbert, Felix. *Machiavelli and Guicciardini: Politics and History in Sixteenth-Century Florence.* Princeton: Princeton University Press, 1973.

Go-Hōkōin-ki. See Konoe Masaie.

Gorai Shigeru. "Fūryū no odori." In Geinō-shi Kenkyū-kai, ed., *Butō—kinsei no uta to odori. Nihon no koten geinō* 6:147–65. Tokyo: Heibon-sha, 1970.

———. *Odori to nenbutsu.* Tokyo: Heibon-sha, 1988.

Grossberg, Kenneth Alan. "Bakufu *Bugyōnin*: The Size of the Lower Bureaucracy in Muromachi Japan." *Journal of Asian Studies* 35, no. 4 (August 1976): 651–54.

――――. *Japan's Renaissance: The Politics of the Muromachi Bakufu*. Cambridge: Harvard University Press, Council on East Asian Studies, 1981.

――――, ed. *The Laws of the Muromachi Bakufu*. Trans. Grossberg and Kanamoto Nobuhisa. Tokyo: Sophia University, 1981.

Guicciardini, Francesco. *The History of Italy*. Trans. Sidney Alexander. (1969).

Haga Kōshirō. "Chanoyū no kaiso." In Kuwata Tadachika, ed., *Cha ni ikita hito* 1. *Zusetsu chadō taikei* 6:73–97. Tokyo: Kadokawa Shoten, 1963.

――――. *Sanjōnishi Sanetaka*. Tokyo: Yoshikawa Kōbun-kan, 1960.

――――. *Sen no Rikyū*. Tokyo: Yoshikawa Kōbun-kan, 1963.

――――. "The Wabi Aesthetic Through the Ages." In H. Paul Varley and Kumakura Isao, eds., *Tea In Japan: Essays on the History of Chanoyū*, 195–230. Honolulu: University Press of Hawaii, 1989.

Haga Kōshirō and Nishiyama Matsunosuke, eds. *Cha no bunka-shi*. *Zusetsu chadō taikei* 2. Tokyo: Kadokawa Shoin, 1962.

Haga Norihiko. "Muromachi bakufu-ron." In Nihon Rekishi-gaku Kenkyū-kai, ed., *Nihon-shi no mondai-ten*, 93–107. Tokyo: Yoshikawa Kōbun-kan, 1965.

――――. *Sōryō-sei*. Tokyo: Shibun-dō, 1966.

Hall, John Whitney. *Government and Local Power in Japan, 500–1700*. Princeton: Princeton University Press, 1966.

――――. "Japan's Sixteenth-Century Revolution." In George Elison and Bardwell L. Smith, eds., *Warlords, Artists, and Commoners: Japan in the Sixteenth Century*, 7–21. Honolulu: University Press of Hawaii, 1981.

――――. "Kyoto as Historical Background." In John Whitney Hall and Jeffrey P. Mass, eds., *Medieval Japan: Essays in Institutional History*, 3–38. New Haven: Yale University Press, 1974.

――――. "The Muromachi Bakufu." In Kozo Yamamura, ed., *The Cambridge History of Japan: Volume 3, Medieval Japan*, 175–230. Cambridge: Cambridge University Press, 1990.

Hall, John Whitney, and Jeffrey P. Mass, eds. *Medieval Japan: Essays in Institutional History*. New Haven: Yale University Press, 1974.

Hall, John Whitney, Nagahara Keiji, and Kozo Yamamura, eds. *Japan Before Tokugawa: Political Consolidation and Economic Growth, 1500–1650*. Princeton: Princeton University Press, 1981.

Hall, John Whitney, and Toyoda Takeshi, eds. *Japan in the Muromachi Age*. Berkeley and Los Angeles: University of California Press, 1977.

Harada Tomohiko. *Chūsei ni okeru toshi no kenkyū*. Tokyo: Dai Nihon Yūbenkai Kōdan-sha, 1942.

Harada Tomohiko and Nishikawa Kōji, eds. *Kinki no shigai kozu*. *Nihon no shigai kozu* 3. Tokyo: Kojima Shoten, 1978.

Harrington, Lorraine F. "Regional Outposts of Muromachi Bakufu Rule: The Kanto and Kyushu." In Jeffrey P. Mass and William B. Hauser, eds., *The Bakufu in Japanese History*, 66–99. Stanford: Stanford University Press, 1985.

Hayashiya Tatsusaburō. *Chūsei bunka no kichō*. Tokyo: Tōkyō Daigaku Shuppan-kai, 1953.

――――. *Kyōto*. Tokyo: Iwanami Shoten, 1962.

――――. *Machishū: Kyōto ni okeru "shimin" keisei-shi*. Tokyo: Chūō Kōron-sha, 1964.

————. "Machishū no seikatsu to geijutsu." In Hayashiya, *Chūsei bunka no kichō*, 187–285. Tokyo: Tōkyō Daigaku Shuppan-kai, 1953.

————, ed. *Zuroku chadō-shi*. Kyoto: Tankō-sha, 1980.

————. *Zusetsu chadō-shi*. Kyoto: Tankō Shinsha, 1964.

Hayashiya Tatsusaburō, with George Elison. "Kyoto in the Muromachi Age." In John Whitney Hall and Toyoda Takeshi, eds., *Japan in the Muromachi Age*, 15–36. Berkeley and Los Angeles: University of California Press, 1977.

Hirota, Dennis. "The Practice of Tea 1: Heart's Mastery—The *Kokoro no fumi*, The Letter of Murato Shukō to His Disciple Chōin." *Chanoyū Quarterly: Tea and the Arts of Japan* 22 (1979): 7–24.

————. "The Practice of Tea 2: The *Wabi* Tea of Takeno Jō-ō, The Letter on *Wabi* and Selected Documents." *Chanoyū Quarterly: Tea and the Arts of Japan* 23 (1980): 7–21.

Hoff, Frank. "City and Country: Song and the Performing Arts in Sixteenth-Century Japan." In George Elison and Bardwell L. Smith, eds., *Warlords, Artists, and Commoners: Japan in the Sixteenth Century*, 133–62. Honolulu: University Press of Hawaii, 1981.

————. *The Genial Seed: A Japanese Song Cycle*. New York: Grossman, 1971.

Honda Yasuji. "Fūryū." In *Katarimono, fūryū. Nihon no minzoku geinō* 4. Tokyo: Kiji-sha, 1970.

Horiguchi Sutemi and Inagaki Eizō, eds. *Cha no kenchiku to niwa. Zusetsu chadō taikei* 4. Tokyo: Kadokawa Shoin, 1962.

Huizinga, Johan. *Homo Ludens: A Study of the Play-Element in Culture*. Boston: Beacon Press, 1970 [1950].

Hurst, G. Cameron, III. "The Development of the *Insei*: A Problem in Japanese History and Historiography." In John Whitney Hall and Jeffrey P. Mass, eds., *Medieval Japan: Essays in Institutional History*, 60–90. New Haven: Yale University Press, 1974.

————. "The Structure of the Heian Court: Some Thoughts on the Nature of Familial Authority." In John Whitney Hall and Jeffrey P. Mass, eds., *Medieval Japan: Essays in Institutional History*, 39–59. New Haven: Yale University Press, 1974.

Iguchi Minoru and Nagashima Fukutarō, eds. *Genshoku chadō daijiten*. Kyoto: Tankō-sha, 1980.

Ike Susumu. "Daimyō ryōgoku-sei no tenkai to shōgun, tennō." In Rekishi-gaku Kenkyū-kai and Nihon-shi Kenkyū-kai, eds., *Kōza Nihon rekishi 4, chūsei 2*, 233–44. Tokyo: Tōkyō Daigaku Shuppan-kai, 1985.

Ikegami Hiroko. "Sengoku daimyō ryōgoku ni okeru shoryō oyobi kashindan hensei no tenkai." In Nagahara Keiji, ed., *Sengoku-ki no kenryoku to shakai*, 35–103. Tokyo: Tōkyō Daigaku Shuppan-kai, 1976.

Imai Sōkyū. *Imai Sōkyū chanoyū nikki nukigaki*. In Sen Sōshitsu, ed., *Chadō koten zenshū* 10:1–64. Kyoto: Tankō-sha, 1961.

Imatani Akira. *Kyōto 1547 nen: Egakareta chūsei toshi*. Tokyo: Heibon-sha, 1988.

————. "Muromachi Local Government: *Shugo* and *Kokujin*." Trans. Suzanne Gay. In Kozo Yamamura, ed., *The Cambridge History of Japan: Volume 3, Medieval Japan*, 231–59. Cambridge: Cambridge University Press, 1990.

————. *Ōnin no ran. Shūkan Asahi hyakka Nihon no rekishi 18, chūsei 2,* no. 7. Tokyo: Asahi Shinbun-sha, 1981.

————. *Sengoku-ki no Muromachi bakufu.* Tokyo: Kadokawa Shoten, 1975.

————. *Sengoku Miyoshi ichizoku.* Tokyo: Jinbutsu Ōrai-sha, 1985.

————. *Shugo ryōgoku shihai kikō no kenkyū.* Tokyo: Hōsei Daigaku Shuppan-kyoku, 1986.

————. *Tenbun Hokke no ran.* Tokyo: Heibon-sha, 1989.

————. *Tokitsugu kyō-ki: Kuge shakai to machishū bunka no setten.* Tokyo: Kabushiki Gaisha Soshiete, 1980.

Imatani Akira and Takahashi Yasuo, eds. *Muromachi bakufu monjo shūsei, bugyō-nin hōsho hen.* 2 vols. Kyoto: Shibunkaku Shuppan, 1986.

Imatani Akira, with Kozo Yamamura. "Not for Lack of Will or Wile: Yoshimi-tsu's Failure to Supplant the Imperial Lineage." *Journal of Japanese Studies* 18, no. 1 (Winter 1992): 45–78.

Inoue Toshio. *Ikkō ikki no kenkyū.* Tokyo: Yoshikawa Kōbun-kan, 1968.

————. *Yama no tami, kawa no tami—Nihon chūsei no seikatsu to shinkō.* Tokyo: Heibon-sha, 1981.

Ishida Hisatoyo, Naitō Akira, and Moriya Katsuhisa, eds. *Rakuchū rakugai-zu taikan.* 3 vols. Tokyo: Shōgaku-kan, 1987.

Ishii Ryōsuke. *Nihon hōsei-shi teiyō.* Tokyo: Sōbun-sha, 1952.

Ishii Susumu. "Chūsei shakai-ron." In *Iwanami kōza Nihon rekishi 7, chūsei 3,* 305–46. Tokyo: Iwanami Shoten, 1976.

Itō Teiji. *Chūsei jūkyo-shi.* Tokyo: Tōkyō Daigaku Shuppan-kai, 1973 [1958].

Iwahashi Koyata. *Nihon geinō-shi: Chūsei kabu no kenkyū.* Tokyo: Geien-sha, 1951.

Iwasaki Yoshie. *Shokunin uta-awase.* Tokyo: Heibon-sha, 1988.

Kadokawa Nihon Chimei Daijiten Hensan Iinkai, ed. *Kyōto-fu. Kadokawa Nihon chimei daijiten* 26. Tokyo: Kadokawa Shoten, 1983.

Kamiki Tetsuo. "Chūsei kōki ni okeru bukka hendō." *Shakai keizai-gaku* 34 (1968): 21–38.

Kamiya Sōtan. *Kamiya Sōtan nikki.* Sen Sōshitsu, ed., *Chadō koten zenshū* 6. Kyoto: Tankō-sha, 1958.

Kangin-shū. In Asano Kenji, ed., *Shintei chūsei kayō-shū,* 41–161. Tokyo: Asahi Shinbun-sha, 1973.

Kanrōji Chikanaga. *Chikanaga kyō-ki.* Sasakawa Taneo, comp., *Shiryō taisei* 39–41. Tokyo: Naigai Shoseki Kabushiki Gaisha, 1940–41.

Kanrōji Motonaga. *Motonaga kyō-ki.* Haga Kōshirō, ed., *Shiryō sanshū* 23. Tokyo: Zoku Gunsho Ruijū Kansei-kai, 1973.

Kasahara Kazuo. *Rennyo.* Tokyo: Yoshikawa Kōbun-kan, 1963.

Kasamatsu Hiroshi. "Chūsei no seiji, shakai, shisō." In *Iwanami kōza Nihon rekishi 7, chūsei 3,* 305–46. Tokyo: Iwanami Shoten, 1976.

————. *Hō to kotoba no chūsei-shi.* Tokyo: Heibon-sha, 1984.

————. "Youchi." In Amino Yoshihiko et al., *Chūsei no tsumi to batsu,* 89–102. Tokyo: Tōkyō Daigaku Shuppan-kai, 1983.

Kasamatsu Hiroshi and Katsumata Shizuo. *Tokusei-rei: Chūsei no hō to saiban. Shūkan Asahi hyakka Nihon no rekishi 8, chūsei 1,* no. 8. Tokyo: Asahi Shinbun-sha, 1981.

Katsumata Shizuo. "Ie o yaku." In Amino Yoshihiko et al., *Chūsei no tsumi to batsu*, 15–26. Tokyo: Tōkyō Daigaku Shuppan-kai, 1983.

———. *Ikki*. Tokyo: Iwanami Shoten, 1982.

———. "Mimi o kiri, hana o sogu." In Amino Yoshihiko et al., *Chūsei no tsumi to batsu*, 27–42. Tokyo: Tōkyō Daigaku Shuppan-kai, 1983.

———. *Sengoku hō seiritsu shiron*. Tokyo: Tōkyō Daigaku Shuppan-kai, 1979.

———. "Shigai tekitai." In Amino Yoshihiko et al., *Chūsei no tsumi to batsu*, 43–58. Tokyo: Tōkyō Daigaku Shuppan-kai, 1983.

Katsumata Shizuo, with Martin Collcutt. "The Development of Sengoku Law." In John Whitney Hall, Nagahara Keiji, and Kozo Yamamura, eds., *Japan Before Tokugawa: Political Consolidation and Economic Growth, 1500–1650*, 101–24. Princeton: Princeton University Press, 1981.

Kawai Masaharu. *Ashikaga Yoshimasa*. Tokyo: Shimizu Shoin, 1972.

———. *Chūsei buke shakai no kenkyū*. Tokyo: Yoshikawa Kōbun-kan, 1973.

Kawai Masaharu, with Kenneth A. Grossberg. "Shogun and Shugo: The Provincial Aspects of Muromachi Politics." In John Whitney Hall and Toyoda Takeshi, eds., *Japan in the Muromachi Age*, 65–86. Berkeley and Los Angeles: University of California Press, 1977.

Kawasaki Chizuru. "Muromachi bakufu no hōkai katei." In Murata Shūzō, ed., *Kinki daimyō no kenkyū*, 49–82. Tokyo: Yoshikawa Kōbun-kan, 1986.

Keene, Donald. "Jōha, a Sixteenth-Century Poet of Linked Verse." In George Elison and Bardwell L. Smith, eds., *Warlords, Artists, and Commoners: Japan in the Sixteenth Century*, 113–31. Honolulu: University Press of Hawaii, 1981.

———. "Nikki ni miru Nihon." *Asahi shinbun*, January 18, 1984.

Kefukigusa. Ed. Takenaka Wakae. Tokyo: Iwanami Shoten, 1943.

Kenmu shikimoku. In Satō Shin'ichi and Ikeuchi Yoshisuke, eds., *Muromachi bakufu hō. Chūsei hōsei shiryō-shū* 2:3–10. Tokyo: Iwanami Shoten, 1957.

Kiley, Cornelius J. "Estate and Property in the Late Heian Period." In John Whitney Hall and Jeffrey P. Mass, eds., *Medieval Japan: Essays in Institutional History*, 19–24. New Haven: Yale University Press, 1974.

Kingen wakashū. In Hanawa Hokiichi, comp., *Zoku gunsho ruijū*, ser. 33, pt. 2, vol. 983, pp. 40–59. Tokyo: Zoku Gunsho Ruijū Kansei-kai, 1963.

Kishida Hiroshi. "Chūsei kōki no chihō keizai to toshi." In Rekishi-gaku Kenkyū-kai and Nihon-shi Kenkyū-kai, eds., *Kōza Nihon rekishi 4, chūsei 2*, 83–158. Tokyo: Tōkyō Daigaku Shuppan-kai, 1985.

Kissa ōrai. In Sen Sōshitsu, ed., *Chadō koten zenshū* 2:163–213. Kyoto: Tankō-sha, 1958.

Kitazume Masao. "Kokujin ryōshu to dogō." In Rekishi-gaku Kenkyū-kai and Nihon-shi Kenkyū-kai, eds., *Hōken shakai no tenkai. Kōza Nihon-shi* 3:117–38. Tokyo: Tōkyō Daigaku Shuppan-kai, 1970.

Kobayashi Seiji. "Sengoku sōran no tenkai." In *Iwanami kōza Nihon rekishi 8, chūsei 4*, 1–44. Tokyo: Iwanami Shoten, 1976.

Kobayashi Tadashi. "Shinshutsu no shoki rakuchū rakugai-zu byōbu ni tsuite." *Kokka*, no. 1105 (1987): 19–24.

Kodama Kōta, Nakada Yoshinao, Hayashi Hideo, Bitō Masahide, Kimura Motoi, Nishiyama Matsunosuke, and Hayashi Ryōshō. *Kinsei-shi handobukku.* Tokyo: Kintō Shuppan-sha, 1972.

Kokushi Daijiten Henshū Iinkai, ed. *Kokushi daijiten.* 14 vols. Tokyo: Yoshikawa Kōbun-kan, 1979–93.

Konoe Masaie. *Go-Hōkōin-ki.* Takeuchi Rizō, ed., *Zoku shiryō taisei* 5–8. Kyoto: Rinsen Shoten, 1967.

Koyama Yasunori. "Chūsei senmin-ron." In Rekishi-gaku Kenkyū-kai and Nihon-shi Kenkyū-kai, eds., *Kōza Nihon rekishi 4, chūsei 2,* 159–98. Tokyo: Tōkyō Daigaku Shuppan-kai, 1985.

KR. See Kyōto-shi, ed., *Kyōto no rekishi.*

Kugyō bunin. Kuroita Katsumi, ed., *Shintei zōho kokushi taikei* 53–57. Tokyo: Kokushi Taikei Kankō-kai, 1934–38.

Kumakura Isao. *Chanoyū no rekishi: Sen no Rikyū made.* Tokyo: Asahi Shinbun-sha, 1990.

———. *Chanoyū nyūmon.* Tokyo: Heibon-sha, 1985.

———. *Chanoyū: Wabicha no kokoro to katachi.* Tokyo: Kyōiku-sha, 1977.

———. "Kan'ei Culture and *Chanoyū.*" In H. Paul Varley and Kumakura, eds., *Tea in Japan: Essays on the History of* Chanoyū, 135–60. Honolulu: The University Press of Hawaii, 1989.

Kundaikan sōchō-ki. In Hanawa Hokiichi, ed., *Shinkō gunsho ruijū,* ser. 15, vol. 361, pp. 767–79. Tokyo: Meicho Fukyū-kai, 1977 [1928].

Kuroda Hideo. *Kyōkai no chūsei, shōchō no chūsei.* Tokyo: Tōkyō Daigaku Shuppan-kai, 1986.

Kuroda Toshio. *Rekishi-gaku no saisei: Chūsei-shi o kuminaosu.* Tokyo: Azekura Shobō, 1983.

Kurokawa Naonori. "Chūsei kōki no nōmin tōsō." In Rekishi-gaku Kenkyū-kai and Nihon-shi Kenkyū-kai, eds., *Hōken shakai no tenkai. Kōza Nihon-shi* 3:227–50. Tokyo: Tōkyō Daigaku Shuppan-kai, 1970.

Kuwata Tadachika. *Cha ni ikita hito* 1. *Zusetsu chadō taikei* 6. Tokyo: Kadokawa Shoin, 1963.

———. *Sadō no rekishi.* Tokyo: Tōkyō-dō Shuppan, 1967.

———. *Taikō-ki no kenkyū.* Tokyo: Tokuma Shoten, 1965.

———. *Taikō no tegami.* Tokyo: Bungei Shunjū-sha, 1959.

———, ed. *Taikō shiryō-shū.* Tokyo: Jinbutsu Ōrai-sha, 1971.

———. *Yodogimi.* Tokyo: Yoshikawa Kōbun-kan, 1958.

Kuwayama Kōnen, ed. *Muromachi bakufu hikitsuke shiryō shūsei.* Tokyo: Kondō Shuppan-sha, 1980.

Kuwayama Kōnen, with John Whitney Hall. "The *Bugyōnin* System: A Closer Look." In John Whitney Hall and Toyoda Takeshi, eds., *Japan in the Muromachi Age,* 53–63. Berkeley and Los Angeles: University of California Press, 1977.

Kyōto Kokuritsu Hakubutsu-kan, ed. *Rakuchū rakugai-zu.* Tokyo: Kadokawa Shoten, 1966.

———. *Tokubetsu tenrankai yonhyaku-nenki Sen no Rikyū ten.* Kyoto: Mainichi Shinbun-sha, 1990.

Kyōto-shi, ed. *Kyōto no rekishi.* 10 vols. Tokyo: Gakugei Shorin, 1968–76.

————, ed. *Shiryō Kyōto no rekishi*. 16 vols. projected. Tokyo: Heibon-sha, 1979 (vol. 3); 1980 (vols. 4 and 7); 1981 (vol. 12); 1983 (vol. 2); 1984 (vol. 5); 1985 (vols. 8 and 9); 1987 (vol. 10); 1988 (vol. 11).

Maeda Gen'i. *Gen'i Hōin gejijō*. In Hanawa Hokiichi, comp., *Zoku gunsho ruijū*, ser. 23, pt. 2, vol. 666, pp. 329–42. Tokyo: Zoku Gunsho Ruijū Kansei-kai, 1961.

Mass, Jeffrey P., ed. *Court and Bakufu in Japan: Essays in Kamakura History*. New Haven: Yale University Press, 1982.

————. *The Development of Kamakura Rule, 1180–1250: A History with Documents*. Stanford: Stanford University Press, 1979.

————. "The Kamakura Bakufu." In Kozo Yamamura, ed., *The Cambridge History of Japan: Volume 3, Medieval Japan*, 46–88. Cambridge: Cambridge University Press, 1990.

————. *The Kamakura Bakufu: A Study in Documents*. Stanford: Stanford University Press, 1976.

————. *Lordship and Inheritance in Early Medieval Japan: A Study of the Kamakura Sōryō System*. Stanford: Stanford University Press, 1989.

————. *Warrior Government in Early Medieval Japan: A Study of the Kamakura Bakufu, Shugo, and Jitō*. New Haven: Yale University Press, 1974.

————. "What Can We Not Know About the Kamakura Bakufu?" In Mass and William B. Hauser, eds., *The Bakufu in Japanese History*, 13–30. Stanford: Stanford University Press, 1985.

Mass, Jeffrey P., and William B. Hauser, eds. *The Bakufu in Japanese History*. Stanford: Stanford University Press, 1985.

Matsunaga Teitoku. *Taion-ki*. Odaka Toshirō, ed., *Nihon koten bungaku taikei* 95. Tokyo: Iwanami Shoten, 1964.

Matsuya Hisamisa, Matsuya Hisayoshi, and Matsuya Hisashige. *Matsuya kaiki*. Sen Sōshitsu, ed., *Chadō koten zenshū* 9. Kyoto: Tankō-sha, 1957.

Matsuya kaiki. See Matsuya Hisamasa.

MBMS/BHH. See Imatani Akira and Takahashi Yasuo, eds., *Muromachi bakufu monjo shūsei, bugyōnin hōsho hen*.

Minegishi Sumio, ed. *Honganji, Ikkō ikki no kenkyū. Sengoku daimyō ronshū* 13. Tokyo: Yoshikawa Kōbun-kan, 1984.

————. "Ikkō ikki." In *Iwanami kōza Nihon rekishi 8, chūsei 4*, 127–74. Tokyo: Iwanami Shoten, 1976.

Misumi Haruo. "Fūryū-ko." In *Geinō-shi no minzoku-teki kenkyū*. Tokyo: Tōkyō-dō Shuppan, 1976.

————. "Minzoku to geijutsu no aida: Matsuri, asobi, odori, mai, to geki." In Geinō-shi Kenkyū-kai, ed., *Butō—kinsei no uta to odori. Nihon no koten geinō* 6:7–64. Tokyo: Heibon-sha, 1970.

Miura Keiichi. "Chūsei no bungyō ryūtsū to toshi." In Minegishi Sumio, ed., *Taikei Nihon kokka-shi, chūsei* 1:159–205. Tokyo: Tōkyō Daigaku Shuppan-kai, 1975.

————. "Jūroku seiki ni okeru chiiki-teki bungyō ryūtsū no kōzō." In Nagahara Keiji, ed., *Sengoku-ki no kenryoku to shakai*, 231–63. Tokyo: Tōkyō Daigaku Shuppan-kai, 1976.

———. "Sengoku-ki no kōeki to kōtsū." In *Iwanami kōza Nihon rekishi 8, chū-sei 4*, 90–125. Tokyo: Iwanami Shoten, 1976.

Miyagawa Mitsuru, with Cornelius J. Kiley. "From *Shōen* to *Chigyō*: Proprietary Lordship and the Structure of Local Power." In John Whitney Hall and Toyoda Takeshi, eds., *Japan in the Muromachi Age*, 89–107. Berkeley and Los Angeles: University of California Press, 1977.

Miyata Teru. *Shō-Kyōto hyakusen*. Tokyo: Akita Shoten, 1975.

Momose Kesao. "Ōnin, Bunmei no ran." In *Iwanami kōza Nihon rekishi 7, chū-sei 3*, 177–218. Tokyo: Iwanami Shoten, 1976.

Mori Teru, ed. *Nihon emakimono zenshū* 28. Tokyo: Kadokawa Shoten, 1980.

Morisue Yoshiaki. "Nō to hogosha." In Nogami Toyoichirō, ed., *Nō no rekishi. Nōgaku zensho* 2:198–235. Tokyo: Sōgen-sha, 1942.

Morita Kyōji. "Hosokawa Takakuni to Kinai kokujin-zō." In Murata Shūzō, ed., *Kinki daimyō no kenkyū*, 240–75. Tokyo: Yoshikawa Kōbun-kan, 1986.

———. "Sengoku-ki Kinai ni okeru shugo-dai, kokujin-zō no dōkō." In Murata Shūzō, ed., *Kinki daimyō no kenkyū*, 276–310. Tokyo: Yoshikawa Kōbun-kan, 1986.

Motonaga kyō-ki. See Kanrōji Motonaga.

Murai Yasuhiko. "A Biography of Sen Rikyū." *Chanoyū Quarterly: Tea and the Arts of Japan*, 61 (1990): 7–56.

———. "The Development of *Chanoyū*: Before Rikyū." In H. Paul Varley and Kumakura Isao, eds., *Tea in Japan: Essays on the History of Chanoyū*, 3–32. Honolulu: University of Hawaii Press, 1989.

———. *Sen no Rikyū*. Tokyo: Nippon Hōsō Shuppan-kyōkai, 1971.

Murata Shūzō, ed. *Kinki daimyō no kenkyū. Sengoku daimyō ronshū* 5. Tokyo: Yoshikawa Kōbun-kan, 1986.

———. "Sō to do ikki." In *Iwanami kōza Nihon rekishi 7, chūsei 3*, 135–76. Tokyo: Iwanami Shoten, 1976.

Nagahara Keiji. "Chūsei no shakai kōsei to hōken-sei." In Rekishi-gaku Kenkyū-kai and Nihon-shi Kenkyū-kai, eds., *Kōza Nihon rekishi 4, chūsei 2*, 317–57. Tokyo: Tōkyō Daigaku Shuppan-kai, 1985.

———. "Daimyō ryōgoku seika no nōmin shihai gensoku." In Nagahara Keiji, ed., *Sengoku-ki no kenryoku to shakai*, 105–53. Tokyo: Tōkyō Daigaku Shuppan-kai, 1976.

———. "The Decline of the *Shōen* System." Trans. Michael P. Birt. In Kozo Yamamura, ed., *The Cambridge History of Japan: Volume 3, Medieval Japan*, 260–300. Cambridge: Cambridge University Press, 1990.

———. "The Medieval Origins of the *Eta-Hinin*." *Journal of Japanese Studies* 5, no. 2 (Summer 1979): 385–405.

———. "The Medieval Peasant." Trans. Suzanne Gay. In Kozo Yamamura, ed., *The Cambridge History of Japan: Volume 3, Medieval Japan*, 301–43. Cambridge: Cambridge University Press, 1990.

———. *Nairan to minshū no seiki. Taikei Nihon no rekishi* 6. Tokyo: Shōgaku-kan, 1988.

———. *Nihon chūsei no shakai to kokka*. Tokyo: Nippon Hōsō Shuppan-kyōkai, 1982.

———. *Nihon rekishi taikei 2: Chūsei*. Tokyo: Yamakawa Shuppankai, 1985.

———, ed. *Sengoku daimyō ronshū*. 18 vols. Tokyo: Yoshikawa Kōbun-kan, 1983–86.

———, ed. *Sengoku-ki no kenryoku to shakai*. Tokyo: Tōkyō Daigaku Shuppan-kai, 1976.

———. *Sengoku no dōran*. *Nihon no rekishi* 14. Tokyo: Shōgaku-kan, 1975.

Nagahara Keiji and Kozo Yamamura. "Shaping the Process of Unification: Technological Progress in Sixteenth- and Seventeenth-Century Japan." *Journal of Japanese Studies* 14, no. 1 (Winter 1988): 77–109.

Nagahara Keiji, with Kozo Yamamura. "Village Communities and Daimyo Power." In John Whitney Hall and Toyoda Takeshi, eds., *Japan in the Muromachi Age*, 107–23. Berkeley and Los Angeles: University of California Press, 1977.

Nagashima Fukutarō. *Chūsei bunkajin no kiroku: Cha-kaiki no sekai*. Kyoto: Tankō-sha, 1972.

———. *Ōnin no ran*. Tokyo: Shibun-dō, 1968.

Nakabe Yoshiko. *Kinsei toshi no seiritsu to kōzō*. Tokyo: Shinsei-sha, 1967.

Nakamikado Nobutane. *Nobutane kyō-ki*. Shiryō Taisei Keigyō-kai, comp., *Zōho shiryō taisei* 44–45. Tokyo: Rinsen Shoten, 1972.

Nakamura Hiraku, ed. *Nihon kochizu taisei*. Tokyo: Kōdan-sha, 1973.

Nakamura Kichiji. *Do ikki kenkyū*. Tokyo: Azekura Shobō, 1974.

Nakao Takashi. *Nichiren-shū no seiritsu to tenkai*. Tokyo: Yoshikawa Kōbun-kan, 1973.

Nanbō-roku. In Sen Sōshitsu, ed., *Chadō koten zenshū* 4:1–333. Kyoto: Tankō-sha, 1956.

Nanzenji monjo. See Sakurai Kageo and Fujii Manabu, eds.

Naramoto Tatsuya, ed. *Ōtsu-shi shi*. 3 vols. Otsu: Ōtsu Shiyakusho, 1963.

Nihon-shi Kenkyū-kai, ed. *Ōnin-Genroku*. *Kōza Nihon bunka-shi* 4. Tokyo: San'ichi Shobō, 1962.

Nihon-shi Kenkyū-kai and Rekishi-gaku Kenkyū-kai, eds. *Yamashiro kuni ikki: Jiji to heiwa o motomeru*. Tokyo: Tōkyō Daigaku Shuppan-kai, 1986.

Ninagawa Chikatoshi. *Chikatoshi nikki*. Takeuchi Rizō, ed., *Zoku shiryō taisei* 13–14. Kyoto: Rinsen Shoten, 1967.

Ninagawa-ke monjo. Tōkyō Daigaku Shiryō Hensanjo, comp., *Dai Nihon komonjo, Iewake monjo*, ser. 21. Tokyo: Tōkyō Daigaku Shuppan-kai, 1984.

Nishikawa Kōji. *Toshi no shisō: Hoson shukei e no shihyō*. Tokyo: Nippon Hōsō Shuppan-kyōkai, 1973.

Niunoya Tetsuichi. *Kebiishi*. Tokyo: Heibon-sha, 1986.

Nobutane kyō-ki. See Nakamikado Nobutane.

Noda Tadao. "Shimogyō monjo, Sanjō-Karasuma Manjūya-chō monjo." *Nihon-shi kenkyū*, nos. 35, 36, 38, 39, 41 (January 1958–March 1959).

Nogami Toyoichirō, ed. *Nōgaku zensho*. 5 vols. Tokyo: Sōgen-sha, 1952–58.

Noma Seiroku and Oyama Fujio, eds. *Cha no bijutsu to kōgei*. *Zusetsu chadō taikei* 5. Tokyo: Kadokawa Shoin, 1964.

Okami Masao and Satake Akihiro, eds. *Hyōchū rakuchū rakugai byōbu*. Tokyo: Iwanami Shoten, 1983.

Okuno Takahiro. *Kōshitsu go-keizai-shi no kenkyū*. Tokyo: Chūō Kōron-sha, 1944.

Ōnin-ki. In Hanawa Hokiichi, comp., *Shinkō gunsho ruijū,* ser. 16, vol. 396, pp. 252–97. Tokyo: Meicho Fukyū-kai, 1977 [1928]. (*Also see* Wada Hidemichi.)

Ōmura Yukō. *Tenshō-ki.* In Kuwata Tadachika, ed., *Taikō shiryō-shū,* 11–145. Tokyo: Shinjinbutsu Ōrai-sha, 1971.

Ōta Gyūichi. *Shinchō kō-ki.* Ed. Okuno Takahiro and Iwasawa Yoshihiko. Tokyo: Kadokawa Shoten, 1970.

———. *Taikō gunki.* In Kuwata Tadachika, ed., *Taikō shiryō-shū,* 147–224. Tokyo: Shinjinbutsu Ōrai-sha, 1971.

Owada Tetsuo. *Ōmi Asai shi.* Tokyo: Shinjinbutsu Ōrai-sha, 1973.

Ōyama Kyōhei. "Chūsei no mibun-sei to kokka." In *Iwanami kōza Nihon rekishi 8, chūsei 4,* 261–314. Tokyo: Iwanami Shoten, 1976.

———. "Kugonin, jinnin, yoriudo." In Asao Naohiro, ed., *Shakai-teki shoshūdan,* 249–84. *Nihon no shakai-shi* 6. Tokyo: Iwanami Shoten, 1988.

———. "Medieval *Shōen.*" In Kozo Yamamura, ed., *The Cambridge History of Japan: Volume 3, Medieval Japan,* 89–127. Cambridge: Cambridge University Press, 1990.

Oyudono no ue no nikki. In Hanawa Hokiichi, ed., *Ho-i gunsho ruijū* 1–10. Tokyo: Taiyō-sha Daisan Kōjō, 1932–34.

Oze Hoan. *Taikō-ki.* Ed. Kuwata Tadachika. Tokyo: Shinjinbutsu Ōrai-sha, 1971.

———. "Toyotomi daimyōjin sairei-ki." In Hanawa Hokiichi, ed., *Zoku gunsho ruijū,* ser. 3, vol. 63, pp. 223–31. Tokyo: Zoku Gunsho Ruijū Kansei-kai, 1980 [1924].

Radcliffe-Brown, A. R. *Structure and Function in Primitive Society.* New York: Free Press, 1965.

Rekishi-gaku Kenkyū-kai and Nihon-shi Kenkyū-kai, eds. *Kōza Nihon rekishi.* 2 vols. Tokyo: Tōkyō Daigaku Shuppan-kai, 1984–85.

Rodd, Laurel Rasplica, trans. *Nichiren: Selected Writings.* Honolulu: University Press of Hawaii, 1980.

Rodrigues, João. *História da Igreja do Japão. See* Michael Cooper, ed. and trans., *This Island of Japon.*

Ruch, Barbara. "The Other Side of Culture in Medieval Japan." In Kozo Yamamura, ed., *The Cambridge History of Japan: Volume 3, Medieval Japan,* 500–543. Cambridge: Cambridge University Press, 1990.

Sakai Kimi. Review of *Toyotomi heiwa-rei to sengoku shakai. Rekishi-gaku kenkyū,* no. 563 (January 1987): 56–61.

Sakurai Eiji. "Jūroku seiki Kyōto no shokunin soshiki." *Rekishi-gaku kenkyū,* no. 579 (April 1988): 19–32.

Sakurai Kageo and Fujii Manabu, eds. *Nanzenji monjo.* 3 vols. Kyoto: Nanzenji Shomu Honjo, 1974.

Sakurai Yoshirō. *Chūsei Nihon no ōken, shūkyō, geinō.* Tokyo: Jinbun Shoin, 1988.

Sanetaka kō-ki. See Sanjōnishi Sanetaka.

Sanjōnishi Sanetaka. *Sanetaka kō-ki.* 13 vols. Tokyo: Taiyō-sha, 1931–38 (vols. 1–5); Kokusho Shuppan Kabushiki Gaisha, 1944 (vol. 6:1); Zoku Gunsho Ruijū Kansei-kai, 1962–67 (vols. 6:2–13; Takahashi Ryūzō, ed.).

Sasaki Gin'ya. *Chūsei shōhin ryūtsū-shi no kenkyū*. Tokyo: Hōsei Daigaku Shuppan-kyoku, 1972.

———. "Nihon chūsei toshi no jiyū jichi kenkyū o megutte." *Shakai keizai shigaku* 38, no. 4 (1972): 96–111.

———. "Rakuichi rakuza-rei to za no hoshō ando." In Nagahara Keiji, ed., *Sengoku-ki no kenryoku to shakai*, 157–230. Tokyo: Tōkyō Daigaku Shuppan-kai, 1976.

Sasaki Gin'ya, with William B. Hauser. "Sengoku Daimyo Rule and Commerce." In John Whitney Hall, Nagahara Keiji, and Kozo Yamamura, eds., *Japan Before Tokugawa: Political Consolidation and Economic Growth, 1500–1650*, 125–48. Princeton: Princeton University Press, 1981.

Sato, Elizabeth. "The Early Development of the *Shōen*." In John Whitney Hall and Jeffrey P. Mass, eds., *Medieval Japan: Essays in Institutional History*, 91–108. New Haven: Yale University Press, 1974.

Satō Shin'ichi. *Muromachi bakufu shugo seido no kenkyū 1*. Tokyo: Tōkyō Daigaku Shuppan-kai, 1967.

———. *Nihon no chūsei kokka*. Tokyo: Iwanami Shoten, 1983.

Satō Shin'ichi and Ikeuchi Yoshisuke, eds. *Muromachi bakufu hō. Chūsei hōsei shiryō-shū 2*. Tokyo: Iwanami Shoten, 1957.

Satō Shin'ichi, Ikeuchi Yoshisuke, and Momose Kesao, eds. *Buke kahō. Chūsei hōsei shiryō-shū 3*. Tokyo: Iwanami Shoten, 1965.

———. *Kamakura bakufu hō. Chūsei hōsei shiryō-shū 1*. Tokyo: Iwanami Shoten, 1965.

Satō Shin'ichi, with John Whitney Hall. "The Ashikaga Shogun and the Muromachi Bakufu Administration." In John Whitney Hall and Toyoda Takeshi, eds., *Japan in the Muromachi Age*, 45–52. Berkeley and Los Angeles: University of California Press, 1977.

Sen Sōshitsu, ed. *Chadō koten zenshū*. 12 vols. Kyoto: Tankō-sha, 1957–62.

———, ed. *Chadō zenshū*. 15 vols. Tokyo: Sōgen-sha, 1946 [1936].

———, ed. *Chanoyū: The Urasenke Tradition of Tea*. Trans. Alfred Birnbaum. New York and Tokyo: John Weatherhill, Inc., 1988.

Sen Sōsa, Sen Sōshitsu, and Sen Sōshu, eds. *Rikyū daijiten*. Kyoto: Tankō-sha, 1989.

Sencha-shū. In Sen Sōshitsu, ed., *Chadō zenshū* 12:99–184. Kyoto: Sōgen-sha, 1946 [1936].

Shibusawa Keizō. *Nihon jōmin seikatsu ebiki*. 5 vols. Tokyo: Kadokawa Shoten, 1965–68.

Shimada Sōchō. *Sōchō shū-ki*. Shimazu Tadao, ed., *Sōchō nikki*. Tokyo: Iwanami Shoten, 1975.

SKR. See Kyōto-shi, ed., *Shiryō Kyōto no rekishi*.

Sōchō shū-ki. See Shimada Sōchō.

Spencer, Paul, ed. *Society and the Dance: The Social Anthropology of Process and Performance*. Cambridge: Cambridge University Press, 1985.

Steenstrup, Carl. "The Middle Ages Survey'd." *Monumenta Nipponica* 46, no. 2 (1991): 237–52.

———. "*Sata mirensho*: A Fourteenth-Century Law Primer." *Monumenta Nipponica* 35, no. 4 (1980): 405–36.

Suzuki Ryōichi. *Daijōin jisha zōjiki: Aru monbatsu sōryō no botsuraku no kiroku. Nikki, kiroku ni yoru Nihon rekishi sōsho* 18. Tokyo: Kabushiki Gaisha Soshiete, 1983.

────. *Ōnin no ran.* Tokyo: Iwanami Shoten, 1973.

Suzuki Susumu, ed. *Edo-zu byōbu.* Tokyo: Heibon-sha, 1971.

Tabata Yasuko. "Chūsei kōki Kinai dogō no sonzai keitai." In Murata Shūzō, ed., *Kinki daimyō no kenkyū,* 161–204. Tokyo: Yoshikawa Kōbun-kan, 1986.

Takahashi Yasuo. *Kyōto chūsei toshi-shi kenkyū.* Kyoto: Shibunkaku Shuppan, 1983.

────. *Rakuchū rakugai-zu: Kyōkai bunka no chūsei-shi.* Tokyo: Heibon-sha, 1988.

────. "Shoki rakuchū rakugai-zu byōbu no kaiga shiryō ronteki saikentō." *Kokka,* no. 1105 (1987): 25–46.

Takayanagi Kōji and Takeuchi Rizō, eds. *Kadokawa Nihon-shi jiten.* Tokyo: Kadokawa Shoten, 1966.

Takeda Tsuneo, ed. *Fūzoku-ga: Sairei, kabuki. Nihon byōbu-e shūsei* 13. Tokyo: Kōdan-sha, 1978.

Tamon'in nikki. See Tsuji Zennosuke, ed.

Tamura Yoshirō and Miyazaki Eishu, eds. *Nichiren shinkō no rekishi. Kōza Nichiren* 3. Tokyo: Shunshū-sha, 1972.

Tanaka Michiko. "Sengoku-ki ni okeru shōen sonraku to kenryoku." In Murata Shūzō, ed., *Kinki daimyō no kenkyū,* 2–48. Tokyo: Yoshikawa Kōbun-kan, 1986.

Tanaka Toyozō. "Hōkoku-sai no byōbu ni tsuite." In *Nihon bijutsu no kenkyū,* 291–300. Tokyo: Nigen-sha, 1960.

Tani Shin'ichi. "San'ami." In Kuwata Tadachika, ed., *Cha ni ikita hito* 1. *Zusetsu chadō taikei* 6:58–72. Tokyo: Kadokawa Shoten, 1963.

Tanuma Mutsumi. "Muromachi bakufu, shugo, kokujin." In *Iwanami kōza Nihon rekishi 7, chūsei 3:* 1–50. Tokyo: Iwanami Shoten, 1976.

────. "Muromachi bakufu to shugo ryōgoku." In Rekishi-gaku Kenkyū-kai and Nihon-shi Kenkyū-kai, eds., *Hōken shakai no tenkai. Kōza Nihon-shi* 3:85–115. Tokyo: Tōkyō Daigaku Shuppan-kai, 1970.

Teishitsu Rin'ya Kyoku, comp. *Go-ryōchi shikō.* Tokyo: Kunai-shō, 1937.

Tennōjiya kaiki. See Tsuda Sōtatsu.

Thucydides. *The Peloponnesian War.* Trans. Rex Warner. New York: Penguin Books, 1980 [1954].

Tōhō Gakkai, under the auspices of the Japan Foundation, comp. *An Introductory Bibliography for Japanese Studies,* vol. 6, pt. 2, *Humanities 1983–86.* Tokyo: Bonjin-sha, 1990.

────, comp. *An Introductory Bibliography for Japanese Studies,* vol. 7, pt. 2, *Humanities 1987–88.* Tokyo: The Japan Foundation, 1991.

Tōkyō Bijutsu, with Gakubu Seinen-kai, eds. *Bijutsu techō.* Tokyo: Shufu no Tomo-sha, 1982.

Torii Kazuyuki. "Ōnin, Bunmei no ran-go no Muromachi bakufu." *Shigaku zasshi* 96, no. 2 (1987): 38–60.

Totman, Conrad. *The Green Archipelago.* Berkeley and Los Angeles: University of California Press, 1989.

Toyoda Takeshi. *Chūsei Nihon shōgyō-shi no kenkyū.* Tokyo: Iwanami Shoten, 1952.

———. *A History of Pre-Meiji Commerce in Japan.* Tokyo: Kokusai Bunka Shin-kōkai, 1969.

———. *Nihon hōken toshi.* Tokyo: Iwanami Shoten, 1952.

———. *Sakai: Shōnin no shinshutsu to toshi no jiyū.* Tokyo: Shibun-dō, 1966.

Toyoda Takeshi and Sugiyama Hiroshi, with V. Dixon Morris. "The Growth of Commerce and the Trades." In John Whitney Hall and Toyoda Takeshi, eds., *Japan in the Muromachi Age,* 129–44. Berkeley and Los Angeles: University of California Press, 1977.

Tsuda Sōtatsu, Tsuda Sōgyū, and Tsuda Sōbon. *Tennōjiya kaiki.* Sen Sōshitsu, ed., *Chadō koten zenshū* 7–8. Kyoto: Tankō-sha, 1959.

Tsuji Nobuo. "Uesugi iemoto rakuchū rakugai-zu saikō, Imatani-shi no setsu ni taishite." *Kokka,* no. 1105 (1987): 47–59.

Tsuji Zennosuke, ed. *Tamon-in nikki.* 6 vols. Tokyo: Kadokawa Shoten, 1967.

Turner, Victor. *The Ritual Process: Structure and Anti-Structure.* Ithaca: Cornell University Press, 1979 [1960].

Uejima Tamotsu. *Kyōkō shōen sonraku no kenkyū.* Tokyo: Haniwa Shobō, 1970.

Varley, H. Paul. "Ashikaga Yoshimitsu and the World of Kitayama: Social Change and Shogunal Patronage in Early Muromachi Japan." In John W. Hall and Toyoda Takeshi, eds., *Japan in the Muromachi Age,* 183–204. Berkeley and Los Angeles: University of California Press, 1977.

———. "*Chanoyū:* From the Genroku Epoch to Modern Times." In Varley and Kumakura Isao, eds., *Tea in Japan: Essays on the History of Chanoyū,* 161–94. Honolulu: University Press of Hawaii, 1989.

———. *The Ōnin War.* New York: Columbia University Press, 1967.

Varley, H. Paul, and George Elison. "The Culture of Tea: From Its Origins to Sen no Rikyū." In George Elison and Bardwell L. Smith, eds., *Warlords, Artists, and Commoners: Japan in the Sixteenth Century,* 187–222. Honolulu: University Press of Hawaii, 1981.

Varley, H. Paul, and Kumakura Isao, eds. *Tea in Japan: Essays on the History of Chanoyū.* Honolulu: University Press of Hawaii, 1989.

Wada Hidemichi, ed. *Ōnin-ki.* Tokyo: Koten Bunko, 1978.

Wakita Haruko. "Chūsei hisabetsu-min no seikatsu to shakai." In Buraku Mondai Kenkyū-jo, ed., *Buraku no rekishi to kaihō undō,* 69–182. Tokyo: Buraku Mondai Kenkyū-jo Shuppan-bu, 1986.

———. "Chūsei Kyōto no tochi shoyū." In Wakita, *Nihon chūsei toshi ron,* 119–80. Tokyo: Tōkyō Daigaku Shuppan-kai, 1981. *Also in* Nagahara Keiji, ed., *Sengoku-ki no kenryoku to shakai,* 265–329. Tokyo: Tōkyō Daigaku Shuppan-kai, 1976.

———. "Chūsei sangyō no hatten, Ōmi no baai." In Wakita, *Nihon chūsei shōgyō hattatsu-shi no kenkyū,* 523–93. Tokyo: Ochanomizu Shobō, 1969.

———. "Muromachi-ki no keizai hatten." In *Iwanami kōza Nihon rekishi 7, chūsei 3,* 51–98. Tokyo: Iwanami Shoten, 1976.

———. *Nihon chūsei shōgyō hattatsu-shi no kenkyū.* Tokyo: Ochanomizu Shobō, 1969.

———. *Nihon chūsei toshi-ron.* Tokyo: Tōkyō Daigaku Shuppan-kai, 1981.

———. "Nihon chūsei toshi to ryōshu kenryoku." In Wakita, *Nihon chūsei toshi ron*, 345–86. Tokyo: Tōkyō Daigaku Shuppan-kai, 1981.

———. *Sengoku daimyō. Taikei Nihon no rekishi 7.* Tokyo: Shōgaku-kan, 1988.

———. "Towards a Wider Perspective on Medieval Commerce." *Journal of Japanese Studies* 1, no. 2 (Spring 1975): 321–45.

Wakita Haruko, with Susan B. Hanley. "Dimensions of Development: Cities in Fifteenth- and Sixteenth-Century Japan." In John Whitney Hall, Nagahara Keiji, and Kozo Yamamura, eds., *Japan Before Tokugawa: Political Consolidation and Economic Growth, 1500–1650,* 295–326. Princeton: Princeton University Press, 1981.

Wakita Osamu. *Oda seiken no kiso kōzō.* Tokyo: Tōkyō Daigaku Shuppan-kai, 1975.

———. "Shinpojiumu chūsei mibun-sei no kenkyū jōtai to kadai." *Buraku mondai kenkyū* 78 (1984): 1–40.

Wakita Osamu, Asao Naohiro, Sasaki Junnosuke, Fujiki Hisashi, and Miyagawa Mitsuru. *Shinpojiumu Nihon rekishi 10: Shokuhō seiken-ron.* Tokyo: Gakusei-sha, 1972.

Wang Yi-T'ung. *Official Relations Between China and Japan, 1368–1549.* Cambridge: Harvard University Press, 1953.

Watanabe Morimichi. *Ōmi shōnin.* Tokyo: Kyōiku-sha, 1980.

Weinstein, Stanley. "Rennyo and the Shinshū Revival." In John Whitney Hall and Toyoda Takeshi, eds., *Japan in the Muromachi Age,* 331–58. Berkeley and Los Angeles: University of California Press, 1977.

Wintersteen, Prescott B., Jr. "The Early Muromachi Bakufu in Kyoto." In John Whitney Hall and Jeffrey P. Mass, eds., *Medieval Japan: Essays in Institutional History,* 201–9. New Haven: Yale University Press, 1974.

———. "Muromachi Shugo and Hanzei." In John Whitney Hall and Jeffrey P. Mass, eds., *Medieval Japan: Essays in Institutional History,* 210–20. New Haven: Yale University Press, 1974.

Yamamura, Kozo, ed. *The Cambridge History of Japan: Volume 3, Medieval Japan.* Cambridge: Cambridge University Press, 1990.

———. "The Development of *Za* in Medieval Japan." *Business History Review* 47 (Winter 1973): 438–65.

———. "The Growth of Commerce in Medieval Japan." In Yamamura, ed., *The Cambridge History of Japan: Volume 3, Medieval Japan,* 344–95. Cambridge: Cambridge University Press, 1990.

———. "Returns on Unification: Economic Growth in Japan 1550–1650." In John Whitney Hall, Nagahara Keiji, and Kozo Yamamura, eds., *Japan Before Tokugawa: Political Consolidation and Economic Growth, 1500– 1650,* 327–72. Princeton: Princeton University Press, 1981.

Yamanoue Sōji. *Yamanoue Sōji-ki.* In Sen Sōshitsu, ed., *Chadō koten zenshū* 6:49–130. Kyoto: Tankō-sha, 1958.

Yamashina Tokitsugu. *Tokitsugu kyō-ki.* 4 vols. Tokyo: Kokusho Kankō-kai, 1914–15.

Yamazaki Masakazu. *Muromachi ki.* Tokyo: Asahi Shinbun-sha, 1976.

Yampolsky, Philip, ed. *Selected Writings of Nichiren.* Trans. Burton Watson. New York: Columbia University Press, 1990.

Yokoi Kiyoshi. *Chūsei minshū no seikatsu bunka.* Tokyo: Tōkyō Daigaku Shuppan-kai, 1975.

————. "Chūsei minshū-shi ni okeru 'jūgo-sai' no imi ni tsuite." In Yokoi, ed., *Chūsei minshū no seikatsu bunka,* 193–203. Tokyo: Tōkyō Daigaku Shuppan-kai, 1975.

————. "Gekokujō no bunka." In Rekishi-gaku Kenkyū-kai and Nihon-shi Kenkyū-kai, eds., *Kōza Nihon-shi 3: Hoken shakai no tenkai,* 297–321. Tokyo: Tōkyō Daigaku Shuppan-kai, 1970.

————. *Gekokujō no bunka.* Tokyo: Tōkyō Daigaku Shuppan-kai, 1980.

————. "'Kyōki' no koto." In Yokoi, *Gekokujō no bunka,* 87–117. Tokyo: Tōkyō Daigaku Shuppan-kai, 1980.

————. "Machishū no seikatsu bunka." In Yokoi, *Gekokujō no bunka,* 149–75. Tokyo: Tōkyō Daigaku Shuppan-kai, 1980.

————. "Minshū bunka no keisei." In *Iwanami kōza Nihon rekishi 7, chūsei 3,* 219–52. Tokyo: Iwanami Shoten, 1976.

Yonehara Masayoshi. "Sakai no machi no chajin." In Kuwata Tadachika, ed., *Cha ni ikita hito* 1:98–122. Tokyo: Kadokawa Shoin, 1963.

Yoshida Nobuyuki. "Kōgi to chōnin mibun." *1980 nendo rekishi-gaku kenkyū-kai taikai hōkoku,* 96–114.

Index

Alliances: between farmers and courtiers, 184; between Harumoto and Ikkō sectarians, 148; between workers and patrons, 178–179; formation of block federations (*machi-gumi*), 295; formed through tea parties, 281; formed to replace medieval power structure, 287; *ikki* forms of, 42–43; surrounding Ōmi and Sakai shogunate conflict, 135–141; surrounding successions, 15–18; upward mobility through patronage, 201–208. *See also* Block associations; Faction politics

Ashikaga house: Ōnin quarrel of, 15; resolution of succession of, 45, 48

Ashikaga Shogunal Line (1429–1573), 44

Ashikaga Yoshiaki, 47

Ashikaga Yoshiharu, 46–47, 63, 120, 140, 222–224

Ashikaga Yoshihide, 47, 119, 121

Ashikaga Yoshihisa: becomes shogun, 33, 45, 48; biographical sketch of, 120; death of, 37; marches against the Rokkaku house, 36–37; succession quarrel of, 15; supports Hatakeyama Yoshinari, 35

Ashikaga Yoshimasa: actions provoke Ōnin war, 24–25; criticism of, 19–21; the incumbent shogun, 15; orders Silver Pavilion construction, 35–36; supports Hatakeyama Masanaga, 35

Ashikaga Yoshimi, 15, 48

Ashikaga Yoshitane: biographical sketch of, 120; defeat of, 49–50, 74–75; Hosokawa Masamoto's rebellion against, 45, 48–49; marches against the Rokkaku house, 37; reinstalled as shogun, 75

Ashikaga Yoshiteru, 63, 120–121, 222–224

Ashikaga Yoshitsuna, 137–138, 140–141, 222

Ashikaga Yoshizumi, 50, 75, 120

Awa Hosokawa, 52

Barracking duty, 83, 226, 235

Battles (*kassen*): described, 6; of Katsura River (1527), 139; in Kawachi (1493), 49–50; Ōnin war, 28; politics of demonstration as alternative to, 54; protocols to control violence during, 31–32; of shogunate law regarding, 21–24; of Shōkokuji, 28–29; Yamashiro (1485–1486), 37–38. *See also* Private battles; Tax battles

Block associations: class composition of, 232–234; defense of, 214–218; elders (*shukurō*) presiding over federations of, 231; formation of block federations (*machi-gumi*), 219, 231, 331, 333; *furyū* dancers identified with, 252, 336; *gachi gyōji* (monthly magis-

Block associations (continued)
trates) of, 217, 231; Gion festival controversy and, 217; grievance/redress mediated through, 238–239; history from 1539 to 1553, 225–231; increased political authority of, 234–235, 239–241; naming of, 212–213; political organization of, 209, 229–231, 289; political truce between shogunate and, 230, 235–239, 331; population of, 313; shogunate orders for rebuilding of moats by, 218–219; survey mapping of Kyoto, 210–212; tax exemptions of, 235; tax withholding of, 219–220

Block federation (machi-gumi), 219, 231, 331, 333

Board of Administration (mandokoro): aligned with Ashikaga Yoshimasa, 35; disbanded by Miyoshi Chōkei, 223–224; forced to flee Kyoto, 75

Board of Retainers (samurai-dokoro), 88–89, 163–164

Buddhism: Hokke (Lotus) movement within, 153; Ikkō ("single-minded") movement within, 148

Bugaku dancing, 301

Bugyō-nin (council of magistrates), 35, 120–123

Burckhardt, Jacob, 257

Business taxes: collected by nōsengata, 187, 201–202; collected from sake-brewing industry, 187; paid by importers to patrons, 180–181; paid by producers to patrons, 186–187; privileged population exempted from, 202–203; shogunal income from, 191; shogunate documents regarding withheld, 199–201; used to buy off patrons, 184–186. See also Taxes

Byōdōin temple, 38, 43

Capital governorship (shugo), 18

Chō (blocks), 210, 333. See also Block associations; Ryōgawa chō

Chronicle of Ōnin (anonymous): on battle of Shōkokuji, 28–29; on beginning of Ōnin war, 11–13; on combined battle forces, 27; criticism of Ashikaga Yoshimasa by, 20–21

Class system: depicted within screen paintings, 300–302; of fūryū dancing, 255–256; as primary locus of political/social organization, 289; of tea society, 264–268, 281–283; upward mobility within, 201–208; within block associations, 232–234

Code of war: during Ōnin war (1467–1477), 31–32; grievance/redress outside of, 9; restrained violence as part of, 71–74, 93. See also Word wars

Commoners: appropriation of tea culture by, 260–261, 266–268, 273; (jige) elders, 233; land ownership by, 213–214, 330; as main body of fūryū dancers, 252; military disengagement of, 224; political power through block associations, 235–239, 293; population estimates of, 315; screen painting depiction of, 301–302; upward mobility through patronage attachment, 201–208

Culture of lawlessness: arson and theft incidents of, 100–104; changes in social order manifested by, 243–244; described, 13, 243; Jiriki kyūsai (self-redress) as part of, 94–100; as Ōnin legacy, 13–14; rōnin contribution to, 70–71. See also Urban conflict

Daimyo houses: goyō shōnin (merchants) in service of, 185, 195–196; Sengoku daimyō ronshū history of, 303; as shogunate replacement, 287

Dancing: bugaku, 301; changes in wartime fūryū, 248–249, 336; class structure of fūryū, 255–256; connections between obon and fūryū, 250–251; diary entry on sponsorship of, 244–245; Kyoto prohibition against, 55, 245; participants in fūryū, 251–252; political context of fūryū, 257–259; politics of demonstration and fūryū, 253–255; significance of forbidden fūryū, 245–253; song lyrics of fūryū, 336; wartime tea parties compared to fūryū, 279–281, 284. See also Politics of demonstration

Debtors' rebellions, 39, 89–93, 136. See also Tax battles; Tokusei-rei

Deputies of provincial governors (shugo-dai), 41

Eastern camp: location of, 28; political actions of, 30–31
Echigo guild, 185
Economic structure (Kyoto): crises of wartime, 61–63, 179–180, 182–185, 190–196; distribution of goods within, 188–190; export sector of, 192–194; *goyō shōnin* (merchants) emerge as part of, 184–185; import sector of, 180–186; licensed purveyors as part of, 180–182, 184; production sector of, 186–188; provincial commerce as threat to, 193–195; reduced internal consumption in, 191, 192, 195; wartime illicit peddling, 182–184. *See also* Guilds (*za*); Patronage structure; *Sake*-brewing industry
Elders (*shukurō*), 231, 233
Enryakuji. *See* Hiei
Era of Warring States (1467–1568): authority of government sectors during, 119–121; beginnings of, 11; collapse of medieval polity during, 286–287; faction politics during, 285–286; Hokke uprising (1532–1535), 145–167; map of Kyoto during, 62; Ōmi vs. Sakai shogunate struggle (1526–1532), 135–145; the purge during, 74–82; rupture force of, 35–36, 285–286; Yakushiji Motoichi's rebellion during, 4. *See also* Code of War; Ōnin war (1467–1477)
Exports: domestic, 192–194; from Kyoto to China, 192. *See also* Economic structure (Kyoto)

Faction politics: during Era of Warring States, 285–286; impact of *Ikkō* movement on, 148–151; medieval standards of, 20–21; in Ōmi vs. Sakai shogunate conflict, 135–142; succession and, 17. *See also* Alliances
Famine of 1461, 20
Fūryū odori (dance of the wind flowing). *See* Dancing

Gachi gyōji (monthly magistrates), 217, 219, 231
Gion festival, 216, 217, 256, 297
Goyō shōnin (merchants), 184–185, 195–196

Grievance: *Jiriki kyūsai* (self-redress) cases of, 94–100; justification through, 24, 48; mediated through block associations, 238–239; Ōmi vs. Shakai shogunate conflict provoked by, 135–145; retribution rites due to, 30, 32; Tōji vs. Tōjiin temples, 93–94; war trophies as redress for, 8–9; Yamashiro uprising as act of, 39–40. *See also* Private battles
Guilds (*za*): changes in wartime, 188; described, 181; Echigo, 185; evolution into *ton'ya*, 181–185, 195–196; export, 187; import, 181; Ōyamazaki oil, 185–186, 193; petitions, public suits, and edicts regarding, 114–116, 123, 177–179, 189–190, 199–200, 206–208. *See also* Economic structure (Kyoto); Labor

Hachiman shrine, 43
Hana no gosho, 63, 311–312
Hanzei (half-tax) levy, 83–86
Hatakeyama house: overextension of, 17–18; succession quarrel within, 14, 22; Yamashiro assembly demands against, 40
Hatakeyama Masanaga: burns own mansion and marches on shogun, 25; as *kanrei*, 35; succession quarrel of, 14, 22; in Yamashiro battle (1485–86), 37–38
Hatakeyama Yoshinari: attacks adoptive brother, 25; succession quarrel of, 14, 22; in Yamashiro battle (1485–1486), 37–38
Hiei, Mount (Enryakuji temple): destruction by forces of, 164–167, 171, 209; Hokke defense against, 169; opposition to Hokke by, 153–154; opposition to Ikkō by, 148; victory over Hokke alliance by, 208
Hikan (deputies), 202
Hino Tomiko, 20, 35
Hokke (Lotus) movement: destruction during suppression of, 60; emergence of, 153–156; fighting between Ikkō and, 149–167; Hiei victory over, 166–167, 171, 208; Hosokawa Harumoto alliance with, 157–159, 161; identity of participants in, 167–170; Kyoto temples burned, 165–166; rise of the,

Hokke (Lotus) movement *(continued)* 46–47; role in Kyoto of, 159–164, 215–216; social and political confusion following defeat of, 240; temples of, 154–155. See also *Uchimawari;* Yamashina Honganji

Hōkōshū (shogun's personal guard), 35, 63, 88

Hōkoku sairei-zu byōbu (screen paintings), 245–247

Honekawa Kōken, 70

Honganji temple, 149

Hosokawa Harukuni, 156–157

Hosokawa Harumoto: alliance with Hokke sectarians, 157–159, 161, 163; alliance with Ikkō sectarians, 148, 162–163; becomes *kanrei,* 46; campaigns conducted by, 220–223; challenges Hosokawa Takakuni, 75; grievance of, 137; returns to Kyoto, 171

Hosokawa house: battle of heirs of (1507–1508), 44–46, 50–52; *kanrei* line of the (1430–1563), 45; military networks of, 88

Hosokawa Katsumoto: conflict with Yamana Sōzen, 18–19; death of, 33; eastern camp of, 28

Hosokawa Masamoto: attitude toward throne of, 62; conflicts with deputies of, 103; death of, 51; defeats Ashikaga Yoshitane, 74–75; heirs of, 125; rebellion against Ashikaga Yoshitane by, 45–46, 48–50; taxes of, 83–85; victory over Yakushiji Motoichi by, 1–8; Yakushiji Motoichi's rebellion against, 4

Hosokawa Sumimoto: ousted by Hosokawa Takakuni, 75, 137; portrait of, 124; split between Kōzai Motonaga and, 50–51, 75

Hosokawa Sumiyuki, 50–51

Hosokawa Takakuni: alliances as Ōmi *kanrei,* 141, 142; becomes *kanrei,* 75, 137; compels Kōzai Motomori to commit suicide, 135; conflict with Hosokawa Sumimoto, 51–52; split between Yoshitane and, 46–47; suicide of, 141

Hosokawa Ujitsuna, 47, 156–157, 221–222

Ibaragi Nagataka, 122, 123, 141–142, 149, 218, 225, 333

Ikki movement: described, 39, 89; in Hokke form, 145–179; new alliances of, 41–43; suppression of, 286; in *tokusei* form, 89–93; *uchimawari* as, 147; in Yamashiro, 37–44, 72–73, 87

Ikkō movement: alliance with Hosokawa Harumoto of, 141; conflict between Hokke and, 153–167; emergence of, 148–150; suppression of, 286–287; war between Harumoto and, 163; Yamashiro armed farmers march against, 163. See also Yamashina Honganji

Illicit peddling, 182–184

Imai Sōkyū, 259

Ima Mairi no Tsubone, 20

Imperial enthronement ceremony, 36, 63

Imports: illicit peddling of, 182–184; sector described, 179–180; as vital to wartime economy, 192. See also Economic structure (Kyoto)

Ise Sadachika: appointed Yamashiro military governor, 38–39, 43; contributions to Shiba quarrel, 18; guardian of Hino Tomiko's infant son, 20

Ishiyama Honganji fortress, 156

Izumi uprising (1473), 41

Japan. See Medieval Japan

Jinbo house, 18

Jiriki (power of the self), 43–44, 50, 97

Jiriki kyūsai (self-redress of grievance), 93–100

Jizamurai, 39–42

Kai house, 18

Kamigoryō-sha shrine, 25, 27, 28

Kamiya Sōtan, 259

Kanō Seisen, 174

Kanrei (chief minister): authority of, 121; conflict between civil proprietors and, 85–86; exercise of authority by, 122–123, 125–128; growing division between shogunate and, 117–118, 120–128; Hatakeyama and Shiba claims to, 18; Hosokawa Harumoto as Sakai, 141; Hosokawa house line of (1430–1563), 45; Hosokawa Takakuni as Ōmi, 141; identity significance of, 48–49; rivalry over, 48

Kanrei-dai, 119–121

Kanrei line (Hosokawa house), 45

Kanrōji Chikanaga, 88–90

Katsura River battle (1527), 75, 139

Kawachi: battle (1493) in, 49–50; western camp moves to, 34

Kemari, 301

Kenbutsu (watching spectacles), 71, 146, 253–254

Kitano document (1493), 117–118

Kitano shrine, 87–88, 112, 116, 187

Kōzai Motomori, 135–137

Kōzai Motonaga (or Mataroku), 50–51, 57, 71–73, 85

Kuni ikki, 39

Kunin (public people), 202

Kyoto: alliance with warlords to save, 151–152; armies gathered in, 26–27; burning of, 29–30, 61, 60–61; changes in authority assumptions in, 293–294; conditions after death of Hokke movement, 171–174; creation of two urban "islands" in, 64–69; crime in, 100–104; debtors' rebellions in, 89–93, 136; defeated Ashikaga Yoshitane paraded through, 74–75; destruction by Hiei invasion of (1536), 165–166, 171, 209; diary entries regarding conflict in, 57–59, 60–61, 294–295; economic decline following Ōnin war, 61–63; economic structure of, 179–196; enemy hunts conducted in, 79–82; exploitation of resources of, 82–89; *furyū* dancing forbidden in, 244–259; government transitions (1467–1568) within, 46–47; impact of occupation years on, 32–33; *kenbutsu* (watching spectacles) in, 253–254; land sales in 213–214, 330; map during Era of Warring States, 62; map prior to Ōnin war, 60; mass tax delinquency practiced in, 164, 219–220; neighborhood purges in, 142–145; organized marches (*tokusei ikki*) into, 39; political action within, 30–31; population of, 68, 313; post-Ōnin years in, 35–36, 312; prohibitions introduced for, 55–56, 81–82, 245; refuge sought through word wars, 106–109; screen paintings depicting, 294–302, 344–345; shogunal mansions in, 311–312; *shokunin* (people of skill) in, 174–176, 374; survey mapping of, 210–212; tax battles within, 114–117, 144–145; uprising of 1484 in, 88–89; Yanagimoto Kataharu victoriously en-

ters, 139, 142. *See also* Block associations; Economic structure (Kyoto)

Labor: commercial documents governing, 177–179, 199–200; crisis of wartime, 187–188; economic structure of Kyoto and, 179–185; informal conventions governing, 176–177; Kyoto *shokunin* (people of skill), 174–176, 374; as part of neighborhood reciprocal agreement, 219; reorganized stratification of, 208–209; within neighborhood economies, 186–187. *See also* Guilds (*za*); Patronage structure

Land tenure, 213–214

Lotus Sutra, 153

Lotus uprising (1532–1536). *See* Hokke (Lotus) movement

Machi-gumi (block federation), 219, 231, 331, 333

Matsunaga Hisahide, 47

Matsuya Hisamasa: account of trips in diary of, 271; diary entries on tea by, 259, 263, 265–266

Medieval Japan: code of war within, 9, 31–32, 71–74, 93; consent to shogunal authority by houses of, 16; described, xxii–xxxii; historical impact of Ōnin war on, 13–14; importance of succession in, 15; justification for private battle within, 24; law of shogunate regarding battle in, 21–24; perception of battle and quarrel in, 6–8; practice of *tokusei ikki* in, 39, 89; rejection by Miyoshi Chōkei of order, 239, 287; rule of force vs. rule of law in, 26, 53–54; standards of faction politics in, 20–21; succession norms in, 16–17; tax battles of, 83–86; threat of *ikki* movement to, 42–43; tolerance for private battles within, 13

Military authorities: attempts to neutralize block associations by, 237; block association's authority recognized by, 234–235, 239–240, 334

Military conscription, 86–88

Miyoshi Chōkei: attempts to dismantle medieval order, 239, 287; campaigns of (1539–1553), 221–224; disbands Board of Administration, 223–224;

Miyoshi Chōkei (continued)
  military challenges of, 47; as Warring
  States daimyo, 332
Miyoshi Motonaga, 52, 137, 221, 224; alliance with Ōmi shogunate, 137–139;
  power struggle between Yanagimoto
  and, 140, 143; speculations on political vision of, 142, 287; suicide of,
  141, 148; victory against Ōmi party,
  141
Miyoshi Yukinaga, 50–52
Monthly magistrates (*gachi gyōji*), 217,
  219, 231

Nakamikado Nobutane: on arson and
  theft incidents, 101–103, 106; on battle, 1–6, 8–10, 290; on conscription,
  86–87; mansion of, 62
Nanajū ichiban shokunin uta-awase
  (poem contest), 174–175, 324
Neighborhoods. *See* Block associations
Nichiren school of Buddhism, 153. *See
  also* Hokke (Lotus) movement
Ninagawa Chikatoshi, 95–96, 99, 114
Nisui-ki, 102, 128, 130, 146, 150, 152,
  157, 244, 251
Noh troupes, 328
Nōsengata, 187, 201–202. *See also* Business taxes

Obon, 250–251. *See also* Dancing
Oda Nobunaga, 47, 339
Ōmi: collapse of, 141; incumbent government in exile in, 139–140
Ōnin-ki. See Chronicle of Ōnin
Ōnin war (1467–1477): armies gathering
  in Kyoto, 27; background quarrels preceding, 11–12, 14–24; code of conflict
  during, 31–32; destruction in Kyoto
  during, 29–30, 60–61; economic crisis
  following, 61–63; events following,
  34–37; historical impact of, 13–14; Kyoto government during, 46; provocation of, 24–25; Shōkokuji battle of,
  28–29; social and political attachments
  before and after, 53–54. *See also* Era of
  Warring States (1467–1568); Succession
Onoyama petition (1515), 109–112
Ōuchi house, 33–34
Ōuchi Yoshioki, 51, 53
Ōyamazaki oil guild, 185–186, 193

Patronage structure: abuse by clients of,
  199–201; attachment as social economic status indicator, 201–208;
  block associations' separation from,
  234–235, 239; changes in wartime,
  184–186; regulatory functions of,
  196–197; tribute/services paid
  through, 180–181, 184. *See also* Economic structure (Kyoto); Labor
Petitions. *See* Word wars
Politics of demonstration: as alternative to
  violence, 54, 244; code of war imple-
  mented by, 71–74, 93; during Kyoto
  neighborhood tax battles, 144–145;
  enacted during purge, 76; *jiriki kyūsai*
  (self-redress) as, 94–100; Kyoto townspeople evoke *samurai-dokoro* duties,
  163–164; similarities between *furyū*
  dancing and, 253–255; social reconfiguration through, 104–105, 288–
  289; *tokusei ikki* as, 39, 89–91; urban
  conflict and, 59; used by soldiers of
  the land, 43–44; word wars and, 107–
  108. *See also* Hokke (Lotus) movement; Yamashiro
Private battles: between Hosokawa Takakuni and Yanagimoto Kataharu, 135–
  141; between Tōji and Tōjiin temples,
  93–94; change in legitimacy of, 289;
  conduct of shogunate during, 21–24;
  jiriki kyūsai (self-redress) and, 94–
  100; justification for, 24, 48; medieval
  law tolerance for, 13. *See also* Battles
  (*kassen*); Grievance
The purge: enemy hunts during, 79–82;
  fiction of legitimate shogun following,
  77–78; in Kyoto neighborhoods, 143;
  politics of demonstration during, 76;
  structure of, 74–75
Purveyors (*kugonin*), 180–181

Quarrel (*kenka*), 6. *See also* Private battles

Rakuchū rakugai-zu ("Scenes In and
  Around the Capital"), 294–302,
  344–345
Ran, 25–26
Realm under heaven uprising (1532–
  1535), 145–148
Redress. *See* Grievance
Rodrigues, Jesuit João, 61, 62
Rokkaku house, 36–37, 221

Rōnin, 69–70

Rule of force: mode of control emerging from, 31; rule of law vs., 26; uprising as experiment in, 53–54

Rule of law: political theater as substitute for, 252; rule of force vs., 26

Rupture: power structure crisis due to, 285–286; restoration images following, 35–36; tension between expectations and, 36

Ryōgawa chō (two-sided block), 210, 212. *See also* Block associations

Sakai party: Hosokawa Harumoto *kanrei* of, 141; members of, 135; parallel government set up by, 139–140; power struggle within, 140; victory of, 141

Sake-brewing industry: malt quarrel, 115–116; *nōsengata* in, 178–179; smuggling in, 189; statutes for, 122–123, 199–200, 201–202; trade, 89, 187; uprisings against, 89–93

Salt taxes (1507), 36

Sanjōnishi Sanetaka: on attack against Ashikaga Yoshitane, 78; on half-tax levy collections, 84, 127; on Kanrōji's sponsorship of dancing, 244–245; records Kyoto regulations, 55, 95, 159; reports on purge of enemies, 80, 96; sale of manuscript of, 62; on withholding of taxes in Kyoto, 144

Sanmon sectarians. *See* Hiei

"Scenes In and Around the Capital" (screen paintings), 294–302, 344–345

Self-redress. *See* Grievance

Sen no Rikyū: condemned to death, 242–243, 279; contribution as wartime tea man, 283; debut, 263, 339; as guest, 342; Takeno Jōō's remarks on *wabi* to, 277. *See also* Tea parties

Settsu uprising (1477–1482), 41

Shiba house: Ōnin quarrel of, 15; overextension of, 17–18; succession issue, 33

Shiba Yoshikado, 15, 18

Shiba Yoshitoshi, 15

Shinran, 148

Shogun: biographical sketches of wartime, 119–120; ideal role of, 20–21; selection following purge, 77–79; transitions in office of (1467–1568), 46–47; Yoshitane taken prisoner while, 49–50

Shogunal edicts: on Hokke (Lotus) sect, 166–167; on Kyoto administration, 122–123; on licensed traders/trade privileges, 199–200; to *obi* guild, 189–190; prohibitions, 55–56, 81–82, 245; on repair of palace moats, 218–219; on *sake* imports, 189; symbolic shogunate and lack of, 118

Shogunate: administrative powers within, 15; authority bypassed by Miyoshi Chōkei, 224; authority within provinces of, 52–53; claims of authority over Yamashiro by, 39; decrees responding to word wars by, 91–93, 129–130; elimination of Board of Retainers, 88; elimination of *hōkōshū* (personal guard) of, 63, 88; Gion festival controversy and, 217; growing division between officials and, 117–118, 119–128; impact of Ōnin war on, 34–35; income derived from business taxes, 191; institutional constraints within, 15–16; *jiriki kyūsai* (self-redress) vs. authority of, 94–100; Kitano shrine officials independence from, 112; law regarding battle and, 21–24; Ōmi vs. Sakai (1526–1532), 135–145; Onoyama petition (1515) to, 109–112; orders for military conscription by, 87–88; perceived as source of order, 117; political relationship between block associations and, 230, 235–239, 331; purge and fiction of legitimate, 78–79; rivalry between Yoshiharu and Yoshitsuna, 46–47, 135–141; tax battles threaten authority of, 113–117; word wars to redefine, 108–109. *See also Bugyō-nin* (council of magistrates); *Kanrei* (chief minister)

Shōkokuji, 28–29

Shokunin (people of skill), 174–176, 374. *See also* Labor

Shugo funyū (laws under), 112

Silver Pavilion, 35–36

Six blocks, 219, 331. *See also* Block federation

Smuggling, 182–184

Sōchō: description of Kyoto by, 291; on disordered state of Kyoto, 134, 142; expresses moment of peace, 106–107; laments destruction in Kyoto, 60–61; on *suki,* 278; on a teahouse, 130

Social economic status: changing structures of labor, 208–209; language and symbols indicating, 203–205; patronage attachment as indicator of, 201–208; tea party as indication of, 273–276, 282–283; within block associations, 232–234

Social order: changes in authority and legitimacy, 293–294; culture of lawlessness reflecting changing, 243–244; debtors' marches as protest of, 244; reconfiguration through politics of demonstration, 104–105, 288–293; reflected in transformation of tea party, 261–263, 272–273; trauma of upheaval of, 257; wartime tea parties' challenge to, 279–281

Succession: Ashikaga Yoshitsuna quarrel over shogunate, 137–145; battle over Hosokawa house, 46, 50–51; dual purpose of quarrels over, 32; governor-deputy relationship and, 18; importance of, 15; medieval approach to, 16–17; partible and unitary inheritance, 306; shogunal authority over, 23–24. See also Ōnin war (1467–1477)

Suki, 278. See also Tea parties

Survey maps: Kyoto, 210–212. See also Block associations

Takeno Jōō, 271, 277

Tanba uprising (1489–93), 41

Tariki (power of the other), 97

Tax battles: Kyoto neighborhood purges as, 144–145; over half-tax (hanzei) levy, 83–86; word wars over, 113–117; Yamashiro farmers march against Ikkō armies, 163

Taxes: exemptions granted to blocks, 230, 235–236; extraordinary (hibun) wartime, 82–87; mass delinquency in Kyoto, 164, 219–220; military, 121; privileged commoners exempted from, 202–203; shogunal magistrate decrees regarding, 123, 199–201. See also Business taxes

Tea diaries: accounts in, 259–261, 271–272; aesthetic transformation revealed in, 262–263; description of class mingling in, 265–266; literacy evident in, 268; social functions of, 278–279

Tea parties: authority exercised in environment of, 274–276; background of, 260, 273; changes in wartime, 265–266, 274, 278, 338; class composition of, 264–268, 272–273; connection between linked verse and, 337; fūryū dancing compared to wartime, 279–281, 284; role of host in, 274–276; role of tea objects in, 269–272, 275–277; social features of, 263–268, 272–273; social transformation of, 260–263; suki of, 278; tea huts used for, 338; wabi of, 262, 277–278

Tōjiin temple, 93–94, 98

Tōji temple, 93–94, 98, 101, 151, 164, 214

Tokusei ikki (debtors' rebellions), 39, 89–93, 136. See also Urban conflict

Tokusei-rei (debt-cancellation edicts), 192–193

Ton'ya: code of blue ash, 205–208; control of manufacture, 188; described, 181–182, 189; import, 181–182; movement toward wholesale, 195–196; transport, 183. See also Economic structure (Kyoto)

Toyotomi Hideyoshi: condemns tea master to death, 242–243, 279; fūryū dancing at death anniversary of, 245–247

True Pure Land school of Buddhism, 148

Tsuda diary (1548–1590), 259

Tsuda Sōgyū, 268

Tsuda Sōtatsu, 259, 267, 272

Tsujikiri (armed street assault), 71

Uchiki Shōtarō Munemori petition, 131–132

Uchimawari: Hokke sectarians conduct, 151, 156, 164; significance of, 145–148

Unification era (1568–1615), xvii–xviii, 285

"Upheaval of Ōnin," 11. See also Ōnin war (1467–1477)

Upward mobility: manifestations of, 204–205; through patronage attachment, 201–208. See also Social economic status

Urban conflict: arson and theft incidents in Kyoto, 100–104; between Ikkō and Hokke armies as, 149–152, 159–167; Kyoto tax battles as, 114–117, 219–

220; politics of demonstration within, 59, 104–105; purges as, 74–82; *rōnin* contribution to, 70–71; *tokusei ikki* (debtors' rebellions) as, 39, 89–93, 136; uprising of 1484 as, 88–89. *See also* Culture of lawlessness; Kyoto

Violence. *See* Code of war

Wabi (quality of modesty), 262, 277–278. *See also* Tea parties
War trophies, 8–9. *See also* Grievances
The Way: described, 117; guild petitions which invoke, 207–208; half-tax and loss of, 84; tea party as practice of, 266–267
Western camp: abandonment of, 33; location of, 28; political actions of, 30–31
Word wars: become blood wars, 135; Kitano shrine independence declaration, 112; monthly magistrates win concessions with, 217–219; *nōsengata* appointment petition (1539), 201–202; Onoyama petition (1515), 109–112; over tax matters, 113–117; political pressures created by, 127–128; politics of demonstration and, 107–108; shogunate decrees responding to, 91–93, 129; *shugo funyū* rallying cry of, 112–113; significance and motivation of, 106–109, 129–133, 173, 287–288; Uchiki Shōtarō Munemori petition, 131–132

Yakushiji Yōichi Motoichi: Hosokawa Masamoto's victory over, 8–9; rebellion of, 1–4, 6, 50–51

Yamana Sōzen: attacks against the Akamatsu by, 22; conflict with Hosokawa Katsumoto, 18–19; death of, 33; dispatches troops to Yoshinari, 25; western camp of, 27–28
Yamashina Honganji, 72–73, 149, 151–152, 156, 166
Yamashina Tokitsugu: account of Katsura River battle, 139; on crime in Kyoto, 102; on daily events, 130, 159–160, 227–228; describes forces gathered in Settsu, 156; on enemy purges, 79–80; on fish quarrel, 115, 190; identifies *fūryū* performers, 252, 255–256; on *jiriki kyūsai*, 96, 97; observations on *fūryū* dancing, 249–251; on orders for palace moats repair, 122, 218; on privations, 62; reports on Miyoshi's defeat, 148; reports on six blocks, 233–234, 238; on taxes, 85–86; on terror of Kyoto neighborhood purges, 143–144
Yamashiro: armed farmers march against Ikkō armies in, 163; development of *shōen* in, 308–309; Hatakeyama as *shugo*, 35; impact of uprising in, 43–44; protests against half-tax levy in, 84–86; soldiers of the land (*jizamurai*) of, 39–40; tax levy imposed on, 35; tax withholding as protest in, 145; uprising of (1485–1493), 37–44
Yamashiro assembly: collapse of, 41; demands of the (1485), 40; described, 38
Yanagimoto Kataharu: defeat and death of, 141; grievance quarrel of, 134–136, 138; power struggle between Miyoshi and, 140; victory over "Kyoto party," 139
Yusa house, 18

Compositor:	Graphic Composition, Inc.
Text:	10/13 Galliard
Display:	Galliard
Printer:	Maple-Vail Book Manufacturing Group
Binder:	Maple-Vail Book Manufacturing Group